D1501223

Information Design as Principled Action

Making Information Accessible, Relevant, Understandable, and Usable

JORGE FRASCARA,
EDITOR

Information Design as Principled Action

Making Information Accessible, Relevant, Understandable, and Usable

JORGE FRASCARA,
EDITOR

COMMON GROUND PUBLISHING, 2015

First published in 2015 in Champaign, Illinois, USA
by Common Ground Publishing LLC
as part of the On Design book series

Library of Congress Cataloging-in-Publication Data

Information design as principled action : making information accessible, relevant, understandable, and usable / Jorge Frascara, editor.
  pages cm. -- (On design)
  ISBN 978-1-61229-626-5 (pbk : alk. paper) -- ISBN 978-1-61229-627-2 (pdf)
  1. Visual communication. 2. Graphic arts. 3. Graphic design (Typography) 4. Communication of technical information. 5. Human information processing. I. Frascara, Jorge, editor.

P93.5.I479 2014
302.2--dc23

    2014038074

Table of Contents

Preface

This is a book about the joy of learning.

As an information designer, every project is a learning experience. Learning about new users, new contexts, new purposes. It is learning about how general knowledge about perception, cognition, memory, feelings, and behavior can be adapted to the needs of a new project. It is always a moment of joy when one finds a way to support design decisions on reliable ground, when assumptions get confirmed, when other assumptions get challenged, and when a new synthesis must be built.

It is also a moment of joy when the solution proposed works! When the careful building of a document, a signage or any other information system achieves what it is intended to achieve, and when one keeps on discovering ways to improve the performance of a design product.

This book is a celebration of a type of practice and the ethos behind it, hence, "Information Design as Principled Action." Because despite the variations in situations to face and problems to solve, there are two constant principles in information design: the passion to help people attain their information-related goals, and the passion to do things well. The first is ethical, and is based on a commitment to a user-centered design approach, where the users, "the others," are recognized as different, and as respectable in their ways of seeing, understanding, learning, feeling, and behaving. The second is technical, and is based on knowledge and tenacity, to pursue all possible avenues and to look at every detail with attention and with a sense of accountability.

This book is a learning tool for those interested in information design. It is also a homage to the pioneers that in the 1970s began to define its field and its methods. Previous systematic work had been done in the 1930s and '40s by Otto and Marie Neurath, but without extensive impact on the profession through discussion and publication. The 1960s had been years of imagination explosion, years of exploration and spontaneity. But they also were years of self-consciousness for visual communication design, i.e., the founding of Icograda, and for the specifics of information design, through the practical work of Jock Kinnear and Margaret Calvert for signage systems in the UK, and the founding of the Open University's Institute of Educational Technology. In here, the explicit articulation of teaching and learning methods hinging on information design involved Michael MacDonald-Ross and Robert Waller. A self-conscious move on different fronts of performance-oriented design began with the design methods movement, led, among others, by Bruce Archer, John Chris Jones, Christopher Alexander, Nigel Cross, and Robin Roy. Other contribution to note was the creation of the Readability of Print Research Unit, initially directed by Herbert Spencer, with Linda Reynolds as a collaborator, and in 1976 successor to Spencer.

This book also celebrates the vision of the organizers of events that in the 1970s contributed to focusing on communication design's *performance, relevance*, and *accountability,* three characteristics that are essential to information design. ICSID's 1975 "Design for Need;" Icograda's 1978 "Design that Works!" organized by Bob Vogel and Patrick Whitney in Chicago; and the third, and most central event for the development of information design, "Visual Presentation of Information," organized in 1978 by Ron Easterby and Harm Zwaga in Het Vennenbos, the Netherlands. Its proceedings, edited by Easterby and Zwaga, were later on published by Wiley in 1984 as the book "Information Design." Its content is still current, and is an indispensable tool for information design: human cognition and perception do not change in 30 years. The definitive sanction of Information Design as a discipline came in 1979 with Robert Waller's foundation of the *Information Design Journal*. This created a forum for a growing body of knowledge where the information design community found a place to both contribute and consult. Among the most prolific contributors, there and elsewhere, I want to recognize Patricia Wright and James Hartley. Writing for other publications, our community must thank John Sweller, whose work on cognitive psychology provided significant insights to our understanding of instructional design. Credit is due to David Sless, for all the work produced in the last 30 years by the Communication Research Institute (CRI), and for the generous dissemination of his work and ideas; and to Peter Simlinger, for his endless tenacity to create and sustain the International Institute for Information Design (IIID). Karen Schriver merits my attention and gratitude, first for her landmark book: *Dynamics in Document Design*, second, for her always generous disposition to offer advice, including suggestions for the title of this book.

A special thank goes to the pioneers that have gracefully helped build this volume, and to the younger researchers that joined in.

The learning continues, and the joy too.

Jorge Frascara
Vancouver, Canada
August 2014

Part I: Introduction

Chapter 1: What is Information Design?

Jorge Frascara

Abstract

Information design aims at the creation of effective communications through the facilitation of the processes of perception, reading, comprehension, memorization and use of the information presented. Knowledge use in information design must always be framed by due attention to **who** is our public, **what** are we talking about, **why** we address them, and **where**, **when** and **through** what media. My introduction will deal with the conception of a design project and the importance of its final objective, the organization of the design process, the organization of content and its impact on visual structures, the importance of the user, the consideration of cultural differences, perception, legibility and readability, notions of color, the importance of the context of implementation and use, the role of images (representation and symbolism), diagrams, data design for decisions, and the need for research and evaluation.

Introduction

Information design aims at the creation of effective communications through the facilitation of the processes of perception, reading, comprehension, memorization, and use of the information presented. It is of necessity user-centered. It is ethical because it recognizes "the others" as different from the designer and deserving respect in their difference. There are no recipes for information design: there is knowledge to be applied, but its application must always be framed by due attention to who is the public, what one is talking about, why one addresses them, and where, when and through what media.

We information designers must recognize that people are not electronic devices, and that Claude Shannon's terminology, which comes from information technologies and defines the poles of communication as transmitter and receiver, overlooks differences in cognitive styles, cultures, expectations, feelings, interests, value systems, and levels of intelligence. The messages that we broadcast are not received, but are interpreted by people. But information management does not end with interpretation. In information design, people must not only understand the messages but also act according to them. They might have to organize the connections of a sound system, to fill in a form, to take medicine, or to find a specific office in a building or the right exit from a highway.

The design process in this field involves two distinct moments: 1) the organization of the information (the content and its units of meanings, texts and illustrations), and 2) the planning and implementation of the visual presentation. These tasks require knowledge and skills to process, organize and present linguistic and non-linguistic information. They also require an understanding of cognitive and perceptual processes, as well as the legibility of symbols, letters, words, sentences, paragraphs and complex texts.

The areas of work include the following:

- presentation of texts (technical reports, instruction manuals, school books, scientific documents);
- alphanumeric tables (timetables, directories, financial statements);
- graphs and diagrams (statistical graphs, visualization of physical structures or abstract information);
- teaching aids (information-centered wall-charts, technical illustrations);
- administrative documents (forms, tickets, receipts, contracts, bills);
- instructions (in gadgets, medicines, electronic products, electro-domestics, game rules);
- control panels (cars, aircraft, sound systems, control rooms);
- wayfinding (symbols, signs, systems);
- maps and plans (without getting into products of cartography, architecture or engineering, that are not created by graphic designers);
- catalogues, programs, brochures, exhibitions; and
- interfaces.

All this can apply to printed or electronic media or to three-dimensional media, and these media could be static or dynamic (educational games, CDs, web pages, online forms).

Information design uses objective methods to evaluate the efficiency of its products. Evaluation is used to determine in which aspects and to what extent the design has improved the performance of a previous product or has achieved the desired performance in the case of new products. Performance in information design is measured as the ability of the users to see, understand, memorize and use the information presented. The evaluation methods are objective because they are based on observable behaviors, for instance, the amount of information remembered, its accuracy, the time required to find a specific piece of information in a document or to fill in a form, the time required to remember a cooking recipe, or any other measurable action that the document is supposed to support.

Information design is not defined by what one does, but by how one does it. The person who designs a sign system that imitates other systems is not doing information design. Information design responds to the needs of people, with regard to the understanding and use of products, services and facilities, on the basis of interdisciplinary knowledge arising from ergonomics, linguistics, psychology, sociology, anthropology, graphic design and computer science – among other fields. Good information design makes information accessible (easily available), appropriate (to its contents and users), attractive (inviting), concise (clear and without embellishments), relevant (connected to the purpose of the user), timely (available when the user needs it), understandable (without doubts or ambiguities), appreciated (for its utility) (IIID, 2007a), and usable.

Interdiscipline is not invented by information design nor is it exclusive to it: advertising agencies and organizations such as the International Standards Organization (ISO) have for a long time gathered designers, psychologists, sociologists and anthropologists to make sure that design decisions are taken with due attention to the capacities and profiles of user populations. The design of teaching aids, for instance, cannot be the sole responsibility of teachers, or bank notes of economists, or traffic signs of traffic police. The effectiveness of any piece of information design requires an interdisciplinary team.

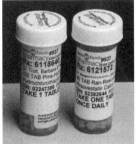 

Figures 1, 2 and 3

Without good information design, forms are tiring to fill in and generate errors, documents are not inviting to read, instructions cannot be understood (but can create frustration or even be dangerous), educational materials do not help learning, websites are difficult to navigate, and control panels produce undue fatigue among users. An example from Italy (illegible and overwhelming instructions in a spray can), another from Canada (confusing labelling where the final user is neglected and two different drugs challenge visual discrimination), and a third one from Argentina (instructions for taking a medication all set in condensed type 5pt/4), prove that the problem is international and affects the use of dangerous substances (Figures 1, 2 and 3).

Conversely, good information design is inviting, reduces fatigue and errors in information processing, speeds up the tasks, and renders the information attractive and adapted to the situation in which it appears.

The International Institute for Information Design (IIID), in Vienna, defines information design as follows: "Information design is the defining, planning, and shaping of the contents of a message and the environments in which it is presented, with the intention of satisfying the information needs of the intended recipients" (IIID, 2007b, p. 8).

The analysis of the information flow in an organization helps to diagnose possible communication problems that can be resolved by information design. Institutions are frequently satisfied with the effectiveness of their functioning, without having critically evaluated the effectiveness of their communications, that is, the internal communications that relate to management but not to the communications between the institution and the public. In these situations, there is normally a conservative tendency ("this is the way we do things here"). If the communication instruments and protocols are not optimal, the workers tend to compensate through their personal efforts, thereby covering the deficiencies of the system. This effort has a cost, though, because processes take longer, are more exposed to errors, and increase fatigue in people (Wright, 1978, p. 258).

A task always requires attention and participation: to follow a sign, to fill in a form, or to respond to a question always involves a cognitive effort. To help people to act with efficiency when performing a task in a given situation, we need to learn how they solve problems, and only then will we be able to design properly. "Efficiency" in this case means to reduce the cognitive effort required by a given situation. To solve a problem might mean having to decide whether or not one can take an aspirin and an anticoagulant at the same time, or trying to understand whether or not part A and part B of a blender should be already attached when plugging in the device. To carry out any task, it is necessary to understand the information, to memorize it, and to implement it. The more units of information to process, the more demanding the cognitive effort becomes.

There are three types of memory: sensorial, short-term (or working memory) and long-term. Sensorial memory is immediate and does not require effort. For instance, when entering an airport, multiple sources of information fall upon us, but only the name of an airline is of interest to us. Once the location of the airline is found, this passes to working memory, but an effort is required to keep that information in mind until one actually reaches the right counter. If someone calls us while on our way, we might lose the information. If we had to remember the information so as to be able to pass it on to someone else on the following day, then it would become necessary to develop mnemonic strategies to take that into long-term memory. Good information design presents the information in ways that facilitate memorization at all three levels.

George Miller (1956) said that one can accumulate seven units of active information in mind, perhaps two more or two less, depending on several factors. In mass communications, it is advisable not to expect that people will be able to process more than five units, and three is better. If one has to present a message with 20 information units, it is advisable to group the information into five groups of four units, or something similar – as long as the groupings make some sense– instead of presenting a continuous list. In this way, it is easier for the reader to manage the information, regarding understanding just as much as remembering. If the intention is to facilitate memorization, conspicuous numbering of the parts of a document is useful. Subtitles are also useful because they act like a sign system in the text.

The Conception of a Design Project and the Importance of its Final Objective

If the final objective of every design project is to respond to a human need, then the enunciation of the purpose of a project must be articulated in two stages. First, for instance, in describing what will happen as a consequence of the design product: "It is hoped that with this form the form-fillers' errors will be reduced by 50%." Or, "This new signage will cut by 30% the number of questions visitors ask medical personnel concerning how to find their way around the hospital." The objectives must be defined in ways that allow performance evaluation. Second, the product should be devised so that the objective is attained.

Every design project must be based on the identification of a reality that one wishes to change. Further to this, one must set up operative objectives to define what the product *must do,* and not just how it *should look* (Cross & Roy, 1975). One must also define the intermediate objectives that are required to reach the final ones. Final objectives must be focused on the responses of the public, regarding changes in knowledge, attitudes, feelings or behaviors.

Guillermina Noël and I offered a workshop at the Philadelphia University for the Arts on user-centered design. One of the groups of students redesigned the prospect of a medical drug so as to respond to the needs of seniors.

When the new design was shown to the users, they indicated that they preferred the existing one. It took some effort for the students to reconsider their approach and to do something that would really be better (not just look better) than the existing design. (Figure 4)

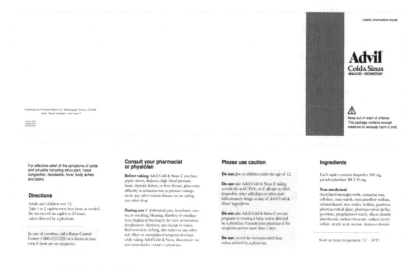

Figure 4

The encounter with the users was decisive for the students to reach the understanding that the problem was not esthetic but persuasive, because the users, rather than complain about specific features of the design, confessed that they had never read the prospect. It became clear that the first objective of all information design product must be to be inviting, to motivate people to engage with the information. Something must persuade the reader that the message is worth the cognitive effort. This means that every information design must first address a persuasive dimension.

When the objectives of a design project get defined, these must be achievable and measurable. One should not establish objectives that are impossible to reach, such as "avoid all errors in the administration of pharmaceutical drugs." It is not advisable either to set vague objectives, such as "improve the quality of life," because it is difficult to create design criteria that could help to reach them or methods that could measure the results. It is always useful to measure the impact of a project to evaluate the degree to which the objectives were met, as well as to identify the strengths and weaknesses of the strategy used. This implies an iterative approach that alternates design with research, and that, of necessity, involves the users.

Programming the Design Process

Design and research methods contribute to the design process. Research methods are used to study problems, to generate knowledge, and to evaluate outcomes.

Design methods serve to make decisions about strategies and ways of implementing them in the products. Research and design intertwine in the process.

There is no universally valid way of organizing the design process. What I propose here is based on my personal experience and on readings that I have consulted through the years. These include works by Christopher Alexander, Nigel Cross, Robin Roy, John Chris Jones, Bruce Archer, Gregory Bateson and David Sless, but I have also borrowed ideas from Ron Easterby, Harm Zwaga, Anthony Wilden, Edward Hall, Ronald Shakespear, Richard Saul Wurman, Juan Carrera, Claude Lévi-Strauss, Jean-Paul Sartre, Gilles Deleuze, Felix Guattari, James Gibson, Herbert Spencer, Jean Piaget, Edgar Morin and Maria Montessori, as well as many others who appear in the references of this book.

The method and the substance are always integrated; ways of working are ways of thinking, and they affect not only how we do things but also what we do. My design process is generally based on nine main steps:

1. Contact with the client (or identification of a need)
2. Collection of information (publications, experts and users)
3. Development of the design strategy
4. Design development and production of prototypes
5. Evaluation
6. Redesign
7. Fabrication and implementation
8. Evaluation of final performance
9. Design revision/adjustment

Steps 4 and 5 are normally repeated several times. Design methods involve all the processes of interaction with the client, interpretation of information, visualizations, drafts, prototypes and final design. Research methods relate to the collection of information, and the evaluation of specific aspects of prototypes and of full-scale productions. Research is almost always necessary in information design, because there are usually specific aspects of the project in question for which there might not be reliable existing information.

Contact with the Client (or Identification of a Need)

The project normally starts with a request from a client, but it can also be originated by the designer. In this case, the designer identifies a problem or an opportunity and seeks resources to develop a design response. In the case of a client-initiated project, the scope of a first meeting is to define what the client *wants* and what the client really *needs*. From a management point of view, the objective of this first meeting is also to generate trust. Final and intermediate objectives of the project are discussed at this point, as well as strategies to reach them. Normally, this oral meeting is followed by a letter from the designer that summarizes the topics discussed and the agreements arrived at, describing what the client expects, what the designer promises, what the client will contribute, as well as a schedule, a budget, and a form of payment. This takes the form of a letter of agreement or of a contract, depending on the case. Clarity, completeness and precision in this communication are pivotal to the success of the engagement. The letter of agreement is an information design project.

Collection of Information (Publications, Experts, and Users)

Once the objective of the project has been defined, it is necessary to identify the full spectrum of users for the project. Users are the most important source of information to identify needs, possibilities and constraints, and to guide the development of a design solution. Users involve not only final users but also all those involved in the generation, handling, distributing, receiving, and collecting of the document, in other words all those who come in touch with or are somehow affected by the document. The collection of information requires *imagination* (to conceive the entire range of problems that must be confronted and the strategies to do this), *understanding* (of situations different from one's own) and *tenacity* (to lift all the covers, to pose all the questions, and to thoroughly analyze all that is collected). It is necessary to avoid an excess of self-confidence and the production of quick responses based on personal experience. This experience is always insufficient and at times misleading. One needs to identify the missing information and to learn where to find it.

User interviews are important, and it is necessary to make an effort to leave aside one's convictions and to avoid filtering or judging the information provided by users until the next step where one analyses the information produced. Social anthropology has developed methods that are extremely useful for visual communication design, particularly in what relates to the observation of users. But it is important that the designer acquires the skill and does the observing. There is nothing that can replace the direct interaction with reality when one needs to collect actionable information. Reality shows all the differences that one must consider. Users come to a communication engagement with their personal history, possibilities, limitations, preferences, interests, expectations and specific needs.

Interviews with users – as much on the client's side as on the public's side – can be complemented by focus groups and by observations of users interacting with the communicating product. It can also be useful – despite the method's limitations – to play user, that is, to use the product. Finally, bibliographic consultations complement the search for information at diverse moments of the project's development. A project normally requires diverse methods for the collection of the necessary information.

Development of the Design Strategy

One begins with the analysis of the information obtained. On this basis, the problem is normally redefined. The strategy usually includes a list of operative objectives. Diagrams are sometimes useful to map the situation and the strategy. These can take diverse forms, such as: a) objectives tree, to visualize how the final objective requires intermediate ones at several levels, and to arrive down at the level of design criteria; b) flows, to visualize the steps that must be followed and the corresponding responsibilities (Figure 5); c) net, or structure of an organization, to show how objectives, functions or other factors affect one another, so as to identify relations and possible conflicts (Figure 6); and d) comparison of quantities to study the relative intensity a problem. (figure 7)

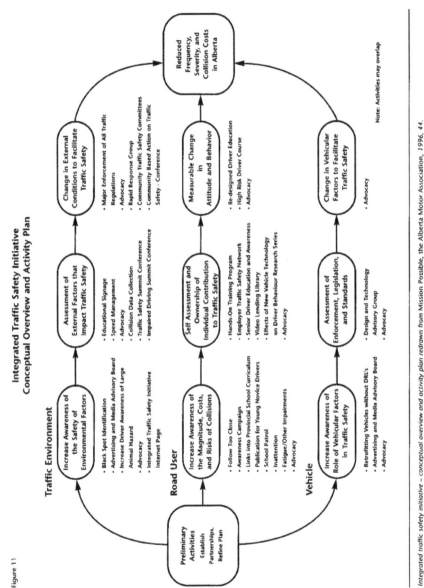

Figure 5

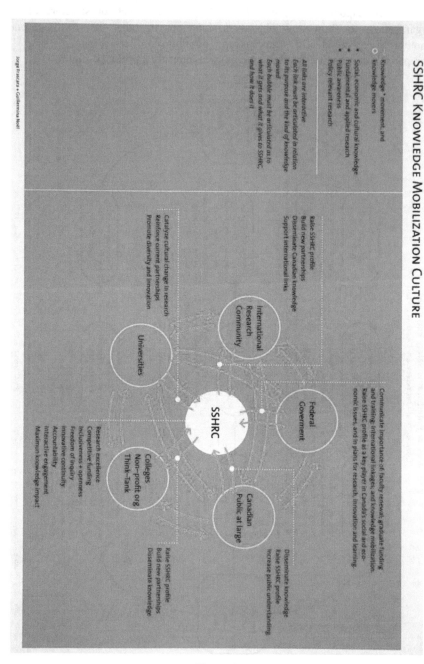

Figure 6

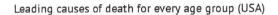

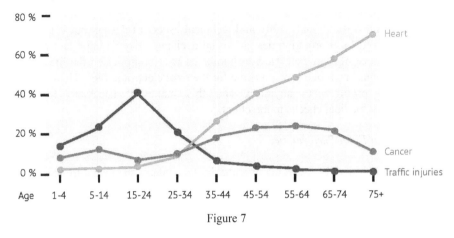

Figure 7

Fundamentally, diagrams can help us to recognize the *components of a problem*, their possible *grouping into categories*, the *relative importance* of each factor and each category, and the *flows and connections* among them.

Design Development and Production of Prototypes

Once the objectives and the strategies have been defined, a prototype is designed with its correspondent rationale. Every important design decision must be supported by evidence, coming either from the literature or from tailor-made experiments developed specifically for the project.

Evaluation

This is the point at which the performance of the prototype is measured to find out what works, what does not, and how to fix it. The evaluation can involve the full prototype or specific aspects of it. The evaluation of the product must go beyond a comparison between alternative solutions, because this only takes us to the *best existing solution*, not necessarily to the *best possible one*. It is important to establish desirable levels of performance and to find ways to reach them. The cycle "prototype improvement and evaluation" can be repeated several times, until the available information and resources, human and material, do not allow any further improvement of the product.

Redesign

Improve the design based on the information obtained from tests and interviews with users.

Fabrication and Implementation

This is the most traditional, crafty and technical aspect of design, but it is not a mechanical act. In information design, visual decisions play an important part in the performance of a product. New technologies have complicated the life of the designer because now one is responsible for the final electronic files. There are no professional proofreaders anymore, and this makes it necessary to pass responsibility for final checks to the client.

Evaluation of Final Performance

Every design project is a working hypothesis. To evaluate the extent to which the objectives of a project have been reached, these must be clearly articulated from the beginning, along with the criteria to evaluate the success of the product(s). Even though evaluations could take place at the prototype level, a full-scale evaluation is necessary after implementation, even though often this does not happen.

Design Revision/Adjustment

The information provided by the evaluation helps to adjust the design of the product. The evaluation after implementation normally offers rich results because it is the first time that the product works in its real context, with real users, under real constraints.

The use of this information is, again, not a mechanical event. One should remember what Niels Bohr told a colleague: "You are not thinking, you are just being logical" (Frish, 1979, p. 1). Methods allow one to arrive at reasonable solutions, but to get to excellent solutions one needs to go beyond and to use all resources available. A few examples might help to clarify this point:

> 1) Michael Burke was designing diagrams and pictograms to explain how to assemble an artifact to illiterate Africans when he noticed that they could not understand the visual information expressed in two dimensions. Instead of trying to make the diagrams clearer, or larger, or better supported by oral explanations, he made a three-dimensional paper model that could be cut out and assembled, just as it would happen with the real object.
>
> It is to be noted that Burke clearly had the objective in mind "to help the Africans be able to build the product," and not just "to produce explanatory graphics." This allowed him to step back from the problem to conceive and implement an efficient solution.
>
> 2) In an evaluation of the effectiveness of warning messages on the backs of school busses, for example, "Stop when red lights flashing", I found that the most important strategy to put the message across was not to change the typeface, its color, or its size but to wash the busses frequently. This implied a redefinition of the problem. I had been

contacted to improve the typographic message; however, in the process of looking into this problem, I found that the existing messages could only be improved marginally, but the backs of the buses were generally covered by mud and snow, which obliterated the messages (Figure 8).

Figure 8

3) Tom Nelson (1981)found that, during World War II, pilots could roughly assess their altitude based on the details they could see in the landscape, that is, forests, trees and leaves. He later learned that animals with simple brains, such as cats, cannot distinguish between a square and a triangle, but they can distinguish visual patterns from one another. He then thought that visual patterns could help children with severe working memory limitations to learn to differentiate the shapes of letters. We developed together an alphabet for this purpose, assigning a different pattern to the back of each letter. We found that once the children had learned to differentiate the letters they were able to recognize the letters without the patterns (Frascara, 1980; Nelson et al., 1981). It was not possible to solve the problem with large or three-dimensional letters; instead, it was necessary to appeal to a lower function of the brain that was able to operate without working memory (Figures 9 and 10) (Frascara, 2006a, pp. 114-117).

Figures 9 and 10

4) When Ronald Shakespear (2009) changed the name of his client from "Subterráneos de Buenos Aires" to "Subte," he was capitalizing on an ingrained brand in the minds of the users who referred to the subway service by this name. As he says, the designer must have a big ear (Figure 11) (Shakespear, 2009).

Figure 11

Some Things to Remember

- The more one knows a problem, the easier it is to solve it.
- Any design project needs information that is *sufficient, precise* and *reliable.*

- • The existing knowledge is generally not enough to solve a new design problem; there is always a need for research to generate the missing information.
- The limits of applicability of the information collected must be clear. These define its validity.
- Research is always useful, not only to generate a good proposal but also to defend it.
- Every design problem is interdisciplinary.
- The interpretation of results must not only carefully identify causes and effects but also collect criteria to face future situations more efficiently.
- The presentation of the design project to the client is an information design project.

Contents and Visual Presentation

The Organization of the Contents

Understanding Texts

Reading can be divided into two aspects: legibility, which refers to the facility with which letters can be recognized (a perceptual problem), and readability, which refers to the facility with which a text can be understood (a cognitive problem). The legibility of a text can be assured through the use of standards for normal vision to define lettersize, lettershape and layout. The comprehensibility of a text varies more from reader to reader because it is based on knowledge of the topic, interest, and general intellectual development (Klare, 1984), as well as on the way in which the text is written. Some indicators of readability are the number of syllables per word, the number of words per sentence, and the number of sentences per paragraph. It is suggested that a text formed by short words, single-clause short sentences, and few paragraphs will be easier to understand than the opposite. This, however, omits consideration of the conceptual complexity of the content and the preparation of the reader to confront the text. Wittgenstein will always be difficult for people who ignore his writings, even if he had written short words and short sentences. Adequate titles, logical sequence of paragraphs, and good use of grammar and punctuation can help comprehension (Cutts, 2007).

In addition to the already mentioned factors, one should differentiate the texts according to their purpose: the act of reading is different when reading a novel, a newspaper, a technical report, or a bank account, and even when one looks for a name in the phone book.

A usual mistake of design schools is to teach page layout using dummy text. How can communication efficiency be evaluated with dummy text? How can text layout be assessed without considering communication efficiency? How is it possible to design a product in a communication design department where the content is not comprehensible? In this way, students get formed into visual cosmetics, and these are students who do not read what they design, and who do not become sensitive to what Robert Waller (1980) calls "macro-punctuation."

That is the way in which column width, number of words per line, typographic variations, management of space, and line changes contribute or not to the efficient comprehension of a text. To allow the reader to choose a reading strategy, it is necessary to visually codify diverse types of information, segmenting the text when needed to change the tone of voice through changes in type and in the use of the space (that is, marginalia, captions, titles, questions or footnotes). These changes send meta-messages to the reader regarding how to take in every bit of information.

Organization of the Contents and Usability

Information design is generally used in connection with taking action or making decisions. The usability of information, in addition to depending on expositive clarity and internal coherence, also depends on other important factors: the reader's motivation, the reader's knowledge, the actions through which the reader obtains the information, and the actions the reader must undertake to use the information.

Obviously, a user-centered design approach becomes indispensable. The type of use and the situation of use also affect the definition of design criteria. The organization of the instructions to assemble a piece of furniture, centered on the use of working memory, requires different strategies from those required by a scientific document that must be remembered for the rest of a surgeon's life.

User-centered Communication Design

People, not Graphics

The notion of user-centered design begins from the principle that design is not about the creation of products, but about the impact that those products have on people, about obtaining desirable reactions. The fundamental problem for the information designer is the creation of tools to help people to learn, remember, act, interact (with objects, people and information), realize wishes and satisfy needs.

Every product of information design has an operative objective; it must affect the knowledge, the attitudes, the feelings, or the behavior of people in a desired way. But every object placed in the public space also has a cultural impact because it affects the way that people relate to information and to other people, and because it creates habits and cultural consensus (this second impact is a subject for the social sciences). The designer creates cognitive habits. An authoritarian design fosters the creation of authoritarian or submissive people. A design that respects people fosters respect for others. A design that invites thinking invites the public to think independently. In this way, the task of the designer is not only one of facilitating the management of daily life but also of educating through the promotion of actions loaded by positive social values.

Learning about the User

User-centered design is ethical because it supposes accepting the users as different, and being acceptable in their difference; the user is seen as independent, with thoughts, opinions, tastes and preferences that can be different from those of the designer.

The effectiveness of a communication depends to a great extent on its adaptation to the user. This implies a change from the notion of the user as a receiver to another of the user as a partner, and thus regards communication as an act of negotiation, where the originator of the information and its interpreter try to establish a common terrain. This emphasizes the need to study the particularities of each situation and calls for tests and an iterative approach to designing (Mackenzie, 1993; Penman & Sless, 1994). Iterative designing is based on the creation of working prototypes, and their testing, modification and retesting until it is judged that one has achieved the best possible result given current possibilities. Donald Norman (1990) has been a strong advocate of products that respond to the needs, motivations and skills of the users. If information design is not user-centered, then it becomes inefficient, and even possibly dangerous, such as in the case of obscure warnings in medications that concern allergies, dosage or interaction with other drugs (Figure 12).

Figure 12

Several strategies are useful to include the user in the design process: these include interviews, focus groups, ethnographic observations, statistics, and performance testing. The aim of these methods is to improve the product before it goes to industrial-scale production and after implementation.

The preoccupation for the user began in the application of physical ergonomics to the design of useful objects. It was intuitive and practical at the beginning, such as in the case of the medieval shoemaker who measured the feet of his clients, and more systematic later, such as in the industrialization of the clothing industry, vehicle manufacturing, workstations or tools.

The conscious notion of user-centered design was pushed further by the physical ergonomics studies of Alphonse Chapanis (1996) during World War II, and was later extended to the cognitive, emotional and cultural aspects. Taken to its final consequences, user-centered design not only tries to get to know the user in order to reach the public but also in order to assist in the generation of well-being. This is, for instance, the case of information design in the urban environment that helps daily life, or in the design of interfaces for electronic media that facilitate the tasks of users.

In sum, user-centered information design is interdisciplinary, involving several branches of psychology (perception, cognition, emotion, development and behavior), as well as some aspects of sociology (statistics, surveys and demographics) and anthropology (ethnographic observation and cultural studies). User-centered information design emphasizes the needs of the users, their capacities and wellbeing; it is based on scientific research, it involves tests, and it uses an iterative process. It uses qualitative and quantitative evaluation methods to assess the performance of its products.

Information Design and Cultural Difference

Information Design, Culture, and Globalization

Information design, that is, the organization of the contents of a message and the conception and production of its visual presentation, has traditionally been developed as a discipline based on logical thinking. The quality of this logical thinking was conceived as definable in the universally valid principles that resulted from the study of human cognition.

Several aspects of life today challenge these assumptions: given that geographical distances are eliminated by fast transportation and class separations are less a determinant of human interaction, daily experience confronts us with more different people than in the time of our grandparents. In addition, it is common for a designer in an industrialized country to develop a project for another country, or for implementation in several countries at the same time. This contact with a wide variety of people has come to demonstrate that logical processes do not necessarily take place in the same way in different human groups. This is not because different people define and use logic in different ways, but because people's interest in logic varies, because many other processes take place in a cognitive task, and because cognitive tasks are framed by other inescapable human dimensions. I will not expand on this concept any further because I have dealt with it in detail elsewhere (Frascara, 1999, 2000).

The Visual Presentation

Perception

Gestalt theory is one of the most useful conceptual tools for the visual communication designer. Understanding its principles helps in the development of perceptually and cognitively efficient solutions.

Let us begin from the principle that the *main objective* of perception is survival, and that its *strategy* is to understand the environment that surrounds the subject. To understand, it is indispensable to organize. The principle that permits the first step toward organizing perception is the duet *integration-segregation*. This process is based on the well-known "laws" of *proximity* (the simplest one), *similarity* and *good form*. The three laws work based on relations, that is, *proximity* brings together objects that are *closer* from one another *than* from others. The proximity that brings them together, or the distance that separates them, are not physically defined, but they depend on the situation. The same applies to *similarity* and to *good form* versus disorder. These principles are fundamental for reading: the distance between letters determines the limits of words through letterspacing and wordspacing. These set the bases for line-spacing and margins. Proximity also serves to separate captions from main texts and to connect images to their right texts. Typographic differences in shape (roman, italics, or different fonts), tonal differences (regular, bold, light) and size (points) allow readers to recognize emphases, titles, subtitles, captions, notes, etc. The principle of *good form* helps us to integrate elements into totalities, to highlight relations between components, and to establish spatial codes.

The relation between letter-spaces and word-spaces is key to the facilitation of reading. Lack of good spacing can be witnessed in many newspaper columns where sometimes the composition is compressed without allowing reasonable space between words. Reading is based on fast jumps (saccadic movements) and brief fixations. For efficient reading, the reader must – in peripheral vision – be able to determine where the next fixation should be. This is done to a great extent through the perception of the space before an important word, and by ignoring brief words such as articles and prepositions that – in general – can be guessed from the text being read. If the space between words is erratic or insufficient, reading becomes slower and more tiring (Figure 13a and 13b). In this case, it becomes necessary to explore the text in more detail to decide where the next fixation should be. Good letterspacing and wordspacing are sheer applications of Gestalt theory.

Erratic spacing

If the space between letters and words is erratic (as it happens in narrow newspaper columns) reading becomes tiring and slow, because it becomes necessary to explore the text in detail to be able to chose the following fixation. All this is pure Gestalt Theory, and it can be proved empirically.

Normal spacing

If the space between letters and words is erratic (as it happens in narrow newspaper columns) reading becomes tiring and slow, because it becomes necessary to explore the text in detail to be able to chose the following fixation. All this is pure Gestalt Theory, and it can be proved empirically.

Figures 13a and 13b

Another important element for the facilitation of reading is consistency in the visual codification adopted. The conventions adopted to solve a given text composition problem must be maintained throughout the document or the series of documents. The reader who understands the visual language of a text can read it with more efficiency. This consistency not only facilitates reading but also contributes to the reader's pleasure.

Esthetic pleasure was defined by Theodor Lipps as "the realization of an expected activity" (cited by Worringer, 1997, pp. 4-7); in other words, when one can predict what will be coming, its arrival will be enjoyable. Through understanding the structure of something, one can become able to predict. In music, for instance, rhythm, melody and key create frames that shape the expectations of listeners. When music develops within predictable frames, and certainly with an adequate degree of novelty (information), the audience experiences pleasure. It seems that the creation of these frames is essential as much for pleasure as for understanding. This has been called "priming" in cognitive psychology. If a person knows the objective of the text to be read, and its visual conventions, it will be easier to understand it (Meyer & Schvaneveldt, 1971).

Legibility and Readability/Choosing Alphabets

Typefaces as Systems/Choosing Alphabets

The alphabet is a system of combinable components. These are essentially 26 capitals, 26 lower cases, 10 numerals, and some 20 additional signs. These 82 components should be compatible and harmonious in any combination possible, so that reading does not become hampered by uneven weights, random heights, and variable tonal densities, spaces or shapes. The basic 52 letters imply 2704 possible cases of sequences of two letters. They are designed to relate to each other in any sequence.

Clearly, it is impossible to design a typeface by trial and error, and it is also easy to believe that many poorly designed typefaces crowd the market. Choosing a typeface requires attention to the system's ability to perform well for the kind of reading required. Attention-grabbing and continuous reading is quite a different function. Ease in continuous reading is based on a good balance between consistency of style and tonal weight across an alphabet and, at the same time, sufficient distinction between letters. The alphabet is a combinable system composed of units (letters) that can be classified in subsystems according to their form. The letters *abcdeopq*, for instance, have common characteristics and their solutions should be similar, but, at the same time, these letters should differ as much as possible from each other to avoid confusion. Several basic characteristics should be kept consistent in their subsystem, such as their width, and the profile of the almost circular shape of their central portion. Within this system, *a, b, d, p* and *q* will have to be similar in the visual resolution of the relation between the vertical stroke and their circular core. (Figure 14)

abcdeopq **abcdeopq**

Times   Futura

Figure 14

Other subsystems are formed by other lower-case letters, and different relations are established for capitals. Height, tonal weight, and style should maintain coherence in a given font. The tonal weight is the ratio of black to white in the area of a letter, as created by the strokes and the spaces between them.

One of the basic elements for ease of reading is word recognition. The fundamental cues are the initial letter, the length of the word, and its profile – mainly ascenders and descenders and the internal tonal structure of the word (Schiepers, 1976, p. 51). As already mentioned, the fixation points separated by the saccadic movements of the eye are guided by the blank space between important words. One reads words by fixating foveal vision around the second letter of a word, letting peripheral vision make up whatever is there to the right. According to Herbert Spencer (1968), only four letters of normal size fall within foveal vision at a usual reading distance. The other 12 to 15 letters that we normally recognize with accuracy fall away from foveal vision, and therefore away from our maximum ability to resolve their details (Spencer, 1968, p. 19). Reading speed relates to using peripheral vision efficiently, and taking a number of guesses. For this to happen, words must maintain tonal homogeneity. The tonal density of each letter, despite variations of shape, should be similar to every other one, so that the ability of the visual system to spot its next useful fixation point can be enhanced. In support of this, Spencer cites several researchers, including W. B. Pillsbury, who showed that a typing error in the first part of a word is more easily recognizable than in the second part. This happens because the second part of a word is normally guessed, and only seen in peripheral vision (Spencer, 1968, pp. 17-18).

Guided by a stylistic search for simplicity, Herbert Bayer designed his Universal font, in 1925, in an attempt to make letters as simple as possible (Figure 15).

abcdefghi
jklmnopqr
stuvwxyz
a   d d

Figure 15

He therefore eliminated the capital letters, and designed an alphabet heavily based on geometry. The result is a conspicuously illegible font because it ignored the need for a good balance between the similarity of style and the distinctiveness of each letter. This design ignored 400 years of type design traditions in Western Europe, beginning with Claude Garamond (around 1540) and other designers of his time. The influence of the 1920s' love for geometry also affected Paul Renner and his Futura typeface an extremely popular one, revisited in the 1960s by Herb Lubalin with his Avant Garde. Variations of tonal density between letters are extreme in this typeface and create random points of visual attraction in words, negatively affecting legibility. These variations fool the eye in its task of searching for the most efficient places to focus on during its brief fixations.

The alphabets created in the 1950s, such as Univers (Adrian Frutiger) and Helvetica (Max Miedinger, figure 16a) recovered the traditional interest in optical corrections. Their legibility, however, has been surpassed by later alphabets whose letters have wider apertures and are more distinct from one another (Officina Sans, figure 16b). This improvement in legibility is based on increasing the opening left by inward turning strokes – as in the *e* or *a* – and is supported by research related to the Landolt Ring (Sanders and McCormick, 1993, p. 94). The Landolt Ring measures visual resolution by allowing a small opening in the ring, one that at certain distances becomes invisible (Figure 16c).

ABCabcdefghijklm

Figure 16a

Figure 16b

Figure 16c

Increasing the gap will increase its visual detection. This same phenomenon applies to the resolution – and therefore the distinction – of several small letters such as *a, e, c* and *o*.

Letter size and stroke width alone do not therefore guarantee the best possible performance in legibility. Letterform, letter separation, word separation, line separation, and margins are also important dimensions for legibility.

The intention to improve legibility in small sizes led type designers of the 1950s to abandon the 5 to 8 proportion between lower case and upper case, and to change it to a 6 to 8 proportion. This, however, generated the need to increase line separations to avoid the visual jamming of lines. This is often ignored in the design of product packaging where, in an attempt to save space and to comply with requirements related to information content, highly unreadable texts are produced (Figure 17).

Figure 17

It could be argued that the height of the characters of these texts falls easily within the range of legible sizes as defined by the Snellen chart (Figure 18). They become discouraging, however, because setting a text in all caps, or setting without leading (line separation) a contemporary typeface that maximizes the x-height of the lower cases, will result in an overwhelming appearance. There is always a need to add about 20% leading up to 12-point type, and at least 10% for 14-point and up.

Figure 18

The different height of lower cases and capitals within a given type size suggests that, when determining the size of a text in a sign, one should specify the x-height (actual height of the face of a lower-case or upper-case printed letter) and not the body size (the size of the block of lead that used to support the letter in old technology; now meaning the distance between two lines of text if no extra line space is added). Poulton (1972, p. 161) found that to attain a similar x-height of about 1.2 mm, Times New Roman and Univers required 6.5-point type, and old style Perpetua required 8.5-point type. The legibility of text is supported by the size of the face of the letters, and not by their body size. Miles Tinker has been criticized for referring to point size rather than face size in his studies. When he began his studies, all alphabets were designed in a 5 to 8 proportion. It is possible to deduct the face size of those fonts because we have still old-style fonts around. The proportion of 6 to 8 developed in the 1950s by Univers and Helvetica has increased legibility in small sizes, but it has required a reduction in the length of the descenders and ascenders (a negative factor in legibility), and requires extra leading. This has been inherited by Arial, compared here to Baskerville in figure 19.

Arial   Baskerville

Figure 19

Considering a 127-point size font (44.6 mm), the x-height of a Helvetica upper case is 28 mm, whereas that of an old-style Times Roman is 25.5 mm. The descender of a lower-case *q* in Helvetica will be 8 mm for that point size and 9 mm for Times Roman. Measuring from the bottom edge of the descender to the top of the upper-case X, the Helvetica will measure 36 mm and the Times Roman 34.5 mm. The height of their lower-case x shows the most significant difference: 21 mm for Helvetica and 15.9 mm for Times Roman. We can, therefore, assess that Tinker's studies referring to a 12-point type relate to a face whose size is approximately 75% of the size of a face designed after the 1950s. Figure 20 shows a comparison of x-height between Arial and Baskerville, where a 48 point Arial has the same height as a 52.5 Baskerville, whose lowercase is much smaller.

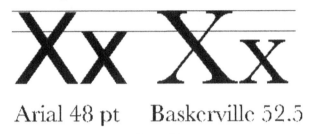

Figure 20

The basic dimensions to control in order to assess the quality of a typeface are height, width, weight and letterspacing.

Height: There should be an apparent constant x-height of all lower-case letters, an apparent constant height of capitals, and an apparent constant height of all ascenders and descenders in lower-case letters. Movements away from the norm are possible, but ascenders higher than capitals are not practical because they might invade the space of text lines above. Fonts with the *l* higher than the *t* are no exceptions, however, because the *t* has more distinctive features, and therefore it does not need a long ascender above its horizontal stroke to be recognizable. It is not advisable to use alphabets with short ascenders for *d* or *b* because these are essential for the achievement of distinction from other lower-case letters. Distinctive shapes for the solution of these letters is also advisable if one is dealing with users who suffer from some form of dyslexia, or just have plain low literacy level: lowercases *bdpq* tend to be confused by these users when differences rely on spatial orientation only.

Width: This will vary according to the complexity of the letterform. The guiding criterion to ensure that no letter stands out in an alphabet is to maintain a constant tonal density, that is, to maintain a similar ratio of black to white in all letters. To achieve this, the letters *a-b-c-d-e-g-o-p-q* may have equal width. Other groups with similar width are *f-r-t; h-n-s-u; i-j-l; k-v-x-y-z;* and *m-w.*

In addition to the relative differences between letters, type width as a variable relates to the possibility of condensing the form of type. A strong trend of product label designers to cram as much information as possible in a label has resulted in discouraging texts. Type density, however, can be negative in relation to not only the ability of people to read the texts but also their willingness to read (Young, Laughery & Bell, 1992, p. 504).

Weight (tonal weight): Consistency in weight means consistency in tone. It is necessary to provide an even weight throughout a word. This is necessary because reading is led by tonal contrast. Strokes should have an apparently consistent thickness across letters, and across horizontals, verticals, diagonals and curves. Changes in their thickness from thick to thin should be based on the same rationale for every letter. Ascending diagonal strokes (from left to right) are thinner than descending diagonal strokes (this partly comes from the tradition of calligraphy); vertical strokes are thicker than horizontal strokes (this possibly derives from architecture, where the column that supports should be thicker than the supported roof); curved strokes change smoothly their thickness according to the evolution of their direction, thinner in the diagonal sections that go from left to right, thicker in the vertical ones (deriving from calligraphy), and thinner in the horizontals.

Letterspacing: The letterspacing should be designed so that letters forming a word can be seen as a unit. The spacing program, however, should maintain easy identification of each letter. A typeface such as *Super Clarendon* (Figure 21), for instance, set with tight spacing, renders the spaces inside the letters (counters) clearly more visible than the spaces between the letters, hampering reading efficiency in continuous texts. Tight spacing in an expanded letter will frequently shift tonal cues from helping to guide the fixations between saccadic movements efficiently to attracting the eyes to meaningless configurations created by the meeting of two contiguous letters.

Super Clarendon

A text set tight in super Clarendon will show too much the counters of the letters due to their large size. The individuality of the letters will fight against the configurations created by neighboring characters, resulting in tiring reading.

Figure 21

There are other factors that affect typographic selection. Preferences will depend on length of text, use of text, economy and technology of production, context of implementation, and purpose of the message. For example, the following list identifies several factors to consider:

- *Length of text:* a) a few words b) a few sentences c) long text
- *Use of text:* a) continuous reading b) lists for information scanning/searching

- *Economy and technology of production:* a) space available b) production technology available
- *Context of implementation:* a) printed on small products' surfaces b) printed on paper for close range reading c) printed on signs for wall mounting d) produced on plastic for internally lit signs e) designed as part of dials or other types of control panels f) electronic signs
- *Purpose of the message:* a) to inform b) to direct c) to persuade

Typefaces as System /Choosing Alphabets/Summary

An alphabet is a system of elements that should show a good balance between similarities and differences: similarities so that a reader can subordinate letters to words and words to sentences; and differences because the reader must be able to distinguish letters from one another to be able to easily distinguish words from one another. All letters in a given weight of a typeface should have a similar tonal density. Apertures of letters should be generous, avoiding closing-in hooks for letters such as 'a' or 'e'.

Legibility of Letters/The Resolving Power of the Eye

The previous section discussed criteria regarding the quality of a type font. This section instead discusses the size of letters, which is a second fundamental factor in the preparation of efficient visual presentation of words.

One way of establishing reliable criteria for the sizing of type to ensure the legibility of print is to resort to optometry. Visual acuity can be defined as the visual angle subtended by the eye when perceiving a shape, and is measured in minutes of degrees. The viewing angle is formed by the relation between lettersize and viewing distance. In the case of what is considered normal vision, for instance, the height of the letter *E* should be 5 minutes of arc, or .0015 radians – the ratio of required letter height to viewing distance (Smith, 1984, p. 176). This means that at one meter viewing distance the letter should measure 1.5 mm (Grether & Baker, 1972, p. 58). This is the standard used today for the definition of normal vision. According to this standard, and given that the letter *E* is formed by five horizontal elements (three strokes and two spaces), a person with normal vision should be able to resolve details that measure one-third of a millimeter per meter of viewing distance. One is easily able to detect the presence of such elements in the visual field, and something even thinner could be spotted. Regarding legibility, however, we must address the capacity of the eye to *resolve* details, and not merely to *detect* their presence. If we look at several parallel lines, we will be able to count them if we have normal vision, and if their thickness and the separations between them are at least one-third of a millimeter per meter of viewing distance.

The Snellen chart works with square forms similar to the upper-case *E* in different orientations. Subjects are supposed to clearly indicate the direction of the elements (Figure 22).

Figure 22

In this system, the smallest readable *E*, which establishes whether one does or does not have normal vision, is five times the height of the resolution threshold (three horizontal strokes and two spaces). Mark Sanders and Ernest McCormick (1993) argue that, when the overall size of the letter is constant, people can equally distinguish the letter *E* when the strokes are thinner. They recommend a stroke-width to letter-height ratio of 1:6 to 1:8 for black type on white ground, and 1:8 to 1:10 for the opposite. They go on to recommend that, when illumination is reduced, thick letters become more readable, and a ratio of 1:5 is more efficient (Sanders and McCormick, 1993, p. 103).

With regard to reading, however, it is one thing to consider a threshold value but another to define "comfortable reading." If one observes a person approaching a written notice, this person will get much closer to the text than what the threshold value requires. This will result in a comfortable reading value of two to three times the threshold value, increasing the size of the letters to 3 or even 4.5 millimeters per meter of viewing distance.

Jerry Duncan and Stephan Konz (1976) report that, when subjects were asked to read numerals, they approached them until subtending an angle of 23 minutes of arc, instead of the 5 required for error-free reading. Numerals require larger visual angles because they do not form units such as words that can be recognized in a holistic manner. The reading of letters involves guessing and probability of occurrence. In numbers, instead, this is not the case, and therefore a reader will require a greater size for sign reading. Among the military, the recommendation for the size of critical data is three to five times the threshold value. Other factors affect this decision, such as viewing angle, tonal contrast, and light conditions. Thus, the maintenance of signs and the emotional contexts are in this case considered (Smith, 1984, p. 173). In the military, personnel in a war zone might be frightened, tired, stressed, and in a hurry, and the signs might be dirty, poorly lit, and located at less than ideal visual angles. Many typefaces are good for most situations, but in adverse conditions special considerations must guide the careful selection of type (Sanders and McCormick, 1993, p. 103).

Grether and Baker (1972) indicate that the recommended letter size depends on the viewing distance and the illumination conditions. For a viewing distance of 70 cm, they recommend a lettersize of 5 mm, well in line with the "comfortable" size discussed above. They also recommend that for less critical functions – and when light levels are above 1 foot-candle (ft-c) – the letter height could be reduced to 2.5 mm. This is still consistent with the dimensions discussed by Smith. If we consider normal vision and the threshold established by the Snellen chart, at a viewing distance of 70 cm, the minimum size of a letter should be 1.05 mm (Grether & Baker, 1972, p. 107).

According to the U.S. Military Standard 1472B (Section 5.5.5.12, p. 94 and Table X, p. 95, 1974, cited by Smith, 1984, p. 174), intensity of light is relevant to the determination of type size. Recommendations therein have established a difference between non-critical data and critical data. For critical data with variable positions on a display, the standard recommends character heights of 3.0 to 5.0 mm for a high luminance level and 5.0 to 7.5 mm for low light intensity, considering a viewing distance of 710 mm. Smith notes that the subtended angles of this Military Standard's recommendations range from 6 to 37 minutes, that is, from barely above the normal acuity threshold of 5 minutes to a generous 7.4 times higher.

Sanders and McCormick (1993) concur with much of this. Translating their feet and inches formulae to metric, they recommend 7.2 to 10.7 millimeters per meter of viewing distance for low luminance signs with variable position and critical use, as opposed to 5.3 to 10.5 mm for fixed positions; and 1.8 to 7.2 mm for non-critical use. For high luminance (1.0 foot-lambert [fL] and above), they reduce the minimum size acceptable in the first two cases but not for the non-critical use. They go on to suggest that for comfortable reading one should consider a 20/40 vision standard, that is, twice as large a visual angle as that required by normal vision, as defined by the Snellen chart. This will result in typesizes of 3.5 to 4.6 to 5.8 millimeters per meter of viewing distance, depending on whether the stroke width-to-height ratio is 1:6, 1:8 or 1:10 (Sanders and McCormick, 1993, pp. 107-108).

According to Grether and Baker (1972), the intensity of light is a major factor in the determination of visual acuity. The visual angle required for the legibility of letters and other symbols might shift from a wide 10 minutes for a low light condition to a 0.4 minute for a high luminance situation.

In the history of requirements for minimum sizes in all kinds of warnings or mandatory notices, it has been common among manufacturers to address minimum height requirements by producing ultra-narrow letters with hairline strokes. This is not a good interpretation of the intentions of such regulations, which are meant to help users and consumers to read sizes, contents, warnings, expiry dates, and the like. Consistent with this discussion, for a letter to maintain a good level of legibility, the thickness of its elements must be approximately one-fifth (or somewhat thinner) of the height of the character, and the width of the character should be no less than three-fifths of its height. This derives from the letters *E, B* and *S*, for instance, having three horizontal strokes and two spaces separating them, that is, five elements to be discriminated. They have three vertical elements. The same maximum number of elements applies to almost all lower-case letters, with the exception of *m* and *w,* which should therefore be wider than the rest. In old typewriters, given their fixed space allowance for all letters, it was normally quite possible to spot these letters in a typescript because their strokes jammed together and their tone was darker than the rest. No letter has more than five horizontal elements and normally no more than three vertical ones. This coincides with Grether and Baker who, in connection with printed information, recommend that "letter width-to-height ratio should be 3:5" (Grether & Baker, 1972, p. 107). Studies of the legibility of type have found no significant performance differences when comparing two fonts of similar proportions. Benjamin Somberg (1990) studied type in CRT displays and found no significant difference between 1:0.70 and 1:0.57 proportions (Somberg, 1990, p. 1463). It seems that people accept a certain range of proportions before performance deteriorates. In the market, however, there are many examples of condensed type where legibility is hampered.

Extensive research on the relative legibility of typefaces with different widths has been reported by Young, Laughery and Bell at the 1992 Human Factors and Ergonomics Society meeting in Santa Monica, California (cited by Wogalter and Vigilante, 2003, p. 328). They found that any reduction of the width of a given font affected its legibility in a significant way. Philip Anderton and B.L. Cole (1982) reported earlier their findings about how letter separation affects legibility. As common knowledge in typography indicates, when characters are set too tight, the legibility performance of any font deteriorates, particularly for reading at a distance, such as in signs posted for reading in large or open spaces.

As mentioned above, tonal direction is a factor to consider when deciding the stroke thickness of a letter. If the letter is black on a white ground and another version is white on a black ground, this second version should lose about 10% of stroke thickness to appear equal to its black counterpart. White elements tend to appear thicker to the eye. Grether and Baker (1972) report that, though visual acuity increases as light intensity increases, for internally illuminated signs there is a drop point when luminance continues to grow beyond 10 fL. At this point, "acuity for white on black targets drops off quickly." This is called irradiation, that is, the blurring of the edges of forms that results from a high contrast of light between figure and ground (Grether & Baker, 1972, p. 51). It has been found that white letters on black ground result in about 10% slower reading (Tinker, 1963, p. 130). Nilsson reports: "Black letters on white backgrounds were slightly, but consistently, more legible than white-on-black" (Nilsson, 1999, p. 5).

The context of implementation has a bearing on letterspacing. Letterspacing for signs in the street should be generous as opposed to the spacing between letters in a book to be read at a short distance. But reading at a close range requires a wider visual angle for comfortable reading than signs to be read at a distance (Smith, 1984, p. 183). The legibility of signs is in turn affected by weather conditions and other visual difficulties, and a safety factor always has to be estimated for each situation in question. Giese (1946) condemns the habit of testing prospective employees for visual acuity with the traditional Snellen chart at the 20 feet (6 meters) distance when the actual work of the laborers would involve close range vision. The acuity a person can demonstrate at 20 feet is not necessarily an indication of how someone would perform at 30 cm from the object. Luckiest and Moss (1933) concur in this. They found that the subject's acuity (measured as the subtended visual angle) increased with the increase of distance between observer and stimulus (the distances ranging from 60 to 280 cm). Giese (1946) concludes that variations of acuity performance relate to the distance from the target and to the variations of distance required by a job. He argues that a 30 cm difference in distance from 20 to 50 cm sounds insignificant, but it requires a change of 3 diopters of focal power, whereas the same 30 cm difference at 5 or 10 meters distance requires only a fraction (.01 and .003 respectively) of a diopter (Giese, 1946, p. 105). This suggests that warning signs that are to be read from close range require a visual angle larger than those placed at medium distance. As well, if an operator of equipment is expected to work while focusing at different distances and eventually reading the text of a warning, it is advisable to define the type size with generosity, recognizing the difficulties of focal accommodation.

Age has a bearing on legibility, and also on readability and speed of reading. Although Grade 1 children might be able to read quite a lot of words, text signs directed at children should be designed while considering that reading maturity reaches a reasonable level at age 10 (Buswell, 1937, p. 158). A good level of reading ability is not achieved until 13 years of age (Ballantine, 1951, p. 63).

The context of use must always be considered. In a study of the ability of older drivers to read street names in relation to the reflectivity of the material, it was found that information overload affected the legibility of type. To maintain comparable legibility without overload conditions, letters had to be more reflective in complex traffic (Chrysler, Tranchida, Stackhouse and Arthur, 2001, p. 1597). Warning signs often appear in industrial settings where a high concentration of attention is required from workers. Information overload might affect younger people less than older adults, but it is still a factor to be considered when defining the conspicuousness of a warning sign. Pure legibility studies in laboratory settings might not respond to the full scope of information required for a given case.

Legibility of Letters/The Resolving Power of the Eye/Summary

- Minimum legibility height for normal visual acuity: 1.5 millimeters per meter of viewing distance.
- Comfortable reading size: 4.5 millimeters per meter of viewing distance.
- Minimum size for critical information under low light conditions: 7 millimeters per meter of viewing distance.
- Required stroke width to height of letters: 1:5 to 1:8.
- Required correction for white type on dark ground: 10% thinner strokes.
- Letterspacing for medium distance reading should be more open than for close range reading.
- Close range vision requires larger visual angles than medium and long reading distances.

According to the Canadian Federal Identity Manual, as the reading distance grows, the letter size must grow at a slower pace. They propose the following scale:

- 1 m: 5 mm
- 2 m: 6 mm
- 4 m: 8 mm
- 6 m: 10 mm

- 9 m: 15 mm (At this level, we are quite close to the threshold of the resolution power of the eye; however; the recognition of the profile of a word requires less visual acuity than an isolated letter. If the signs are properly coded visually, it is possible to identify the sign and to come closer to read it.)
-
- 12 m: 20 mm (threshold: 18 mm)
- 15 m: 25 mm (threshold: 22.5 mm)
- 24 m: 40 mm (threshold: 36 mm)

The purpose of this recommendation is to avoid excessively large signs. The size of the letters should always be maintained at 10% above the threshold.

For road signs, the Canadian government recommends the following x-heights:

- 50 to 60 mm for 30 km/h;
- 80 to 100 mm for 50 km/h; and
- 120, 150 or 200 mm for speeds up to 100 km.

Placement of the signs is also important. For it to be seen, a sign must fall within a radius of 15° from the centre of the direction of the observer's vision. This means roughly 25 cm displacement for every meter of distance between the observer and the sign.

For warning or danger signs, the sign must be placed within 5°, that is, 8 cm displacement for every meter of distance between the observer and the sign.

Upper Case versus Lower Case

Much has been discussed about the relative legibility of words in upper case as opposed to lower case. In signage, the usual reading of one to three words does not show significant differences. For long texts, however, the situation is different because texts in all caps remove differences in word profile – one of the strategies of the visual system to discriminate words – and this deteriorates reading performance. In an experiment that compared the legibility performance of texts in Univers all caps with other texts in lower-case letters, working in small sizes, E.C. Poulton (1972) found that the caps had to be 1.44 mm high to be as legible as the lower-case Univers with an x-height of 1.19 mm (E.C. Poulton, 1972, p. 160). Poulton refers readers to Tinker and Paterson (1928) when he states that, in 9-pt and 10-pt body sizes, caps are not read as quickly as mixed caps and lower-case letters (Poulton, 1972, p. 158). Tinker, after a later experiment (reported in 1940), indicated that, according to reading speed tests (and readers' opinions), lower-case type is much more legible than text set all in caps (Tinker, 1963, pp. 57, 60). The same is supported by Hartley (2004, p. 921).

Paterson and Tinker report that, working with 60-pt. type, headlines were more easily read when set in upper and lower case than when set all in caps (1946, pp. 187-188).

Confusion concerning the superiority of either caps or lower-case letters probably originated with early legibility studies that compared the legibility of individual letters, upper and lower case. These studies were often flawed on two counts: 1) they measured exclusively the legibility of individual letters, and 2) they often worked within a given point size, disregarding the different actual size of the letters.

In the signage for a hospital in Edmonton, Alberta, it was decided to compose the word *exit* all in lower case, on the basis that lower-case letters are more legible than caps. The speed with which one reads a single word, as already mentioned, does not show significant differences. In addition, North Americans are routinely used to reading the word EXIT from a long distance, all in caps, as an icon, even when individual letters cannot be distinguished. The configuration *exit* in lower case challenges our stored memory of the sign and might weaken its performance (Figures 23a and 23b)

Figures 23a and 23b

Jock Kinneir (the designer who created the road sign system for the United Kingdom) used to say that people speak in lower case and scream in caps. In the case of the design of danger-related signs, it makes sense to set the word *DANGER* all in caps, but any longer explanatory text to follow would be more appropriate if set in upper and lower case.

Habit has much to do with readability. We are used to reading texts in upper and lower case. To us, initial letters in upper case indicate proper names or the beginning of sentences. Herbert Bayer, for the sake of simplicity, designed the text for the Bauhaus exhibition catalogue around 1970 without caps at all. He did this partly as a reaction against the German tradition of capitalizing every noun, but even English speakers find the texts difficult to read without the cues provided by capital initials after periods or for proper names. By the same token, it could be that habit supports serif against sans serif faces when reading long texts, such as books and magazines. In his famous article on the legibility of small typefaces, Poulton found that Times New Roman and Perpetua were more legible than Univers, even when the Univers texts were enlarged to 1.48 mm x-height, well above the 1.24 and 1.28 mm used for Times and Perpetua respectively (Poulton, 1972, p. 161).

Upper Case Versus Lower Case/Summary

- Lower-case letters are more legible than upper-case letters for reading texts.
- Upper-case letters are more legible when used individually.
- Word recognition is based on the initial letter, the length of the word, and its profile (ascenders and descenders and the internal pattern).

Color

There are several national and international standards concerning the codified use of color, which sometimes leave little option to the designer of traffic or other kinds of regulatory signs. One must look into local uses in every case. The sign for exit, for instance, is red in North America but green in Europe. It has been internationally established that traffic lights and signs are red for stop, yellow for caution, and green for proceeding. Brown and blue are used for parks and information respectively. The enclosing shape of traffic signs and the position of lights in traffic lights help color-blind people to interpret the system. This is possible because to obtain a driver's license one has to learn the code. When using color to communicate with the general public, one has to rely on more natural color symbologies. About 6% (some authors say 8%) of healthy adult males have some form of color blindness (Grether & Baker, 1972, p. 71). These people tend to confuse red with yellow, and green with white; moreover, in many situations, they confuse red with green. Although green is not a warning color, the poor perception of red calls for making sure that warning signs do not rely on color alone. When designing a color system within the design of warnings, care should be taken to ensure that the shades are distinct also for people with severely reduced sensitivity to color. The US Army-Navy Aeronautical Specification AN-C-56, the scale of 10 spectral colors developed by Chapanis and Halsey (1956), and the US Government Federal Specification II-C-595 are examples of sets built in search of a reliable distinction level for all sighted people.

The colors of backgrounds affect legibility. Luckiest and Moss measured the visibility of type on 10 colors of paper and found that only the "[f]airly saturated yellowish red or reddish orange" showed significant reduction in both visibility and reading speed. It seems that accommodation to conditions allows for a rather broad range of tonal contrast between type and ground, though black on white or on light shades of sepia, cream and buff tends to be preferred (Luckiest and Moss, 1933, p. 25).

The visibility of black type on color ground, or color type on black ground, depends to a great extent on tonal contrast. Miyake, Dunlap and Cureton studied the ability of subjects to correctly respond to a series of brief exposures of black numerals on color paper (1930, p. 340). They found that black type read well on white, yellow and green (I suppose, a light green), but red and green type on black ground resulted in low legibility scores. Unfortunately, the colors are not reported with precision, and it is therefore difficult to generalize the results. Tests of reading speed show that red print on a dark green background can extend reading time by about 40%. Tonal similarity and hue conflicts are key situations to avoid when planning colored type on colored ground. Color combinations that result in poor legibility cause an increase in regressions, an extension of fixation durations, and therefore an increase in perception time; they also increase fatigue and slow down the overall reading speed. Color does not appear to affect legibility in test situations in which size and tonal contrast appear as leading variables, but Nilsson (1999, p. 2) argues that this is due to using speed of perception as an indicator of legibility. When legibility measures are based on distance and not speed, color appears as a relevant dimension. Nilsson reports on several figure-ground color relations that were significantly more effective than black on white: "green/white, black/yellow, and green/yellow, with white/green, blue/yellow, black/red and blue/white being at least equally effective" (p. 8).

Color also has a bearing on meaning and attention: in certain contexts, red seems to be internationally associated with danger. Adams and Edworthy (1995, pp. 2232-2233) found "that the signal word had to be twice as big in black as in red to give the same perceived urgency."

Color/Summary

Color type on color ground should maintain significant light intensity difference to guarantee legibility. In this context, "significant" means about a 1 to 2 light reflectance relation between letters and grounds. Poor situations such as medium to dark type on black ground can significantly reduce reading speed. Optimal readability favors black type on off-white backgrounds.

The Sign in Context

The actual effectiveness of a sign requires the monitoring of all details of implementation. A highly visible warning sign, placed on the back and sides of a tanker truck that was carrying a corrosive acid, became useless when the truck overturned on a British highway some years ago. A passerby who tried to help the driver suffered severe foot burns. From the direction of approach of the pedestrian, the sign on the back of the tanker was invisible, and so were the ones on the sides: one was against the ground, and the other was pointing at the sky and above the height of the pedestrian. Grether and Baker (1972, p. 42) propose that the information must be presented so that correct decisions and control actions can be undertaken "without unacceptable delay." They also stated generally that "a display must be designed to suit the particular conditions under which it will be used."

The congress *Data Design for Decisions*, Paris, 2009, organized by the International Institute for Information Design (*International Design Journal* 2009), brought together several presentations aimed at arguing that information does not normally have an end in itself, but does constitute an important step in decision-making processes and their implementation, be these decisions related to thinking or acting.

There is also the concept of *scenarios* in design methods (Maschi, 2006) that help designers to consider complete and complex situations, in which not only things but also people's behaviors are described and discussed. When dealing with the design of information that might affect the safety of others, such as in medications or in the handling of potentially dangerous equipment or substances, the designer must be particularly careful, considering the contexts of use and the emotional and physical factors that could affect the users of a device, a drug, or a facility. This problem is confronted by designers who work on the instructions for emergency procedures, such as those in passenger aircraft. If danger reduces cognitive functions, and more so for a person without experience in a given situation, the expected level of skill can fall dramatically. Many years ago, information designer Paul Mijksenaar was approached by the aircraft manufacturer Fokker to redesign the instructions for the emergency opening procedures of one of their aircraft's doors. The client claimed that people found existing instructions difficult. After analyzing the situation, Mijksenaar responded with a recommendation to change the opening mechanism. It was too complex for an ordinary passenger to understand how to operate it without formal training, and particularly in a stress situation.

In the toilets of a university in Brazil, the sign asking people to wash their hands before leaving the place was located on the mirrors above the wash basins. Totally useless. The people who read the signs were those who got close to the wash basins intending to wash their hands. Those who headed for the exit did not see them. The signs should have been on the inside of the exit door, on the inside of cubicles, or above the urinals. The best sign can become useless at the implementation stage, as it was already reported above regarding figure 8.

There has been formal research in support of the need to test things in situation, particularly in the terrain of warnings, instructions and training. Purswell, Krenek and Dorris (1987) observed that to evaluate the performance of a warning label it is necessary to assess how its users are affected by information overload, the stimulus energy level, risk perception, the cost of compliance, and the interaction of warnings, instructions and training. Cost, in this context, is the effort or time required by a user to read, as well as to observe a recommendation. Although these considerations are not purely typographical, they do affect the final performance of warnings and related materials. The design of warnings is a specialized field; however, it is used here as an example because the difficulties that a warning reader experiences are similar to those found by any reader of instructions, only in a more evident way. This helps us to understand where the problems could lie in the visual presentation of any instructional signs.

The Sign in Context/Summary

The final evaluation of a sign must take place in its implementation context. When thinking about design as a strategy to obtain certain responses from people, it is advisable to engage in an iterative process, alternating the development of prototypes with their evaluation by users (Sless, 1996, p. 6).

Every design solution can be improved. Every new solution contributes to the development of the profession and prepares us to face new situations with more sophisticated tools.

Images: Representation and Symbolism

Pictograms

The design of graphic symbols for public information can have different functions and is divided into several categories: operation of equipment, instructions, wayfinding in buildings or open spaces, identification of places or objects, and warning and danger signs. These categories are related to two types of user: the trained professional and the public at large. The first type refers to chemists, engineers and aircraft pilots, and requires symbols that can be easily distinguished from one another, learned, and remembered. The second type, the design of symbols for public information, requires instead that the symbols can be understood without a learning process (ISO/TR 7239, 1984; ISO 7001, 2007/2013/2014).

It should be noted, however, that there are also pictograms used in branding, but I will not refer to these in this book, the focus of which is on information design. Sometimes pictograms must be designed with the sole purpose of providing clear information, such as in the case of aircraft control panels or medical equipment, or in the design of warnings. Other times, however, the information can work along with the creation of a certain type of environmental character, playful, childish, or whatever might be the case, depending on the genre of the facility or context in which it operates.

Pictogram Development Methods

The development of a set of graphic symbols for use within a professional field requires a commission composed of designers and users who, knowing existing standards, can find ways to improve existing symbols or to add new ones while avoiding conflicts with the existing ones. This requires interviews and meetings, and finally tests to evaluate the level of recognition until an acceptable level is achieved.

In the development of graphic symbols for public information, the International Organization for Standardization (ISO) has established a protocol that consists of the following steps: 1) selection of the referents to be included in the system, 2) collection of existing graphic symbols that represent the selected referent, 3) Preference Ranking test for the selected symbols, 4) Comprehension test of the three best symbols for each referent selected through preference ranking, 5) writing of a description of the image content for the finally selected graphic symbol for each referent, and 6) design of one example of visualization to be published along with the standard description in ISO 7001 (ISO 9186, 2008/2014).

Selection of the Referents

When the need for pictograms to communicate information is determined, the first step is to define the number of items that must be included in a system or category. The main criterion here is to determine when a pictogram can be more efficient than a word. It is normally advisable to display the pictogram along with a corresponding word. Redundancy seldom obstructs communication. Sometimes, because of lack of space or multilingualism (in an airport, for instance), the word might not help many people, and can become just noise.

Collection of Existing Graphic Symbols

Once a list of referents has been defined, an international search must be developed to collect the corresponding existing symbols. Once collected, consultation with experts might help to eliminate solutions that are too similar or others that perceptually or cognitively appear as obviously not fit for international standardization. If the expert group decides that before going to testing it would be useful to develop new visual solutions, these must be developed. Before starting a labor intensive testing program, it is advisable to have expert consensus that the existing samples possess sufficient quality to warrant the effort. The adoption of a symbol as a standard in ISO requires the comprehension of 67% of the tested population. For danger related symbols, 83% is required.

Preference Ranking Test (Easterby & Graydon, 1981; Easterby & Zwaga, 1976)

This test is done with each referent independently. 1) All existing alternative designs for a given referent are brought together; 2) the subjects (usually 100 per country in two dissimilar countries) are told what the symbols are supposed to stand for; 3) the subjects are asked to rank the pictograms from the best to the worst, assigning "1" to the best; and 4) the three pictograms that obtain the lowest score are selected for the comprehension test (Figures 24a and 24b).

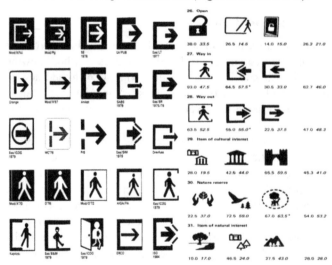

Figures 24a and 24b

Comprehension Test

Normally, 450 subjects are used for this test in each of five countries. In this case, subjects are not informed what the symbols to be seen stand for. 1) Three booklets are compiled, each one with one of the three versions of the selected symbols; 2) other symbols are added to reduce inter-influence between symbols and to get to around 30 to 40 symbols per booklet; 3) page order is randomized for each version of the booklets to reduce sequence effect; and 4) subjects are asked to write down what they think the symbol stands for beneath each pictogram.

The written responses must be interpreted, so they are categorized as follows: 1) certain; 2) almost certain; 3) likely certain; 4) marginally likely certain; 5) unlikely certain; 6) no response; 7) don't know; and 8) wrong (description of image or opposite meaning). The responses are looked at from not only a comprehension perspective but also a behavioral perspective. The original text reads: "Given this response, is the respondent certain, almost certain, likely, marginally likely, or unlikely to have understood the sign and to behave correctly." "Behave correctly" is the key issue here. Depending on the importance of the symbol, that is, whether it involves potential danger, the category "marginally likely" can be counted as a wrong answer. For danger-related symbols, 1% of opposite meaning responses results in the elimination of the pictogram.

Writing of a Description of the Image Content/Design of One Example of Visualization

When the most efficient pictogram has been found, its verbal description has to be formulated. This description of the elements included in the image and their distribution (that is, a side view of stairs with the profile of a human figure climbing them), serves as a guide that could be visualized in diverse ways depending on the visual culture of the place where it will operate. The standard description is published with an example of visualization. The description, not the pictogram, constitutes the standard.

Implementation Criteria

Locations always impose their specific constraints, but some recommendations are worth noting. For each meter of the viewing distance of the observer, the following is recommended.

- Minimum line thickness: 0.5 mm
- Minimum size for significant details: 1 mm
- Symbol size to ensure legibility: 12 mm
- Symbol size to ensure conspicuity: 25 mm
- Maximum displacement from central line of vision: 250 mm
- Maximum displacement for danger symbols: 80 mm

The listed dimensions are to be taken as departure points and must be evaluated in the situations of use. The increase in size is not to be mechanically added as the distance increases. Generally, at great distances, these sizes can be reduced by 30%, particularly when a pictogram is associated with other pictograms. It is important that users can see where to find information, even when this information is not quite legible.

Another factor to consider is the complexity of the environment where the pictogram is going to operate. Final decisions regarding size must be arrived at through prototype testing at real scale in the implementation site. (To study this topic further, consult ISO Technical Report 7239, now replaced by ISO 9186; see also Frascara 2006a, p. 134.)

Graphic symbols have also been used to represent statistical data. A pioneer in this subject was Otto Neurath, and his organization Isotype (Figure 25) (University of Reading, 1975).

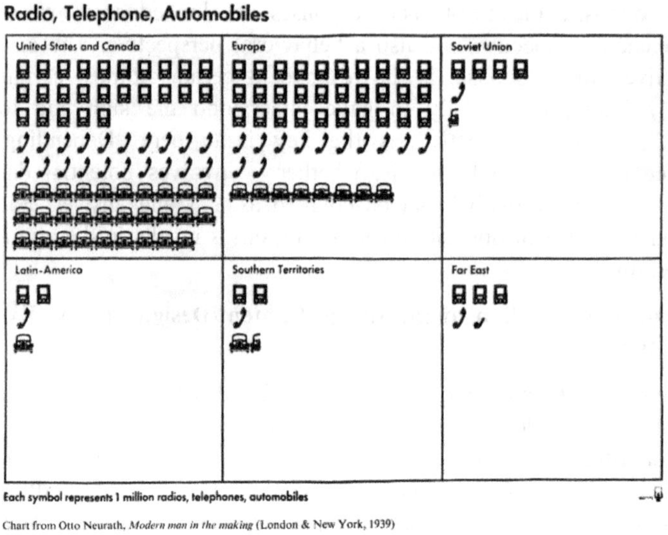

Figure 25

The Importance of Contexts

Several contexts affect the performance of graphic symbols. One is physical, the situation of use. Figure 26a shows a symbol that is difficult to understand away from its context. Figure 26b shows the symbol in context, and then the message becomes clear. Some symbols that look good in the isolation of the design office can become obscure or even disappear in other contexts. One can sketch at the office, but there is nothing like assessing the symbol in its situation of use. Lighting, environmental complexity, viewing angle, even dirt can affect the performance of a symbol.

Figure 26a and 26b

Another context is conceptual, and this is brought in by the user. When I encountered the symbol of Figure 27 for the first time, I did not know what it meant. This was not because of a poor visual quality of the pictogram, but because I did not have an idea of what the referent represented, which was a sandy area to be used as an escape route before a slope when truck drivers could not trust their brakes.

Purpose can be a problem. The purpose of a symbol might be irrelevant and become puzzling for a user who has a different purpose in mind. Redundant symbols can become noise, just like fire extinguisher symbols that are located immediately above much larger and more conspicuous actual fire extinguisher.

Figure 27

Diagrams

Diagrams are traditionally used in visual communications to present quantitative information (Tufte, 1983). This has been widely discussed, and their advantages for some applications have been proved many times, paradigmatically by Jacques Bertin through his classical example of the hotel manager (Bertin, 1981). Bertin (1983) recognizes three basic functions for diagrams: to record, to understand and to communicate, extending the value of diagrams beyond their more usual function as communication devices. One can ponder some times, whether diagrams help the reader come to grips with a text or are rather involved in the creation of knowledge.

Although diagramming as a way of contributing to the process of thinking has been used quite commonly, it has not been systematically studied much at all, and certainly it has penetrated general education even less. As a result, picture making has been relegated to self-expression and recreation, and verbal language has provided the paradigm for thinking, for science, and for general exchanges of information. The structure of verbal language, however, offers a limited capacity to convey information. It promotes linear thinking and sequentiality, and is inadequate for the presentation of hierarchies, inclusions, simultaneity, distinctions of levels, multiplicity of kinds, and complexity of connections. Although all this can be described verbally, the nature of the verbal discourse does not reflect the structure of the signified. The development of thinking habits in Western education has concentrated on language, and therefore on sequential and unilinear thinking. In the long run, this has limited our capacity to understand serious problems of a physical or social nature because of the lack of ability of the verbal language to promote thinking in terms of ecologies of information.

It is possible that this tendency has been fostered by the nature of the verbal language structure, but its influence has also been felt in the terrain of graphic presentations where simplicity, isolation of variables, and reduction of data have been pursued many times as strategies to improve the scientific quality of the graphics developed. In this way, it was attempted to produce clarity of information.

It is evident, however, that our world is an integrated system, as it can be easily seen now that the natural environment is stressed by human overpopulation, chemical contamination, and biological hazards that stem from the need for unprecedented quantities of food production.

Case 1: Diagrams and Statistics

In 1974, I did a study on children's preferences for illustration styles in Buenos Aires. I compared preferences between four types of images: 1) complex versus simpler; 2) natural colors versus intensified colors; 3) soft edges + lights and shades versus hard edges and flat colors; and 4) natural versus simplified shapes. The children were shown two pictures at a time, one differing from the other in only one dimension. Pictures were coded with strings of two letters, and the children were asked to write on a sheet of paper the code of the image that they liked the best. The results were computed after separating the 440-children population into six groups: three ages (7, 9 and 11) and the two genders. The project involved four responses per child for a total of 1760 responses. It was difficult to see patterns in numbers, so the data were transformed into a graph that allowed the viewer to visualize trends (Frascara, 1979; Ladan & Frascara, 1977).

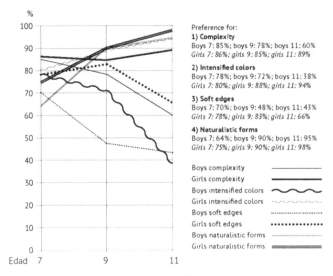

Figure 28

As the graph shows, the information presented in a diagram becomes more understandable than when presented alphanumerically on the right, and aids in the decision-making processes regarding publications for children (Figure 28).

Case 2: Diagrams and Traffic Safety

Traffic safety is another super-complex problem that cannot be addressed properly if one does not look at it in its totality. Although the graphs published in *Mission Possible: the integrated safety initiative for Alberta* (1996) do not intend to represent the totality of the factors that affect traffic safety, they do at least show that, when looking at the traffic safety problem, we have to be conscious of the three basic areas of action that an integrated strategy has to consider: the traffic environment, the road users, and the vehicles (Figure 29).

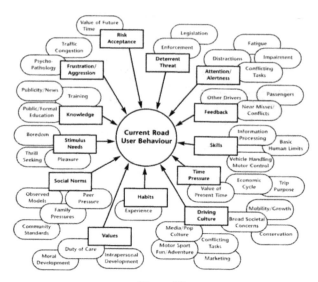

Figure 29

If we focus on one of those dimensions, and try to identify the factors that affect road user behavior, for instance, a driver, cyclist or pedestrian, we get an idea of how each one of the dimensions outlined could be further developed to present the problem with a high degree of richness. One can get closer to each one of the areas to see that they are made up of clusters of information that offer possibilities for insight and action. This need for action that we have in the practice of design benefits more from diagramming as opposed to verbally describing complex situations. Verbal descriptions challenge memory and imagination, and deceivingly present problems as if they were under control.

The first reaction of people who enter traffic safety is to propose solutions that relate to the window through which they see the problem. If they are engineers, they point at road construction and vehicle safety; if they are policemen, they look at enforcement; if they are traffic education experts, they look at driver training, etc. In this connection, diagramming has to fight the power of personal experience, of recent experience, and of the emotional charge associated with what has been lived as opposed to what has been learned beyond that. Diagrams help to develop a bird's-eye view of a problem.

Case 3: Diagrams and the Environmental Problem

The limits to growth is a publication produced by the Club of Rome (Meadows, et al., 1972) that focuses on alerting people to the finite nature of world resources and to the fast way in which we are heading toward disaster. It presents information about the world situation by using both a series of double entry charts and a series of diagrams that illustrate connections among a wide variety of factors. The series of diagrams begins with a simple one on population (Figure 30, p. 34), followed by more complex diagrams that finally propose relations between population, agricultural capital, and industrial capital (Figure 31, p. 97). Other diagrams propose alternative influences, such as the relations between industrial capital, service capital and non-renewable resources (Figure 32, p. 100). Finally, a full graph of world ecology is presented (pp. 102-103, impossible to reproduce here). In this case, it becomes clear that we are in front of an insight that cannot be conveyed by verbal language alone.

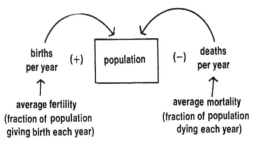

Figure 30

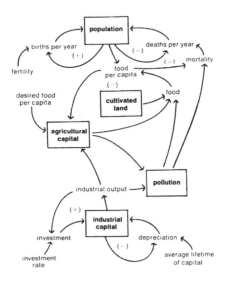

Figure 31

To convey information about something physical, such as the streets of a city or the muscles of an arm, a visual presentation will be more efficient than a verbal description. In the Club of Rome case, however, I am not talking about physical things but about conceptual constructs, where connections are proposed between economic and biological factors, resources, population and pollution: a complex ecology that resists comprehension if one separates its components into discrete pairs.

Although we could argue about the suitability of the specific connections outlined by the authors of this publication, the graph successfully drives home the message that the problem is not simple; moreover, the possible solution to such a complex problem cannot be based upon strategically breaking it down into its component problems because these cannot be addressed independently.

Instead of looking at isolated events in a linear, language-based, binary way, a more responsible and intelligent approach to knowledge would be to look at diagrams as tools that foster the understanding of ecologies of information, and as instruments that assist the development of intelligence. I propose to define intelligence as the ability to connect and distinguish units of information; as the ability to generalize from the particular and to recognize in the individual the applicability of the general; and as the ability to discover patterns, hierarchies and causalities. The intelligent person creates taxonomies and uses information to build propositional knowledge and to guide action. Diagrams provide an alternative possibility to written language. Their relevance depends in part on the problem confronted and in part on the kind of intelligence of the observer (Gardner, 2006).

Information as a Guide for Action

Information design can help to make decisions. In 1980, the Government of the Province of Alberta hired population geographer Dr. Leszek Kosinski to produce statistical posters to inform immigration officers about the population and its changes in Alberta. This was meant to help legislators to assess immigration laws and their implementation. He hired me to visualize the data and to put it into shape in A1-size posters. The project caught the attention of the Federal Government of Canada, and shortly after we did a similar project at the national level (Figures 32 and 33).

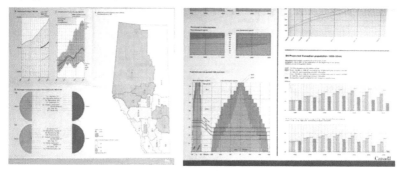

Figures 32 and 33

Diagrams, to be understood, must contextualize the statistics in an adequate way to avoid the distortions frequently found in journalism. If I say "there were 43,100 deaths," I am not indicating where, when or why. But, if I say "there were 43,100 deaths in the USA caused by traffic accidents in 2007," I have a more precise idea. Still, I can wonder: "is this a lot? Is it normal for a country of this size?" Figure 34 gives more information, but it does not take into account the population of the countries included. The information is truthful, but its significance is distorted. Since the populations of the three countries differ considerably, to make a comparison it makes more sense to measure the number of fatalities per 100,000 people. In this case (Figure 35), one can see that the number of traffic fatalities in the USA in 2007 was 1.6 times higher than in Canada and more than twice those in Norway.

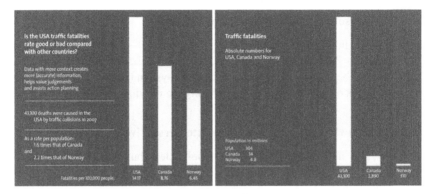

Figures 34 and 35

Contexts can pertain to different categories: one category could be the number of people involved in fatality collisions per age group, and another could be the costs involved. The total cost of non-intentional injuries in the USA in 2006 was 684 billion dollars (without including long-term treatment costs). The public goes through the roof when an exceptional expense is noticed by the media (Figure 36), such as the one-time-only Bush administration bank bailout. It is surprising that neither the media nor the people become outraged over the cost of non-intentional injuries that could be reduced by 50% with good public and industrial education campaigns.

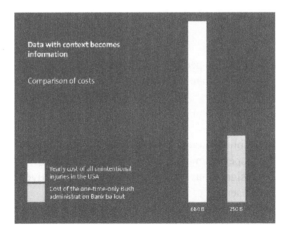

Figures 36

Comparison is a key strategy in applying clarity to information. To make the comparison work, one of the factors must be known by the public. *People can understand only things that relate to things that they already understand.* For instance, everybody knows that the American budget for the army is extremely high. This cost in 2005 represented 4.06% of the GNP; however, the cost of non-intentional traffic injuries in 2008 represented 4.82% of the GNP. The significance of the injuries problem is now much clearer.

More Comparisons: Education and Public Health

Traffic injuries in Canada cost the same as financing K-12 education. If traffic injuries were to be reduced by 50%, 6,250 new teachers could be hired, and 16,500 hospital beds could be added to the health system (in addition to those that would then become available), dramatically improving health as much as education.

The Challenge: How to Transform Data into Persuasive Information

Frequently, the information must be not only clear but also convincing. The presentation of the information must recognize the mentality of its public. Tables might be good for accountants, short texts for politicians, graphs for statisticians, and diagrams for designers. But this refers only to form:

- the content must be related to things that the public already understands;
- it must consider the public's vocabulary;
- the public must see a personal benefit in the adoption of a behavioral change or in the sheer effort involved in reading;
- to warrant a mass media effort, the public must be:
  - *substantial* (must justify the expense);
  - *reachable* (it should be possible to reach the most critical segments exposed to the risk);
  - *reactive* (the public should be able to change); and
  - *measurable* (it should be possible to measure the reduction of the problem).

Some Things to Remember

It is easier to produce well-performing information design when one tries to support cognitive functions than when one tries to promote attitude or behavioral changes.

It is easier to facilitate cognitive tasks:

- when the public belongs to a definable culture, is motivated, and is willing to cooperate in the project;
- when the designer has access to study representatives from the entire spectrum of users;
- when structured interviews can be combined with ethnographic observation of use; and
- when qualitative research can be combined with quantitative research.

Data without context is not information, and the contexts at play are partly brought up by the designer and partly by the public.

The Role of Evaluation in Information Design

Evaluation in information design serves to estimate the degree to which the new design improves upon the performance of the previous one, or, where no previous one exists, achieves the performance expected. This evaluation must be based on the observation of use of the design, not on a survey of opinions conducted with users. The final evaluation of a project of information design should be quantified, such as describing the improvement of a task in reduction of errors or of time required to complete it, or to increase in the memorization of instructions, or efficiency in the use of any device. This measurement sometimes relates to less numerical data, such as the reduction of fatigue in workers who operate visual displays. Efficiency is at the center of information design. Visual and cognitive ergonomics define the field: *information design aims at the optimization of the cognitive and perceptual performance of people.*

Research

Research in information design has no end. One does not have to just learn a bunch of principles and then apply them; every new project has particularities that require systematic attention. Existing knowledge serves as a departure point for the creation of a first prototype, but this knowledge must be complemented by studies of users in action, ideally in the actual situation of use.

Social Relevance

Practice, teaching and research in visual communication design do not respond, for the most part, to social needs but to commercial interests. Ideally, to make a project effort worthwhile, one must find a need that could be satisfied through a design intervention. It can be an urgent need, such as helping Africans to avoid contracting malaria, or a simpler one, such as making telephone service bills more comprehensible. The satisfaction of daily needs can provide a long list of possibilities for information design projects of public utility.

Professional Relevance

The design response to a social problem can also have professional importance if the process followed is both efficient and innovative, and can assume a quality of paradigm, such as in the case of design studio Mijksenaar's solution for the John F. Kennedy airport in New York: a color was assigned to each one of four categories of signs, keeping in mind what users are focused on at different times. The approach is useful not only for any airport but also for other public facilities (Figures 37, 38, 39, and 40).

Figure 37

Figure 38

Figure 39 and 40

Given the reduced presence of design and research methods in design education, the professional practice, when directed at confronting complex social problems in a systematic manner (such as is the case in the global design and consulting firm IDEO), can become a useful source of information to enrich the knowledge base of the profession.

Conclusion: Information Design and Social Well-being

The Information Helps, But the Designer is Key

This book tries to demonstrate the value of systematic methods for information design, as well as the important contribution that cognitive and perception psychology make to our work. Regardless of the amount of knowledge that the designer might possess, to arrive at the best possible result, one always has to be attentive to the specificity of the project, to its public, to the actions it implies, and to the situations in which it operates, and to measure the results after the design has been implemented (Frascara, 1999). Every design project should not be just an opportunity to show what one already knows; *it should be an opportunity for learning*. This is one of the important things that research offers to design: to improve performance and to create new knowledge that is useful for future situations.

There is enough knowledge today to produce good information design, but this knowledge is not getting to where it should. The major need now is not on the development of new knowledge, but on putting this knowledge to use for the improvement of all the communications that support our society daily, from tax forms to medical drug leaflets. Branding today consumes luxurious resources and generates lots of work, but there is much more to be done every day in relation to our everyday life. "It is thanks to clear communications that I can use the subway in London, the telephone in my Oslo hotel or the tax forms in Canada. Lack of design clarity creates dependence: one has to ask. Sometimes one does not speak the language; sometimes one does not get the answer; one is never certain. Going from A to B can become an almost impossible task. Fifty percent of the energy of a person can be wasted on insignificant minutiae, with the corresponding emotional fatigue and loss of productivity, sense of self-worth, and satisfaction. Order in a newspaper page, in traffic, in signage, in consumer products information, in architecture, in public offices, in books and magazines, little by little penetrates in the life of people... The ideal society is organized and transparent. These two principles reinforce each other: it is easy to understand an organized society, and it is easy to organize a transparent society. Opacity protects corruption and chaos" (Frascara, 2009).

It is the responsibility of the designer to identify the needs, to show them, and to have the necessary competence to confront them. It is also our responsibility to have the required political savvy to be able to put intelligent design solutions into practice. I hope that the collective effort that produced this book can contribute to the development of a more effective information design, and to a more ethical and organized life, where energies would not be wasted in incomprehensible bureaucratic procedures, but where one could focus on productive work.

Information design serves to create communications that respond to the possibilities and the needs of all segments of the population. Well-designed public information would avoid form-filling errors in hospitals, would facilitate reading instructions for medicines, would increase workers' safety in industry, would render administrative work more efficient, and would allow common citizens to understand insurance policies, legal documents, and contracts. Information, when it is tailored to the users' needs, is ethical, facilitates tasks, and reduces costs. *Access to information should be regarded as a civil right.* To make this happen now, good information design is not an option: it is a necessity.

References

Alberta Motor Association (1996). *Mission possible: the integrated safety initiative for Alberta.* Edmonton, AB: Alberta Motor Association.

Alexander, C. (1966). *Notes on the synthesis of form.* Cambridge, MA: Harvard University Press.

Anderton, P. J. & Cole, B. L. (1982). Contour separation and sign legibility. *Australian Road Research, 12,* 103-109.

Ballantine, F. A. (1951). Age changes in measures of eye movements in silent reading. *University of Michigan Monographs in Education, #4* (pp. 63-111). Ann Arbor, MI: University of Michigan Press.

Bertin, J. (1981). *Graphics and graphic information processing.* Berlin: Walter de Gruyter.

Bertin, J. (1983), *Semiology of graphics.* Madison, WI: University of Wisconsin Press.

Buswell, G. T. (1937). *Fundamental reading habits: A study of their development. Supplementary Educational Monographs, # 45.* Chicago: University of Chicago Press.

Chapanis, A. (1996). *Human factors in systems engineering.* London: John Wiley & Sons.

Chrysler, S., Tranchida, D., Stackhouse, S. & Arthur, E. (2001). Improving street name sign legibility for older drivers. In *Proceedings of the Human Factors and Ergonomics Society 45th Annual Meeting, volume 2.* Santa Monica, CA: Human Factors and Ergonomics Society.

Cross, N. & Roy, R. (1975). *A design methods manual.* Milton Keynes, UK: Open University.

Cutts, M. (2007). Writing by numbers: are readability formulas to clarity what karaoke is to song? *The Plain Language Association InterNational* (PLAIN) conference, Amsterdam.

Duncan, J. & Konz, S. (1976). Legibility of LED and liquid crystal displays (pp. 180-186). In *Proceedings of the SID, 17(4).*

Easterby, R. & Graydon, I. R. (1981). *Evaluation of Public Information Symbols, ISO Tests 1979/80 Series, Report 70.* Birmingham, UK: University of Aston.

Easterby, R. & Zwaga, H. (1976). *Evaluation of Public Information Symbols, ISO Tests 1975 Series, Report 60.* Birmingham, UK: University of Aston.

Frascara, J. (1979). Children's Picture Preferences, a Comparative Study. *Icographic Magazine,* 13, pp. 2-5.

Frascara, J. (1980). Pattern Design and Literacy for the Retarded. *Icographic,* 14, 14-15.

Frascara, J. (1999). *El Poder de la Imagen.* Buenos Aires, Argentina: Ediciones Infinito.

Frascara, J. (2000). Information Design and Cultural Difference. *Information Design Journal,* vol. 9 # 2-3, 2000, pp. 119-127. Reading, UK: Information Design Journal Ltd.

Frascara, J. (2001). Diagrams as a Way of Thinking Ecologically. *Visible Language,* 35.2, 2001, pp. 164-177.

Frascara, J. (2006a). *Communication design.* New York: Allworth Press.

Frascara, J. (2006b). Typography and the visual design of warnings. In M. Wogalter (Ed.), *The handbook of warnings* (pp. 385-406). Mahwah, NJ: Lawrence Erlbaum.

Frascara, J. (2009). El diseño, el orden y la libertad. In Ronald Shakespear, *Señal de Diseño.* Madrid: Editorial Paidos.

Frish, O. R. (1979). *What little I remember.* New York: Cambridge University Press.

Gardner, H. (1993/2006). *Multiple intelligences.* New York: New Horizons/Basic Books.

Giese, W. J. (1946). The interrelationship of visual acuity at different distances. *Journal of Applied Psychology, 30,* 91-106.

Grether, W. F. & Baker, C. A. (1972). Visual presentation of information. In H. P. Van Cott and R. G. Kinkade (Eds.). *Human engineering guide to equipment design.* Washington: US Government Printing Office.

Hartley, J. (2004). Designing instructional and informational text. In D.H. Jonassen (Ed.), *Handbook of Research on educational communications and technology* (2nd. ed.), pp. 917-947. Mahwah, NJ: Erlbaum.

Horton, J. C., & Jones, R. J. (1997). Warning on inaccurate Rosenbaum cards for testing near vision. *Survey of Ophthalmology, 42/2,* September-October, pp. 169-174.

IIID (2007a). *IDX Information Design Exchange.* Vienna, Austria: IIID.

IIID (2007b). www.iiid.net/Definitions.htm

Information Design Journal 17/3, 2009.

ISO (1984). *Technical Report 7239.* Geneva, Switzerland: ISO.

ISO 7001. Geneva, Switzerland: ISO.

ISO 9186. Geneva, Switzerland: ISO.

Jung, C. (1998). *The essential Jung.* London: Fontana Press.

Klare, G. R. (1984). Readability and comprehension. In R. Easterby and H. Zwaga (Eds.), *Information design* (pp. 479-495). London: Wiley & Sons.

Ladan, C. J. & Frascara, J. (1977). Three Variables Influencing the Picture Preferences of South and North American Boys and Girls, *Reading Improvement,* 14/ 2, pp. 120-128.

Lewis, J., & Ritchie, J. (2003). Generalising from qualitative research. In J. Snape & J. Spencer (Eds.), *Qualitative research practice* (pp. 263-286). London: Sage Publications Ltd.

Luckiest, M. & Moss, F. K. (1933). The dependency of visual acuity on stimulus distance. *Journal of the Optical Society of America, 23(1),* 25-29.

Mackenzie, M., (1993). Appearance & performance. *Communication News,* Vol. 6/3, 1-3.

Maschi, S. (2006). Design-driven innovation. In Frascara, J. *Designing effective communications.* New York: Allworth Press, pp. 78-82.

Meadows, D. H., Meadows, D.L., Randers, J., & Behrens III, W.W. (1972) *The limits to growth.* London: Earth Island Limited.

Meyer, D. E. & Schvaneveldt, R. W. (1971). Facilitation in recognizing pairs of words: Evidence of a dependence between retrieval operations. *Journal of Experimental Psychology* 90: 227–234.

Miller, G. A. (1956). The magical number seven, plus or minus two: Some limits on our capacity for processing information. *The Psychological Review,* vol. 63, pp. 81-97.

Miyake, R., Dunlap, J. W., & Cureton, E. E. (1930). The comparable legibility of black and coloured numbers on coloured and black backgrounds. *Journal of General Psychology, 3,* 340-343.

Nelson, Thomas M., Nilsson, T. & Frascara, J. (1981). Information in letter backgrounds and acquisition of reading skills. *Reading Improvement,* 18/4, 287-294.

Neurath, O. (1939). *Modern Man in the making.* New York: Alfred A. Knopf.

Nilsson, T. (1999). *Legibility and visual effectiveness of some proposed and current health warnings on cigarette packages*. Prince Edward Island: Health Canada-University of Prince Edward Island.

Norman, D. (1990). *The Design of Everyday Things*. New York: Doubleday.

Oberly, H. S. (1924). The range of visual attention, cognition and apprehension. *American Journal of Psychology, 35,* 332.

Paterson, D. G., & Tinker, M.A. (1946). Readability of newspaper headlines printed in capitals and lower case. *Journal of Applied Psychology, 30,* 161-168.

Penman, R. & Sless, D. (1994). *Designing Information for People*. Hackett, Australia: Communication Research Institute of Australia.

Pillsbury, W. B. (1897). A study of apperception. *American Journal of Psychology, 8,* 315-396.

Poulton, E. C. (1972). Size, style and vertical spacing in the legibility of small typefaces. *Journal of Applied Psychology, 56* (2), 156-161.

Purswell, J. L., Krenek, R. F. & Dorris, A. (1987). Warning effectiveness: what do we need to know. In K. R. Laughery, M. S. Wogalter, & S. L. Young. (Eds.). *Human Factors Perspectives on Warnings.* Santa Monica, CA: Human Factors & Ergonomics Society, pp. 174-178.

Sanders, M. S. and McCormick, E. J. (1993). *Human factors in engineering and design* (7th ed.). New York: McGraw-Hill.

Schiepers, C. (1976). *Global attributes in visual word recognition.* Nijmegen, Netherlands: Centrale Reprografie.

Shakespear, R. (2009). *Señal de Diseño*. Madrid: Editorial Paidos.

Sless, D. (1996). The Telecom bill: Redesigning a computer generated report. In R. Penman and D. Sless (Eds.), *Designing information for people* (pp. 77-97). Hackett: Australia: Communication Research Institute of Australia.

Smith, S. L. (1984). Letter size and legibility. In R. Easterby & H. Zwaga (Eds.), *Information design* (pp. 171-186). London: Wiley & Sons.

Somberg, B. L., (1990). *Character aspect ratio and design tradeoffs. In Proceedings of the Human Factors and Ergonomics Society 34th Annual Meeting* (pp. 1461-1464) Santa Monica, CA: Human Factors and Ergonomics Society.

Spencer, H. (1968). *The Visible Word.* London: Hastings House.

Tinker, M. A. (1963). *Legibility of print.* Aimes, IA: University of Iowa Press.

Tinker, M. A. & Paterson, D.G. (1928). Influence of type form on speed of reading. *Journal of Applied Psychology, 12,* 359-368.

Tufte, E. (1983). *The Visual Display of Quantitative Information.* Cheshire, CT: Graphics Press.

U.S. Military Standard 1472B (1974).

University of Reading (1975). *Graphic communications through Isotype.* Reading, UK: Department of Typography and Graphic Communication.

Waller, R. (1980). Graphic aspects of complex text: Typography as macro-punctuation. In P.A. Kolers, M.E. Wrolstad, & H. Bouma, *Processing Visible Language,* Vol. II. London: Plenum Press.

Wogalter, M. S. & Vigilante, W. J., Jr., (2003). Effects of label format on knowledge acquisition and perceived readability by younger and older adults. *Ergonomics,* 46, 327-344.

Worringer, W. (1911). *Abstraktion und Einfühlung*. Munich: R. Piper. Published in English (1953) as *Abstraction and Empathy*. New York: International Universities Press. Cited from: Elephant Paperbacks (1997).

Wright, P. (1978). Feeding the information eaters: Suggestions for integrating pure and applied research on language comprehension. *Instructional Science, 7* (3), 249-312.

Wright, P. (1999). *Using layout for the generation understanding or retrieval of documents*. Menlo Park, CA: AAAI Press.

Young, S. L., Laughery, K. R., & Bell, M. (1992). Effects of two type density characteristics on the legibility of print. *Proceedings of the Human Factors and Ergonomics Society 36th Annual Meeting*. Santa Monica, CA: Human Factors and Ergonomics Society, pp. 504-508.

The following publications deserve to be listed here despite not being mentioned in the text.

Arthur, P. & Passini, R. (1992/2002). *Wayfinding: people, signs and architecture*. Oakville, ON: Focus.

Crosby, T., Fletcher, A., & Forbes, C., (1970). *A sign system manual*. New York: Praeger Publishers.

Easterby, R. & Zwaga, H. (Eds.) (1984). *Information design*. Chichester, UK: John Wiley & Sons.

Frascara, J., Noël, G. (2010). "Evaluation and design of a blood components transfusion request form." *Information Design Journal* 18(3), pp. 241-249. John Benjamins.

Frascara, J. & Ruecker, S. (2007) "Medical Communications and Information Design" *Information Design Journal,* 15 (1) pp 44-63.

Kolers, P. A., Wrolstad, M. E., & Bouma, H. (1980). *Processing of Visible Language*, Vol II, New York: Plenum Press.

Mijksenaar, P. & Westendorp, P. (1999). *Open here*. New York: Joost Eiffers Books.

Schriver, K. (1997). *Dynamics in document design*. New York: John Wiley & Sons.

Wildburg, P. & Burke, M. (1998). *Information graphics*. London: Thames & Hudson.

Wurman, R. S. (2004). *Understanding healthcare*. Newport, RI: Quad Graphics & TOP.

Zwaga H., Boersema, T. & Hoonhout H.C.M. (Eds.) (1994). *Proceedings of Public Graphics: Visual information for everyday use*. Lunteren, Netherlands: Delft University and Utrecht University.

Biographical Note

Jorge Frascara is professor emeritus, Department of Art and Design, University of Alberta; honorary professor, Emily Carr University; fellow of the Society of Graphic Designers of Canada; member of the Former-Presidents Forum of Icograda (International Council of Graphic Design Associations); International

Fellow, Society for the Science of Design (Japan); and Advisor, Doctorate in Design Sciences, Iuav University of Venice. He is a member of the Editorial Boards of *Design Issues* (MIT, USA), *Information Design Journal* (John Benjamins, Netherlands); *Visible Language* (University of Cincinnati, USA), and *Arcos* (Federal University, Rio de Janeiro, Brasil);

He is the author of *Communication Design* (New York, NY: Allworth Press, 2004); and *User-Centred Graphic Design* (London, UK: Taylor & Francis, 1997), and the editor of *Designing Effective Communications* (New York, NY: Allworth Press, 2006); *Design and the Social Sciences* (London, UK: Taylor & Francis, 2002); *Graphic Design, World Views* (Tokyo, Japan: Kodansha, 1990); and the *ISO Technical Report 7239, Design and Application of Public Information Symbols* (Geneva, Switzerland: ISO, 1984). He has also authored four books in Spanish and more than 50 articles internationally. He has been an advisor on graphic symbols to the International Standards Organization, the Canadian Standards Association, and the Canadian Standards Council, and a Board of Directors Member, Communication Research Institute of Australia.

His professional experience includes illustration, film animation, advertising, social marketing, graphic design, and visual aids for special education. After 31 years in Canada and 5 in Italy he now lives in Canada again and concentrates on research and development of visual communications for safety and for information design, particularly in the health sector.

Part II: Conceptual Frames

Theory should emerge from the practice, from the real, from the particular. Theories are often developed looking at social phenomena "from outside," from a God-like point of view. These theories are perfectly coherent systems, are very seductive as such, and provide filters that rather than helping people see reality tend to ignore reality's nuances, discrepancies, and inconsistencies. They some times serve to hide the fear of ignorance but do not provide insights that help solve design problems, which are always situated, different from one another, and particular.

The authors of this section tackle different issues, but show a common thread: discovering the presence of broad principles in specific situations that become operative tools for the confrontation of a variety of communication design problems. These conceptual frames set the basis for a responsible practice in communication design.

Chapter 2: The Use of Worked Examples and Other Forms of Explicit Guidance in Ill-structured Problem Domains

Suna Kyun, Slava Kalyuga, and John Sweller

Abstract

The use of worked examples to assist learners to acquire problem solving skill is well-known and increasingly accepted when dealing with the well-structured problems found in domains such as mathematics, science and technology (Sweller, 2011, 2012; Sweller, Ayres, & Kalyuga, 2011). Research concerning the use of worked examples in ill-structured domains is much more recent and has generated some scepticism (Spiro & DeSchryver, 2009). In this chapter we will outline cognitive load theory that is associated with the use of worked examples, suggest why it should apply equally to all domains whether well-structured or ill-structured, and discuss the empirical evidence, especially evidence associated with language-based areas such as literary appreciation, that indicates the superiority of instruction using worked examples over instruction in general problem solving in ill-structured domains.

Recent versions of cognitive load theory have placed an increasing emphasis on evolutionary biology. Knowledge can be divided into biologically primary information that we have evolved to acquire and biologically secondary information that we need for cultural reasons but that we have not specifically evolved to acquire (Geary, 2007, 2008). Learning to listen and speak provide the clearest examples of biologically primary knowledge. We do not need formal instruction when learning to listen and speak because we have evolved to acquire such skills easily, naturally and without conscious effort. Simply living in a listening/speaking society is sufficient to allow us to learn to listen and speak.

In contrast, we do need formal instruction to learn to read and write. We have not evolved to automatically learn to read and write because reading and writing are biologically secondary skills. For most people, formal, explicit instruction and conscious effort are required to learn these skills. Unlike listening and speaking, without explicit instruction and conscious effort, most members of a society will not learn to read and write. Despite a continuous history extending to thousands of years of some people in many societies being able to read and write, these skills only became common with the rise of near universal education a little more than 100 years ago. Unlike learning to listen and speak, most people do not become literate simply by exposure to other literate people. Literacy is a biologically secondary skill that requires formal, explicit instruction. Schools and other educational institutions were invented in order to deal with the increasing volumes of biologically secondary knowledge required by modern societies.

From this analysis it follows that the cognitive processes involved in reading and writing are different to the processes involved in listening and speaking and the distinction is captured by Geary's concepts of biologically secondary and biologically primary knowledge. We should not confuse the two. They are learned differently and so need to be taught differently. Attempting to teach biologically secondary knowledge that we have not evolved to acquire, as though it is biologically primary knowledge that we have evolved to acquire, is unlikely to be effective.

Cognitive load theory deals with teaching and learning of the biologically secondary knowledge that provides the content relevant to students in educational institutions or who are learning via printed information or via ICT. Current versions of the theory treat biological evolution as an information processing system (Sweller, 2011, 2012; Sweller, Ayres, & Kalyuga, 2011) and suggest that when dealing with biologically secondary information, human cognitive architecture has evolved to mimic the processes of evolutionary biology (Sweller, 2003; Sweller & Sweller, 2006). Both evolutionary biology and human cognition can be considered as examples of natural information processing systems. Such systems can be specified by five principles that form the basis for those aspects of human cognitive architecture relevant to instruction.

The *information store principle* specifies that natural information processing systems require a very large store of information to govern their activities. Long-term memory plays that role in human cognition. Evidence for the central importance of long-term memory in problem solving initially came from the work of de Groot (1965) who found that the only factor explaining the superiority of chess masters over weekend players was the huge store of schemas held by chess masters. Chess masters, briefly shown a board configuration from a real game were superior to weekend players in reproducing that configuration. They were superior problems solvers because from previous experience, they could recognize most of the board configurations encountered during a game and had learned the best moves associated with each configuration. Apart from this difference in long-term memory, there was no evidence that chess masters differed in any other way from less able players. There was no evidence, for example, that they had acquired any superior cognitive or meta-cognitive skills that could explain their problem solving superiority. The only difference was in memory of board configurations. Chase and Simon (1973) replicated de Groot's findings and in addition, found no differences between chess masters and weekend players using random board configurations, thus confirming that the critical factor was the acquisition of knowledge held in long-term memory. Simon and Gilmartin (1973) suggested that chess masters have learned to recognize tens of thousands of board configurations over the many years of practice required to become proficient (Ericsson & Charness, 1994).

Chess requires, of course, problem solving in a well-defined area. It can be argued that in ill-defined areas there are vastly more, even an infinite number, of problem states that would need to be remembered (Spiro & DeSchryver, 2009). The first argument against this suggestion is based on cognitive theory: there is no evidence that our cognitive architecture has evolved to distinguish between well-defined and ill-defined problems. We treat all problems for which we do not have a solution held in long-term memory as ill-defined problems (Greeno, 1976). The fact that (a) chess players with different levels of expertise only differ in their memory of chessboard configurations and the best moves for each configuration despite that (b) every chess game played differs from every other chess game, strongly suggests that there are no cognitive distinctions between well-defined and ill-defined problems. As we gain expertise in an area, we accumulate more and more problem solutions to the problem states we are likely to encounter irrespective whether the problems are well-defined or ill-defined. Those solutions consist of problem states and the best moves associated with those states. The fact that some problems, such as those encountered when playing chess, may have a large or infinite number of potential states and moves associated with those states is irrelevant. We can never acquire all the possible schemas for any but the simplest problems, whether well-defined or not. In other words, the only argument required is that more schemas are acquired as expertise increases. The fact that there are a large or even infinite number of such schemas does not affect the argument. Our problem solving skill will increase with an increased number of schemas held in long-term memory irrespective of the total number that potentially could be acquired.

In accord with the suggestion that de Groot's results are independent of the degree to which the problems are well-defined, are similar results from a variety of areas, including areas heavily dependent on language. For example, similar differences to those obtained in chess have been obtained between high and low knowledge individuals in text processing tasks (Chiesi, Spilich, & Voss, 1979; Spilich, Vesonder, Chiesi, & Voss, 1979). Individuals with a high level of knowledge in a domain are better able to process text associated with that domain and better able to remember that text. Knowledge schemas held in long-term memory are fully able to account for skill differences with no requirement for additional, general, cognitive strategies.

The second argument against the suggestion that problem solving skill in ill-defined areas cannot consist of domain-specific knowledge held in long-term memory and acquired via explicit instruction, is empirical. There now is considerable empirical evidence that we can show people how to solve ill-defined problems. That evidence is associated with the second principle used by cognitive load theory to describe human cognitive architecture: the *borrowing and reorganizing principle.* This principle suggests that the huge amount of information stored in long-term memory under the information store principle is acquired primarily by borrowing information from other people. We imitate what others do, listen to what they say and read what they write. If so, we might expect that one of the best ways for people to acquire problem solving skills is to study worked examples provided by others.

The worked example effect occurs when problem solving skill improves more from studying worked examples than solving the equivalent problems (Renkl, 2005; Sweller, Ayres, & Kalyuga, 2011). The original evidence for the worked example effect was provided using well-defined, primarily mathematics problems (e.g. Cooper & Sweller, 1987; Sweller & Cooper, 1985) but in recent years the same effect has been demonstrated using ill-defined problems (e.g. Rourke & Sweller, 2009). Importantly for present purposes, the effect is just as obtainable using language-based areas as any other area.

Consider a student learning to read, process and understand Shakespearean text. In effect, the student is engaged in a classic, ill-defined, problem solving task. Classical Shakespearean texts are written in Old English that is very different from Modern English. It is usually difficult to comprehend and may impose high levels of cognitive load on readers who need to extensively search through endnotes or refer to footnotes. Deriving meaning from such text can be considered a form of problem solving. If so, according to cognitive load theory, learning will be facilitated by providing direct, explicit guidance to learners concerning the meaning of textual passages. As a form of worked examples designed to assist learners in comprehending such texts, Oksa, Kalyuga, and Chandler (2010) used explanatory notes providing interpretations of Shakespearean play extracts in Modern English that were physically integrated line by line with Shakespeare's original text. Two experiments were run with novice learners who were high school students studying Shakespearean plays as part of an English literature course. These students had no prior knowledge of the texts. The results of the experiments indicated that students who were presented the integrated explanatory notes were better able to comprehend and had lower reported ratings of cognitive load than students required to follow a more traditional, search-based instructional format. Search-based instruction essentially consists of problem solving.

In another experiment reported by Oksa, Kalyuga and Chandler (2010), the same material and experimental design were used with a group of experts. These participants were professional Shakespearean actors rather than the high school students used in the previous experiment. Using these participants, the traditional format without integrated explanatory notes resulted in better comprehension and lower ratings of cognitive load than the integrated notes condition. Think-aloud verbal protocols indicated that the integrated explanatory notes were redundant for these high-knowledge readers and interfered with their fluent processing of Shakespeare's original text. Thus, similar to worked examples in well-defined technical domains (e.g., Kalyuga, Chandler, & Sweller, 2001; Kalyuga, Chandler, Tuovinen, & Sweller, 2001), this form of worked examples in the ill-defined area of literary comprehension was effective for novices, but not for more knowledgeable learners. These results provide an example of the expertise reversal effect (Kalyuga & Renkl, 2010; Sweller, Ayres, & Kalyuga, 2011).

Kyun, Kalyuga, and Sweller (2013) directly tested the hypothesis that worked examples can be just as effective in ill-defined as well-defined areas. Two experiments were designed to compare the instructional effectiveness of worked examples with solving the equivalent problems in the ill-defined domain of English Literature. Problem solving is a traditional method of teaching literature with students expected to discover their own interpretations of textual material. Based on the borrowing and reorganizing principle, we might expect such forms of discovery learning to be less than optimal. Providing learners with possible interpretations to study and consider should be preferable, in the same way as providing mathematics or science students with possible problem solutions to study is preferable to students attempting to discover solutions themselves, especially if the discovered solutions are less optimal than presented solutions.

Korean university students for whom English was a foreign language, participated in Kyun, Kalyuga and Sweller's experiments that were conducted in a realistic university environment. The same four essay questions in the area of Children's English Literature were included in both worked example and problem solving conditions based on two pairs of similar problems. Students were informed of the similarity of the problems. In the worked example condition, students were presented with several model answers to two essay questions, with each question followed by a similar question that they had to answer themselves. In the problem solving condition, students were presented four essay questions all of which they were asked to answer themselves. Instruction time was equalized across the two conditions. In the following post-test, all students were asked to answer questions that were identical to one of the four problems in the learning phase, near transfer questions that were similar to those in the learning phase and far transfer questions that were different from those in the learning phase.

One of the experiments used more knowledgeable students (59 participants) while the other experiment used relatively less advanced students in the area of Children's English Literature (55 participants). While participants were competent in English, they had not previously studied children's English literature. In both experiments, students in the worked example group performed better in answering essay questions during the learning phase, as assessed by independent markers. For the identical, near and far transfer tests, there were no significant effects for more knowledgeable students, while for less knowledgeable students, the worked example group performed significantly better on the identical problem test with no differences on the transfer tests. Similar to previous research in the expertise reversal effect, the worked example effect was not obtained using higher knowledge learners (Kalyuga et al.,2001; Oksa et al., 2010). While novice learners need worked examples, those examples are likely to be redundant for more knowledgeable learners who could use their knowledge to successfully respond to the test problems without needing to study worked examples in the learning phase.

The information store principle suggests that most human cognitive activity involving biologically secondary knowledge is generated by information stored in long-term memory and the borrowing and reorganizing principle suggests that the bulk of that information is obtained explicitly from other people. While information can be obtained from other people, at some point it needs to be created. The *randomness as genesis principle* explains how novel information is created.

We know how biological evolution, a highly creative system, generates novel information. All biological novelty stems from random mutations that are tested for effectiveness with effective (or adaptive) mutations retained and ineffective mutations jettisoned. In effect, biological evolution uses a random generate and test system to generate novel information. If human cognition constitutes a natural information processing system, we might expect generate and test during problem solving to similarly provide the source engine of human creativity (Sweller, 2009).

The major argument in favor of random generation as the source of human creativity is logical rather than empirical. If we do not have information in long-term memory informing us how to solve a problem, all techniques we use to generate problem solving moves rely on random generation and test. Without information in long-term memory, it is only *after* we have made a move and tested it that we can determine whether it is effective. It does not matter whether we use means-ends analysis (Newell & Simon, 1972), problem solving by analogy, or combinations of inductive techniques, none can guarantee a problem solution until after they have been attempted, either physically or mentally. For example, without information in long-term memory, we can never be sure whether an analogy is appropriate or inappropriate until after it has been made. Knowledge may tell us that some analogies are better than others but if we do not have knowledge to inform us, we have no choice but to randomly choose and test one of multiple analogies that may work. Until an effective alternative to random generate and test is clearly specified as a general problem solving strategy, we must assume that there is no alternative.

There are instructional consequences that flow from this formulation. Any instructional recommendation that emphasizes any form of teachable/learnable general problem solving (i.e. problem solving not reliant on the acquisition of domain-specific knowledge) is, in effect, recommending that students learn to engage in random generate and test. While aspects of random generate and test may be teachable under some circumstances, many aspects may be biologically primary and so unteachable. In contrast, the use of explicit instruction and especially worked examples has the potential to reduce random generate and test in all curriculum areas.

The randomness as genesis principle also has structural consequences. If, when dealing with novel information, we must engage in a random generation process, it is important that the amount of information with which we must deal is limited. Dealing with large quantities of novel information will result in a combinatorial explosion that renders effective information processing difficult or impossible. Human cognitive architecture obviates this problem by a limited working memory. According to the *narrow limits of change principle,* only limited amounts of novel information can be processed at any given time by natural information processing systems.

The narrow limits of change principle is central to cognitive load theory. It suggests that one of the major reasons for instructional failure is the unnecessary imposition of an excessive working memory load. A large number of cognitive load theory effects that indicate techniques for reducing cognitive load have been generated with the worked example effect being one of the most important. For novice problem solvers in an area, studying problem solutions taxes working memory far less than attempting to solve the equivalent problems.

The last principle, the *environmental organizing and linking principle,* provides the ultimate justification for the preceding principles. As indicated by the narrow limits of change principle, working memory is limited when dealing with novel information. Those limits disappear when working memory deals with familiar information stored in long-term memory (Ericsson & Kintsch, 1995). Once information is organized in long-term memory, working memory can use that information with neither capacity nor duration limits. The acquisition of knowledge, stored in long-term memory, transforms us. That transformation occurs equally in the case of ill-defined as well-defined areas. While our cognitive system distinguishes between biologically primary and secondary knowledge, there is no evidence that it distinguishes between well-defined and ill-defined problem areas.

In conclusion, according to cognitive load theory, studying working examples is an effective and cognitively efficient instructional procedure, especially with novice learners. Worked examples have been extensively investigated using traditional and online instructional materials in many well-defined technical domains. However, until very recently, they have been rarely studied in ill-defined areas such as instruction in literary areas. That omission can lead to the impression that the theory is solely concerned with well-defined problem areas. While from a theoretical perspective, that view appeared erroneous, there were only limited data from randomized, controlled experiments that could throw light on the issue. In the last few years, that problem has been rectified. Several studies have indicated that exactly the same cognitive load theory principles apply to ill-defined as well-defined problem areas. In particular, studying worked examples can be just as effective in ill-defined problem areas as in well-defined areas. There is every reason to assume that similar results would be obtained in ICT-based instruction. While more data from randomized, controlled experiments needs to be collected, including in ICT-based learning environments, the current data suggest that the use of worked examples in areas such as literary appreciation can be relatively effective compared to the more traditional, problem solving approach.

References

Chase, W. G., & Simon, H. A. (1973). Perception in chess. *Cognitive Psychology,* *4,* 55-81.

Chiesi, H., Spilich, G., & Voss, J. (1979). Acquisition of domain-related information in relation to high and low domain knowledge. *Journal of Verbal Learning and Verbal Behaviour, 18*, 257-273.

Cooper, G., & Sweller, J. (1987). Effects of schema acquisition and rule automation on mathematical problem-solving transfer. *Journal of Educational Psychology, 79*, 347-362.

De Groot, A. (1965). *Thought and choice in chess.* The Hague, Netherlands: Mouton. (Original work published 1946).

Ericsson, K. A., & Charness, N. (1994). Expert performance; its structure and acquisition. *American Psychologist, 49*, 725-747.

Ericsson, K. A., & Kintsch, W. (1995). Long-term working memory. *Psychological Review, 102*, 211-245.

Geary, D. (2007). Educating the evolved mind: Conceptual foundations for an evolutionary educational psychology. In J. S. Carlson & J. R. Levin (Eds.), *Psychological perspectives on contemporary educational issues* (pp. 1-99). Greenwich, CT: Information Age Publishing.

Geary, D. (2008). An evolutionarily informed education science. *Educational Psychologist, 43*, 179-195.

Greeno, J. G. (1976). Indefinite goals in well-structured problems. *Psychological Review, 83*, 479-491.

Kalyuga, S., & Renkl, A. (2010). Expertise reversal effect and its instructional implications: Introduction to the special issue. *Instructional Science, 38*, 209-215.

Kalyuga, S., Chandler, P., and Sweller, J. (2001). Learner experience and efficiency of instructional guidance. *Educational Psychology, 21*, 5-23.

Kalyuga, S., Chandler, P., Tuovinen, J., & Sweller, J. (2001). When problem solving is superior to studying worked examples. *Journal of Educational Psychology, 93*, 579-588.

Kyun, S., Kalyuga, S., & Sweller, J. (2013). The effect of worked examples when learning English literature. *Journal of Experimental Education, 81*, 385-408.

Newell, A., & Simon, H. A. (1972). *Human problem solving.* Englewood Cliffs, NJ: Prentice Hall.

Oksa, A., Kalyuga, S., & Chandler, P. (2010). Expertise reversal effect in using explanatory notes for readers of Shakespearean text. *Instructional Science, 38*, 217-236.

Renkl, A. (2005). The worked out example principle in multimedia learning. In R. E. Mayer (Ed.), *The Cambridge handbook of multimedia learning* (pp. 229-245). New York: Cambridge University Press.

Rourke, A., & Sweller, J. (2009). The worked-example effect using ill-defined problems: Learning to recognise designers' styles. *Learning and Instruction, 19*, 185-199.

Simon, H., & Gilmartin, K. (1973). A simulation of memory for chess positions. *Cognitive Psychology, 5*, 29-46.

Spilich, G., Vesonder, G., Chiesi, H., & Voss, J. (1979). Text processing of domain-related information for individuals with high and low domain knowledge. *Journal of Verbal Learning and Verbal Behavior, 18*, 275-290.

Spiro, R. J., & DeSchryver, M. (2009). Constructivism: When it's the wrong idea and when it's the only idea. In S. Tobias & M. Thomas (Eds.), *Constructivist instruction: Success or failure?* (pp. 106-123). New York, NY: Routledge/ Taylor & Francis Group.

Sweller, J. (2003). Evolution of human cognitive architecture. In B. Ross (Ed.), *The psychology of learning and motivation* (Vol. 43, pp. 215-266). San Diego: Academic Press.

Sweller, J. (2009). Cognitive bases of human creativity. *Educational Psychology Review, 21,* 11-19.

Sweller, J. (2011). Cognitive load theory. In J. M. B. Ross (Ed.), *The psychology of learning and motivation: Cognition in education* (Vol. 55, pp.37-76). Rotterdam: Elsevier.

Sweller, J. (2012). Human Cognitive Architecture: Why some instructional procedures work and others do not. In K. Harris, S. Graham & T. Urdan (Eds.), *APA Educational Psychology Handbook* (Vol. 1, pp. 295-325). Washington, D.C.: American Psychological Association.

Sweller, J., Ayres, P., & Kalyuga, S. (2011). *Cognitive load theory.* New York: Springer.

Sweller, J., & Cooper, G. (1985). The use of worked examples as a substitute for problem solving in learning algebra. *Cognition & Instruction, 2,* 59-89.

Sweller, J., & Sweller, S. (2006). Natural information processing systems. *Evolutionary Psychology, 4,* 434-458.

Biographical Notes

Slava Kalyuga

Slava Kalyuga is professor of educational psychology at the School of Education, the University of New South Wales, Sydney where he received his PhD and has worked since 1995. His research interests are in cognitive processes in learning, cognitive load theory, and evidence-based instructional design principles.

Prof Kalyuga is the sole author of two books (*Instructing and testing advanced learners: A cognitive load approach* and *Managing cognitive load in adaptive multimedia learning*), and a co-author of another book (*Cognitive load theory*). He published more than 70 refereed papers and book chapters (not counting papers and books published in Russian earlier in his career) and guest-edited a special issue of Instructional Science on expertise reversal effect (2010). Three of his papers were listed among the world top 35 (4th, 14th and 32nd) in instructional design for the years 1980-2008 (*Australasian Journal of Educational Technology*, 2009, 25, 559-580). One of these papers, "Expertise Reversal Effect" in *Educational Psychologist*, 2003 (journal with one of the highest impact factors in the field) was placed in the top 1% within its field by Web of Science. He was ranked as the world 10th most productive educational psychologist for the years 2003-2008 by the number of single- and first-authored publications (*Contemporary Educational Psychology*, 2010, 35, 11-16).

Prof Kalyuga is currently a member of editorial board of three major journals in the field *Journal of Educational Psychology, Educational Psychology Review,* and *Learning and Instruction,* and has served as a reviewer for almost all major research periodicals in the field.

Suna Kyun

Suna Kyun received a Ph.D from the School of Education at the University of New South Wales and currently works as a postdoctoral research fellow at the Yonsei University College of Medicine, South Korea. Her research interest is cognitive processes in learning and problem solving, and its application to instructional design of ill-defined domains such as medical domains.

John Sweller

John Sweller holds a BA (Hons), 1969, and a PhD 1972, from the University of Adelaide, Australia.

He has been a lecturer in education, Tasmanian College of Advanced Education (1973), lecturer in education, University of New South Wales (1974-1978), and, at the same university, senior lecturer in Education (1979-1989), Associate Professor of Education (1990-1991), Professor of Education (1992-2005), and now Emeritus Professor of Education, University of New South Wales, since 2006.

His research is associated with cognitive load theory, an instructional theory based on our knowledge of human cognitive architecture. He initiated work on the theory in the early 1980's. Subsequently, "ownership" of the theory shifted to my research group at UNSW and then to a large group of international researchers. The theory is now a contributor to both research and debate on issues associated with human cognitive architecture, its links to evolution by natural selection, and the instructional design consequences that follow. It is one of the few theories to have generated a large range of novel instructional designs from our knowledge of human cognitive architecture. The following instructional design effects have flowed from cognitive load theory: goal-free, worked example, split-attention, redundancy, modality, element interactivity, isolated-interacting elements, imagination, expertise reversal, completion, variable examples, guidance fading, transient information and collective working memory effects. These effects have been studied by many groups of researchers from around the globe.

About a dozen special issues of various journals have been devoted to cognitive load theory. He has authored or co-authored papers in these issues and have acted as a joint editor of the papers published in *Educational Psychologist* (2003) and *Instructional Science* (2004). The special issues have been based on many symposia on cognitive load theory presented at major meetings around the world.

John has been a Fellow of the Academy of Social Sciences of Australia since 1993.

Chapter 3: Designing Information for the Workplace

Patricia Wright

Abstract

Those designing information for the workplace face many problems. Often there are competing pressures on time or costs, or both, arising from clients, suppliers and the intended audience. Nevertheless, creating messages that people ignore is a complete waste of time and money. This chapter shows how a better understanding of what people do when using information in the workplace can not only help information designers make appropriate decisions but can also help them persuade colleagues and managers in other departments of the advantages of supporting good design. Guidelines tend to have limited usefulness, especially when workplace information varies from wall notices, printed materials and email messages. An alternative approach is to base decisions about what and how to communicate on considerations of how people respond to information design options. Information in the workplace is not read in the same way that people read novels because in the workplace information is used as part of some other task, such as finding the answer to a query. Research has shown that people have strategies for dealing with technical materials; they are selective in what they choose to read, can easily misunderstand what they have read, and can be biased in how they apply their knowledge gained from reading – e.g., assuming that an instruction is only relevant in certain contexts or applies only to certain people. The skill of good information design is to help the content providers as well as the readers to achieve their intended goals.

There are many ways of providing information in the workplace. These include notices and signs on walls and doors, messages and forms distributed by print or email, manuals and handbooks that explain company procedures and how to operate complex devices such as the internal telephone system or the print-collate-staple photocopier. Given such diversity of content and location there is little scope for a simple list of guidelines being able to help writers. Nevertheless there are criteria that apply to all well-designed information. Here, listed alphabetically, are ten criteria that few people would dispute. Well-designed information is:

- *Accessible* – making it easy for readers to find the information they need.

- *Appropriate* – the information is relevant to the current product or procedure, and the message design meets the cultural values of the audience.

- *Attractive* – the message appears inviting rather than off-putting to readers.

- *Believable* – the content, tone and appearance encourages trust and confidence in the text.

- *Complete* – the message contains all the information users need rather than directing them to other sources.

- *Concise* – there is no information that is unnecessary for the reader's tasks.

- *Errorless* – even minor typographic slips can undermine readers' confidence in the text.

- *Interpretable* – the information can be applied in the context of the workplace

- *Relevant* – the content has clear links to readers' work tasks

- *Understandable* – the message is free from jargon, uses simple syntax, and includes diagrams/pictures where these help to convey the message.

These criteria are not contentious but writers face the problem of how to achieve these standards in workplace communications. Part of the solution may come from understanding more about how people interact with information in the workplace. For convenience this interaction will be divided into three clusters of activities, all of which can be influenced by the way the information is designed and presented, whether printed or on a computer screen. These activities start with readers finding the information they need, then understanding what the writer is saying, and finally applying that understanding to satisfy their reason for turning to the information in the first place, reasons that may be as diverse as answering queries or getting procedural instructions.

Will Readers Find the Information?

In order for readers to access the information they want they must set a search target, devise a search strategy and carry out the search. A new notice on a crowded notice board may be invisible to many readers unless it uses color or graphics to catch the attention. Footnotes and small print may be ignored by people in a hurry to get on with their main task. If for any reason the information is not accessed then it does not matter how user friendly it might have been because people did not get that far. Checking that the wording of the information matches readers' search targets, and is located where readers expect to find it, are two examples of how writers can cater for and support readers' behavior.

Readers Ignore Information

In spite of their variety, the different kinds of information found in the workplace have at least one thing in common. People do not read them for fun or enjoyment. Research has shown that there is considerable agreement among people about when they will read and when they will ignore material such as written instructions (Wright at al, 1982). Usually work documents are read as part of trying to complete some other task (e.g. trying to reclaim travel expenses or transfer a telephone call). The existence of this higher priority goal influences how people read workplace information. It leads them to read very selectively, searching for the details they think are crucial and ignoring other information.

This point was well illustrated in two studies by Marcel and Barnard (1979) where people were given a sequence of pictures explaining how to operate a machine. When asked to read the message aloud, almost everyone provided a fully correct account of the instructions. This showed there was no problem understanding the pictures. However when people used these instructions to operate the machine many of them jumped to successive pictures showing a hand performing an action. They ignored the pictures showing that they needed to wait for the machine to signal when it was ready for their next action. This 'misreading' resulted in many people failing to operate the machine successfully. One design implication of these findings is that writers need to focus on all the actions readers must take, and in this case 'pausing' was a necessary action. Understanding how readers skipped through the instructions with their focus on *"What do I do next?"* highlighted the need to devise a way of calling attention to this action of pausing and waiting for the machine to catch up. Studies of people using computers have made similar observations. It helps if the screen shows that the computer is busy doing something (e.g. downloading a document) otherwise people continue to press keys or click on the screen, in order to continue their intended action sequence.

Explicit Cues to Structure

Even when the message consists entirely of words, technical information often benefits from the use of typographic and spatial formatting. This may include the use of headings and subheadings. These can help readers know where they are in the document, and move quickly to the information they want, because it shows where the current information fits within the document's hierarchical structure. The levels of headings can be conveyed either by a typographic distinction or by an explicit numbering system (e.g., 3.2.1). Numbering systems can also assist cross-referencing within the document. Here the limitations of the reader's memory must be borne in mind. Three levels may be a safe maximum for a hierarchy because people are likely to make mistakes when trying to remember a four element reference (e.g., 5.17.11.23).

Displaying information in tables can also help readers find answers to their queries. Tables can make contingencies clear (*If A then X, if B then Y, if C then Z*) and readers can quickly scan for the 'If' condition they are interested in, ignoring the other information. Scanning is harder to do for information written as a prose paragraph. However, research suggests that if readers are uncertain about what they should look up in a table then a flow chart, or a dialogue having a similar structure, is likely to be more helpful (Wright et al, 1973). The usefulness of formatting illustrates how different the information on the printed page or computer screen may need to be from the way people talk.

Will Readers Understand What is Read?

Although an oversimplification, the activities relating to how readers understand the writer's message can be thought of as understanding the words, the sentences and the concepts. Unfamiliar terminology is an obvious barrier to communication. Familiar terms given new meanings may be even more problematic because some readers may not realise they have misunderstood. Where technical jargon is needed, e.g., for precision, then a glossary may be essential. This may be more conveniently provided in online documents (e.g., in a pop-up window) than in print. Jargon terms used on wall signs can lead to hand-written 'translations' being stuck underneath the official sign.

Sentences

Much could be said about the relation between sentence structure and understanding but the golden rule is Keep it Simple. Negatives in sentences can cause difficulties. Nearly always sentences with two negatives will be understood more easily if they are rephrased to make a positive statement. For example, readers find it easier to understand *Wait for the light to come on before pressing the button* than to grasp the meaning of *Do not press the button unless the light has come on.*

Readers in a hurry may latch onto just the key words. For example, if the instruction says *Before doing A do B* this may be misremembered as first do A then do B because this was the order the actions were mentioned by the writer. Understanding and memory are linked in several ways. People easily forget what they just read, especially when reading about unfamiliar topics. It can be a convenient heuristic to note that any sentence which cannot be repeated after having been read once is probably too long.

Graphics Often Help Readers

Writers can be tempted to write in a way that is close to how they would talk when face to face with the reader. This can lead writers to overlook the contributions of graphics and the visual layout of the page to the success of a communication. Researchers asked 36 adults to write instructions for a visitor walking from the bus station to a city landmark, and found that only one writer provided a sketch of the route. In contrast, when giving usability ratings to various examples of route directions people gave higher marks when instructions included diagrams (Wright et al 1995). This illustrates a change in information values as people change roles from writer to reader. It will take a conscious effort for writers to keep their focus on the reader.

People who are good with words may not be skilled at drawing. As a consequence technical writers may need to collaborate with other professional communicators. Before this can happen the writer has to appreciate the value of saying things in ways other than sentences and paragraphs. The uses of graphics will vary with content, audience and location. Graphics can expand or repeat the text, possibly replace it. It is not being suggested that graphics are a better form of communication than words. The point is only that there are times when readers will find the inclusion of graphics helpful, yet writers may easily overlook the contribution they can make.

Can Readers Apply Their Understanding?

The third cluster of readers' activities relates to how people use their understanding gained from reading. These activities include remembering what was read, locating specified items in the workplace, interpreting their understanding for the current context.

Remembering

The reader's memory can easily hinder the application of what was read and understood. Writers can help by numbering the steps in a sequence because this can assist people in keeping track of how far they are through the sequence. Bullet lists of steps may be have similar benefits over prose paragraphs. Visually indenting the steps within subgoals will help place-keeping and may also discourage readers from trying to remember too much at any one time.

Reality Checks

When readers are applying the knowledge they gained from reading, referential ambiguity can become an issue. For example readers may feel confident they were told they should download and complete form A, but that confidence evaporates when they are confronted with choices among A1, A2, A3. The information was good as far as it went but it did not go far enough to fully support readers' decision making. In similar vein instructions fail to correspond to reality if they say *Press the green button* but the product button is yellow.

Readers have to guess whether this is the intended button or not. Leaving readers to draw inferences can be risky. One study found that when the instructions on a tin of sealant said *Avoid contact with eyes* only 30% of the adults applying this sealant to a wooden chair chose to put on the goggles that were on the table beside the tin. But 80% put on the goggles when the instructions were changed and specifically told people to do this.

Discrepancies between the text and the final state of the product/system reflect how products and systems continue to evolve after the content specification has been given to the writer. Detecting and correcting these problems can be done with a technique called a 'walk through' in which somebody checks that the information given in the document corresponds accurately to that needed by the reader.

Inferences about Audience and Authors

Readers may interpret the advice or instruction as applying only in specific contexts – e.g. to other people rather than themselves. If readers suspect the information has been provided to protect the manufacturer or organization rather than to help the reader (e.g. labels in synthetic garments saying *Wash by hand*), then information may be disregarded. Providing reasons for the advice/instructions may change the reader's view of the writer's intention.

Compromises

Technical writing is difficult to do well because writers often have competing goals. There can be demands from the client who is paying for the work - e.g. a request for something colorful or something cheap. There can be pressure from the writer's line manager or organization - e.g., to have the work finished quickly. There can be problems with suppliers - e.g., if special artwork is needed. Giving priority to readers' needs can therefore be challenging. If writers have little access to the people who will use the information, they may remain unaware of problems their readers encounter. How are writers to cope with these conflicting pressures? One starting point is a detailed specification of readers' information needs based on an analysis of the tasks they are trying to accomplish when using the information. This specification then provides a bench mark for use in negotiations with other stakeholders.

Stakeholders, especially clients, need to be made aware of the limitations of written communications in the work place. For example, there is no way that good writing can overcome the frustration generated by awkward product design or by complicated organizational procedures. Sometimes it makes better sense and more progress to change the design or procedure rather than accept it in its original form (Sless, 1998). A change to the design can completely remove the need for instructions; for example, ensuring that items will only fit together in one orientation removes the need to explain the correct orientation.

Organizational Support

The calibre of documentation in the workplace reflects the organizational values and procedures for producing it. Organizations can be blind to the need for good design, preferring instead to assume it must be alright because *we have always done it that way*. Unfortunately 'that way' may include leaving the writer with insufficient time to apply the full range of craft skills needed for good documentation. Having the document assessed by experts who know about the content is helpful but it will be text-based. These experts will recognize whether or not the text says what they felt should be said. They will not identify whether all the information that readers want has been included. Furthermore experts' familiarity with the domain makes it hard for them to assess whether other readers can understand the information. For these reasons there is no substitute for user testing. It usually requires only a small number of readers to detect the most glaring problems in documentation. Although testing highlights trouble-spots, solving these problems relies on the craft skills of writers and information designers.

User Testing

Usability testing does not mean asking a few people if they like the information. There are a variety of testing procedures, and often a clearer understanding will be gained when several usability methods are combined. Books describe and discuss a range of usability testing techniques (e.g., Dumas and Reddish, 1994). For most test procedures the evaluation is performance based and readers are asked to use the information to accomplish a relevant work-related task – e.g., using the information to answer a query from a colleague or to cope with a 'low ink supply' message from the printer or locate an office within a complex building. The testing methods may rely on observation of what readers do, noting behavior such as errors, hesitations and backtracking, or the method chosen may ask readers to talk aloud while they are using the information. This can yield insights into the reasons for mistakes, helping the writer distinguish between action slips *(I meant to do X but I must have done Y)* and genuine misunderstandings *(I had expected that the X button would do Y)*. Eliminating problems once they have been found is not always easy and may require considerable creative flair.

Conclusions

The benefits of good technical writing include saving money by reducing waste because it is undoubtedly a waste of money to spend time producing information that few people will read or which they read and misunderstand or wrongly apply. Another financial benefit is that people are more likely to use the product correctly or follow the appropriate procedures. This in turn results in fewer 'faults' being reported by customers and hence greater user satisfaction. So there are benefits for the organization as well as for readers. Achieving successful technical communications becomes easier when writers appreciate how they can support the clusters of activities involved when people interact with information in the workplace.

References

Dumas, J. and J. Redish (1994). *A Practical Guide to Usability Testing.* Norwood, Ablex Publishing Corporation.

Marcel, A.J. and Barnard, P.J. (1979) Paragraphs of pictographs: the use of non-verbal instructions for equipment. In P. Kolers, M.E. Wrolstad, H. Bouma (Eds) *Processing of Visible Language.* NY, NY: Plenum Press.

Sless, D. (1998). Building the bridge across the years and disciplines. *Information Design Journal,* 9, 3-10.

Wright, P., Creighton, P. and Threlfall, S.M. (1982). Some factors determining when instructions will be read. Ergonomics, 25, 225-237.

Wright, P., Lickorish, A., Hull, A.J. and Ummelen, N. (1995). Graphics in written directions: appreciated by readers not by writers. *Applied Cognitive Psychology,* 9, 41-59.

Wright, P. and Reid, F. (1973). Written information: some alternatives to prose for expressing the outcomes of complex contingencies. *Journal of Applied Psychology,* 57, 160-166.

Biographical note

Patricia Wright

Patricia Wright is a behavioral scientist interested in how information design can support communication between organizations and the general public. These communications include printed and online materials, and come both from government and commercial organizations. Research topics have spanned design issues relating to how people fill in forms, and how people consult tables, how they follow instructions and how easily they use online information to answer queries. Much of her recent research has been concerned with health information and multimedia documents, with projects ranging from computer aids for people with memory problems, to web-based decision assistance on screening tests.

Comparisons of interfaces showing how changes in lifestyle can reduce health risks, indicated that older people differ from young men in the interface they prefer and most successfully use. This led to studies involving specific audiences, such as people for whom English is not a first language and adults who consider themselves poor readers. The findings suggest that an interface that lets people choose how information is presented to them, and especially the option of adding spoken text, can accommodate audience diversity more successfully than a design solution that is intended to fit everyone.

After a PhD in Psychology from University College London Patricia joined the Medical Research Council's Applied Psychology Unit (APU) in Cambridge, UK. While there she was elected to a Fellowship at Churchill College Cambridge University and became Director of Studies in Psychology. Following the closure of APU she moved to a Chair in the School of Psychology at Cardiff University, UK. In 1998 she received the Joseph Rigo award from the ACM Special Interest

Group on Documentation for her "individual leadership in documentation." She is a Fellow of the British Psychological Society and an Honorary Fellow of the IEEE Professional Society for Technical Communication from whom she received the Alfred N. Goldsmith Award for "distinguished contributions to engineering communication" in 2005. She has numerous publications (http://psych.cf.ac.uk/patwright) and is currently a member of the Editorial Boards of *Information Design Journal*, *Visible Language* and *Gerontechnology*.

Chapter 4: The Challenge of Information Design: Essential Aspects for the Teaching of Information Design and the Professional Practice of Information Designers

Peter Simlinger

Abstract

Departing from the insight that high-quality information must serve a purpose that information designers need to be aware of, the author requires that information designers have a multi-disciplinary basis. He argues that the creativity of the information designer needs to be drawn from three spheres: subject knowledge, methodical competence and social competence. These spheres, to be developed through consignments of increasing complexity, are to be seen as the basis for information design curriculum development. The current professional situation is characterized by inadequate education in information design and the dominance of 'horizontal invaders.' Information design graduates may endeavor attaining 'achievable' goals – with one indicated example given. If, on the one hand, lurking and often already obvious challenges can be met and, on the other, resentments often projected by art and design schools can be overcome, information design should be able to add incredible value to the well-being of people around the world.

Information Design Aims at Transforming Data into High-quality Information

The idX project (idX 2007) made me aware that high-quality information must serve a purpose. Or more precisely: it must help the recipient(s) of the information to attain envisaged goals. In combination with the concept of 'empowerment,' a term referred to by Richard Saul Wurman as "the word of the new century and the result of inspired instructions" (Wurman 2001) I coined the tag line *High-quality information empowers people to attain goals* (IIID).

When we speak about "high-quality information" we should have the attributes of high quality in mind (Wang 1996), as excerpted from the afore mentioned idX project:

- Accessible
- Appropriate
- Attractive
- Believable
- Complete
- Concise
- Errorless
- Interpretable
- Relevant
- Objective
- Timely
- Secure
- Understandable
- Valuable

"Empowering people to attain goals" is multi-dimensional. Information designers must have the goals of the intended addressees in mind (and the tasks they need to perform), balanced with the goals of the commissioners – in specific cases also considering their employees and suppliers – and certainly their own. Information designers are required to anticipate a common denominator before they proceed to 'scoping,' an activity defined by David Sless (Sless 1997) as step 1 in the process of information design project development.

Information Design Needs an Interdisciplinary Basis

Experts of three universities (Prof. Michael Twyman, University of Reading; Ron Easterby, University of Aston in Birmingham; and Prof. Ryszard Otreba, Academy of Fine Arts, Krakow) assisted me thirty-five years ago – at a time when we still spoke about 'communication graphics' – to draft principles of design related research. The experts advised on an interdisciplinary structure involving graphic communication, linguistics, cognitive psychology and computer science. At that time they felt that all research projects involve at least two disciplines (BÖG 1980).

Today I am convinced that every information designer who aspires to be successful in strategic thinking – and designing – towards an estimated goal must be able to draw from a multidisciplinary knowledge base. Dr Bibhudutta Baral (National Institute of Design, Ahmedabad), quoting Louis Pasteur, reminded me at the IIID Summer Academy 2005 in Bolzano (Italy) of the need for such a knowledge base: "Chance favors only the prepared mind" (the curious reader might like to know that, a couple of years later, I also found this citation displayed in the staircase of the Design Council in London).

If creativity plays a role – I guess, there is no doubt about it – and if it can be developed best through lateral thinking, a term coined by Edward de Bono (Wikipedia/a) then its outcome will depend on the various dimensions that thinking can draw from.

The dimensions creative thinking and acting can draw from are practical, methodical and social. They require subject, methodical, and social competence.

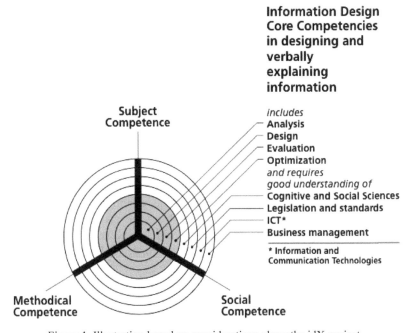

Figure 1. Illustration based on considerations along the idX project

Subject Competence

('Subject competence' is an agreeably poor translation of the 'to the point' German word 'Sachkompetenz.' However, I did not find any other one translation that satisfied me.)

In design education subject competence/knowledge is often considered dispensable: most projects done in schools deal with matters taken from everyday life that do not require any special subject competence/knowledge and allow for the assumption that addressees are familiar with the content. Therefore, it is felt, all that matters is the visual expression of the design.

Information design, however, wants to *empower people to effectively undertake tasks in order to attain anticipated goals.* Thus, the designer needs to understand the tasks, the goals and the frames of reference governing the usefulness of the information he/she is expected to design.

It is a challenge for information designers to acquaint themselves with fields beyond everyday life, especially such in which decisions largely depend on the availability and quality of information.

Familiarity with a specific subject area and its relevant laws, regulations and standards enables information designers to understand the applicable frames of reference and to communicate with subject savvy clients. Designers with prepared minds will discover incredible opportunities of improving information and, more often, by closely working together with their clients, of developing more adequate information systems that *empower people to effectively undertake tasks in order to attain anticipated goals.*

Methodical Competence

A few methods can help get the wheels turning, for example, the 'two things,' Edward de Bono considers essential: provocation and movement (De Bono 1991, p. 90) or even more so the "Six Thinking Hats," proposed by the same author. I may cite: "It is easiest to think of a provocation as a stepping-stone. This stepping-stone is not based on experience and lies outside the main track. The provocation serves to get our mind out of the established track. Using the operation of 'movement' we move forward from the provocation to the new track. Once there, if the idea is valuable, we can see the value in hindsight and can forget about how we got there." (De Bono 1990, p. 90) I guess, the relevance of this for designers is obvious.

Not so obvious is the notion of 'thinking,' especially to people (educators, students) who believe that all that matters is intuition. Of course, we all, once in a while, hope for a heaven-sent brain wave. However, to make this happen, we first need to be able to practice lateral thinking and, second, to also develop operational thinking skills.

To Edward de Bono "thinking is the operational skill with which intelligence acts upon experience." (De Bono 1991, p. 161) He writes: "The main difficulty of thinking is confusion. We try to do too many things at once. Emotions, information, logic, hope and creativity all crowd in on us. It is like juggling with too many balls" and continues:

"What I am putting forward in this book is a very simple concept which allows a thinker to do one thing at a time. He or she becomes able to separate emotion from logic, creativity from information, and so on. The concept is that of the six thinking hats. Putting on any one of these hats defines a certain type of thinking... It is the sheer *convenience* of the six thinking hats that is the main value of the concept." (De Bono 1990, p. 2f)

In a workshop on information design methods, organized by IIID towards the end of 2009 and chaired by Prof. Wibke Weber (then at HdM Stuttgart Media University, now at ZHAW Zurich University of Applied Sciences) over 60 other methods were discussed. Many of them I consider appropriate to constitute an information design rule set. Step-by-step, IIID plans to adequately describe the methods, to structure them and to add even more methods in due course. For the time being, regretfully, IIID does not have a taxonomy that would make it possible to check-off methods for attending to the many attributes of high-quality information, to further investigate other suggested methods and to identify uncharted territories in which hit and miss methods are the only option.

Social Competence

"Information design isn't necessarily about databases, spreadsheets, or even infographics. It's about process – designers and clients working together to solve problems and convey complex information through design systems that are functional and beautiful." What Ann Senechal (Senechal 1997, p. 34) touched in 1997 is of even greater relevance today. Not only did she disprove an all too limited concept of information design. By referring to 'process' and 'designers and clients working together,' she underlined the very condition of successful design – teamwork, involving both designers and clients, plus, I would say, experts whose competencies can facilitate decision making. This type of teamwork should also be considered in project work done at universities.

To successfully contribute to teamwork or even to successfully lead a team, David Sless has defined the social dimensions of information design core competencies as the 5Ps (five essential principles): politics, position, parsimony, politeness, and performance. (Sless 1997)

Essential Aspects for the Teaching of Information Design

A three-year curriculum, originally conceived for the Technikum Joanneum (now FH Joanneum), Graz, Austria, and presented in the previously mentioned idX brochure, may serve as an example of essential aspects required for the teaching of information design. It was designed to ensure subject, methodical and social competencies.

In lectures, tutorials, seminars and project work, students are confronted with assignments of increasing complexity. In the first and second semesters basic knowledge is conveyed and skills taught. These are subsequently enriched by specialized knowledge with regard to business communication, product interface design and orientation systems.

Apart from the subjects which determine the above-cited competencies, the curriculum incorporates elements of general studies which may be adjusted to newsworthy topics relating to information, communication, culture, the humanities, and economics.

The concluding diploma work, stimulated by suggestions by consultants to the school, should relate to real-life situations.

Increasing complexity of project work should concern:

- skills
- media mix and information and communication technology
- project management
- interaction and evaluation
- sort and size of the respective user group(s).

Ever more complex tasks require that the time frame allocated for projects is gradually increased.

Project work makes it possible to convey important content of teaching and practice in a task-oriented way. This concerns:

- strategies of thinking and creativity
- relevant laws, regulations and standards
- precision in expression and rendering
- adequate to perfect presentation of the results
- practice in native and English language.

Consequently, high demands are posed on both students and faculty. No wonder information design courses are rare at the university level.

The Professional Opportunities of 'Horizontal Invaders' and Disconnected Information Design Graduates

Whenever an information design course is developed in consultation with representatives of industries that should have a prime interest in what graduates know and can do, the latter will find it easy to transition from university to professional practice. They will be able to speak to potential commissioners and employers that have acquired an understanding of the subject and the value that qualified information design experts are able to add to their efforts in informing their customers about the products and/or services they wish to sell, to maintain, and to improve. Usually, however, we find other circumstances.

The lack of education in information design and the growing interest in the potential of information among designers of all sorts results in the currently heterogeneous information design profession. 'Horizontal invaders' of other disciplines turn up. Though speaking with rather strange accents, they find ample possibilities for developing the field and occupying its many available niches, often competing with information designers who graduated from "disconnected" universities. I characterize "disconnected" universities as those with low or no interest in the professional challenges waiting to be met by their graduates.

Many years ago, in a private conversation at an *IIID Vision Plus* event, John Thackara, then director of the Netherlands Design Institute and initiator of the "Doors of Perception" conferences, referred to the high standard of Dutch universities and the equally high demands of Dutch industries. At the same time, highly qualified graduates had problems finding adequate jobs whilst the demanding industries had problems in filling challenging vacancies. He indicated a substantial information/communication gap: the industries neither knew exactly what universities were teaching nor what graduates knew and could do, whilst the highly qualified graduates were unable to relate their competencies to the demands of potential employers.

To some extent, I am afraid, this is still the case today with graduates of information design and related subject areas worldwide. Too many potential industry partners do not even realize that information design exists. Still, there are opportunities that can lead up to success whenever adequately qualified experts make the effort to engage in highly complex information challenges. If worst comes to worst, 'problem owners' might be ready to charge an information designer with a task they have difficulty tackling themselves. Information designers ready to grasp such an opportunity and able to deliver beyond the usually limited expectations of such a client will soon find themselves in a situation they no longer wish to deviate from: proceeding along an incomparable career track.

Achievable Objectives in Information Design

When I was young there was nothing like information design I could have studied at university. So I went into architecture. After graduation I had to adjust and gradually succeeded. Due to my background, it was not really difficult to specialize in the design of signage systems for commercial organizations, transport service providers, and hospitals.

The planning and implementation of a signage system of a hospital for about 12000 actively and passively involved people was the farthest I could go. The understanding of the many requirements of an orientation system prompted me to make the client agree to a complete redesign of what turned out to be a most confusing (and at that time, already implemented) room and door numbering system. Towards the end of construction works and the completion of interior fittings, I was known as the one who best understood the function of the building. Thus I was also charged with designing the master key plan for several thousand doors.

Moreover, I was asked whether I could take over the acquisition management and display of art in corridors and in the many lounges of the building. The thinking behind this was: a planner who looks after both the signage and the art would avoid conflicts which otherwise could occur between the two. It gave me an opportunity to convince the deciding jury to favor works visualizing undisputed statements of respected people that had the potential of cheering up both patients and visitors (relatives and friends).

One aspect that made this job stand out was: the complexity of the project, surpassing traditional design (layout and specification of the sign boards and how and where they should be fixed), allowing for modifications by the hospital's administrative staff whenever needed, advising on related organizational matters, and working together with doctors and nurses, architects, facility managers, bureaucrats of all sorts, safety engineers, artists, manufacturers and inspectorates.

Experiences gained through this project and design commissions of Vienna Airport and OeBB / Austrian Federal Railways enabled me to gradually develop – for the International Institute for Information Design (IIID) – a focus on traffic and transport information systems.

Those with other backgrounds might start off with initiatives on improving financial information, healthcare information, tourist information or manual design – to name a few.

Challenges and Lurking Resentments

Demanding powerful clients enable some of the 'strategic' design groups in the USA and elsewhere to develop the field on its cutting edge. However, I believe that the greatest challenges should be identified and acted upon by information designers themselves, independently from those offered by business opportunities.

To become effective, information designers must team up. They may do so in commercially oriented companies or other forms. Being aware of both the cross-national/cross-cultural implications of information, and – due to lacking regional competencies – the need for cross-border cooperation, I conceived the founding of the IIID. This was back in 1986 at a time when I had expected that information design could be developed from an independent basis. Now I know: it can, but it takes a vision, adequate resources and – last but not least – a lot of time.

The vision can be based on the insight that living systems are maintained by flows of information, energy, and matter (wikipedia/b). To design information so that it meets the requirements of living systems in an optimal way is a quite demanding challenge, perhaps the most demanding challenge imaginable in our field.

Aware of the challenge but not ready yet to react adequately many information designers invest their energy in the more familiar activity areas that have developed from a fine arts background. It goes without saying that it is next to impossible to fuse fine arts thinking with the pragmatism of the "horizontal invaders." The first time I became aware of this was many years ago when I learnt of Otto Neurath and what he had summarized in his seminal concept of ISOTYPE (International System Of Typographic Picture Education).

I followed up and convinced my possibly most powerful client at that time, the predecessor of Bank Austria, to invite the Department of Typography and Graphic Communication of Reading University (UK), to show its ISOTYPE exhibition at the bank's Vienna headquarters. The Austrian Minister for Science & Research, Dr Herta Firnberg, alerted the heads of universities of applied arts to visit the exhibition which Reading University had set up to record the 50th anniversary of the foundation of the Gesellschafts- und Wirtschaftsmuseum in Wien/Vienna. At a subsequent meeting the rector of the University of Applied Arts, Vienna, came straight to the point by stating: "Wir lassen uns unsere Kunst nicht verwissenschaftllchen!" ("We won't allow the scientification of our art!")

Since then the resentments I had experienced in 1977 gave way to experimental design approaches at Austrian art and design universities. However, both in Austria and most other countries, the question of how information is to be designed so that it empowers people to attain goals has not yet been made subject of discussions at university level.

Epilogue

To the astonishment of government officials who had never heard of information design I succeeded to attract substantial funding, provided by the European Commission, to develop several information design R&D projects, including

"Substituting/Optimizing (variable) Message Signs for the Trans European Road Network;" "Enhancing interconnectivity of short and long distance transport networks through passenger-focused interlinked information-connectivity;" and "Integrated system for safe transportation of children to school."

Jointly contributing with Veronika Egger (IIID Board Member and Deputy Director) to the 3rd OECD World Forum on "Statistics, Knowledge and Policy: Charting Progress, Building Visions, Improving Life" in 2009 at Busan, Korea, and listening to many other speakers, I became fully aware of the incredible value that high-quality information could add to the well-being of people around the world.

Thus I may hope that more and more of my colleagues understand and react to nowadays most important challenges above and beyond the design of objects and services, of impacting visuals and memorable experiences: the design of high-quality information that empowers people to attain goals.

References

BÖG: (1980)Designorientierte Forschung auf dem Gebiet der Kommunikationsgraphik in Oesterreich/Voraussetzungen und Moeglichkeiten. Bund Oesterreichischer Gebrauchsgraphiker, Wien. March.

CRI: Communication Research Institute, Melbourne, Australia: http://www.communication.org.au/

De Bono, Edward (1991). I am Right – You are Wrong / From this to the New Renaissance: from Rock Logic to Water Logic, p 90. New York, NY: Penguin Books.

De Bono, Edward (1990). Six Thinking Hats, p 90. New York, NY: Penguin Books.

idX = information design exchange / What information designers know and can do / "Development of International Core Competencies and Student and Faculty Exchange in Information Design" (2007). EU/US Cooperation Programme in Higher Education and Vocational Education and Training / Outcome (PDF 600KB) / freely downloadable from www.iiid.net (>"Concluded projects" / "More projects")

IIID = International Institute for Information Design: http://www.iiid.net

Senechal Ann (1997). "It's all in the Process"; Adobe Magazine (US edition), Spring.

Sless David (1997). Theory for Practice / Theorie fuer die Praxis; *Vision Plus Monograph 12 E/D*; International Institute for Information Design. Newly released (in English only) as an e-book by the Communication Research Institute (CRI), 2013.

Wang, Richard Y. and Strong, Diane M.: Beyond Accuracy (1996). What Data Quality Means to Data Consumers. Journal of Management Information Systems. Vol. 12 No. 4, Spring, pp 5–33

Wikipedia/a (2014). http://en.wikipedia.org/wiki/Edward_de_Bono

Wikipedia/b (2014): en.wikipedia.org/wiki/Living_systems

Wurman Richard Saul (2001) *Information anxiety 2*, p 191. Indianapolis, USA: Que Publishing.

Biographical Note

Peter Simlinger graduated in architecture from the University of Technology Vienna. After post-graduate studies at The Bartlett, University College, London, his main interest changed to corporate identity and wayshowing systems.

Work done by Peter Simlinger for the Austrian Railways was honored by a "Brunel Award for Outstanding Visual Design in Public Railway Transportation." The signage system devised by Peter Simlinger for the Vienna airport repeatedly got top evaluation scores in the "Finding your way" category. The project allowed for implementation of public information symbols developed under Peter Simlinger's chairmanship of relevant ISO and National Standards working groups. Other projects realized include orientation systems for hospitals, office/science parks and recreation grounds as well as customer information for Austria's largest bank.

Having been president of "GDA Graphik-Design Austria" (now "DA Design Austria") Peter Simlinger became instrumental in 1986 by founding the International Institute for Information Design (IIID) and in 2013, by founding IIID's 'daughter,' the International Institute for Information Design Research & Education (IIIDre).

Research undertaken by IIID under Peter Simlinger's direction has a focus on curriculum development, traffic & transport information, intellectual property protection, safety & security, and sustainable tourism.

From 2009 to 2013 Peter Simlinger acted as general editor of the *Information Design Journal* (IDJ), published by John Benjamins, Amsterdam, a leading double-blind peer reviewed scientific journal in its field.

Chapter 5: Designing Inclusive Information Spaces

Veronika Egger

Abstract

Every step we take we absorb, process and use information that helps us interact with our environment. In doing so we use all our senses, consciously or unconsciously. We bring our experiences, habits, expectations and knowledge with us into any situation.

In order to use design to support people in this constant process, we must unravel the situation from several angles: What performance does an environment need to deliver to help people achieve their goals? How do people behave, do we want them to behave differently? What abilities do they need to deal with the situation?

This chapter will describe four aspects of successful inclusive information spaces: people, architecture, information, and performance. Never perfect, but always exciting real life projects show how the process unfolds, what we learned, and in what way the perception of design has changed during the project.

When I was asked to write a chapter for this book I jumped at the chance of sharing my experience of inclusive information design with a wider audience. When it came to spelling out what we do on a daily basis it suddenly seemed such an obvious course of action, often simply a case of applying common sense to an information challenge that I briefly wondered whether anyone would want to read about this. This moment of doubt quickly passed with the next project presentation. The clients' surprised and pleased reaction to our results made it abundantly clear that there must be something about inclusive information design that is not as self-evident or as obvious as I have come to believe.

Think "Inclusive"

First and foremost inclusive thinking is not about disability. Accessibility concerns all of us, whether we have an actual physical, sensory or cognitive impairment, are carrying luggage or travelling with small children. Also, we can all experience disabling situations when environmental factors such as loud noise, poor acoustics, inappropriate lighting and adverse weather conditions influence the places and spaces we use.

"Situation" is the key word in this context. Everyone's intentions in a particular situation are basically the same – finding the right train, ordering something on a website, paying a bill, locating a room. It is the designer's job to ensure that this goal can be achieved as easily, safely and independently as possible.

Inclusive information design is about paying attention. Listening and talking to people, observing situations, actions, reactions. Understanding peoples' intentions, how they gain knowledge from the information they find in their surroundings, how each individual piece of information they encounter influences their behaviour and how experience and expectations colour their interpretation. "Ecology of use" (inspired by psychologist James J. Gibson who used the term in his 1979 book *The Ecological Approach to Visual Perception*) is our expression for this complex relationship between a person and their physical and cognitive environment.

Inclusive information design is multidimensional. It encompasses websites, visual and tactile signs, acoustic information, readability, usability, interaction, clear language, contrast and colour, surface material and much more. It is not a separate discipline. It adds a dimension of quality to all application areas of information design.

Though there are many definitions of inclusive design (universal design, design for all) with changing emphasis depending on the application area, the five principles published by the Commission for Architecture and the Built Environment (CABE, 2006) provide a useful framework:

Inclusive Design

1. places people at the heart of the design process,
2. acknowledges diversity and difference,
3. offers choice where a single design solution cannot accommodate all users,
4. provides for flexibility in use, and
5. provides buildings and environments that are convenient and enjoyable to use by everyone.

Approaching a design project inclusively has three distinct advantages:

*   There is one design process for all audiences.
*   Solutions that work for people who face the greatest challenges are easy and comfortable for everyone else.

- The focus shifts from perceived restrictions for the design to an opportunity for innovation.

Legal requirements help drive this change, but it takes more than legislation to create an inclusive environment.

Understanding Spaces and People

Physical dimensions in a building such as entrance width, ramp angle or the placement of control switches are easy to define and measure. While each single item taken by itself may be compliant with standards and building regulations this does not automatically make a building or the activities taking place within it accessible. Achieving this is much more likely to be dependent on how people actually use and understand the building or space they are in.

> The way places are designed affects our ability to move, see, hear and communicate effectively. (CABE, 2006)

Recent research in public transport environments corroborates this statement in a project investigating the distribution of passenger flow in public transport environments and how this can be predicted by simulation of flow characteristics. (MASIMO 2011) Flow characteristics are usually based on average values. They assume that all users know the infrastructure and use the shortest route to reach their goal. They do not however include behavioural characteristics of people with mobility impairments such as wheelchair users, individuals with prams and small children, older people or people with sensory impairments. The quantitative measure revealed an overall slightly slower walking speed (0,84 m/Second) for the research reference groups compared to 1,34 m/Second usually assumed in pedestrian flow simulations. It was surprising, however, that no significant difference was determined in the speed of completing the tasks between the different research reference groups.

> Regardless of physical ability respondents across all reference groups had similar problems when navigating the environment: placement and recognition of functional features or information; readability or audibility of information; clarity of content.

> Leaving us with the observation that the design and organisation of the environment and of information seem to have greater influence on navigation and orientation behaviour than age, gender or any physical requirement.

> (Egger, 2011), Summary of Results; Research carried out by is-design in cooperation with the Austrian Institute of Technology (AIT)

Besides the building itself, functional features of an environment include colour and contrast, artificial and natural lighting, acoustics, surface materials, visual and tactile as well as audible information. We use them all – consciously or subconsciously, and people with limited vision, whether caused by visual impairment or environmental conditions, need to concentrate on the information sources perceivable to them. The design needs to ensure that information is available in the right formats for all audiences.

> Access to information is as important as physical access when using the built environment. Unfortunately, many designs are conceived and developed without early input from an experienced information designer, and for some projects information design is seen as something that simply relates to identifying where the direction and location signs should be placed. (Bright & Egger, 2008)

Information quality is much harder to define and measure than physical features. Regulations can define parameters for lighting levels, surface qualities, levels of contrast, type size, tactile and acoustic qualities. These definitions are buried in different regulatory documents, and each profession only considers documents relevant to their own aspects of service delivery. As a result – particularly in the context of built environments – it often falls to an information designer to ask the pertinent question: What information does the situation provide to help people achieve their goals? Or, in Don Norman's terms: What does the situation "afford" in terms of signals, goals, abilities, values, beliefs and experiences? (Affordance is a term originally coined by psychologist James J. Gibson in 1977 as perceived possibilities for action, appropriated by Norman in the context of human-computer interaction).

Asking such questions and the need to test design for its suitability no longer meets with incomprehension. Since around the start of the Millennium an interesting shift can be observed: disability equality legislation and the demographic change have become drivers for better design. In the past it took a lot of convincing a client that including users in a design process (that was not immediately technology-related) was a good thing and would result in higher quality products and services. Now several powerful arguments speak for inclusive design:

- Older people represent a critical mass of discerning customers that no-one can afford to ignore.
- It is accepted (though sometimes driven by legislation rather than conviction) that people with varying physical, sensory and mental abilities play their full part in society and can no longer be excluded.
- When we talk about designing for the whole population in all its diversity it is obvious even to the greatest sceptics that no designer can be expected to judge someone else's experience based on his/her own point of view.

- The inclusive design approach also overcomes a deep-rooted fear of ugliness in connection with disability, mostly the result of decades of designs being adopted for accessibility which are purely functional and which have not been created to enhance the overall aesthetics of the places and spaces we all use.

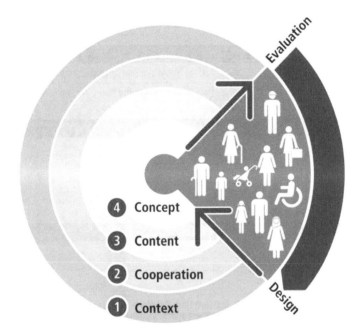

Figure 1: Four C's for quality of use – Context, Cooperation, Content, Concept. Plus an iteration between design and evaluation with people at the heart of the design process.

Assessing Inclusive Qualities in Practice

Qualitative evaluation methods have a long tradition in information design and are exhaustively described in other chapters of this book.

However, to provide an insight into practical aspects of inclusive information design applications two examples for the use of qualitative evaluation shall be discussed at this point.

1. Multimodal Analysis

Multimodal analysis for information design is an adaptation of the framework for multimodal interaction analysis (Norris, 2004). In practice this means taking a "snapshot" of an interaction. The snapshot is representative for a particular point in the interaction process, the person in the snapshot is representative for all other persons in the test with similar experiences at that point. In one frame we describe all elements within the environment (the building, colours, contrasts, text, sounds, interaction options, information sources, etc.) as well as peoples' verbal (what people say in answer to questions, other comments, how they understand written text) and non-verbal interactions (gesture, gaze, posture). The documentation also contains a description of the person and his/her intended action as well as images, voice transcripts, the emotional state of the person, notes from observation and references to the effects of technology. Frames will vary depending on the context and the available data. The result is a one or two page summary of a complex situation.

Frame title	
Categories of analysis	i.e. confusion, frustration, technology restriction
Situation	description of situation in the frame and current task
Participant	description of reresentative participant
Relevant Data	
Images	i.e. video stills, photos
Audio	transcript of what the person says in this situation
Description of activity	what the person is doing / trying to do
Information sources	what the person uses to gain relevant information for completing the task
Observations	
Physical movement	i.e. head movement, gestures
Eye movement	i.e. hectic, jumpy, controlled
Emotions	i.e. frustrated, happy, impatient, surprised
Effects of technology	i.e. reaction time, feedback
Notes for further analysis	
Relevance	what this may mean for the further use quality of the situation/product
Quantity	how many of the other participants had the same experience
Comparable situations / quotes	
Situations	comparison with similar situations in the test or in other documented situations
Quotes	quotes from other participants in the test or from other documented situations

Figure 2: Generic frame structure that needs to be adapted to project requirements.

The method has been applied with great success in an ongoing research project (MOVING, 2012-2014) assessing the use of a virtual environment as a predictor for real world implementation of a public transport building and its orientation system.

The virtual environment is a 3.3 m square box with 3D projections on the floor and three surrounding walls. Someone using the space navigates by their own body movements: forward by walking in place, turning by shoulder and head movement). Forty-two participants were invited to the test, they came from all backgrounds aged 18 to 86 with varying familiarity with technology, as well as a group of blind and partially sighted people. As far as the team is aware this was the first time that people who are blind or have limited vision have tested an immersive virtual environment.

Participants had to complete specific tasks (buy a ticket at the counter, drop off luggage, find a WC and go to a tram stop). In parallel to the tests in the virtual environment a small group of participants carried out identical tasks in the real world, in sections of the railway station that were already built and operational. This comparison was important for the assessment whether results in the virtual world are applicable to reality.

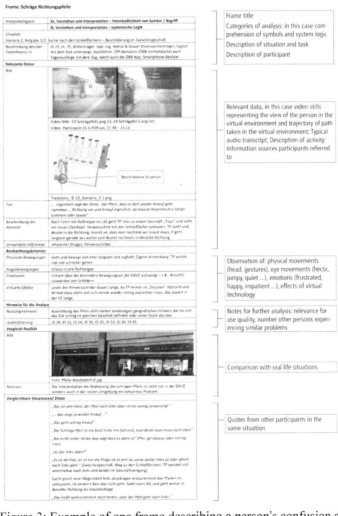

Figure 3: Example of one frame describing a person's confusion at one particular point during the task *(what she can see, her spoken feedback, her track through the building, what information elements she used, her eye-movements, the emotions she displays).*

The following categories for analysis were applied:

- successful search strategies (using signs, a map, a mobile App or environmental features, asking someone),
- confusion (resulting in insecurity, disorientation, frustration)
- understanding and interpretation of information elements (comprehension of symbols, terms or the logic of the signage system)
- getting lost (going the wrong way to such an extent that no relevant information was available)
- technological restrictions (readability, proximity issues, feeling sick, functional problems and system logic)
- abortion of test (feeling sick, technical malfunction, duration).

The frames method was extremely fruitful in two ways. On the one hand the possibilities and limitations of the technology environment could be assessed. On the other hand this way of documenting a situation helped identify specific information, linguistic and spacial design issues for normally sighted people and people with limited vision side by side. Results of this evaluation have the potential to impact on aspects of interior and information design of future railway stations.

2. The Value of Testing in Real Situations

In the real world there is no such thing as an optimal situation as might be found in a usability lab. This was clearly demonstrated when the interaction and information quality of a wall-mounted intercom system was tested.

The starting point: As a public service police stations need to be accessible for all. In rural areas small police stations are not permanently staffed plus they are usually not located on the ground floor. Making all stations physically accessible and staffing them permanently was no option. A new intercom was the proposed solution for getting in touch – either with staff on site or, alternatively, with a central telephone exchange. The device is mainly based on acoustic interaction with supporting LED-backlit graphic indicators and an induction loop for people who are hard of hearing. In order to accommodate deaf users alternative routes of communication and service delivery were discussed in a parallel project. Therefore public authorities decided that the chosen device would not include a screen capable of video or text interaction. The design team was commissioned to evaluate an existing product for its inclusive qualities. (Egger & Ehrenstrasser, 2013)

The chosen reference groups who would test the performance of the intercom were people who are blind or have limited vision, people who are hard of hearing and people aged 70+. After consultation with representatives of the deaf community it was decided that deaf participants would not participate in the test due to the absence of video or screen interaction. The physical suitability of the intercom for wheelchair users (always providing that the mounting position was correct) had already been demonstrated with the product in use and did not need to be validated, therefore wheelchair users also did not participate.

The task for all participants was to report the theft of a purse to the police. The interaction might have been tested in a lab or, to include ambient noise, outside the lab in the street. Instead the team insisted that the new intercom was mounted outside an actual police station at the correct height for wheelchair users. Why? The environment determines actions and reactions. Simply the fact that we were located outside the police station caused our participants to approach the task with a degree of sincerity and intensity that would not have been the case in the lab – even though the device was clearly a provisional setup and they were told that the person on the other end of the intercom connection was one of the researchers. With uniformed personnel and other people walking in and out of the station this was quickly forgotten as soon as the interchange began and participants were fully immersed in the task.

Evaluation combined a mix of pre- and post-task interviews, the participants' answers and comments, observations by a researcher as well as video and audio data.

Results: With a small sample of 17 participants it was possible to propose a change in the sound feedback (ring and hold tones), recorded messages and their timing, the coordination between auditory and visual feedback (LED backlit graphics), tactile information on the push-button, and preferences for mounting the intercom. Ideally in a next step the project would be extended to include people with learning difficulties and a group of non-native speakers.

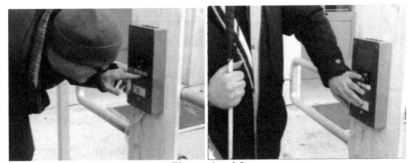

Figures 4 and 5
Left: Participant with poor vision bends down towards the low mounted intercom trying to decipher the graphic elements with LED backlighting. We also observed a tendency with normally sighted participants to lean towards the loudspeaker. Objective measure of acoustic quality allows for an upright position for both speaking and listening within one meter of the device.
Right: A blind participant assessing the tactile qualities of the device.

The Impact of Inclusive Information Design

On a worldwide scale it is difficult to give absolute figures, but drawing on statistics from the World Health Organisation (WHO), Eurostat, OECD and international health and disability organisations around 12-15% of the population of each country can be classified as disabled. Figures fluctuate widely regarding sensory impairments, from 3 to 10% for hearing trouble, 4 to 9% for vision trouble, and learning disabilities affect between 1,5 and 3% of the population depending on the definition of disability in each country. Undisputed is the fact that by 2050 the number of older persons in the world will exceed the number of young people for the first time in history and that this is a global phenomenon. (UN 2002) Whatever is designed now, the likelihood is quite high that the audience for the design has an age-related disability or is strongly affected in their cognitive or motor abilities by environmental factors.

Inclusive (information) design is not a social project and not aimed at a minority. It is good business that contributes to sustainable and enjoyable environments.

The most impressive tool in information designers' toolkits is measuring the quality of what is delivered – way beyond functional aspects. Inclusive design would greatly benefit from an implementation of quality measure for design on a "joy of use" scale similar to the idea of the "happiness index". This efficiency measure was introduced by economists as a measure of sustainable well-being based on global data on life expectancy, experienced well-being and Ecological Footprint to calculate which countries deliver long, happy, sustainable lives for the people that live in them. Good design has the power to shape all these aspects of our lives.

The perfect response from people we design for is: nothing – or quiet satisfaction. Only mistakes and badly designed information attract attention.

References

Bright, K., and Egger, V., Using visual contrast for effective, inclusive environments. *Information Design Journal,16*:3, pp 178-189, 2008

CABE, *The principles of inclusive design*, CABE, London, UK 2006.

Egger, V., Ehrenstrasser, L., Schrom-Feiertag, H., Telepak, G., Creating a Richer Data Source for 3D Pedestrian Flow Simulations in Public Transport. *Measuring Behaviour Conference*, Eindhoven, The Netherlands 2011.

Egger, V. and the Austrian Institute of Technology, VRVis, Rosinak & Partner. *MASIMO* (Multiagent Software for Group-specific Movement and Orientation Behavior of pedestrians), Vienna 2011.

Egger, V. and Ehrenstrasser, L., Design for all Austria. Unpublished project report, 2013.

Gibson, J. J., *The Ecological Approach to Visual Perception*, Hillsdale, NJ: Lawrence Erlbaum Associates, 1986.

Egger, V. and Ehrenstrasser L. in cooperation with the Austrian Institute of Technology, Fraunhofer Austria, Architect Alfred Ritter and Austrian Federal Railways, *MOVING* (Methods for Optimization of Virtual Indoor Navigation Systems), Vienna 2012-2014.

Norman, D., *The psychology of everyday things*, New York, NY: Basic Book, 1988.

Norris, S., *Analyzing multi-modal interaction: A methodological framework.* Routledge, New York, NY and London, UK 2004

UN Department of Economic and Social Affairs, Population Division, *World Population Ageing: 1950-2050,* World Assembly on Ageing 2002

Biographical note

Veronika Egger completed a graphics college in Vienna, Austria, is a graduate of Graphic Design at Derby University, UK, and holds an MSc in Design and Management of Inclusive Environments from The University of Reading, UK.

She has worked at Philips Design in Vienna, and later founded her own company – *is-design GmbH* – in 1997 focusing on Information Design. In her practice Veronika combines information design, product design, user interface design and accessibility to a new field of application: Evidence-based user experience design for the built environment. Veronika has been consultant to the Austrian Federal Railways for the inclusive design of the new Vienna Central Station, several large architectural projects in Austria, Vienna Public Transport, the Austrian Police Service/Ministry of the Interior, pharmaceutical companies such as Merck, Bayer, Sandoz, and many more.

Veronika is a board member and deputy director of the *International Institute for Information Design (IIID) and* Life Fellow of the *Communication Research Institute (CRI)*. She co-founded *design for all*, an organisation promoting inclusive design in Austria and leads the *Experts Cluster Inclusive Design* of Design Austria.

Currently her company is research partner of the project MOVING – Methods for Optimising Indoor Navigation and Orientation Systems, following on from MASIMO – Multiagent Simulation Model for Group Specific Mobility and Orientation Behaviour which was completed in 2010.

Chapter 6: Graphics with a Cause: Otto Neurath and Hans Rosling

Yuri Engelhardt

Millions of dollars yearly are spent in the collection of data. . . We daily see facts presented in the hope of creating interest and action for some really worthy piece of work to benefit the people as a whole. . . Unless the facts are presented in a clear and interesting manner, they are about as effective as a phonograph record with the phonograph missing. . . If the facts were put in graphic form, not only would there be a great saving in the time of the readers but there would be infinite gain to society.

– Willard C. Brinton (1914, pp. 1-2)

Abstract

It has been more than one hundred years since Willard Cope Brinton made these remarks about the potential of graphics to benefit society. Along similar lines, Jorge Frascara has recently talked about "the relevance of information design for things that matter in society." and has argued that design's highest end is "to change an existing reality into a better one." (Frascara, 2010) In what follows here we will look at two well-known initiatives that fit well with these remarks by Brinton and Frascara. Both of these initiatives have focused on producing informative graphics with the intention of raising public awareness about urgent issues in society: Otto Neurath's pictorial statistics and Hans Rosling's "moving bubble charts."

Otto Neurath's Pictorial Statistics: Isotype

Otto Neurath (1882-1945), was a political economist, social scientist and philosopher of science. He was a key member of the group of philosophers known as the Vienna Circle. In addition, Neurath was a pioneer in the field of information visualization. He believed that "visual education is related to the extension of intellectual democracy within single communities and within mankind." (Neurath, O. 1945, p. 247)

In social democratic "Red Vienna," Neurath founded and directed the Gesellschafts- und Wirtschaftsmuseum (social and economic museum) in which he and his team attempted to explain socioeconomic facts and statistics to citizens through the use of graphics. Marie Neurath, his colleague and eventually his wife (they married in 1941), comments on their work for the museum:

> Our object was to make the general public acquainted with the problems the community of Vienna had to tackle (the housing shortage, the amenities needed for children and mothers; the high infant mortality and the tuberculosis), how they were dealt with, and with what success. In colourful charts, which were like simple puzzles which everybody could solve, such problems were brought nearer to general understanding than would have been possible with just words and numbers. – Marie Neurath (1974, p. 130)

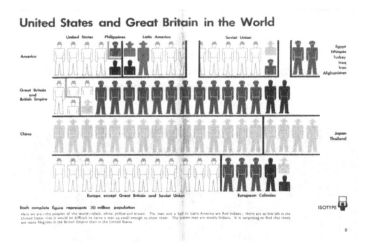

Figure 1. An example of an Isotype chart: the world's population. (Pages 7-8 from L. Secor Florence's book *America and Britain: Only an ocean between*, 1943)

While working for the museum's exhibitions, Neurath and his team, among them the graphic designer Gerd Arntz, developed an iconic language of pictorial statistics, originally called the "Vienna Method" but later renamed as the International System of Typographic Picture Education – Isotype. This iconic language (see figure 1 for an example) uses simplified pictures and specific composition rules to "show up some relationship or development in a striking manner, to arouse interest, direct the attention and present a visual argument which stimulates the onlooker to active participation." (Neurath, M. 1974, p. 146) The Neuraths continued their work while fleeing from fascism, first from Vienna to The Hague (1934), and later to England (1940), where they settled in Oxford.

"The output of the Isotype movement as a whole," says Michael Twyman (1975, p. 17), "draws attention to two things which are of special interest to many designers today. First, it demonstrates that successful designing depends to a large degree on clarity of thinking; secondly, it provides support for the view that the graphic designer's primary role is to serve the needs of society."

Hans Rosling's "Moving Bubble Charts": Gapminder

A much more recent initiative, also based on the aim "to serve the needs of society" by visually presenting socioeconomic statistics, is Gapminder. As the website for the initiative has described it, "Gapminder is a non-profit venture promoting sustainable global development and achievement of the United Nations Millennium Development Goals by increased use and understanding of statistics." (Gapminder 2008) The Gapminder Foundation was created in 2005 by the Swedish medical doctor and researcher Hans Rosling, with his son and daughter-in-law. Their software enables the visual exploration of statistical data such as average income per capita and average life expectancy for all countries of the world in interactive charts with coloured, moving bubbles, with each coloured bubble representing a country (Figure 2). These moving graphics, the data that they can explore, and – above all – Rosling's charismatic performances with these graphics, in which he explains our world to us, have turned out to be very successful in attracting the attention even of people who are usually "allergic" to charts and statistics. The online videos of Rosling's presentations have already been watched by millions of people.

Figure 2. Hans Rosling using an animated Gapminder chart in a presentation. Each coloured bubble represents a country. The size of the bubble stands for the population of the country (e.g., the two biggest red bubbles represent China and India) and the colours of the bubbles stand for the different regions of the world (e.g., red for Asia). In this chart, average child mortality (from bottom to top) is plotted against average number of babies born per woman (from left to right). Gapminder's software is accessible at http://gapminder.org

Seventy Years Apart—The Same Spirit

Although separated by about seventy years of turbulent human history, Neurath's and Rosling's efforts share a spirit that is independent of their time and of the technological means they use. Both Neurath and Rosling are energetic, inspiring, and unorthodox, with a great drive to communicate their ideas and serve society. Neurath's work was strongly connected to exhibitions and museums, and, interestingly, Rosling's team also presents Gapminder as a museum: "Gapminder is a non-profit venture – a modern "museum" on the Internet." (Gapminder 2008)

Four things specifically connect Isotype and Gapminder: first, both Neurath and Rosling believe that statistical data should be accessible to everyone. Second, both believe that making people aware of the relevant statistical data can raise awareness about global issues. Third, they are both convinced of the power of the visual. And fourth, they both employ the latest media technology of their times. Let us have a closer look at each of these four points.

Facts for Everyone

In terms of access to information (and what we now call "open data"), Neurath believes: "The ordinary citizen ought to be able to get information freely about all subjects in which he is interested, just as he can get geographical knowledge from maps and atlases. There is no field where humanization of knowledge through the eye would not be possible" (Neurath, O. 1946, p. 100). After realizing that most Austrians were not aware of national and global socio-economic issues, Neurath hoped to bring such information to the masses through museum exhibitions. Similarly, Rosling's team asserts that "all people, independently of their political agenda, should get free access to already existing statistics about global development to easily improve their understanding about the complex society." (Gapminder 2014a) There is a strong philosophical aspect to the ambitions of both Neurath and Rosling. As a key member of the Vienna Circle, Neurath was one of the main figures in the development and promotion of *logical positivism*, a philosophical position characterized by its trust in rationality, logic, science, empiricism, "facts" and "truth." The trust in these concepts has been heavily criticized by various philosophers since. In this context it is interesting that Gapminder's tagline, "for a fact-based world view," and goal, "to replace devastating myths with a fact-based worldview" (Gapminder 2014b), could be interpreted as a revival of the *logical positivism* that was propagated by Neurath and the Vienna Circle (I am grateful to Jonathan Gray for bringing this to my attention).

Raising Awareness

Both Neurath and Rosling are convinced that disseminating statistical data and presenting it in comprehensible ways can play an important role in raising people's awareness about global issues. Neurath (Neurah, O. 1945, p. 248) argues that: "With visual aids, one could create something that is common to all, we could educate children in various countries. . . Visual education is neutral and satisfies a feeling of having knowledge in common for human brotherhood. Because I believe that visual aids have this peculiarity, I wish to promote visual education, as an element of human brotherhood." Along similar lines, Rosling argues: "We can change how the young generation understands the state of the world if we provide IT-tools that give them a more complex and relevant moving images of world development in the form of animated statistics." (Rosling et al., 2004, p. 526)

The Power of Visual Representations

Another similarity concerns the belief in the benefits of using graphics. Both Neurath and Rosling are passionate advocates of the visual. As Ellen Lupton (1986, p. 47) notes, "Neurath held that vision is the saving link between language and nature, and that, hence, pictorial signs would provide a universal bridge between symbolic, generic language and direct, empirical experience." Neurath believed that "communication of knowledge through pictures will play an increasingly large part in the future" (Neurath, O. 2010, p. 5) and famously stated: "Words make division, pictures make connection." (Neurath, O. 1936, p. 18) Rosling (2007) addresses visualization and animation as services that "unveil the beauty of statistics." For Rosling, it is Gapminder's effective use of visuals that makes development statistics enjoyable and understandable. The Gapminder Foundation aims "to create animated graphics that not only reach and please the eyes, but that also transform statistics into understanding, i.e., goes beyond the eye to hit the brain" (Rosling et al., 2004, p. 523). Gapminder shares this goal with Isotype. As Frank Hartmann (2006) notes: "While the graphic designer wants to catch the eye, Neurath wanted to catch the mind." When, in 1936, Neurath talked about an "education by the eye," his quest was not for better visuals but for getting "the full picture," through perception to imagination.

Making Use of the Latest Media Technology

Would Otto Neurath have used YouTube and Twitter? I believe so. Neurath used a broad range of techniques for producing his displays and reaching his audiences, including the newest available media technologies at the time, especially when he was creating animated graphics for film. Neurath was already experimenting with animated graphics in the late 1920s in his museums in Vienna. Later, in 1941, having fled to Britain, he was approached by filmmaker Paul Rotha, one of the key figures of British documentary film at the time. Neurath and Rotha started working together, with animated Isotype graphics designed by Otto and Marie Neurath being used in seventeen films between 1941 and 1947. At the time these films "were stylistically and technically revolutionary" (Burke & Haggith, 1999, p. 64). Rosling, in turn, is employing state-of-the-art software for creating interactive graphics, and is broadcasting his thoughts via YouTube and Twitter. (Rosling Twitter)

Current Media Technology and Neurath's Vision

Part of Neurath's vision was to engage ordinary people in actively reasoning with statistical data. In recent years we have seen the rise of "open data" and "data journalism," with data being available to the general public to an extent that was unimaginable in Neurath's time. And Neurath could not have foreseen the public availability of visualization software or how easy it is today to make data and graphics available through the Internet. While Isotype graphics were created by a few specialized visualization professionals, current do-it-yourself data visualization software and the Internet now enable basically anyone with basic computer skills to obtain and visualize data, and to publish and discuss such visualizations with others online. Since 2007, various websites have emerged where Internet users create, share, and discuss visualizations of data. (i.e., "Many eyes" http://manyeyes.com) As Kristóf Nyíri (2003, p. 45) points out: "the emergence of computer graphics and multimedia computer networking might lead to a fulfilment of Neurath's vision."

Rosling's Little Men

In recent presentations, Rosling, possibly without realizing it, has been using Isotype's key visual language principles. In a presentation in June 2010, (Rosling video/a) Rosling explains population growth by lining up visual units (plastic boxes in this case; in later presentations he uses toilet paper rolls), with each visual unit standing for a fixed number of people. While Neurath would have used pictures of human figures instead of other objects, Rosling's presentation could be seen as a 3-D Isotype graphic performed live on stage. In a presentation in December 2010 (Rosling video/b) Rosling actually uses a line-up of two-dimensional human figures (again, each one standing for 1 billion people), which strongly reminds us of Neurath's Isotype charts. (Figure 3)

Figure 3. Hans Rosling shows a line-up of little human figures, with each figure standing for one billion people. Rosling explains that two billion people, on the far left, live below. the poverty line, while one billion people, on the far right, live above the "air line" – these are the customers of airlines. (Photograph by Anab Jain, http://superflux.in)

Graphics with a Cause

Noting the various aspects that they have in common, we have discussed Neurath's Isotype and Rosling's Gapminder as examples of how informative graphics may be used to raise public awareness and understanding of social and environmental issues. These are "graphics with a cause". Of course, making charts about socioeconomic statistics is not the only way in which information designers can try to do something for people and the planet. There are many other possibilities. Among my favourite initiatives are those where digital and visual tools are created that can help to serve the public interest, to assist vulnerable populations, to make ethical consumer choices, and to hold governments accountable. To me, all such initiatives are fine examples of what Jorge Frascara has expressed as "the relevance of information design for things that matter in society." (Frascara 2010)

Acknowledgements

Above all, I am grateful to my colleague Raul Niño Zambrano for our joint work, which I present here with his kind permission: a large part of this chapter consists of partly rewritten versions of sections from our joint paper "Diagrams for the Masses" (Niño Zambrano & Engelhardt, 2008). In addition, I would like to thank Anab Jain for figure 3, and Anders Bouwer, Max Bruinsma, Rawley Grau, Jonathan Gray, Frank Hartmann and Wim Jansen for their very helpful comments on the draft versions of this text.

References

Brinton, W. C. (1914). *Graphic methods for presenting facts*. New York: Engineering Magazine Company.

Burke, M., & Haggith, T. (1999). Words divide, pictures unite: Otto Neurath and British propaganda films of the Second World War. *Imperial War Museum Review 12*, pp. 59-71.

Frascara, J. (2010) Data, information, design and traffic injuries. Lecture given at the Museum of Architecture and Design, Ljubljana, 16 March 2010. A video of this lecture is available online at http://videolectures.net/aml2010_frascara_diti/

Gapminder 2014a: website, http://www.gapminder.org/faq_frequently_asked_questions/ (Accessed August 2014)

Gapminder 2014b: website, http://www.gapminder.org/donations/ (Accessed August 2014)

Gapminder 2008: website, http://www.gapminder.org "About Gapminder" (Accessed December 2008)

Hartmann, F. (2006). *After Neurath: The quest for an "inclusive form of the icon."* Lecture given at Stroom Den Haag, The Hague, 31 October 2006. Retrieved from http://www.medienphilosophie.net/texte/neurath.html

Lupton, E. (1986). Reading Isotype. *Design Issues 3* (2), pp. 47-58.

Neurath, M. (1974). Isotype. *Instructional Science 3*, pp. 127-150.

Neurath, O. (1936). *International picture language: The first rules of Isotype*. London, UK: Kegan Paul, Trench, Trubner and Co.

Neurath, O. (1945). Visual education: Humanisation versus popularisation. In M. Neurath and R. S. Cohen (Eds., 1973), *Empiricism and sociology* (Vienna circle collection, Vol 1). Dordrecht, Netherlands: Reidel, pp. 227-248.

Neurath, O. (1946). From hieroglyphics to Isotype. Extract from the manuscript, translated by Marie Neurath. In *Future books 3*, pp. 93-100.

Neurath, O. (2010). *From hieroglyphics to Isotype: A visual autobiography*. Edited by M. Eve and C. Burke. London: Hyphen Press.

Niño Zambrano, R., & Engelhardt, Y. (2008). Diagrams for the masses: Raising public awareness – From Neurath to Gapminder and Google Earth. In G. Stapleton, J. Howse & J. Lee (Eds.), *Diagrammatic representation and inference*. Berlin: Springer, pp. 282–292.

Nyíri, K. (2003). From texts to pictures: the new unity of science. In K. Nyíri (Ed.), *Mobile learning: Essays on philosophy, psychology and education*. Vienna: Passagen Verlag, pp. 45-67.

Rosling, H., Rosling Rönnlund, A., & Rosling, O. (2004). New software brings statistics beyond the eye. In *Statistics, knowledge and policy: Key indicators to inform decision making*. Proceedings of the OECD's first world forum on key indicators (Palermo, Italy, 10-13 November). Paris: OECD Publishing, pp. 522-530.

Rosling, H. (2007). Visual technology unveils the beauty of statistics and swaps policy from dissemination to access. *Statistical Journal of the IAOS 24*, pp. 103-104.

Rosling Twitter; http://twitter.com/hansrosling
    Rosling
    video/a.http://www.ted.com/talks/hans_rosling_on_global_population_g
    rowth.html

Rosling
    video/b.http://www.ted.com/talks/hans_rosling_and_the_magic_washing
    _machine.html

Twyman, M. (1975). The significance of Isotype. In *Graphic communication through Isotype*, exhibition catalogue. Reading: University of Reading.

Biographical Note

Yuri Engelhardt is an assistant professor in data visualization and infographics at the University of Twente (since 2014) and also an assistant professor in digital media at the University of Amsterdam (since 2003). Yuri's path in life has included elementary school in Australia, high school in Germany, college in California, a master degree in medicine and a PhD in computer science in the Netherlands, guest lecturing in Spain, and raising kids in Costa Rica. One of his key research interests is related to the various visual and spatial structuring principles that are the quintessence of all the different forms of presenting information visually. Since the mid-1990s Yuri has been teaching data visualization to students of computer science, digital media, journalism, and graphic design, and he is always learning a lot from them. He is the founder of

InfoDesign, the first global online forum on information design (1995), member of the editorial board of the *Information Design Journal* (since 1999), author of "The Language of Graphics" (2002), and co-founder of the annual "Show me the Data" symposia (since 2008). Yuri is passionate about social and environmental issues, education, health, human rights, sustainability and accountability. He believes in knowledge as a path to positive change, and he loves data-driven "Graphics with a cause."

Part III: Historical Overviews

History defines the meaning of words, the nature of professions, and the sets of values a society holds dearly. Without knowledge of the past it is impossible to understand the present. Winkler, Bakker and Holmes each one takes a different approach to the use of history as a way to capture the present, and as a way to understand and define which have been and which are the preoccupations of information designers, and the conditions that are necessary for its practice.

Chapter 7: Even Cavemen Could Do It Better: The Need for Change in the Design Paradigm[1]

Dietmar R. Winkler

Abstract

From the insights of Bertrand Russell, British philosopher and mathematician, a great sentiment for a distinct and useful mission for a true profession of graphic and communication design could be taken. He maintained, "Any device is useful that sheds light on the otherwise unknown." If one applies his criteria to visual design projects, it becomes clear that the greater majority is of unnecessary, repetitive and ephemeral uselessness. It is forgettable. It is used for shifting momentary attention from the everyday-ordinary and mundane by dressing it up in visual deceptions to appear new and seemly exotic. Yet, the purpose of information design is quite different. It is about the systemic collection of verifiable facts and data, defining the acquired knowledge so it can become a useful and reliable tool for human use in the operational evolution of understanding of society and culture. It is never trivial.

Designers have only within the past four to five decades rediscovered "information design," when in truth efficient visual recording and storing of complex information has been a seamless and timeless necessity, required for building reliable reservoirs of dependable information for instructing each following generation, assuring survival and cultural continuity. This makes visual information design as old as any culture or social group. It was and is produced

---

[1] Note: The illustrations in this chapter are taken from the first edition of the "Encyclopaedia Britannica." It was issued serially in sections from 1768 to 1771. The first bound volume of these sections was completed in 1769, the second in 1770 and the third in 1771. The three-volumes set, subtitles "A Dictionary of the Arts and Sciences," contained 2,459 pages and was accompanied by 160 information graphics, copper-engraved by Andrew Bell.

by curious people, direct and close to the phenomena, searching for clarity in understanding the emerging paradoxes when comparing episodes observed by the community of thinkers and scientists to distinguish between peculiarities and to bring order to small or sensational spectacles. Unfortunately visual design returns late to the table, mainly because it has no deep intellectual ambitions. Suddenly aware that its discipline is losing respect and relevance, it nevertheless is still unwilling to invest in profession-supporting intelligence. In today's world of economic exchange the product is knowledge, and designers can no longer be interested in just packaging knowledge products for those who are visually unskilled. This moment in the history of design is about searching the universe for data and for inventing quality processes for synthesizing information components into useful and reliable knowledge for dissemination to the citizenry.

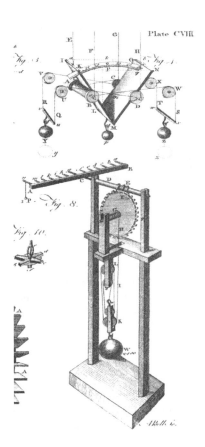

For this world, clambering for more sophisticated contributions from all its members, the intellectual skills of design education and practice have become tepid. Digital technologies instead of expanding design's original visualization skills have stunted them further and they continue their downward spiral in their atrophy. The conditions are hastened by discontinuity of visual studio skills and practices and even more through lacks in intellectual nourishment. Schools are the culprits that instill in design practitioners notions of expediency through technology and notoriety through charisma, rarely responsibilities to social and cultural contexts in which information must perform and in which superficial knowledge is not only useless but also endangering. At this point, information design has become mostly typographic. It is rarely graphic. Budget expediencies substitute photographic forms. Unless one believes that pie and bar charts are great graphic inventions then typographic programming and styling have become the order of the day.

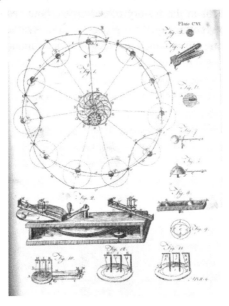

Looking at the majority of practicing designers, there seems to be an extreme lack of involvement in generating information. Outstanding meant in the past to stand above all others' shoulders. But most designers are not better educated or informed than the public on any subject matter. Like the public, they only respond to the latest fads or social, political and technological rumors, delivered in media news bytes. They are as unprepared to critically interpret and separate fads from trends or framing cultural propositions. They rarely feel self-empowered to author their own challenge to emerging conditions. Their realities are shaped by the same media that instructs every member of society, from workers to administrators. Knowing the same, not more, makes designers useless. They have become observers that do not see, communicators that hate to communicate or read and write. They hide behind the hype of contemporary technology. What makes them so indifferent to the emerging intellectual challenges and why do schools continue to foster superficiality and useless expediency, and why are they frittering away their chance to instruct society, expending energies on things that are inconsequential and not worthwhile?

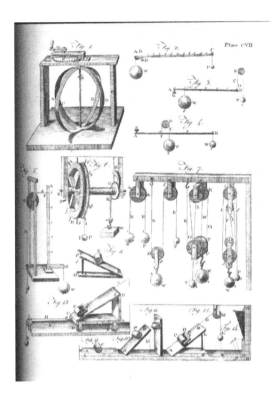

As world history shows, each culture was able to give visual shape to important concepts without the help of so-called designers, framing the first inkling and dawning of understanding of newly emerging phenomena, including the unseen, mythological worlds and the placement of the human within their competitive hierarchies, and forming information resources on tools and strategies to grow food, heal the ailing, traverse ocean distances and evolve tools of communication to foster social relationships.

The early twentieth-century Modernist promise for an increased status of designers has been fast eroding and at the same time the public's needs for more efficient and dependable information has drastically increased. While designers are trying to hold on to the speed-sluggish Gutenberg era, their vocation has been leapfrogged by the digital, high-speed information environment, in which many more participants from other disciplines function as information managers. The new era is not at all different from any other in human history, in that those things vital for survival will be highly regarded, while everything else is delegated to the titillating and ephemeral scrapheap of short-lived entertainment. Even if graphic and typographic styling can sharpen intelligibility of information, in this newly emerging world, a squiggly, hand-drawn diagram may be of greater value, than one that is aesthetically elaborated, if the treatment of essentials has not been enhanced or made more comprehensible through graphic design. The only difference may lie in the fact that the new technology has aided all researchers in casting finer and bigger nets. It has provided ways to follow complex developments and evolutions and therefore, on every day, information is outdating the findings from the day before. Having the abilities to learn the same software applications, used by designers, researchers are also able to apply the same technologies to presenting information. One thing, however, will always stay in the realm of visual design, namely the skills to observe and translate visual data into contextual visual information. But then again, if the information is very important, its value will not be diminished by a crude, non-design styled diagram, as long as the information is not compromised.

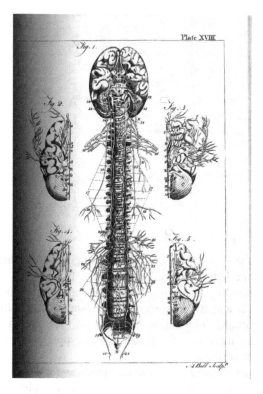

A tough analysis reveals that smart managers and members of business schools and strategic think tanks continue to shape most of architecture, products to be marketed, and the corporate iconography as well – not designers. The owners and controllers of information, delegate to designers the intellectually passive role of merely becoming stylistic graphic and typographic hands for their construction of information presentations. Designers are just not well enough educated to field and stimulate discipline-specific discussions. Unless they begin to critically know and understand the intellectual roots of the material for their projects, can follow various rationales or weigh the value on equal intellectual planes of experts and information researchers, they will not be very useful in determining contents and context. They will stay in the category of beautification experts of which there are too many.

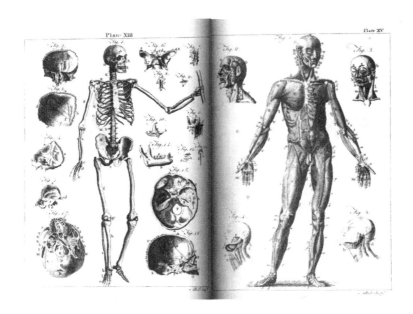

Then, there is the dearth of talented visualizers. A four-year rudimentary design education can provide some of the skills but falls woefully short for professional scientific and information visualization. As beautification specialists, most designers are taught to be expedient in typographic and graphic styling. The field is stagnating by visualizers who have no stake in the development of the contents of the information or who care about the most appropriate application to contexts. For the public, it is never about the aesthetics of type font or graphics. It is about intelligibility. It is never about graphic design, but always about communication. In the next stage of professional evolution designers need to learn and understand that graphic design is subservient to communication and information research, synthesis and management. This must also be the directive to design educators. They must develop curricula antithetical to present modes, which properly relate to the needs of this time. Only then can the badly needed dramatic change occur, from passive graphic stylist to active communication negotiator. Each domain is caught up in coping with its own information explosion and resulting frustration. There is little time for sharing and interfacing with other disciplines. This moment in time presents the unique opportunity for designers to function as information synthesizers, intellectual contents mediators between knowledge domains and disciplines as well as the public.

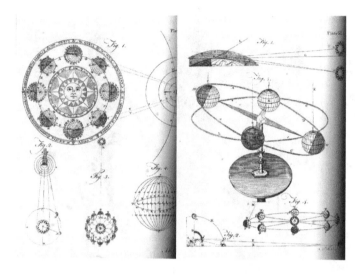

If design wants to revitalize its traditional mission, it must step up to support the citizens' social needs for information in modern, democratic cultures, which automatically, evolving from autocratic and dictatorial systems with fewer truths into a more complex worlds of many but competing truths, it must be eager and want to grow beyond tradition. This completely opposite role from styling, formatting, decorating and entertaining requires of designers new skills, like bringing concepts intellectually together, sharpening them, elaborating on philosophical or political ideas, with the capabilities to select appropriate venues to reach designated audiences, especially those without design awareness, but with communication needs. This evolving design process is about negotiating between segments of the populace and the specific resources, held by individuals, by institutions and corporations, private, public, municipal and federal, profit and non-profit. Design will then participate in the accelerated culture instead of just seeing it pass by.

The basic foundations have been laid by many international information design experts, including Jacques Bertin, Edward Tufte, Richard Wurman and others, which in this paper are reduced to essentials, namely requiring designers to accept full responsibility for the integrity of information (not passive but active knowledge of subject and context); expunge confusing and misleading presentation styles (eliminating mask, lipstick and other beautification make-up, thereby stopping style from entering where fact stops); embracing the audience with respect and sympathy (as there are no general audiences but individual citizens in need of good information for their survival); reducing and eliminating data boredom by presentation of the essentials only, purging the trivial, concentrating on revealing the not so obvious; and intimate collaboration with the project conceptualists, information researchers, and presentation technologists.

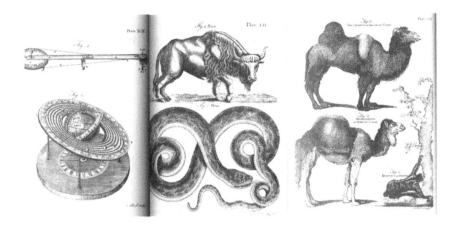

A Case for Sustained, Direct and Hands-on Observation: Information Research, Analysis, Synthesis, and Encoding

But before the eve of photography, the scientific observer and the visual recorder were one and the same. As soon as photography entered the laboratory this seamless process was interrupted. Now neither photographer nor graphic designer may neither have interest, affinity or expertise in the subject matter they are presenting nor the understanding of the context in which the information is used. Schools have short-changed the profession. It is easier to teach the aesthetics of styling than critical thinking. Today, the process of information search is made easier through digital means, but in the process continues to use the designer a passive team-member in the data and information assembling and shaping process. A graduating design major most likely is no more informed by direct experience than any other member of society. That means that they have no better information than the public. The contemporary designer seems to only go into action if there is a client request and an appropriate budget. Even then the idea that expediency is more important than information fidelity is letting them be bystanders rather than active participants.

The invention by Louis-Jacques-Mandé Daguerre (1787-1851) of photography, in the beginning decades of the 1800s ushers in a distinct split between the direct observation and visual recording and the "stand-in" recording by photographers. Between 1844 and 1846, William Fox Talbot (1800-1877) published "The Pencil of Nature," a first book with and about documentary photography, which introduced the naïve belief, prevailing even today, that photography more accurately depicts reality, than the artist/designer as observer ever could. The photographic work of Edward Muggeridge (1830-1904), Thomas Eakins (1844-1916), and Étienne-Jules Marey (1830-1904) fortify the vision of photography as a tool for scientific exploration of reality. In addition the discovery leading to the invention of the X-ray by Wilhelm Conrad Röntgen (1845-1923), a German physicist, further enshrined the use of photography as a scientific observation and recording process. Harold Edgerton (1903-1990) always considered his strobe photography as scientific, never as art. Roland Barthes, French theorist, challenged the concept that photography presents an undisturbed scientific truth, noting that the process of photography distorts reality just like any human observation, which is never neutral but guided by bias, worldview, religion or purpose.

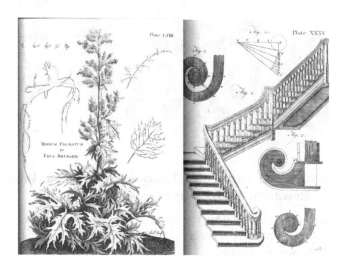

In the same ways in which architect Christopher Alexander believes that great architecture of buildings can only be accomplished by designers who stand in the middle of the social, cultural and physical environment, surrounded by all organic information – about people, their behaviors – namely the fully loaded aggregates of the information ecology, not just understanding, but feeling and anticipating the inherent hierarchical or organic flow, then design has to go back to direct observation, not just waiting to give shape to information, which has been assembled and authored by others. Universities should focus on specific knowledge areas and develop disciplinary concentrations for information design experts (i.e., medicine, law, hard and soft sciences, etc.).

Nicolaus Copernicus, 1473–1543, Renaissance astronomer, influenced Galileo Galilei 1564-1642, Italian physicist, mathematician and astronomer, and also Johannes Kepler, 1571–1630, mathematician, astronomer and astrologer. All three played major roles in the dawning of the Scientific Revolution ushering in the period of European Enlightenment. All three were direct observers of the nightly firmaments, and recorded their findings in charts, diagrams and three-dimensional mechanical working models or like Galileo in beautifully rendered watercolors. Their sensitivity and skill to accurately visualize what they saw through their scopes rivaled contemporary photography. They were extraordinary information designers.

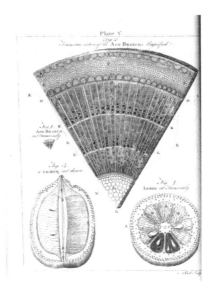

Just to make clear the vastness of information reservoirs, encyclopedias present among the histories of disciplinary accomplishments over ancient and contemporary epochs in all cultures, Islamic, Hindu, Buddhist, Shinto, Christian, socialist or capitalist, the astonishing work of myriads of contributors to human knowledge, even if each filters the individual importance according to a cultural bias. That is why we find out from Chinese maps that the South American continent was known long before it was "discovered" by Europeans. The encyclopedic lists and numbers include about 1700 major contributors to botany, 2700 to zoology, 75 geometers who contributed to mathematics among 1400 mathematicians. 800 were and are physicists, 750 astronomers, 500 archeologists, 100 physicians, 300 geographers and 200 cartographers, 600 sociologists and 950 historians, among many other disciplines.

The exact number does not really matter. What truly matters is that one culture learns from another, instructs the other and one generation learns from the former and instructs another. It is also quite a task to do justice to all world cultures, which have labored to make sense of the universe and convey this survival knowledge to their peoples. For example, only in the middle of the 17th century in Europe, relatively late in comparison with Islamic alchemy, which matured into chemistry already in the 1st century, does Europe's alchemy turn away from sorcery and magic to the foundations of what is western chemistry, which begin to support this vital discipline. Still, everything known is based on careful documentation, manifested in measures, frozen in processes encapsulated in drawings, charts and graphs by the hundreds of early alchemists, now called chemists.

Each culture produced outstanding observers and thinkers. The visual recordings of Leonardo Da Vinci, a keen scientific observer and early visual and industrial designer will always astound the historian. The medical studies by Claudius Galenus or Galen of Pergamum, a prominent Roman physician, dominated and influenced Western medical science for over a millennium, even though his research in human medical anatomy was flawed, borrowed from studies of monkeys and other animals. He erroneously believed that blood vessels originated in the liver, not the heart. It is not until Andreas Vesalius presents his seven-volume research in *De Humani Corporis Fabrica* (On the Fabric of the Human Body), profusely illustrated with woodcuts, in 1543, that many of the obvious errors were corrected. His studies stayed as preferred teaching tool for many centuries. Vesalius was a student both of art and medicine, studying and working in Paris, Padua, Bologna, and Basel, becoming the invited physician to the court of Emperor Charles V.

In the hierarchy of most often published texts, *The Elements of Geometry* by the Greek mathematician Euclid, who originally published it in Alexandria around 300 BC, stands close to few others at the top that have continued to influence generations of mathematicians. It has and is continuing to instruct students. But in 1847, the British mathematician Oliver Byrne presented a peculiar edition of The Elements. It concentrated on the first six volumes, covering elementary plane geometry and theory of proportions. It featured strong graphic visuals for instructions. The book is especially unusual in the instructive use of color. One can surmise that this colorful text, which presents each theorem in solid signal-color fields, may have informed the work of the Russian Suprematism movement, its founder Kasimir Malevich, and its members like El Lissitzky and Liubov Popova.

John James Audubon, 19th century French-American ornithologist, left an invaluable legacy of his encounter with indigenous bird-life on the North-American continent. Johann Wolfgang Goethe, renown German humanist and man of letters of the 18th and 19th centuries, nevertheless observed the visual phenomena of color, developing independently the understanding of the chromatic scale and color wheel. He influenced the color understanding of Johannes Itten, Wassily Kandinsky and other students and faculty of the Bauhaus.

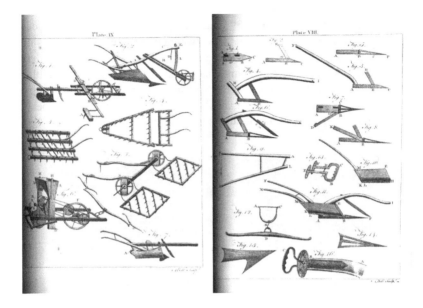

The hand-produced diaries, recording the first overland expedition of Meriwether Lewis and William Clark (1804–1806), undertaken for the United States to gain accurate information on the new resources acquired through the 1803 land purchase of the State of Louisiana from France, instructed the citizenry with rationales for opening the road to the West. The diaries of Henry David Thoreau, a 19th century American author, poet, political and environmental philosopher, reveal his extraordinary skills as keen daily observer of his environment. His observational awareness is even more astonishing since he was not a "visual person," neither designer nor artist. In comparison, while today's artist/designers are trained to inform and instruct, they traverse their world out of awareness, in Ersatz experiences, void of any critical recognition, and without greater sophistication than the public, Thoreau was able to point to the fact that a certain plant had over seasons morphed into a different shape, size or color. The Denis Diderot (1713-1784) *Pictorial Encyclopedia of Trades and Industry* froze information on processes, materials and methods in history, books that Shakespeare's Prospero would have liked to have had when he was separated when shipwrecked from the rest of the known civilization.

Alexander von Humboldt, following the examples set by Marco Polo (1254–1324), the Venetian merchant who introduced Europe to the rich and sophisticated cultures of Central Asia and China, Amerigo Vespucci (1454–1512), Italian explorer, Vasco Da Gama (1460–1524), Portuguese explorer and Captain James Cook (1728–1779) English explorer, navigator and cartographer. On the basis of his painstakingly collected data in South America he observed the interrelation of all physical sciences, biology, meteorology, and geology that have an inference on the growth of plants or their propagation. During their time, there was no designation that made them into scientists. They were just interested and committed individuals. They and others formed the understanding of the world by recording everything of importance, as seen through the eyes of their epochs of course. Captain James Cook in 1769 made it possible through his contact, for others to record some customs of the Maori, which make contemporary designers aware of other ways of creating social identities. In Maori tattoos, each pattern or ornament reads like a passport, making clear to any tribal member the status and rank within the tribal hierarchy, levels of skills in war and statesmanship and social prestige and accomplishment, setting the initial stage for interpersonal conduct and etiquette. It is information design in its best form.

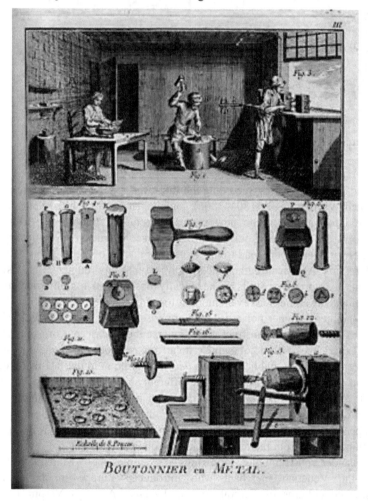

Even missionaries as well as the conquistadores of Maya and Inca cultures were early information gatherers and designers. They needed to bring back proof to their governmental sponsors about what was accomplished and about the size and quality of the riches they conquered and the natives they converted. Conquistadores, like Hernán Cortés or Pizarro were indirectly forced to be diligent in covering anything of possible importance for their monarchs. We would not have known much about cultures and societies that contrasted with those in Europe and which since have died out. They brought back the Florentine Codex (circa 1540 to 1585), which was copied from original source materials, namely records of conversations and interviews with indigenous peoples of Tlatelolco, Texcoco, and Tenochtitlan, organized into a series of 12 volumes, and codices like it or the Codex Zouche-Nuttall or Codex Dresdensis help us even today to establish the parameters of these cultures. The Codex Dresdensis, a pre-Columbian Maya book of the eleventh or twelfth century of the Yucatecan Maya is believed to be the earliest known book written in the Americas. These documents are still aiding anthropologists today in understanding Maya and other indigenous cultures.

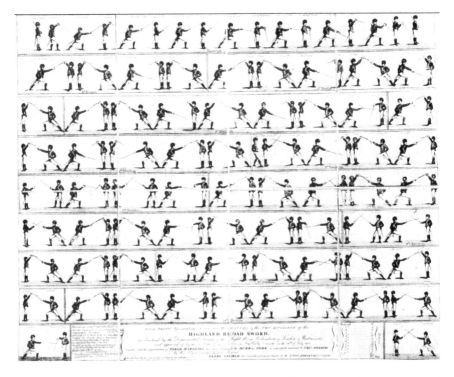

There are many examples in contemporary times. Vincent F. Luti, composer and professor of music at the University of Massachusetts Dartmouth, from a youthful age showed great interest in the exquisite designs of 18th Century gravestones by regional stone carvers of Newport, Rhode Island. Continuously, over sixty years, he took stone-rubbings and photographs, assembling an astonishingly detailed and exquisite collection of information from which the contents for his seminal text was developed. The information is so self-explaining and explicit, that several design and art historians had to rewrite portions of their much more generalized presentations. His book has become a bible for archeologists because of its meticulous approach.

This means that if designers want to get back into information graphics, they must get their hands and minds dirty, observing, describing, authoring, drawing, painting, photographing and providing text and image about the phenomena. For designers, living in a world of ephemera, in which technologies change and in which one style fad is chasing the next, the only thing lasting is the integrity of information design. Even when data becomes obsolete caused by additions of better and more precise insights, the phenomenon of information design will always be a significant contributor to the knowledge of human evolution. Society will hold it in esteem. It is and will always be important.

Biographical Note

Dietmar R. Winkler, educated in design in Hamburg, Germany, is professor emeritus at the University of Massachusetts Dartmouth. He believes that design theory cannot be separated from evolving contemporary and future professional practices. He is the former director of the School of Art and Design at the University of Illinois at Urbana-Champaign. He also held the Joyce C. Hall-Chair as director of the Center for the Study of Form, Image, and Text at the Kansas City Art Institute. Prior, for approximately twenty years, he was a senior faculty member of the Design Department, the dean of the College of Visual and Performing Arts, and an adjunct faculty member in the cognitive science program of the Psychology Department at the University of Massachusetts Dartmouth.

Since 1960, he has been examining professional design practice and the education of design and communication subjects. His interdisciplinary interests have been to expand narrow traditional visual and form/function literacies to include user-based design in behavioral, social, and cultural contexts. He is a member of the editorial board of advisors to *Visible Language* journal for which he has written on design and educational issues. Other papers have appeared in publications of AIGA, ICOGRADA, and *TipoGráfica*.

In design practice, he has worked as type and design director, responsible for the development and implementation of various long-term publication programs, identity systems, and design and production staffing plans at Brandeis University, Harvard Business School, Massachusetts Institute of Technology, University of Massachusetts Dartmouth, as well as the WGBH Educational Foundation. His design work has been awarded, exhibited, and published by art director clubs of Boston, New York, and St. Louis, the Type Directors Club of New York, the American Institute of Graphic Arts. Reviews and visual presentations have also appeared in publications and books of the national and international professional media: Art Direction, Communication Arts, Graphis (Switzerland), Idea Magazine (Japan), Novum Gebrauchsgrafik (Germany), Print, among others.

Chapter 8: Pictopolitics: Icograda and the International Development of Pictogram Standards: 1963–1986

Wibo Bakker

Abstract

The rise of pictograms in the nineteen sixties is usually associated with the Olympic games (Tokyo 1964, Mexico City 1968, München 1972) or world exhibitions (Montréal 1967). It is often suggested that the designers of the symbols for these events, played a pioneering role in its development. Remarkably the role of international organisations that contributed to the development of pictograms in these years has seldom been researched. An organisation that was most active in this area was the International Council of Graphic Design Associations (Icograda). President Willy de Majo and his close collaborator Peter Kneebone held the opinion that ideally a standardized and tested pictogram set for general traveller information should to be developed. Through its activities Icograda eventually contributed to raising awareness about the necessity of standards for public information symbols. By using the archives of Icograda and researching the organisations and individuals it was dealing with like the ICBLB, UIC, Glyphs Inc., C.K. Bliss, Henry Dreyfuss, ISO and Masaru Katzumie, a far more balanced picture of the development of pictograms emerges. This study gives a new, more institutional twist to the history of a popular design theme within the graphic design profession.

Icograda and Student Project Nr. 1: Designing an International Symbol Language

Icograda was founded in a time that the design world was obtaining an increasingly international outlook.[1] In 1963 a small British working committee that was led by the designer Willy de Majo (1917-1993)–Icograda's first president–organised a first inaugural meeting in London. Delegates from 28 of the leading graphic design associations in 17 countries were present and voted unanimously to set up Icograda. Most of them applied for membership too.[2] On an idealistic level Icograda strove "to encourage the better use of graphic design as a means towards the advancement of humanity, regardless of race or creed."[3] Its immediate aim however was to "raise the standards of graphic design and the professional status of graphic designers." To support this it initiated activities that benefited the profession as whole.

Icograda established for example guidelines for international design competitions and contracts. Also it set up committees for important subjects such as the "Unification of Typographic Measurements Commission" and the "Commission on International Signs and Symbols."[4] Highlights of Icograda's activities were the two-yearly congresses that were hosted by a member body. Congresses in Zurich (1964), Bled (Yugoslavia 1966) and Eindhoven (Holland 1968) each attracted hundreds of visitors who listened to lectures by designers, psychologists and sociologists.

One of the main priorities of Icograda in 1963 was the improvement of design education. To aid this it decided to organise so called 'student projects' with 'universal usefulness' in which graphic design students from all over the world could participate. These projects were presented and judged at Icograda congresses with the intervening two years being used for the actual work on the project. One of the themes De Majo suggested for the first project was a 'Symbol Language for directional signs in-doors and out'.[5] This idea soon evolved into the "Student project nr. 1" with the title "Designing an International Symbol

---

[1] The establishment of Icograda was preceded by that of the Alliance Graphique Internationale (AGI) in 1955, and the Association Typographique Internationale (ATypI) and the International Council of Societies of Industrial Design (ICSID) in 1957.

[2] Michael Middleton, 'Icograda London 63' [Reprint from a SIA journal report on the inaugaral meeting of the International Council of Graphic Design Associations held in London, 26-28 April 1963, pp. 9-12]; Wynkyn de Worde Society, *ICOGRADA, the first five years,* London 1968; ICOGRADA [Jorge Frascara (ed.)], *Graphic design, world views: a celebration of 25 years' achievement,* Kodansha International, New York 1990.

[3] Michael Middleton, 'Icograda London 63' [Reprint from a SIA journal report on the inaugaral meeting of the International Council of Graphic Design Associations held in London, 26-28 April 1963, pp. 9-12 (12)].

[4] See for the 'Unification of Typographic Measurements Commission'; Andrew Boag, 'Typographic Measurement: a chronology', *Typographic papers* (1), 1996, pp. 105-121.

[5] University of Brighton, Design Archives: Icograda [not catalogued] (DAIC): 'Minutes General Assembly 1963-1968; Board Meeings 1963-1966' (BM).

Language." Chairman of the project was the designer Peter Kneebone (1923-1990) who had collaborated with De Majo in establishing Icograda.

Interestingly it was probably the United Kingdom's widely publicised adoption of a newer version of the international road signs in 1963 that had given De Majo the idea for the project.[6] In a broader sense it was grounded upon the fascination of the design and business world at the time with trademarks and symbols. Scientific research had recently discovered that abstract and pictorial symbols–as exemplified by their use in visual identities–were important carriers of meaning and could transcend language barriers. It was to be expected that in an increasingly internationally orientated world, visual symbols would become core elements of communication.[7]

Despite the ambitious title of the project students would have to develop a limited integrated set of 24 symbols for verbal concepts such as telephone, toilet and emergency exit, stand alone symbols that catered to immediate needs of international travellers.[8] Since it was an educational effort it was not Icograda's intention for their first student project to deliver a pictogram set for real world application. The project was announced in the summer of 1964 at the first Icograda congress in Zurich and at the end of the year entry forms were sent to over 600 design schools worldwide.[9] Press coverage was given in *Design* and

---

[6] The adoption, and the history of road traffic signs in general, were extensively described by the graphic designer Anthony Froshaug in an article published in the British design magazine *Design* 1963: Anthony Froshaug, 'Roadside traffic signs', *Design* (178), October 1963, pp. 37-50. Kneebone would regularly send this article to organisations interested in signs and symbols.

[7] Wibo Bakker, *Droom van helderheid: Huisstijlen, ontwerpbureaus en modernisme in Nederland: 1960-1975*, Uitgeverij 010, Rotterdam 2011, pp. 13-29.

[8] The 24 verbal concepts for the symbols were; entrance, exit, no smoking, do not touch, danger, w.c. (ladies), w.c. (gentlemen), fire alarm, telephone, post office, police, doctor, hospital, chemist. information bureau, exchange bureau, petrol, railway station, airport, harbour, hotel, museum, historical monument, directional arrow. In the letter introducing the project to educational institutions Kneebone described it as 'the first of a series of projects enabling students to collaborate on international design problems to benefit both themselves and the community.' In: Letter Kneebone to 'Principal', December 1964 in: DAIC: 'Icograda: 1964-1968: Signs & Symbols Commission: Peter Kneebone' (64).

[9] A complete list of entries is lacking. An early list from July 1965 shows 77 applications from the following countries and schools; Belgium; Stedelijke Akademie voor Tekenkunst (Kortijk), Académie des Beaux Arts et des Arts Décoratifs (Tournai). France; Ecole Régionale des Beaux Arts (Besançon), Lycée Technique de Jeune Filles (Paris). Germany; Folkwangschule für Gestaltung (Essen-Werden), Werkkunstschule Wuppertal (Wuppertal-Barmen), Kunst + Werkschule (Pforzheim), Hochschule für Grafik und Buchkunst (Leipzig), Werkkunstschule der Freien und Hansestadt Hamburg. Great Britain; Hereford Art School (Hereford), School of Advanced Studies: Regional College of Art (Manchester), College of Arts Gandy School (Exeter), Graphic Design Department Chelsea School of Art (London), High Wycombe College of Art and Technology (High

Graphis.[10] Icograda knew that they were entering virgin territory with this project. The only other known symbol or pictogram systems for public space were those of the 1964 Tokyo Olympics (Figure 1)–conceived after Icograda came up with the idea of their student project–and that of the international road signs.

Figure 1. Tokyo Olympics information pictograms designed by Katzumie's team, 1964.

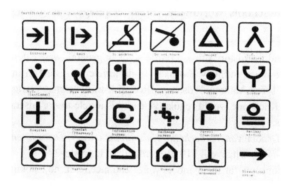

Figure 2. Entry for the Icograda "Student project nr. 1" by Jacobus Le Grange (Manchester College of Art and Design), awarded with a 'Certificate of Merit,' 1966.

Wycombe), Kingston College of Art, South West Essex Technical College and School of Art (Walthamstow), Cardiff College of Art (Cardiff). The Netherlands; Academie voor Kunst en Industrie (Enschede), Akademie voor Industriële Vormgeving (Eindhoven), Koninklijke Academie van Beeldende Kunsten (Den Haag); U.S.A; Museum Art School (Portland), San Francisco Art Institute. Switserland; Kunstgewerbeschule Zürich. New Zealand; School of Fine Arts (Christchurch). In; Letter Wim Crouwel to Kneebone, 19 July 1965 in: DAIC-64. Later also applications were received from Austria, Brazil, Canada, Finland, East-Germany, Italy, Poland, South Africa, Sweden and Yugoslavia.

[10] Stanley Mason, 'Towards an International Symbology', *Graphis* (116), 1964, pp. 514-517; Margit Staber, 'Icograda Congress, Zürich 1964', *Graphis* (116), 1964 p. 518; 'An international sign language starts badly', *Design* (201), September 1965, p. 26.

Two years later at the Icograda congress in Bled over a 100 entries for "Student project no. 1" were assessed by a jury of known designers such as Abraham Games, Josef Müller-Brockmann, Paul Rand and Masaru Katzumie, the art director of the Tokyo Olympics pictograms. Typical for the prize-winning entries was that they showed a high degree of abstraction that ensured a clear visual coherence (Figure 2). The jury favoured this approach because they thought a more pictorial solution would cause ambiguity, attributed to intercultural differences. Curiously the jury also stated that ideally a pictorial system was needed. Only at a later stage this was to be replaced by a thoroughly researched abstract system, although they did acknowledge that such a system needed more time to gain international acceptance than a pictorial one.[11]

The somewhat roundabout assessment of the jury shows that they had given considerable thought to the development and introduction of pictograms. This was a reflection of the increased knowledge they had gained in this subject in the past years. By 1966 Icograda had established Icograda "Commission on International Signs and Symbols" (CISS) and had contacted dozens of organisations and individuals who had started working on similar projects. According to Icograda these projects were not coordinated and missed a scientific foundation that guaranteed a successful design process and application. Naturally as designers they were also afraid that in the future they would be forced to use haphazard collections of pictograms that lacked visual quality.

Icograda Tries to Steer the ICBLB, the UIC and Other Organisations in the Right Direction

De Majo and Kneebone played a key role in establishing relations with other parties working on pictogram systems.[12] They became first aware of other

---

[11] Peter Kneebone 'Student Seminar' [Speech about the results of 'Student project nr. 1'], 11 July 1966 in: DAIC: Folder 'ICOGRADA–Bled, Yugoslavia–1966'; Peter Kneebone, 'Communicating across frontiers–with and without words', *Design* (214), October 1966, pp. 44-47. ICOGRADA, 'Press Release: ICOGRADA Student Project Nr. 1', 16 July 1966 in: DAIC-64. The winning entry was that of: Jan Olov Sundström & Sunniva Kellquist (Konstfackskolan, Stockholm). Runners up were Jacobus Le Grange (Manchester College of Art and Design) and Rolf Erikson & Jan Olov Sundström (Konstfackskolan, Stockholm).

[12] It is fair to say De Majo and Kneebone were highly experienced in international organisational affairs. De Majo was of Yugoslavian heritage, but was born and educated in Vienna. During the war he served at the BBC Overseas Service, The Royal Yugoslavian Air Force and the Supreme Headquarters of the Allied Expedition Force (SHAEF). Later he became a consultant designer to several companies in the United Kingdom. Kneebone was born out of an English father and a French mother. During the war he served as a naval liaison officer in Italy and as broadcasting representative for the Government Information Office (GIO) in Cairo. After the war he finished a study of modern languages

activities in the field of symbols when in January 1965 they were passed on a bundle of letters from an organisation called "The International Committee for Breaking the Language Barrier" (ICBLB). Enclosed was a questionnaire the ICBLB had sent earlier to organisations around the globe. [13] It listed 38 expressions–such as toilet, baggage-check or exit–that travellers should be able to recognize. [14] Each expression was illustrated by one or more symbols. The participants in the questionnaire had to circle the symbols they thought most suitable for an expression or could draw their own proposal. In another letter the ICBLB announced the preliminary results: They had received 300 entries and concluded that "cooperation between organisations," and "symbol consistency" were "essential."[15]

The ICBLB was based in New York and was headed by the Japanese businessman Soichi Kato. Upon arriving in America in the late nineteen fifties he had major problems finding his way in public life. According to him this had to do with bad quality of information signs in public space. That is why in 1963 he established the ICBLB. Despite the ambitious name originally it was only active locally, proposing for example new bus signs for the City of New York. It quickly gained the support of local businesses and organisations, most importantly the Port of New York Authority that was responsible for the local infrastructure and border traffic.[16] When in 1964 the United Nations issued a statement urging "cooperation in expanding the use of symbols" in connection with their upcoming

---

at Oxford. From 1948 on Kneebone was closely involved with the organisation and promotion of the 'Festival of Britain' after which he started a career as an illustrator and designer. See for Willy de Majo: Dick Negus, 'Obituary: Willy de Majo', *The Independent,* 23 October 1993. See for Peter Kneebone:
http://www.museumoflondon.org.uk/archive/exhibits/festival/kneebone.htm.

[13] Letter ICBLB (Soichi Kato) to ICSID (D. des Cressonnieres), stamped 14 December 1964. Attached to the letter a survey and the results of the survey as received by February 1965 in: DAIC-64.

[14] The 38 expressions surveyed by the ICBLB were; toilet, men, women, exit, emergency exit, entrance, elevator [entrance], elevator [indication], information, first aid, police, danger, don't smoke, don't enter, airport, seaport, railway station, bus, taxi, gasoline station, hotel, restaurant, pharmacy, currency exchange, arrival, departure, gate, ticket, bagagae check, bagage claim, passport control, customs, fasten seat belts, telephone, post, telegram, wet paint, travel agent.

[15] Letter ICBLB (Soichi Kato) to ICSID (D. des Cressonnieres), stamped 14 December 1964. Attached to the letter a survey and the results of the survey as received by February 1965 in: DAIC-64.

[16] 'Breaking the Language Barrier', *Congressional Record* (185), Vol. 108, 9 October 1962; 'World language of signs sought', *New York Times,* 3 June 1962; 'Paris and London leave Manhattan behind when it comes to helping the rider find the right bus', *The New York Times,* 2 December 1963; 'The Sorry Plight of Our Buses', *The Sun,* 23 October 1964.

"International Cooperation Year 1965" the ICBLB jumped to the opportunity to expand its mission.[17]

Another organisation that caught De Majo's and Kneebone's eye in the beginning of 1965 was the Union Internationale de Chemins de Fer (UIC), the international organisation for railway companies in the western world. Since 1961 it had been working on a symbol set that was intended to "ease transportations by railway." This set may well have been the first pictogram set designed for general traveller information. Just like Icograda and the ICBLB the UIC had chosen to symbolize a limited amount of expressions. The final designs for the set were handpicked by a committee of railway officials out of the entries of a competition. Since 1963 this set had been offered on a provisional basis to UIC-members (Figure 3).[18] In June 1965 Kneebone participated in a conference of the UIC dedicated to this set. The UIC had invited international travel and transport organisations with the intention of convincing them to accept it as a standard for international traveller symbols. At a subsequent conference in January 1966 the UIC wanted to propose more symbols.[19]

Figure 3. UIC-symbol selection as sent to the Dutch Railways, 1965.

---

[17]United Nations: General Assembly: Committee for the International Co-operation Year, 'Facilitating Communication' [A/AC.118/L.5], 19 March 1964 in: Library of Congress: Margaret Mead Papers: Mead K64-1.

[18] 'Signs of the times', *The New York Times*, 4 April 1965; Letter UIC secretary-general to members, 'Emploi des pictograms', 4 July 1963; Minutes CRV-meeting, 1 May 1963; letter CRV to Dutch Railway-directors Wansink and Koster, April 1963; Letter chairman CRV to directorate, April 1963. All in: The Utrecht Archives: Dutch Railways (UA) 943-95.

[19] Letter Kneebone to De Majo, 'Student Project Progress Report', June 1965 in: DAIC-64.

Icograda's acquaintance with the activities of the ICBLB and the UIC was a turning point for its subsequent involvement with symbol development worldwide. De Majo and Kneebone considered the symbols that were presented by these organisations as totally unsatisfactory. Upon receiving the ICBLB questionnaire De Majo wrote to Kato: "your questionnaire, as it stands at present, is almost like asking people 'do you prefer cyanide or heroin?' In other words, there seems little point in choosing between two or more bad solutions." [20] Kneebone made similar statements at the UIC conference, where he proposed to regard all work in the field of symbols as experimental research directed towards a fully integrated, rational and international system.[21] Kato however did not seem to take in the criticism and Kneebone's proposal was flatly rejected.

According to Icograda the problem with these organisations was that they wanted to develop a symbol system by selecting and combining symbols. However, the considerations for selecting these symbols were not transparent. Also the visual quality–and coherence of the symbols as a set–was doubtful at the least. Most important of all it was not clear whether the symbols would be understood by the general public worldwide. Icograda found similar problems with the activities of almost every other organisation dealing with symbols. De Majo and Kneebone became convinced, that thorough scientific research was needed to develop a pictogram set for general traveller information that would be applicable worldwide. And of course designers should be involved.

After the UIC conference Kneebone wrote to De Majo: "The situation is not a happy one and calls for immediate action by Icograda (…) International symbols are the most basic graphic problem that we, as an organisation, can be concerned with."[22] Icograda regarded the matter of symbols as a test case that would show the invaluable contribution designers could make to society. But if it wanted to be on top of the alarming development rate of symbol systems it had to act swiftly. Already in the entry forms for the "Student project no. 1" Kneebone had outlined Icograda's plans to establish–in cooperation with other interested parties–a symbol council and to hold a symbol conference.[23] This plan was likely to be executed after the presentation of the student project in 1966. Now it had to be moved forward.

As a first step it established in October 1965 an Icograda "Commission on International Signs and Symbols" (CISS). To legitimate the CISS an impressive selection of designers like Kneebone, De Majo, Erik Ellegaard Frederiksen, Roger Excoffon, Hans Weckerle, Masaru Katzumie, Paul Rand and Josef Müller-Brockmann, and scientists like Martin Krampen and Gilbert Cohen-Seat sat on its commission. The CISS also spoke for the design community as a whole

---

[20] Letter De Majo to Kato, 25 June 1965 in: DAIC-64.

[21] 'Special Session on International Signs and Symbols in Transport & Tourism' [ICC] , 1 April 1966 in: DAIC-64.

[22] Letter Kneebone to De Majo, 'Student Project Progress Report', June 1965 in: DAIC-64.

[23] Letter Kneebone to De Majo, June 1965 in: DAIC-64.

representing the International Council of Societies of Industrial Design (ICSID) and the International Union of Architects (UIA) in matters regarding symbols.[24] Despite the impressive list of commission members in fact Kneebone and De Majo were taking care of all most all correspondence and activities of the CISS.

In an exposé about the CISS Kneebone wrote:

> The purpose of the Icograda Commission is to act as a dispassionate, professional, co-ordinating and advisory body (...) the commission will endeavour to prevent duplication and ensure that official organisations concerned with international signs and symbols will be able to carry out their work with full knowledge of what is happening in this field in other parts in the world. All official signs and symbols suggested for international use could then be established with the assistance of professional expert designers rather than only by administrators, and be based on valid principals and a coherent vocabulary.[25]

To aid in the collection and dissemination of information on symbols, Icograda envisioned the establishment of international signs and symbols centers in Europe, Africa, India, the Far East and Central America.

An interesting side effect of the UIC-conference was that it not only pressed Icograda into action but also aviation organisations like the Western European Airport Corporation (WEAC), the International Civil Aviation Organization (ICAO) and the International Air Transport Association (IATA), the equivalent of the UIC for air transport. The quickly developing aviation sector did not allow itself to be meddled with by an organisation that had only just escaped the age of steam. It instated working groups for developing its own pictogram systems.[26] Other organisations just went along for the ride but some of them lent their ears towards De Majo's and Kneebone's active lobby for a coordinated symbol effort, like the earlier mentioned WEAC, the International Chamber of Commerce (ICC) and the World Touring and Automobile Organisation (OTA).[27]

At the second UIC conference in January 1966 Icograda proposed to establish an International Council for Signs and Symbols. Icograda would take care of research and development and the public relations angle would be

---

[24] Peter Kneebone, 'Icograda Commission on International Signs and Symbols', ca. 1967 in: DAIC-64.

[25] Peter Kneebone, 'Commission on International Signs and Symbols: Exposé', October 1965 in: DAIC-64.

[26] See for example: IATA Meeting [21/565], 'Airport and directional signs', ca. 1965. The IATA set was presented in 1966. According to Icograda they only repeated the mistakes of organisations like the UIC. In: letter De Majo to Michael Lax, 10 March 1966. All in: DAIC-64. Also the ICAO, ATA and WEAC instigated work groups,

[27] Peter Kneebone, 'Commission on International Signs and Symbols: Exposé', October 1965; Letter De Majo to A. Jarniou, 11 June 1965. Both in: DAIC-64.

addressed by the ICBLB.[28] Unfortunately the only thing everybody hesitantly agreed upon was that "Steps should be taken to establish machinery for proper collaboration between the various bodies." In the mean time UIC would continue to introduce new pictograms.[29] It was clear to Icograda now that no progress was to be expected within an institutional framework dominated by the UIC.

Luckily with the help of the ICC, Icograda was able to organize a session dedicated to travel signs and symbols at the World Conference on Transport and Tourism, organised by the International Union of Official Travel Organisations (IUOTO) in April 1966.[30] Organisations like the ICC and IUOTO supported Icograda because they represented businesses or travellers who would benefit from effective and standardized symbols worldwide. Icograda carefully prepared the session and even convinced the UIC to take part.[31] For the first time they were also able to present a proposal for the scientific research needed to develop pictograms.

Krampen's Scientific Research and the International Commission on Travel Signs and Symbols (ICTSS)

Although Kneebone and De Majo regularly emphasised the need for scientific research in developing symbols they had only a vague idea of what this research should constitute. This weakened their negotiating position with other organisations. Initially De Majo and Kneebone had meddled with semiotics.[32] It helped them describing the nature of existing signs and symbols but it did not contain clues for the development of new symbols. This all changed in the end of 1965 when Kneebone came in touch with the German scientist Martin Krampen (1928-). Krampen had also studied Visual Communication at the Hochschule für Gestaltung (HfG) in Ulm and had an interest in symbols. In the late nineteen fifties he moved to Canada were he became an assistant professor in design and communication at the University of Waterloo.

Krampen was also an advisor to the world exhibition in Montreal, called Expo '67. He wanted to use this opportunity to develop a scientific method that spelled out–as he wrote to Kneebone–"step by step the operations a designer or non-designer should go through, today and 200 years from now, to produce elements of a self-renewing pictorial language which has maximum cross-cultural

---

[28] Peter Kneebone, 'Icograda Commission on International Signs and Symbols: Exposé and Proposal', January 1966 in: DAIC-64.

[29] Draft report of UIC Conference on Pictograms, 20 January 1966; Letter De Majo to Bliss, 7 March 1966 in: DAIC-64.

[30] 'Special session on International Signs + symbols in transport & tourism', 1 april 1966 in: DAIC-64.

[31] Letter De Majo to Stanley A. Mason, 22 February 1966 in: DAIC-64.

[32] For this De Majo and Kneebone used the 'Glossary of Semiotics'. See: T. Maldonado, 'Glossary of Semiotics', *Uppercase* (5), London 1962, pp. 44-62.

and international impact."[33] He assumed that communication only took place if "sender" and "receiver" shared a "common stock of signs." To discover this "stock," visitors at the Expo '67 would be asked to produce symbols based on verbal expressions, a method also known as the "production method." The image contents of the symbols that were produced most for a certain expression would potentially also be the ones best understood.[34]

Krampen's research method was the first step in an extensive proposal for symbol development that Kneebone presented at the signs and symbol session at the World Conference on Travel and Tourism. Further steps consisted of the actual design of the symbols by designers and psychologists, followed by field tests, periodical retesting and redesign. To carry out this proposal 400.000 dollars were needed, some of which would also be used for the earlier mentioned symbols centers.[35] The participants in the session however were hardly aware that there was a symbol problem, let alone that money and serious research were needed to solve it.[36] Some of them were even under the impression that Icograda was just representing craftsman who were there to deliver some "pretty designs," thus providing the quick fix they wanted.[37] Of course this was exactly the kind of attitude towards the design profession that Icograda intended to change.

Although Icograda's proposal was rejected it did manage to convince a dozen non-governmental organisations like the ICC, IUOTO and the UIC to establish an International Committee for Travel Signs and Symbols (ICTSS) that should strive for a coordinated development of pictograms. Icograda took part as an expert body in a consultative capacity.[38] Much to their frustration the outcome of later meetings of the ICTSS proved to be a repetition of the earlier efforts of the

---

[33] Letter Martin Krampen to Kneebone, 3 November 1965 in: DAIC-64. It was only logical that Krampen suggested to the designers of the signage system–the Canadian firm of Paul Arthur & Associates–that symbols should be used as much as possible. In: Michael Large, 'Communication among All People, Everywhere: Paul Arthur and the Maturing of Design', *Design Issues* (2), Vol. 17, Spring 2001, pp. 81-90 (84).

[34] Martin Krampen, 'The Production Method in Sign Design Research', *Print*, November-December 1969, pp. 59-63. Krampen tested the following referents; antidote, interpreter, veterinarian, non-edible, interpreter, edible, insecticide, do not lean out the window, wash and wear, tourist information, inflammable, fertilizer, elevator, high voltage, no entry, baggage, poison, gasoline, hospital, boiling water.

[35] 'Special Session on International Signs and Symbols in Transport & Tourism' [ICC], 1 April 1966 in: DAIC-64. Interestingly the proposal also notes general requirements for pictograms not mentioned before. International symbols should: '1. Be unambiguous, 2. Mean the same thing to all people who will use it, 3. Be read quickly, 4. Be acted upon'.

[36] Letter De Majo to Kling, 6 June 1966 in: DAIC-64.

[37] Letter Kneebone to Rojinsky, 25 May 1966; letter De Majo to executive board Icograda, 7 April 1966; letter Kling to 'Working Party on Signs and Symbols connected with Tourism', 5 April 1966. All in: DAIC-64.

[38] 'Special Session on International Signs and Symbols in Transport & Tourism' [ICC], 1 April 1966 in: DAIC-64.

ICBLB and the UIC to come to a symbol system. That is why Icograda decided to carry out itself a limited version of the research it had proposed earlier. This was discussed during the Bled conference were "Student project nr. 1" was presented. Krampen was to do the research during his upcoming stay at the HfG from 1967 onwards.[39] Icograda hoped that it would serve as a fundament for future activities of the ICTSS. For the moment however the ICTSS would only agree that the research program was "an example of a possible method," which left the possibility open to dismiss the results of the research.[40]

After much delay–partly attributed to the definitive closure of the HfG in 1968–the project started in May 1968. 63 verbal expressions were tested with almost 3000 questionnaires that were–aided by the WEAC–obtained from air travellers in European, US and other airports. In Germany Krampen carried out retests and additional tests with university students and foreign military men stationed there.[41] As such it was the largest research project in the development of symbols yet. However, during this project Krampen increasingly drew his own course. Icograda was aware of this this but there was not much it could do. Krampen's long awaited research report was presented in April 1969 at a meeting that proved to be the last one of the ICTSS.[42] It is likely that its members had

---

[39] Krampen was to be aided in this by the designer Herbert Kapitzki–than head of the visual communication department–who had in interest in symbols on his own. In 1967 Kapitzki was commissioned by the German Airports Association (ADV) to design guidelines for the use of signage and pictograms at German airports, eventually complying with the existing pictogram sets of the UIC and IATA. Around the same time his predecessor at the HfG–Otl Aicher–received commissions for the graphic design of the 1972 Olympics in Münich and the design of the signage for Frankfurt Airport. This last signage system adhered to Kapitzki's ADV design guidelines. Interestingly the opinions of Aicher on pictograms partly rested upon Krampens research. In 1977 they worked together on the book *Zeichensysteme der visuellen Kommunikation: Handbuch für Designer, Architekten, Planer und Organisatoren* (Alexander Koch, Stuttgart 1977). Of course their paths had crossed before at the HfG in the nineteen fifties. See: Letter Kapitzki to Kneebone, 9 August 1966 in: DAIC-64; Martin Krampen & Günther Hörmann, *The Ulm School of Design: Beginnings of a Project of Unyielding Modernity*, Berlin 2003, pp. 55, 183, 188; Herbert W. Kapitzki, *Design: Method and Consequence : A Biographical Report*, Edition Axel Menges, Stuttgart/London 1997, pp. 105-106; German Airports Association, *Pictographs for Orientation at Airports*, Stuttgart 1968; Markus Rathgeb, *Otl Aicher*, Phaidon Press Ltd., London 2006, pp. 116-118.

[40] International Committee for Travel Signs and Symbols, 'Joint Statement', June 1967 in: DAIC-64.

[41] Martin Krampen, 'The Production Method in Sign Design Research', *Print*, November-December 1969, pp. 59-63.

[42] CISS (Peter Kneebone), 'Summary Report 1966/68', for Icograda Congress 19-24 August 1968; Letter Henrion to ICC, 9 April 1969; Letter Kneebone to Katzumie, 13 April 1969. All in DAIC: 'Peter Kneebone: Signs & Symbols Commission: 1968-' (68); In the report Icograda was mentioned only once: "Icograda through its Icograda/Ulm project and

become wary of the project. After three years they still had no symbol set. The efforts of Icograda to coordinate and steer the development of pictograms within the International Committee for Travel Signs and Symbols (ICTSS) –and with this transport and travel organisations in general–had come to a dead end.

Also within Icograda support for the project slowed down. The subtle diplomatic tandem of Kneebone and De Majo had been broken when at the Icograda conference in 1966 a new Icograda president was appointed: the Norge designer Knut Yran. While Kneebone's working relations with De Majo had been close this was not the case with his successor. As a chairman of an almost defunct Commission on International Signs and Symbols (CISS) Kneebone practically worked alone. From a publicity point of view however it was a fruitful time. In 1969 Kneebone was guest editor of a "signs and symbols" special of the American graphic design magazine *Print*.[43] In addition to an expose dedicated to the CISS and its activities it also carried articles from several other organisations and individuals Icograda had come to know like Margaret Mead and Rudolf Modley from Glyphs Inc., C.K. Bliss and Henry Dreyfuss. These persons haven't been addressed so far but are essential for a better understanding of Icograda's involvement in the worldwide development of symbols.

International Language and Machine Instructions: Glyphs Inc., C.K. Bliss and Henrey Dreyfuss

Icograda, the International Committee for Breaking the Language Barrier (ICBLB) and the Union Internationale de Chemins de Fer (UIC) were striving for a basic symbol set for a few dozen expressions, addressing practical and basic

---

other constitutions has speeded up the present survey project'. International Committee for Travel Signs and Symbols (M. Krampen & B. Sevray), *International survey on pictographs,* June 1968-March 1969, p. 2. In: Cooper-Hewitt / National Design Museum, Henry Dreyfuss Archive, Symbol Sourcebook, Preliminary Data Bank; General, General Discussion (18-k); During the project Krampen and another ICTSS-member were hired by the ICAO to design new air transport pictograms. In 1967 Icograda had sent Krampen to an ICAO conference to convince it to join the Icograda Ulm project. The ICAO was a UN-organisation and other aviation organisations were likely to take its lead. ICAO did not join the project but did hire Krampen later on. He adjusted the survey to also meet ICAO's need: since ICAO needed pictograms these might be useful for ICTSS members too. He did not agree with what he called the 'half-hearted design-research approach' of De Majo and Kneebone. In: email Martin Krampen to Bakker 24 July 2012; Icograda seemed not to be wholly aware of this, nor the implied name change of the project. When the ICAO symbols were finally introduced in 1970 Kneebone considered them bad, and called for an emergency ICTSS meeting, to no avail.

[43] *Print,* November-December 1969. The special was a result of a visit of the designer FHK Henrion–Icograda-president between 1968 and 1970–to the United States in the beginning of 1969 where he met the editor of *Print*. See: letter Martin Fox to FHK Henrion, 27 March 1969 in DAIC-64. Henrion also visited Dreyfuss.

needs of the individual traveller or civilian. Nevertheless De Majo and Kneebone also dealt with organisations and individuals that had greater and more idealistic ambitions like Glyphs Inc. and C.K. Bliss. According to them the purpose of symbols was to facilitate human communication in general, bringing together people from different cultures and nations. In that case symbols would act as an international language. Their support could help Icograda in building a stronger lobby for symbols. This was also the reason why Icograda had stated in a CISS statement that it wanted to collect and study all kinds of symbols, ranging from those for electronics till those for astronomy.[44]

Glyphs Inc. was co-chaired by the symbol consultant Rudolf Modley (1906-1976) and the anthropologist Margaret Mead (1901-1978).[45] Modley originally came from Vienna where he had assisted Otto Neurath. This Austrian mathematician and philosopher became famous with the pictorial symbol system that he, his wife Marie Neurath (maiden name Reidemeister), and the graphic artist Gerd Arntz designed for visualising statistics, later to be called the International System of Typographic Picture Education (Isotype). In 1930 Modley went to the United States. Here he founded Pictorial Statistics Inc. in 1934. The company developed and propagated a lose approach to Isotype using a mix of pictorial symbols and illustrative information diagrams.[46]

Margaret Mead was one of the most prominent figures in cultural anthropology. In an article she wrote in 1965, called *The Future as the Basis for Establishing a Shared Culture*, Mead found that the world was increasingly becoming "disjuncted" while at the same time it was at risk of developing a monoculture. To prevent this a "shared culture" was needed, in which all cultures, "primitive" and "developed" could interact on the same level and learn from each other. The key to this was good communication. "World languages" such as English or French were not fit for this. They gave mother tongue speakers an advantage and were culturally biased. "Glyphs" however, could be used as an unbiased intermediary.[47] "Glyphs" were "graphic representations, each of which stand for an idea: male, female, water, poison (...) What is needed, internationally, is a set of glyphs which does not refer to any single phonological

---

[44] Peter Kneebone, 'Commission on International Signs and Symbols' [Exposé], October 1965 in: DAIC-64.

[45] Memorandum Modley to designers, 'Guidelines on designing universally usable graphic symbols', 23 June 1965 in: DAIC-64.

[46] Hisayasu Ihara, 'Rudolf Modley's Contribution to the Standardization of Graphic Symbols', Proceedings of IASDR2011, the 4th World Conference on Design Research, 31 October - 4 November 2011, Delft; Nader Vossoughian, *Otto Neurath: The Language of the Global Polis*, NAi Publishers, Rotterdam 2008; Marie Neurath & Robin Kinross, *The Transformer: Principles of Making Isotype Charts*, Hyphen Press 2009.

[47] Margaret Mead, 'The Future as the Basis for Establishing a Shared Culture', *Daedalus* [*Science and Culture*] (1), Vol. 94, Winter 1965, pp. 135-155. See also: Peter Mandler, 'One World, Many Cultures: Margaret Mead and the Limits to Cold War Anthropology', *History Workshop Journal* (68), 2009, pp. 149-172.

system or to any specific cultural system of images but will, instead form a system of visual signs with universally recognized referents."[48]

The development of this was to be a collaborative project in the widest sense of the word. Indeed it was Mead who had suggested in 1964 to the United Nations to take on the resolution about the development of glyphs that the ICBLB had acted upon. Glyphs Inc. had sent out a letter inviting proposals for a system of "glyphs." "Combination of two or possible more glyphs should be possible" (Figure 4).[49] The proposals were to be shown at a "World Communication Exhibit" Glyphs Inc. wanted to organise. The exhibit–which was Glyphs Inc. main focus for some years–would also incorporate prehistoric symbols, the history of alphabets and numerals, experiments of children with glyphs, visual symbols in the sciences and professions, and a "chamber of horrors" with abused symbols.[50] Since the use of symbols was beneficial to international business it hoped that companies would finance the exhibition.

Glyphs Inc. replaced the ICBLB in 1966 as Icograda's main American partner: Kato had not kept Icograda updated about his activities and had difficulty explaining how the ICBLB was run. As a result Icograda regarded him increasingly as an "amateur."[51] Modley on the other hand was a reasonable person to deal with, an experienced networker like De Majo and Kneebone. This also increased the possibility for Icograda to obtain American funding. Modley

---

[48] Margaret Mead, 'The Future as the Basis for Establishing a Shared Culture', *Daedalus* [*Science and Culture*] (1), Vol. 94, Winter 1965, pp. 135-155 (146-147).

[49] Glyphs Inc., 'Specifications for Participants in the Glyphs for World Communications Exhibit', 1966 in: DAIC-64. Glyph designs to be submitted included 5 of the following; Man, Woman, Toilet, Information, Do not drink, Do not enter, Mail, Smoking permitted, Smoking prohibited, Nursery, Drinking water, In-out (Entrance-exit), Danger-radioactivity, Poison-do not take internally, Do not cross tracks, Hot-cold, Fire alarm, Fasten seat belts, Medical aid (First aid), Do not feed the animals.

[50] 'What's New in Glyphs', *Glyphs* (1), October 1966.

[51] Kato became a liability for Icograda after it had guided the ICBLB –with the aim of gaining more influence– in 1966 in becoming a fellow consultative member in the ICTSS. Around the same time Rand and Katzumie–jury members for 'Student project nr. 1'–wrote to Icograda that Kato had approached them to act as jury members to a symbol competition the ICBLB was organising. Kato had not informed Icograda about any this. Still surprised by this turn of events Icograda was informed that Glyphs Inc.–an organisation they had not yet heard of–had taken over all responsibilities regarding this ICBLB-competition. Following this Icograda refrained from further professional contacts with the ICBLB and succeeded in having it removed from the ICTSS. Kato had complained about problems within the ICBLB in vague terms to De Majo for some time. He felt hindered by a 'power full figure' in the New York art world. He might be talking about Mildred Constantine, curator of the New York Museum of Modern Art. She became a board member of Glyphs Inc. and had an interest in symbols. See: Letter Kneebone to Kato, 11 January 1966; Letter Herman Limberg to all, 14 January 1966; Letter Michael Lax to De Majo, 21 February 1966; Letter De Majo to Kato, 21 March 1966. All in: DAIC-64.

became the CISS representative in the United States and was asked for the jury of "Student project nr. 1."[52] Unfortunately the exhibition that Glyphs Inc. wanted to organize was never realized due to a lack of funding.

Interestingly a glyphs like system already existed in the form of "Blissymbolics," designed by Charles K. Bliss (1897-1985). He was a chemical engineer by training, and was just like De Majo and Neurath born in the Austro-Hungarian Empire. After the Nazi's overtook Austria Bliss and his wife fled to family in Shanghai, only to be interned when the city was over run by the Japanese in 1942. During this time Bliss learnt to read Chinese characters. He noticed that although hundreds of languages were spoken in China, these symbols could be read by anyone. Inspired by this he developed his own system of pictorial writing.[53] The basic version of this so called "semantography" knew about a hundred highly abstracted pictorial symbols. By combining these symbols a great number of new "words" and "sentences" could be formed, which made it seem very much like the glyphs, Glyphs Inc. was looking for (Figure 5).[54]

After Bliss and his wife emigrated to Australia in 1946, he described this system in the three volume set of *International Semantography: A Non-Alphabetical Symbol Writing Readable in All Languages* published in 1949.[55] Strengthened by the growing interest in symbols worldwide Bliss published in 1965 a 2nd edition of his work, called *Semantography (Blissymbolics) : A Logical Writing for an Illogical World.*[56] In 1966 he approached Icograda in the hope that they would finance a visit to the Icograda congress in Bled. There he hoped to receive the recognition he wanted.[57] Icograda acknowledged Bliss considerable work but had trouble digesting his book. It totalled almost a thousand pages and carried religious undertones. Also Bliss bitter personality was hard to handle, even for the diplomatic Kneebone and De Majo.[58] Nevertheless at the time "Blisssymbolics" was the most evolved synthetic 'symbol language' available. So what did Glyphs Inc. think of Bliss work?

---

[52] This last duty was later delegated to Krampen who not only worked with Icograda but also served on the 'scientific committee' of Glyphs Inc.

[53] For more information on C.K. Bliss see; http://www.blissymbolics.us/biography/.

[54] Letter Bliss to De Majo, 15 February 1966 in: DAIC-64.

[55] C.K. Bliss, *International Semantography: A Non-Alphabetical Symbol Writing Readable in All Languages,* Sydney 1949.

[56] C.K. Bliss, *Semantography (Blissymbolics) : A Logical Writing for an Illogical World* [2nd enlarged ed.], Sydney 1965.

[57] Letter Bliss to De Majo, 27 January 1966 in: DAIC-64.

[58] Letter De Majo to Bliss, 7 March 1966 in: DAIC-64.

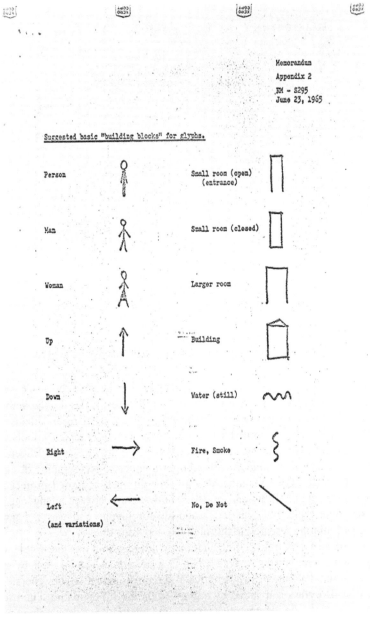

Figure 4. Glyphs' 'building blocks'-suggestions drawn by Modley, 1965.

Figure 5. Blissymbolics in a spread from Bliss' Semantography, 1965.

In 1966 Modley wrote in a letter to Kneebone that he saw the basic symbol elements of Bliss as a step in the right direction. However, despite the ambitions of Mead, Modley thought "a graphic language" was "a snare and delusion."[59] What he wanted was a "a limited set of logically coherent graphic symbols which permit a gradual expansion when new needs become urgent; ten or fifteen basic designs which can be combined with a larger number of pictographic designs as needed." It is difficult to imagine how he thought such a limited project could take shape. Despite his comments on Bliss, he wavered between a language and a set. Also Glyphs Inc. only invited proposals for glyphs and was not actively pursuing or initiating research in this area like Icograda did.[60]

Icograda's hopes for getting international symbols in the international limelight were temporarily revived when it was approached in 1968 by Henry Dreyfuss (1904-1972), one of America's foremost industrial designers.[61] Ten years earlier Dreyfuss had–aided by a grant of the Ford Foundation Fund for the Advancement of the Humanities–made an attempt at developing an all encompassing symbol dictionary. As a first step a "Study through Communication through Symbols," was carried out, involving Modley and

---

[59] Letter Modley to Krampen, 2 April 1966 in: DAIC-64.

[60] Letter from Modley to Kneebone, 11 March 1966; Letter Modley to Krampen, 2 April 1966. Both in: DAIC-64.

[61] Letter Dreyfuss to Pieter Brattinga, 21 October 1968 in DAIC-64.

Krampen in an executive role. The project had halted in 1959 with proposals for the classification of symbols by Krampen.[62] With his upcoming retirement Dreyfuss wanted to make a new attempt at developing such symbol dictionary.

Dreyfuss interest in symbols originated in the nineteen forties when his design agency started designing symbols for the operation of machinery. According to him "Symbols" could "be used on small controls where limited space would prohibit lengthy written captions."[63] Besides safety and efficiency advantages he also saw "Economic advantage (…) gained when symbols are used to obviate the necessity of translating legends and directions in other languages for the international market." Modley–while working on Dreyfuss symbol dictionary in 1959–shared a similar opinion "(…) American, British, French, German and other machine tools are exported to strange countries, all over the world. Machine operators find language barriers a handicap in the use of these machines."[64] Of course this was of particular interest to the United States since it exported large amounts of cars, airplanes and other highly evolved machinery and electronics.

Dreyfus new project drew a lot of support in America including that of the United States of America Standards Institute (USASI). He had good hopes of attracting large funds, possibly to be shared in exchange for cooperation with Glyphs Inc. and Icograda. Even the United Nations Educational, Scientific and Cultural Organisation (UNESCO) expressed an interest and thought about supporting a symbol conference. Despite pressure from Icograda, that wanted to use this opportunity to finally realise their own symbol conference, Dreyfuss deemed he was not ready for this. The moment passed and so did his sponsors. Dreyfuss project eventually materialised in his famous *Symbol Sourcebook* in 1972.[65] His suicide in the same year made further cooperation impossible.

---

[62] The first time Modley was approached for this project was in 1956. Interestingly he had also approached Neuraths widow, Marie Reidemeister to work on this. See: Letter Modley to Marie Neurath, 13 June 1956; Letter Modley to Marie Neurath, 13 May 1958; Letter Marie Neurath to Modley, 15 May 1958. All in; Otto & Marie Neurath Isotype Collection: University of Reading; Martin Krampen, 'Signs and Symbols in Graphic Communication', *Design Quarterly* (62), 1965, pp. 1-31 (22-23, 30); Rudolf Modley, 'The Challenge of Symbology', in: Elwood Whitney (ed.), *Symbology : The use of Symbols in Visual Communications* [A Report on the Fourth Communications Conference of the Art Directors Club of New York], New York 1959, pp. 17-31 (27).

[63] Memorandum Dreyfuss to Donald Peyton, 'Symbols–An Instant language', 26 July 1968 in: DAIC-64.

[64] Rudolf Modley, 'The Challenge of Symbology', in: Elwood Whitney (ed.), *Symbology : The use of Symbols in Visual Communications* [A Report on the Fourth Communications Conference of the Art Directors Club of New York], New York 1959, pp. 17-31 (24).

[65] Henry Dreyfuss, *Symbol Sourcebook: An Authoritative Guide to International Graphic Symbols,* McGraw-Hill, New York 1972.

The United Nations and the Example of International Road Signs

Already in 1964 Icograda had asked the United Nations (UN) for financial aid and assistance in regulating the development of symbols. After all they urged "cooperation in expanding the use of symbols" in connection with their upcoming "International Cooperation Year 1965."[66] However, the UN did not want to give support. Still De Majo and Kneebone were of the opinion that ideally it was the UN that should provide an institutional framework for the development of international traveller symbols.[67] The UN and her fore runner–the League of Nations–had been instrumental in setting world wide standards for the most successful standardised symbol system yet: that of the international road signs.[68] At the time there was a large interest in these signs because of the quickly rising use of cars in the Western world.

In Great Britain and Japan this interest reached a peak in 1963, with the decision to introduce a more internationally valid version of these signs. Around the same time the designer Anthony Froshaug wrote an extensive analysis of British road signs for *Design,* copies of which Icograda would regularly send to its contacts.[69] Froshaug may have gotten his inspiration from Krampen and Aicher. In 1961 they each wrote an article about traffic signs for the Italian design magazine *Stile Industria.*[70] Knowing all this it can hardly be a surprise that one of the two other themes De Majo's suggested for the first Icograda student project was the design of new "Traffic Signs." International road signs also were an important frame of reference for rise of public information symbols.

In his press release for "Student project nr. 1" Kneebone wrote for example: "The problem posed is that of designing a single, coherent vocabulary of symbols

---

[66] United Nations: General Assembly: Committee for the International Co-operation Year, 'Facilitating Communication' [A/AC.118/L.5], 19 March 1964 in: Library of Congress: Margaret Mead Papers: Mead K64-1.

[67] Letter De Majo to Kato, 1 April 1965 in: DAIC-64. Icograda had been striving for recognition by the UNESCO since its establishment. Recognition would confirm its right to act on behalf of the graphic design profession and would elevate their status in dealing with other organisations. Although Icograda did develop good working relations with UNESCO it was only in 1971 that they were recognised as a class C and later, a class B member.

[68] Frank Schipper, 'Unravelling hieroglyphs : Urban traffic Signs and the League of Nations', *Metropoles* (6), 2009, pp. 65-100.

[69] Anthony Froshaug, 'Roadside traffic signs', *Design* (178), October 1963, pp. 37-50. Kneebone would regularly sent this article to organisations interested in signs and symbols.

[70] Froshaug taught at HfG Ulm until 1961. Aicher also worked there. M. Krampen, 'Appunti per una semantica visiva: Storia dei signali stradali', *Stile industria* (32), 1961, pp. 23-24; Otl Aicher, 'Per une revisione degli attuali segnali stradali', *Stile industria* (33), 1961.

to cover the information outside the scope of the international road signs."[71] According to Katzumie "the first great success in this direction [visual language] was the international directive for traffic signs."[72] *The New York Times* wrote that UIC symbol system was "patterned on the highway signs system that is already common in Europe and in many other parts of the world."[73] The fascination with road signs might be best conveyed by the designer Josef Müller-Brockmann who wrote in 1966; "stand still, drive on, walk on, get off, get on, drive right, don't turn, don't park, stop etc. The information given in most of these signs is optimal, the form suitable to the content, the shapes typical and easily remembered, and very often recognizable from a distance."[74]

There were limited attempts to make use of visual characteristics of road signs for pictograms. In 1965 for example Modley proposed that the meanings attached to (American) road signs shapes–triangular (danger), diamond shaped (warning) and rectangular (obligatory)–could also be used for public information signs.[75] Indeed in 1967 the Air Transport Association of America (ATA) would introduce pictograms at major airports in America that used this idea (Figure 6).[76] In the same year the International Committee for Travel Signs and Symbols (ICTSS) advised the International Civil Aviation Organization (ICAO) to bring its proposed airport pictograms in concordance with the road signs around airports. This way foreign travellers would not be confused.[77] The limited interest in using road sign shapes soon gave way to a more practical focus on the image contents of pictogram systems being introduced. Studies into the new road signs in Great Britain did show an important thing though: even years after their introduction their meaning was hard to decipher by the public.[78] This did not plead for the development of pictogram systems with totally new image contents, nor shapes.

---

[71] Icograda, 'Icograda Student Project 1 : An International Symbol Language' [Press Release], April/May 1965: DAIC-64.

[72] Masaru Katzumie, 'Towards an International Sign language', [lecture Icograda Congress Bled], 1966: DAIC-64.

[73] 'Signs of the times', *The New York Times,* April 4 1965.

[74] Müller-Brockmann, 'International Signs', 11-16th July 1966: DAIC Bled 1965-1966

[75] Memorandum Modley to designers, 'Guidelines on designing universally usable graphic symbols', 23 June 1965 in: DAIC-64.

[76] According to Dreyfuss these 'ATA'-signs could even be found at the Moscow airport. In: Henry Dreyfuss, 'Speaking in a Thousand Tongues : Breaking the language barrier with symbols', *Confessional Board Record,* March 1969, pp. 16-20 (17) in: DAIC-64.

[77] International Committee for Travel Signs and Symbols. 'Reply to the International Civil Aviation Organization (ICAO)' [398/32], 14 April 1967 in: DAIC-64.

[78] Peter Kneebone, *International Signs and Symbols: an approach to the problem,* Lecture 10th ATypI congress, 10 November 1967. In: DAIC 68. See also: Road Research Laboratory: Ministry of Transport (A.M. Mackie), *A national survey of knowledge of the new traffic signs* (RRL Report 51), Crowthorne 1966.

Figure 6. ATA pictograms with traffic sign shapes in an Icograda *Sign Information Sheet*, 1967.

The Development of International Pictogram Standards: DOT and ISO

It was only in the middle of the nineteen seventies that the first symbol standards for public information symbols for general use saw the light of day. The first standard was that of the United States Department of Public Transportation (DOT). In 1974 the DOT commissioned the American Institute of Graphic Arts (AIGA) to design public information symbols. AIGA established a committee of five graphic designers: Thomas H. Geismar, Seymour Chwast, Rudolph de Harak, John Lees and Massimo Vignelli. They determined which symbols from 24 existing symbol systems matched the desired referents best, by judging them on three dimensions; the semantic, syntactic and pragmatic value. In other words; do people know what a symbol means, does it have a good "form grammar." and is it easy to reproduce and see. For each dimension a maximum of five points could be awarded.79

"All of these ratings are of course subjective," the designers wrote, "However, they are based on many years of personal and professional experience

---

79 AIGA (for the Department of Transportation), *Symbol Signs* [DOT-OS-40192], National Technical Information Service, Springfield, November 1974. For more reviews of the development process see: Edward K. Carpenter, 'Travelers' Aid: More DOT Symbol Signs', *Print,* September-October 1979, pp. 78-81.

by five individuals with varied interests and backgrounds."[80] After a review of their recommendations by the DOT and AIGA, they selected the design agency Cook and Shanosky Associates to redraw the symbols deemed best. This resulted in a visually coherent set of 34 symbols that was introduced in 1974, a remarkable short timeframe for such a project. In 1979 another 16 symbols were added to this so-called DOT set.[81] It covers a lot of generally used symbols for public information and is copyright free. This not only means that it can be found in the public domain, adding to its visibility, but also that it can be used freely.[82]

Much to the surprise of Icograda around this time also the International Standardization Organisation (ISO) had become involved. Already in 1965 Icograda had asked ISO for help, but had received no for an answer. ISO could only negotiate standards once a considerable percentage of its national members had voted to do so. For a long time this was not the case, despite the fact that the national standardization organisations in the United Kingdom, France and the United States showed an interest in public information symbols.[83] It was only in 1971 that ISO established a Technical Committee (TC) 145 for "Graphical Symbols." Its main task was to function as a clearinghouse for signs and symbols developed by other TC's. Also it was to develop symbols for areas where hitherto no standards existed such as public information symbols.

During the first years of its existence TC 145 carried out preparatory work such as developing ISO standards for classifying and drawing symbols.[84] In 1975–its 'official' start date–TC 145 existed of three subcommittees (SC) dedicated to "Public information symbols" (SC 1), "Safety identification, signs, shapes, symbols and colours" (SC 2) and "Graphical symbols for use on

---

[80] AIGA (for the Department of Transportation), *Symbol Signs* [DOT-OS-40192], National Technical Information Service, Springfield, November 1974, p. 6.

[81] AIGA (for the Department of Transportation), *Symbol Signs 2* [DOT-OS-60510], Technical Information Service, Springfield, March 1979. Compilations of DOT-OS-40192 and DOT-OS-60510 titled *Symbol Signs* [etc.] were published in 1981 and 1993.

[82] http://www.aiga.org/archivedmedia/symbol-signs/symbol_signs.zip

[83] ISO-representatives were invited at the first UIC conference. They made it clear that they saw the normalisation of pictograms as their area. This seemed to incline the UIC to make their pictograms obligatory, 'to prevent that ISO will start all over again'. In: Letter Dutch Railways Economic Affairs Department to CRV, 'Pictogrammen', 29 December 1965 in: UA 943-98. At the second UIC conference it was suggested that ISO should serve as a convening and administrative body. According to ISO-representatives this was not the function of ISO. See: 'Draft report of UIC Conference on Pictograms', 20 January 1966 in: DAIC-64.

[84] ISO TC 145 (UK-3) (R.S. Easterby), 'Co-ordination of symbol design and usage', May 1973 in: Paul Mijksenaar Foundation: ISO correspondence (PMF); ISO 3461:1976, *Graphic symbols–General principles for presentation*. The successors to this standard focused on equipment symbols. See: ISO 3461-1:1988 and ISO 80416-1:2001.

equipment" (SC 3).[85] SC 1 decided in 1976 that–due to technical and cultural differences between countries–the image contents of public information symbols should only be laid down textually, although eventually also visual examples were given. This resulted in the first ISO-standard for "Public information symbols," introduced in 1980: ISO 7001 (Figure 7). This standard has been revised and expanded twice, most recently in 2007. It currently covers the image contents for 79 symbols. [86] Contrary to the DOT standard ISO 7001 is a copyrighted standard. Like all ISO standards organisations have to buy ISO 7001 to use it. This carries not favourably on the design world's familiarity with it.

The research procedure for establishing ISO 7001 was developed from 1975 onwards by Ronald Easterby and Harm Zwaga of SC 1's Working Group for psychologists (WG 1). [87] An important step in this procedure was the "appropriateness ranking test" in which respondents were asked to rank all symbols that had been collected internationally about a given referent. These symbols had to be ranked according to their perceived recognition. This pre-selection saved considerable time and money; further testing showed that the symbols ranked highest also were the symbols best recognised in the "recognition" or "comprehension test." In this test respondents were presented with a symbol and a description of the environment where it could be found (Figure 8).

---

[85] See reports on ISO/TC 145 by the German Standards Institution over the years 1972-1974 in: PMF.

[86] ISO 7001:1980, *Public Information Symbols*; ISO 7001:1990, *Public Information Symbols*; ISO 7001:2007, *Public Information Symbols*. In 2007 also ISO 22727:2007, *Graphical symbols – Creation and design of public information symbols – Requirements* was published, to assist ISO technical committees and others in proposing new symbols.

[87] Harm Zwaga, Ron S. Easterby, 'Developing effective symbols for public information' in; Ron S. Easterby and Harm Zwaga (Ed.), *Information design: The Design and Evaluation of Signs and Printed Material*, J. Wiley & Sons, New York 1984, pp. 277-297.

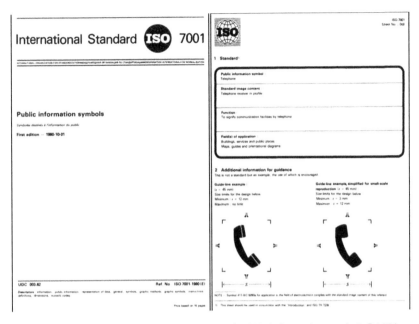

Figure 7. Cover and page of ISO 7001: 1980 "Public information symbols," 1980.

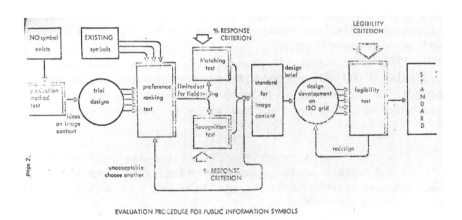

Figure 8. Pictogram evaluation as proposed by Easterby and Zwaga to ISO TC 145/WG 3, 1975.

Based on the outcome of these tests a textual description was made for the symbol that could be included in the ISO 7001 norm. To rule out intercultural differences the procedure and the descriptions of the image contents were tested in many countries spanning several continents. If the meaning of a symbol was comprehended by at least 67 per cent of the respondents it was deemed fit for introduction. Although this all sounds laborious, the ISO procedure actually limited the amount of respondents necessary to come to a statistically sound outcome. It was laid down in the ISO 9186 standard introduced in 1989. Since then this standard has been updated several times, keeping up with new scientific insights.[88] By using this standard one can develop pictograms successfully, by testing their probable effectiveness.

Peter Kneebone was involved in TC 145 almost from the beginning. It is likely he had heard about the ISO-initiative by way of Icograda's "Unification of Typographic Measurements Commission"–led by Ernst Hoch–that had been in close liason with ISO for some time. When in 1975 TC 145 SC 1 finally came up to steam also a Working Group 2 (WG 2) for graphic designers was established. SC 1 was quick to recognise the important role of Icograda. In a memorandum it sent to Icograda's Edugraphic Conference in 1975 it wrote: "Icograda (...) has participated through experts from the very beginning of the endeavors of SC1. Close collaboration with Icograda is essential also in further stages of this pilot work of standardizing graphic symbols!"[89] SC 1 specifically asked for the cooperation of designers in critically following its activities, designing test symbols and motivating national ISO-members in participating in its work.[90]

Around this time Kneebone's role as the main instigator of Icograda's involvement in symbol standardization, was taken over by the graphic designer Jorge Frascara. Disappointed in the quality of symbols used for the tests leading up to the ISO 7001: 1980 standard, he set up the Icograda student project "Graphic Symbols for Public Information: Design of Test Symbols." The project was approved at the Icograda congress in Lausanne in 1977 and can be seen as a successor to Icograda's "Student project nr. 1." Remarkably one of the few persons who objected was De Majo because he thought students would not deliver symbols of sufficient quality. The new student project produced over 1200 symbols. A considerable amount of symbol descriptions that ended up in ISO 7001: 1980, originated in this project.[91] All in all the development and introduction of ISO 7001 and ISO 9186 should be considered as a triumph for Icograda. The big question is whether the development of a symbol standard came in time for a design world, that they–one way or another–represented.

---

[88] In 1984 SC 1 decided to develop a procedure for the preparation and standardization of public information symbols. See: ISO/PLACO 720, 'Agenda item 18–Coordination of standardization of public information symbols', July 1985 in: PMF; ISO 9186:1989, *Procedures for the development and testing of public information symbols*; ISO 9186:2001, *Graphical symbols–Test methods for judged comprehensibility and for comprehension*; ISO 9186-1:2007, *Graphical symbols–Test methods–Part 1: Methods for testing comprehensibility*; ISO 9186-2:2008, *Graphical symbols–Test methods–Part 2: Method for testing perceptual quality*. An earlier document giving recommendations was ISO/ TR 7239: 1984, *Development and principles for application of public information symbols*–edited by Frascara–which was partly integrated in ISO 9186:1989.

[89] ISO (Manfred Machek), 'ISO/TC 145/SC 1 Graphic Symbols for public information' [Special document for ICOGRADA Edugraphic conference 1975], June 1975 in: PMF.

[90] Nederlands Normalisatie-Instituut, Minutes of the informative meeting 'Graphic Symbols' at 2 September 1975, 15 October 1975 in: PMF.

[91] E-mail Jorge Frascara to Bakker ,10 September 2011.

Graphic Designers and Olympic Games and Fairs

The development of ISO standards for public information symbols took almost a decade. During this time the 'symbol explosion' that Kneebone and De Majo had feared in 1965 fully blossomed. Besides the UIC, ICAO, IATA and ATA, also business started introducing them as part of their visual identity, just as institutions like hospitals or local and even national governments. The best known and most widely admired symbol systems were those designed by graphic designers for games and fairs. After the ground-breaking symbol set for the Tokyo Olympics in 1964, similar sets were designed for the world exhibitions in Montreal (1967) and Osaka (1970), and other Olympic Games such as Mexico City (1968), Munich (1972) and Montreal (1976). Especially the sport symbols for the Olympics were admired.

When discussing Olympic designs, magazines like *Graphis, Print* and *Design* showed them before public information pictograms. Also they were likely to be depicted larger and in colour.[92] Designers were impressed too. In 1970 for example, Crosby, Fletcher and Forbes (Pentagram) wrote the first practical signage handbook: *A Sign Systems Manual*. They depicted only two public information pictograms, but used a three-page spread to show 60 sport symbols.[93] Even today there is a preference for showing sports symbols over information symbols. In recent books like *Graphic Design a New History* by the art historian Stephen Eskilson and *Typography* and *Graphic Design: A History from Antiquity to Present* by design historian Roxane Jubert, the only pictograms shown are the sport symbols for the 1972 Olympic Games.[94] They were designed by the German

---

[92] Masaru Katzumie, 'Design Policy of the Olympics Tokyo', *Graphic Design* (17), 1964, pp. 13-40, 82-83; Stanley Mason, 'Towards an International Symbology', *Graphis* (116), 1964, pp. 514-517; Jake Brown, 'All set for Mexico 68', *Design* (237), September 1968, pp. 26-33; Heiner Jacob, Masaru Katzumie, 'Sign Systems for International Events: Munich, Sapporo, Osaka & Co.', *Print*, November-December 1969, pp. 40-49; Alastair Best, 'Munich Olympics', *Design* (285), September 1972, pp. (29-59) 46; Brigitte Beil, 'The Graphic Image of the XX Olympic Games', *Graphis* (160), September-October 1972, pp. 148-161; Fritz Gottschalk, 'The Image of Montreal's 1976 Olympic Games 76', *Graphis* (185), November-December 1976, pp. 268-279. Only when the symbols of the previous Olympics where reused-as was the case with the Montreal Olympics (1976)– more attention was given to the public information symbols. See; Ellen-Jane Opat, 'Here it is, folks! What the world has been yearning for! Another Olympic signing system!', *Print*, May-June 1976, pp. 31-35. Often sports symbols were designed years before the actual start of the Games. This way they could be used for marketing efforts. Public information pictograms followed later.

[93] Crosby, Fletcher, Forbes, *A Sign Systems Manual*, Studio Vista Ltd., London 1970, pp. 42-43, (74-75).

[94] Stephen J. Eskilson, *Graphic Design: A New History*, New Haven 2007, pp. 298-299, 321; Roxane Jubert, *Typography and Graphic Design: From Antiquity to the Present* [o.e. *Graphisme, Typographie, Histoire*, Paris 2005], Paris 2006, p. 361.

designer Otl Aicher and his team and have become the embodiment of the rise of pictograms.[95]

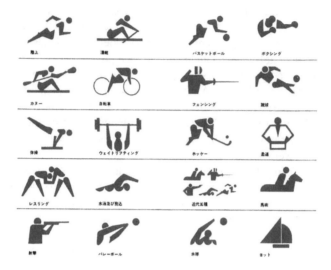

Figure 9. Tokyo Olympic 1964 "Design Guide Sheet" with sports pictograms, 1964.

One of the reasons why designers were so fascinated by sports symbols might be the use of human figures that gave them an instant visual coherence (Figure 9). Almost each new Olympic Game gave opportunity for a new stylistic treatment of these symbols, making it attractive to show comparisons between them, as is often done. The varied contents of the much larger group of public information symbols for these events were harder to bring visually in line. On the one hand image contents were derived from existing sets such as the UIC or Tokyo Olympics set. On the other hand new symbols were designed according to the specific needs of the event.

---

[95] Kerry William Purcell, 'Olympic Pictograms', *Grafik* (178), 2011 in: (http://kerrywilliampurcell.tumblr.com/post/2500521898/olympic-pictograms-published-in-grafik-178-2009).

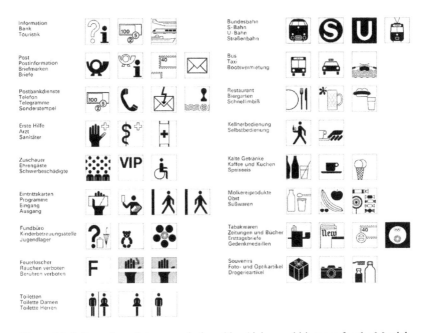

Figure 10. Information pictograms designed by Aicher and his team for the Munich
Olympics, 1972.

Aicher's information symbol set for the Munich Olympics is a case in point.
Besides the usual symbols for toilet or entrance, it also contained no more then
eight symbols showing postal paraphernalia [Figure 10]. Since symbols for fairs
and Olympic Games were not tested it is not known until what extend symbols
like these and others were understood by the public.[96] In fact the decisions that
designers took regarding the image contents of symbols seemed no different from
those of the members of the ICTSS heavily criticised by Icograda. Knowing this
it is remarkable that Icograda did not take into account the possible impact of
these temporary pictogram systems on the graphic design world. The only person
who pointed this out to Icograda was Katzumie.

The Japanese Masaru Katzumie (1909-1986) was the editor-in-chief of the
Japanese magazine *Graphic Design* and affiliated with almost every design

---

[96] Rob Dewar, 'Design and evaluation of public information symbols' in; Harm Zwaga,
Theo Boersema, Henriette Hoonhout ,*Visual information for everyday use: design and
research perspectives,* Taylor & Francis, London 1999, pp. 285-303 (296-297). Email
Martin Krampen to Bakker, 24 July 2012; 'There was no research on Paul Arthurs
pictographs for EXPO 67'; Email Lance Wyman to Bakker, 13 July 2012; 'We didn't
formally test the sports, cultural and service symbol systems'; Email Ian McLaren to
Bakker, 15 July 2012: 'it is VERY unlikely that any testing was undertaken.' Also
Icograda would have been very keen on receiving any testing results in the area of
Olympic and fair symbols. It didn't.

organisation in Japan.[97] As a design coordinator to the Tokyo Olympics it was his idea to develop also information symbols. Katzumie hoped that the Olympic symbols would be gradually "perfected as a common cultural property on an international scope." In 1965 he wrote to Kneebone that international events could be used to promote "the international sign language," and mentioned that he could influence the "Osaka World's Fair in adopting the systematic use of international signs and symbols."[98] Icograda failed to follow up on this and would maintain only superficial contacts with designers developing symbols for large international events.[99] Moreover, in its internal correspondence as well as in its publicity, symbol designs from designers were hardly mentioned, let alone evaluated. One may wonder as to whether Icograda was afraid to alienate itself from the graphic design world by criticising it.

Katzumie's idea of using events to develop a symbol standard caught on in the design world in the nineteen seventies. In *Graphis* it was written that the Osaka World Fair symbols were "approaching very near to a finalized vocabulary." The idea of this evolutionary development was also carried forward by Aicher; "Aicher has said that the Tokyo Olympics created the vocabulary of picture language and that the Munich Olympics will create the grammar."[100] In 1976 the designers for the Montreal Olympics said that they took "credit for having retained the best of earlier systems, thus contributing to the establishment of a unified design standard."[101] They had used the sports pictograms of the Munich Olympics but did make some changes to the information pictograms for the event, that totaled the amazing amount of 173 symbols.

The continuing introduction of new and ever larger pictogram systems by designers made their claims of contributing to an effective "unified design standard" sound increasingly preposterous. As a critic wrote in 1976 about the

---

[97] See: Letter Katzumie to Kneebone 'Bird's Eye View of Japanese Design World', 26 April 1966 in: DAIC: De Majo correspondence (DM).

[98] Letter Katzumie to Kneebone, 29 November 1965. Katzumie's idea of using temporary events to develop better symbols in evolutionary way did not interfere with his support for Icograda. In a lecture Katzumie held in 1965 he accepted that in practice maybe two or three symbol sets would be around. He foresaw–rather optimistically as he confessed later–that around 1980 the UN would organise a conference to sort out the systems. See: Masaru Katzumie, 'On problems of International Symbology' [Lecture 'Vision '65' conference], 21 October 1965. Katsumie gave a slightly adjusted version of this lecture at the Icograda Congress in Bled in July 1966. All in: DAIC-64.

[99] Kneebone, 'Icograda Commission on International Signs & Symbols: Progress Report February 1967', 27 February 1967 in DAIC-64.

[100] Masaru Katzumie, 'Aspects of the Official Graphic Design Programme of Expo '70', *Graphis* (150), January-February 1971, pp. 364-372 (369). See also; Brigitte Beil, 'The Graphic Image of the XX Olympic Games', *Graphis* (160), September-October 1972, pp. 148-161.

[101] Fritz Gottschalk, 'The Image of Montreal's 1976 Olympic Games 76', *Graphis* (185), November-December 1976, pp. 268-279 (268).

Montreal Olympic symbols; "Here it is folks! What the world has been yearning for! Another Olympic signing system!"[102] Or as an ergonomist wrote in 1979 in *Design*: 'Take Moscow's Olympic Games graphics: they have become an art form first and foremost–if they work as information displays that's a bonus (...) Graphic designers haven't done much to counter act this'. In a similar vein he lamented the slow pace of standard development at ISO, and its inability to make various other symbol standards accessible to designers.[103] It was in these years that Isotype was rediscovered, which was to have important consequences for the historiography of pictograms.

Isotype and Pictogram Historiography

After the nineteen fifties Isotype had drifted into oblivion. Now it became subject to several articles and exhibitions (Figure 11).[104] The first Isotype exhibition was organised in 1975 by the educator and designer Michael Twyman. In the accompanying catalogue he testified to Neuraths importance in to the area of visual statistics. Interestingly he also connected Isotype with pictograms:

> "the pioneer work done by Otto Neurath and his team in Vienna in the 1920s has for the most part been forgotten. (...) though the International Organization for Standardization has been concerned in recent years with rationalising symbols for international use, in general, the essential message of the Movement [Isotype ed.] that there should be standard ways of representing things has been ignored. (...) What can be more irresponsible in this context than the re-design every four years of a new set of symbols for the Olympic Games."[105]

---

[102] Ellen-Jane Opat, 'Here it is, folks! What the world has been yearning for! Another Olympic signing system!', *Print,* May-June 1976, pp. 31-35 (31).

[103] Barry Drake, 'Symbols: Less of an Art, More of a Science', *Design* (367), July 1979, pp. 58-63 (58).

[104] The retirement of early modernist pioneers often resulted in exhibitions dedicated to their work. In the nineteen seventies Marie Neurath and Gert Arntz retired. Marie Neuraths archive was shelved at the University of Reading. Arntz' archive was obtained by the The Hague Municipal Museum. See: Michael Twyman, 'Isotype and the University of Reading' in: Friedrich Stadler (ed.), *Arbeitbildung in der Zwischenkriegszeit: Otto Neurath–Gerd Arntz,* Österreichisches Gesellschafts– und Wirtschaftsmuseum/Löcker Verlag, Vienna/Munich 1982, pp. 185-188.

[105] Michael Twyman, 'The significance of Isotype' in: *Graphic Communication Through Isotype,* Reading 1975, pp. 6-17 (17). Twyman erroneously suggests that –except for ISO– the message of symbol standardization was specific to the 'Movement'. Icograda had been emphasizing the need for such a standard for almost a decade. Then there is the example of the international road signs to be considered.

Isotype provided designers with an example of a successful symbol system, in a time that their own efforts increasingly drew fire and an 'official' ISO standard was far away. Isotype was the only (relative) recent symbol system aimed at an international general public that had known a modest success as a 'standard,' notwithstanding road signs. However, contrary to road signs Isotype seemed to be the work of a designer. It was also 'good' in a moral sense. According to Twyman; "The Isotype Movement [was] an excellent example of innovation in graphic design resulting from an attempt to meet social needs."[106] In the nineteen eighties Isotype was included in general graphic design histories where it came to represent the early rise of a symbol system or information design. Since then historians have often suggested that Isotype influenced pictogram development in the nineteen sixties.

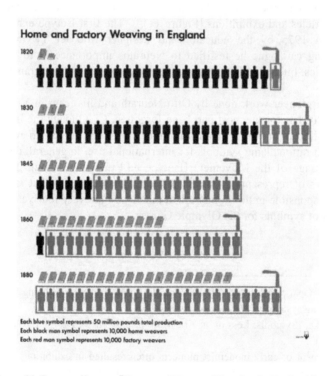

Figure 11. Isotype diagram "Home and Factory Weaving in England," 1939.

---

[106] Michael Twyman, 'The significance of Isotype', *Icographic* (10), 1976, pp. 2-10 (3). Kinross shared a similar view, highlighting the role of the 'transformer'–the person selecting the data and configuring the visual design–as central to Isotype, in 'visual' as well as in 'moral' terms. Its most fruitful influence he saw in 'recent attitudes' in the museum world. In: Robin Kinross, 'On the influence of Isotype', *Information Design Journal* (2), 1981, pp. 122-130 (128).

Eskilson for example writes in *Graphic Design : A New History*: "Aicher approached this project (Munich pictograms) with the 1920s work of Otto Neurath (1882-1945) as a precedent."[107] Interestingly his careful wording does not show whether Aicher even knew Isotype. Although it might be that Isotype influenced the development of pictograms during the nineteen sixties there is hardly evidence to substantiate this.[108] Still, when Isotype and pictograms for

---

[107] Stephen J. Eskilson, *Graphic Design: A New History*, New Haven 2007, p. 321.

[108] Isotype's influence on pictogram development seems an invention of the nineteen eighties. It was only in 1986 that Ellen Lupton stated in *Design Issues* that 'Isotype's legacy includes both the design of statistical charts and the more generalized production of visual symbol sets, from travel signage to corporate identity marks.' This (unsubstantiated) statement might lead people to believe that Isotype influenced the design of pictograms in earlier decades. In: Ellen Lupton, 'Reading Isotype', *Design Issues* (2), Autumn 1986, pp. 47-58 (47). It is likely to be true for the time when the article was written. In 1985 information graphics designer Nigel Holmes–a known Isotype enthusiast–prominently showed Isotype in the introductory chapter of his book about symbol development. In: Nigel Holmes, Rose DeNeve, *Design Pictorial Symbols*, Watson-Guptill Publications, New York 1985, pp. 9-10. Only a few years later Meggs wrote somewhat vaguely about Isotype in his *History of Graphic Design*: 'The impact of their work ['Isotype group'] on post-World War II graphic design includes research toward the development of universal visual-language systems and the extensive use of pictographs in signage and information systems'. In: Philip B. Meggs, Alston W. Purvis, *Meggs' History of Graphic Design* [4th ed] [o.e. Philip B. Meggs, *A History of Graphic Design*, New York 1989], John Wiley & Sons Inc., New Jersey 2006, p. 327. Eskilsons' statement shows that Isotype's possible influence is voiced increasingly more certain, without being substantiated. In a recent historical article for the *Journal of Design History* statistician Wim Jansen wrote 'In the field of design, Otl Aicher sketched the 1972 Munich Olympics Games pictograms, drawing from the Isotype example (…)'. In: Wim Jansen, 'Neurath, Arntz and ISOTYPE: The Legacy in Art, Design and Statistics', *Journal of Design History* (3), 2009, pp. 227-242. When asked for an elucidation Jansen wrote: 'I don't think Isotype was mentioned by Aicher, but the similarity with Isotype in grammar and simple rules has been mentioned explicitly by design researchers' in: email Wim Jansen to Bakker 30 July 2012. Despite knowing only a visual similarity is noted, Jansen assumes a cause and effect relationship. Typical for the lack of evidence for even a general interest in Isotype in the nineteen sixties is, that in the several thousands of pages of reports and letters sent and received by Icograda regarding signs and symbols in the period 1963-1972, it was mentioned only a few times and then only in passing. The most significant reference being the following in a lecture Katzumie held in 1965 at 'Vision 65': 'Pioneers of modern design have already made many experiments in the use of visual language. In the 1920's, Otto Neurath, Vienna, had developed a system of graphic symbols called Isotype [details about names and places] However, the first great success in this direction was the international directive for traffic signs.' The most tangible reference–being known only in Japan for a long time– is that to the design of the sport symbols for the Tokyo Olympics. Its designer–Yoshiro Yamashita–later recalled: 'I was asked to design the event pictograms, just then I was

world fairs and Olympic Games became the selected topic of symbol systems in graphic design histories, it was only logical–if only for storytelling continuity–to assume a relation between all of these symbols. This resulted in what can be called an "Isotype-Aicher-construct." It conveys the attractive impression that designers work in a tradition of aesthetically and morally good symbol design. This also means that pictogram systems that are not 'designed' are excluded.

It might explain why design historians tend to ignore road signs, or the pictogram systems that transport and tourism associations introduced in the nineteen sixties. Sadly by doing so, also possible mutual influences between these systems and those of the fairs and Olympic Games are not explored. In what is a fascinating paradox this makes it harder to substantiate the 'noted' influence of Isotype in the realm of pictogram systems. Even then it begs the question whether Isotype might have been–as implied by Twyman–a good example of standardization. Neurath did not have, nor called out for, an organizational structure to jointly develop standards with others. His 'standard' was a private one.[109]

Conclusion

The nineteen sixties were a formative period in the development of pictogram systems. Icoagrada caught on early with their "Student project nr. 1:" "Designing an International Symbol Language." Noticing the introduction of various pictogram systems of doubtful merit, Icograda became convinced that a standard for effective public information symbols was needed. To contribute to the development of such a standard De Majo and Kneebone sent carefully written opinions, plans, and articles about symbol developments, to parties involved with symbols, acting as intermediaries and lobbyists. It was British diplomacy at its finest and led to the establishment of the Commission on International Signs and Symbols (CISS) (1965) and the International Committee for Travel Signs and Symbols (ICTSS) (1966). Although these committees were not successful in fulfilling Icograda's main goal of developing a standard, they did lead to an

---

attracted to Otto Neurath's Isotype.' in: Yoshiro Yamashita, 'Sign : My way of thinking', *Designers' Workshop* (100), December 1998, p.40. Another interesting reference comes from Krampen. He suggested in 1965– after introducing international road signs–that since Isotype was already known it 'still seems to represent a basically sound starting-point' for the development of symbols'. He did not follow up on this. In: Martin Krampen, 'Signs and Symbols in Graphic Communication', *Design Quarterly* (62), 1965, pp. 1-31 (23). Krampen and Yamashita–the latter through Katzumie-could have influenced Aicher's work in the area of pictograms. Still this possible influence during the nineteen sixties seems to have been limited to that of the sport symbols, and not that of public information symbols.

[109] Hisayasu Ihara, 'Rudolf Modley's Contribution to the Standardization of Graphic Symbols', Proceedings of IASDR2011, the 4th World Conference on Design Research, 31 October - 4 November 2011, Delft. p. 2.

information exchange and cooperation between design, transport and travel organisations and ngo's in general, that without Icograda would not have existed. By doing so Icograda tried to prove its value as an association.

By drawing attention to the effectiveness of symbols it also represented the interests of the general public. Icograda concentrated its efforts on transport (infrastructure) organisations like the Union Internationale de Chemins de Fer (UIC), the International Civil Aviation Organisation (ICAO), WEAC, IATA etc. Contrary to the sets designed for events like the Olympics their symbol sets had a more permanent and public character. Sadly most of these organisations during the nineteen sixties had difficulty seeing possible problems with which was essentially painting or printing images on signs. It was probably the increase in symbol systems altogether–with the encouragement of organisations and individuals like Icograda, Glyphs Inc. and Dreyfuss–that had the DOT and ISO decide to get involved in symbol standardization in the beginning of the nineteen seventies. All in all the development of public information symbol standards came about rather quickly. Standard development for international road signs took considerably longer.

During the nineteen sixties there were two strains of symbol set development. The first strain is that of transport organisations, developed anonymously and not acknowledged in design history, starting with UIC set (1963). The second strain is that of 'designed' symbol sets for world fairs and Olympic Games, with as a starting point the Tokyo Olympics symbols (1964), culminating in the Munich Olympics pictograms (1972). Further research might show that the image contents for public information symbols in these strains influenced each other to a large degree. This could be researched by reconstructing the evolution of the image contents of the pictogram systems of the nineteen sixties, starting for example with the symbol sets for the UIC and the Tokyo Olympics. These were the first modern sets that stood at the foundations of the pictogram craze in the decade thereafter.

Icograda never addressed the fact that many graphic designers developed their own pictogram sets and ideas about symbol design. This might have undercut its strive for some kind of symbol standard. The design world hardly acknowledged the symbols developed by the organisations Icograda was dealing with either. Despite its lofty talk about developing "a symbol language" it seemed more interested in the aesthetics of symbols than in the standardization of the image contents of symbols. This is still visible in graphic design histories that emphasize the Isoype-Aicher construct. These histories often suggest that Isotype was an important influence on the early development of pictogram systems in the nineteen sixties. However, it is more likely that international road signs served as a frame of reference. Their success showed the value of a symbol system for the public good and their coming about served as institutional model for the standardization of symbols.

On a closing note the Icograda archive shows an almost encyclopaedic overview of persons and organisations involved with symbols in the nineteen sixties, making it an important source of information for the history of semiotics, and design and communication in general. It unearths figures like Soichi Kato with his ICBLB, Margaret Mead of Glyphs Inc, C. K. Bliss and Martin Krampen, who was an early pioneer in symbol development connecting many important figures and institutions.

Biographical Note

Wibo Bakker (1974) is a Dutch researcher, consultant and educator. He is specialized in design history, branding, and the professionalization of graphic design. Lately he has become interested in information design and pictograms, carrying out research in the Netherlands, France, England, Germany and Japan. He worked as a lecturer at several Dutch and Belgium art colleges and universities. More recently he was part time affiliated with the Research Group Visual Rhetoric of AKV|St. Joost (Avans University of Applied Sciences) in Breda.

In 2009 Bakker obtained a PhD in design history at Utrecht University for his study of the development of visual identity in the Netherlands. His dissertation was titled "Droom van Helderheid: huisstijlen, ontwerpbureaus en modernisme in Nederland: 1960-1975" (A Clear Dream: Visual Identity, Design Agencies and Modernism in The Netherlands : 1960-1975). For this he won the Jan van Gelder-prize of the Dutch Society for Art Historians for the best art historical research for a researcher until 35 years of age (2010). A year later the dissertation was published by 010 Publishers (Rotterdam) as the third volume in the prestigious Prince Bernhard Fund for Culture "Visual Culture in the Netherlands" series.

Bakker started his career studying graphic design at the ArtEZ Institute of the Arts in Arnhem (1991-1996). Early on an internship at Pentagram Design (San Francisco) made him aware of national differences in design cultures. After his graduation he worked as an art worker and designer in visual identity design at several Dutch design agencies. While freelancing he continued his studies at Utrecht University (2000-2003), where he obtained a bachelor of humanities and a master degree in cultural history of the modern age with a minor in international corporate communication.

Chapter 9: Case History—Alcoholism in America, *American History* Magazine, December 2008

Nigel Holmes

Abstract

The development of a large graphic that was commissioned by American History Magazine. It shows how drinking habits in the US have changed, starting in 1770, going up to 2008 (Americans drink much less today than they did in the 1700s). Various time periods, such as the Prohibition era from 1920 to 1933, are detailed in text blocks. As well as the final piece, a number of initial designs and sketches are included.

As its title implies, *American History* magazine is devoted to aspects of America's past. The magazine is part of the Weider History Group. Because the Weider Group includes magazines that cover the Civil War and World War II, *American History* concentrates on social, political and economic subject matter, leaving military history to its sister publications.

For many issues from 2008 to 2012, I was commissioned to produce large information graphics on subjects that ranged from The Library System, Trade with China, Mortgages, Farming, Banking and Income Tax.

The brief for all the work I did was simple: the graphic must include some sort of timeline that stretched back as far as possible; back to the 18th century if data could be found. I worked closely with a terrific researcher at the magazine, Lorraine Moffa, and with Executive Editor, David Grogan.

The graphic examined here was about alcohol consumption in the U.S.

Working with the research material developed by Lorraine, my first approach was to divide alcohol into three groups: beer, spirits and wine, each with its own timeline.

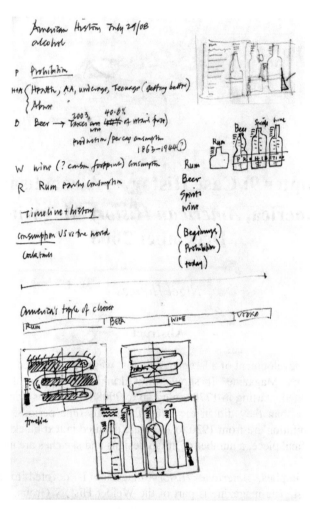

Figure 1

I typically start with small pencil or pen illustrations (Figure 1). This kind of sketching is often made during phone conversations about the job with an editor, when we are discussing the intent of the graphic in broad strokes. Drawing allows me to think of the graphic as a whole, before getting down to the details of the data.

The beer timeline started in 1587, when Virginia colonists started to brew ale using corn. In 1640, spirits were used in Boston as salaries, and in 1770, winemaking arrived in Northern California. The three large, distinctly-shaped bottles would immediately signal to the reader what the graphic was about. Since the overall idea was to show total alcohol consumption, I also included that as a bar chart with horizontal "bars" made up of bottles: one bottle per gallon drunk annually. This chart read from 1750 at the top, down to 1990 at the bottom. (Figure 2)

Figure 2

Lorraine found many interesting snippets of information that made the overall graphic lively and interesting. I included some of these in the first iteration of the graphic.

But editors at the magazine felt that this approach was too densely populated with text and numbers, and indeed the ratio of text to imagery became a running discussion throughout the time I did graphics for the magazine: editors always wanted fewer words and fewer facts, but bigger pictures. My position was that readers (who were typically from older age groups, and definitely history enthusiasts) would lose themselves in the detail. I saw them "reading" the graphics more than "looking" at them. The magazine was a bimonthly, with just six issues a year—plenty of time to take the time to read! Not to mention that there was always a great deal of detail that could be included.

But of course, editors win battles like that! It's their magazine. As the series of graphics continued, the editors were sometimes right to rein me in a bit, but sometimes I felt they were wrong. They were, in effect, assuming their readers would not read the kind of detail that I thought the subject warranted.

In this case the piece was refocused to show alcohol consumption as a series of vertical bars going all the way across the spread. As before, the bars consisted of countable rows of bottles, only now each single bottle represented one-fifth of a gallon, since there are 5 bottles to a gallon. (Figure 3) The three bottle images from the first iteration now become much smaller, forming the background to a chart of excise tax: the amount of money the government collects. Most of the information about the three main beverages was dropped.

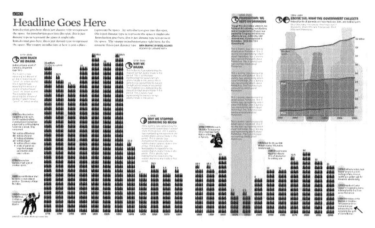

Figure 3

Much of the text at this stage is just dummy type, but the intent of the text blocks is clear—three periods of time are defined, and would be explained in later versions: How Much We Drank (1770-2000); Why We Drank (1770-1830); Why We Stopped Drinking So Much (c.1840). Prohibition (1920–1933) became a tall, light red bar, with texts explaining some of what happened during that time. Many of the interesting facts that Lorraine's research unearthed were added to the large consumption chart in a slightly more casual way, with pointers and small drawings overlaying the columns of bottles.

A further change was made to the excise tax chart (Figure 4), to make that a vertical bar chart instead of the fever chart in figure 3 (A fever chart shows change of a variable over time).

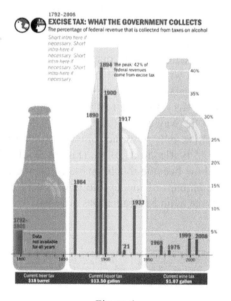

Figure 4

Finally the background to that same chart was changed again, this time to show Uncle Sam conversing with a young man who is holding a beer bottle (Figure 5). This change removed the possibility that the three bottles might be viewed as representing three separate time periods.

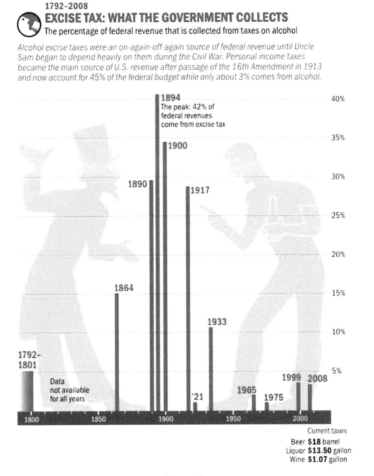

Figure 5

The making of this kind of complex graphic is a collaborative effort: editors, researchers, proofreaders, and myself. Normally, there would also be an art director involved, but my arrangement with *American History* left all the design decisions to me: I was to deliver a complete spread, with all the words and images on one file. The only part that was inserted by the magazine was the headline and short introduction. The final piece as it appeared in the magazine is figure 6 (Figure 6).

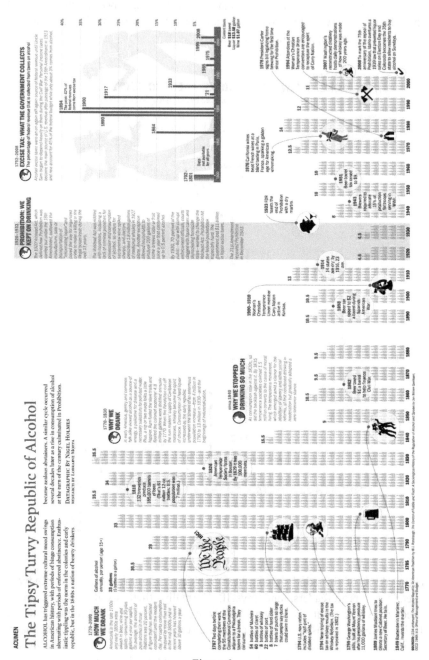

Figure 6

My work often includes humor. It was not really inappropriate in this case, but some of the tiny illustrations accompanying the marginal notes allowed me, perhaps, to raise a small smile (Figure 7). I do not believe that using of humor trivializes the information or data in information graphics. But humor is a valuable tool that is too often overlooked by designers, for fear that they won't be taken seriously. Getting readers' attention and interest is important, even necessary, in our information-overloaded era. Of course the data must be delivered clearly as well!

1799 George Washington's stills, built at Mount Vernon after his presidency, produce 11,000 gallons of whiskey.

1849 Bartender in Martinez, Calif., invents the martini.

1976 California wines beat French wines at a blind tasting in Paris, France, sparking a golden age for American winemaking.

Figure 7

As to the ongoing argument about how much should be included in a graphic of this nature, I remain committed to the idea that in a monthly magazine of this type (as opposed to a similar graphic's appearance on a poster or accompanying a newspaper article, for instance) readers can be relied upon to take the time to read the graphic in much the same way that they might read a text-only piece. I have always thought that information graphics should be studied as closely as written pieces. Information graphics have the advantage that they include pictures as well as words, but they should be "read" rather than just looked at.

Biographical Note

Born in England, Nigel Holmes studied illustration at the Royal College of Art in London and then freelanced for 12 years in London before moving to *Time Magazine* in New York in 1978. He became graphics director and stayed there for 16 years.

At *Time,* his pictorial explanations of complex subjects gained him many imitators and a few academic enemies who thought he was trivializing information. He remains committed to the power of pictures and humor to help readers understand otherwise abstract numbers and difficult scientific concepts.

Since 1994 he has run his own business, Explanation Graphics. Clients have included American Express, Bertelsman, Taschen and The Smithsonian Institution. He does information graphics for many publications, including *The Atlantic, National Geographic* and the *New York Times.* (For the *Times,* his drawings attempting to explain the Higgs Boson won a Gold Medal at the Malofiej Awards in 2014).

In 2009, the Society for News Design gave him its Lifetime Achievement Award. A retrospective exhibition of his work was shown at Stevenson University, Baltimore in 2011.

He has written eight books on aspects of information design. *The Book of Everything* was published by Lonely Planet in 2012. It's a compendium of loosely travel-related information graphics ranging from how to wear a kilt, to delivering a baby in an emergency. *Instant Expert*, a "sister" book, was published by Lonely Planet in 2014.

Part IV: Case Studies in Design Practice

Reflective practitioners create the foundations for respectable professions. It would have been impossible for me to explore the wide scope covered by information design in a book without asking colleagues whose practice I admire to report on their practice.

From instruction manuals in Brazil to hospital forms in Italy through computer based information systems, this section outlines part of the broad terrain covered by information design.

Chapter 10: Mobile Information Design + Persuasion Design—The Money Machine and the Story Machine

Aaron Marcus

Abstract

The Money Machine and the Story Machine projects researched, analyzed, designed, and evaluated powerful ways to change people's behavior: improving "baby boomers'" behavior regarding their personal wealth-management and improving story-sharing across generations among distributed families. The projects intend to persuade and motivate people to change their behavior by means of well-designed mobile smartphone/tablet concept prototype applications (with associated Web portals). The Machines combine information design/visualization with persuasion design. This chapter explains the development of each Machine's user interface, information design, information visualization, and use of persuasion design; showcases the results; and considers the next steps of development.

General Introduction

This chapter introduces two conceptual design projects, the Money Machine and the Story Machine, two in a series of research and development projects that seek to combine principles of information design and persuasion design in the user-centered design (UCD) process of user interfaces for mobile application development. These projects derive from earlier projects: The Green Machine (Marcus and Jean, 2009) and the Health Machine (Marcus, 2011b). In all cases, the Machines seek to change people's behavior by providing usable, useful, and appealing dashboards, high-level system/process model views, focused social networking among people devoted to the user and/or subject matter, just-in-time focused tips and advice, and subject-matter-oriented competitions such as games, incentives, as well as stores and other offerings that encourage continued and improved behavior change. Each of the two case studies of the Money Machine and the Story Machine introduces itself, the subject matter, the process, the results, and the next steps of development.

Case 1: The Money Machine

Introduction to the Money Machine

Between 1 January and 31 December 2011 in the United States, an average of 7000 people each day turned 65 years old, resulting in a recent and significant rise in their financial activities (AARP, 2010). Baby boomers now constitute 40% of the US population, controlling about 67% of the nation's wealth. As they approach retirement, they are facing important decisions about their present and future.

Wealth management information, products, and services are available but many of these tools do not focus on innovative data visualization, are often targeted to the desktop computer, and do not incorporate persuasion to change people's behavior. A further challenge is that many baby boomers are not as familiar as their children and grandchildren with mobile financial management.

The author's firm, Aaron Marcus and Associates, Inc., developed the Money Machine to answer the following two critical questions:

- How can information visualization and design promote sustainable change in wealth-management behavior both short- and long-term?
- How can mobile technology assist in presenting persuasive information and promote behavior change of medium-high income and educated people? (Marcus 2011)

Market Research

In order to have a clearer vision of the target market for the Money Machine, we conducted qualitative research with potential customers. For its interviews, we prepared and distributed a questionnaire to approximately 20 people that asked about the following topics:

- Smartphones and Social Media
- Money Management
- Technology and Money
- Quick Background Information
- Demographics

Results of the Questionnaire

Key results of the questionnaire are depicted in the following charts (Figures 1, 2 and 3):

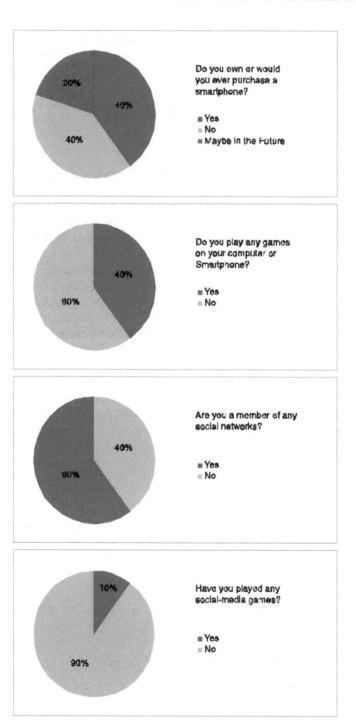

Figure 1

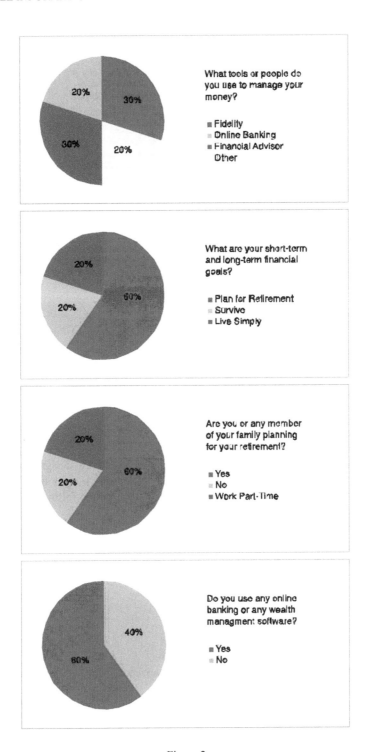

Figure 2

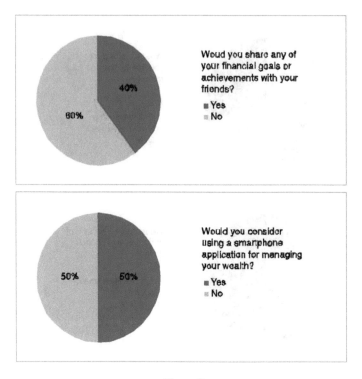

Figure 3

Personas

Based on the data collected, we followed a user-centered design process by constructing personas and use scenarios. We decided on younger baby boomers who would more likely use mobile devices. We proposed the following personas:

- 52-year-old African-American housewife, college educated, married, two children
- 47-year-old Caucasian software engineer, Bachelor in Computer Science from Carnegie Mellon, married, no children
- 50-year-old Caucasian construction worker, high school graduate, single, cares for his elderly father
- 55-year-old Caucasian senior executive at Merrill Lynch; MBA from Yale; married, no children
- 48-year-old Asian grade school teacher and tutor, graduate degree in education from Berkeley, divorced, no children

An example persona follows.

- Persona: Sheila Jones
- 52-year-old African-American housewife, college educated, married, two children
- Proficient with iPad and Excel
- Manages household bills with Excel
- Annual household income: $72,000
  Net worth: $750,000
  Investments: college fund

Design Implications Summary

Objectives

- Monitor budget simply and effectively
- Categorize money for each member of the family
- Manage her children's college fund accounts
- Context
- User is accustomed to older technology, like Excel spreadsheets
- Keeps track of the family finances

Behavior

- Manages budget daily with Excel spreadsheets
- Uses an iPad and has downloaded applications that she uses frequently
- Physical environment: uses iPad at home and while running errands
- Social environment: stays in touch with friends at book club and yoga classes
- Information sharing: shares her financial information with her husband, and shares financial objectives and goals with her friends from time to time

Design Implications

- Design the Money Machine for iPad users like Sheila
- Create a way to partition the budget for each family member, including their dog Bruno. For example, the Money Machine could show how much money can be given to her son for his weekly allowance, and alert her if her son spends too much on sports gear.
- Create a feature where she can identify and be alerted to cash drain(s)
- Create an alert for when her kids use their gift cards
- Have a simple information visualization to show budget monitoring

Use Scenarios

We constructed the following use scenario topics from analysis of our personas.

Financial Monitoring

- View the assets in chart format (*e.g.,* line chart, bar chart, pie chart, or other data visualization, depending on user preference)
- Partition the user's budget into categories (*e.g.,* set up one's own section, as well as sections for one's spouse/partner, dependent child, or dependent parent)
- Connect to investment accounts via bank, brokerage, or telecom company (*e.g.,* AT&T, Google)
- Receive up-to-date articles, advice, and tips regarding monitoring future or current investments. This information may come from professionals, family and friends, or the general public
- Set customizable alerts for investment fluctuations, whether up or down, positive or negative
- Receive overspending alerts
- Establish and maintain objectives (*e.g.,* "I want to retire soon")
- Establish and maintain goals (*e.g.,* specify date of retirement, allocate money for a parent, save for a car, *etc.*). See the ramifications of this goal on current and future budgets, including a timeline and new budget to fund the goal
- Follow and customize pre-set financial templates (best practices) to achieve goals
- Visualize and monitor the user's net worth
- Plan for retirement with a variety of different tools and templates.

Security

- Share financial goals with specific friends and family
- Alert users to any unusual activity in their accounts.

Social Media

- Post financial achievements on the users' own walls and possibly their friends' walls, similar to a merit-badge system
- Connect with financial advisors by text messaging or chat to ask questions and react to their strategy suggestions
- Share tips and strategies with specific friends or family
- Import personal information from social media sites (*e.g.,* race, sex, age). Users not connected to a social media site can add their information manually through the Money Machine
- Resolve any urgent ethical issues.

Gamification

- Set and use pre-existing achievements to help manage finances
- Compare estimated spending with actual spending (*e.g.,* find cash drains)
- Purchase digital items using currency earned from meeting achievements

- Reward valuable tipsters with currency or credit for advice taken by others (*e.g.*, recommending particular investments, creating plans to spend less or save more)
- Develop an "economy of tipsterism," likes and dislikes, bribes and no bribes, objective *vs.* biased opinion, *etc.*

Competitive Products Research

We studied approximately 20 financial and wealth management Websites and iPhone applications. Through screen comparison analysis and customer review analysis, we derived these applications' major benefits and drawbacks.

Money management Websites/mobile products examined include the following:

- Ameritrade
- ASI Wealth Manager Software
- ASI's Goalgami
- Charles Schwab
- iBank
- iFinance
- Investoscope
- Mastock
- Microsoft Money
- Mint.com
  mvelopes.com
- mPortfolio
- Quicken
- Real Estate Investment Calculator
- SmartMoney.com
- You Need a Budget Software (YNAB)

Use of Persuasion Theory

In alignment with Fogg's persuasion theory (Fogg, B. J., and Eckles, D., 2007), we have defined five key processes to create behavioral change via the Money Machine's functions and data:

- Increase frequency of using application
- Motivate changing some living habits: save, plan, invest
- Teach how to change living habits
- Persuade users to plan short-term change
- Persuade users to plan long-term change.

We also drew from Maslow's *A Theory of Human Motivation* (Maslow, 1943), which he based on his analysis of fundamental human needs. We adapted these to the Money Machine context:

- The safety and security need is met by the possibility to visualize the amount of expenses saved

- The belonging and love need is expressed through friends, family, and social sharing and support
- The esteem need is satisfied by social comparisons that display improvement in financial control and skill, as well as by self-challenges that display goal accomplishment
- The self-actualization need is fulfilled by the ability to visualize improvement of financial indexes and mood, and to predict change in users' future economic scenarios.

Impact on Information Architecture

Increase Use Frequency

Games and rewards are among the most common methods to increase use frequency. We developed several financial game concepts for the Money Machine. In terms of rewards, the users might be awarded both virtual rewards (such as "star" designations and new skins for blogs) as well as real money rewards.

In addition, we chose social comparison as another incentive to increase use frequency. Users can form groups with family and friends, and participate in various group competitions. Although these competitions are based around financial controls and exercises, users do not have to reveal personal financial data, which most prefer to keep securely private.

Increase Motivation

In the Money Machine, we set the users' potential financial conditions as an important incentive for their behavior change. Viewing their current versus predicted economic status over the next 20 to 30 years gives users greater understanding of the strengths and weaknesses to their financial strategy.

Because setting goals improves learning outcomes and provides quantitative performance data, the Money Machine asks users to set time-based goals for budget reduction (*e.g.*, saving on consumer items or maintenance services, both required and optional), savings, and retirement. Users receive suggested step-by-step plans of action in order to achieve each goal.

In addition, we created 10 monthly challenges. In meeting these challenges, users are making short-term financial behavior change that will generate long-term positive impacts.

Social interaction is another strong motivator of behavior change, both through community support and informal competition or comparison. The Money Machine leverages social networking by integrating features found in forums and on blogs, Facebook, and Twitter. Users can send messages to and share ideas with their social groups. These social ties serve as additional incentive to motivate behavior change.

Improve Learning

For many people with significant financial challenges, understanding long-term wealth management is crucial. To improve learning, the Money Machine integrates contextual tips on the following topics:

- Consuming more wisely
- Increasing financial control
- Tackling complications associated with debt and poor investments
- Coping with principle burn rates that are either too high or too low

Users can also choose to receive updates on latest research articles and news about wealth management.

We seek to make the education process entertaining as well as informative. Proposed games teach users to choose the right proportion of investments, amount and type of each instrument, *etc.* Through playing games featuring educational information, users learn to manage their wealth like a skilled financial advisor, without getting bored.

Information Architecture

Based on the preceding, we developed the following information architecture. Note that Emotional Management and Time Management were considered to be possible future areas for investigation. They were not explored in the current version of the Money Machine. (Figure 5)

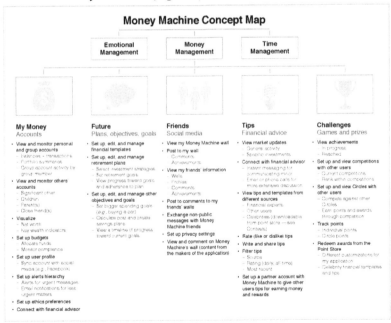

Figure 5

Screen Designs

Based on the personas, use scenarios, and product comparison, after many rounds of discussions, and initial designs, these revised mobile screen designs emerged. They are the result of several rounds of design, originally brainstorming and concept mapping to wireframes, and then initial paper sketches to these revised versions. Space limitations precludes detailed discussion of the evolutionary process.

Landing screen

User-selected priority information is displayed at the top of the screen, with arrows for scrolling at either side. The bottom half of the screen displays market updates as well as social networking and competition notifications. (Figure 6)

Figure 6

My Money/Submenu

This My Money screen typifies submenus throughout the Money Machine. (Figure 7)

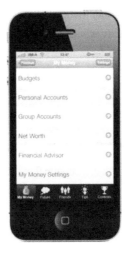

Figure 7

My Money/Budgets

User-filtered budget categories are displayed at the top. "Total" displays total earnings, expenses, and savings for a given timeframe (weekly, monthly, yearly, lifetime, *etc.*). Users can view specific budgets by clicking on the associated icon above. (Figure 8)

Figure 8

My Money/Retirement Planner

This sample chart illustrates users' current assets, allowing them to view a their retirement plans graphically and create a more intuitive understanding of factors like risk, savings rates, and tax management. (Figure 9)

Figure 9

My Money/Group Accounts

Group accounts lets users manage shared funds easily. Selecting a group account member from the top bar displays the total money in the account, versus that member's contributions and expenses for a given timeframe (weekly, monthly, yearly, lifetime, *etc.*). (Figure 10)

Figure 10

Future/Goals

Under the heading of Future, users set financial goals (acquisition, savings, *etc.*), each of which has an associated status bar showing the users' progress toward their goal. Users can access further details, such as expected date of accomplishment, by clicking on the arrow at right. (Figure 11)

Figure 11

Friends/Main page

This screen displays a search-enabled list of users' friends on the Money Machine. Users click on a friend's name or icon to view a complete profile. A privacy indicator sits next to each friend, representing that friend's access to sensitive financial information (red signifies zero access, yellow signifies limited access, and green signifies complete access). (Figure 12)

Figure 12

Friends/Announcements

Announcements falls under the heading of Friends, the Money Machine's social media network. This is a list of posts from friends and circles on the application. The user can give posts a thumbs up. The posts can be filtered by person or

subject through clicking on the filter button. The inbox button will take the user
to his/her messages.(Figure 13)

Figure 13

Tips /Main page

This is a news feed of financial tips from users on the application. Tips can be
filtered by person or subject through clicking the filter button. Users can write
their own tip by clicking on the "write" button. Users can also search through the
tips. Each tip can be rated with a thumbs up or down, and more detail about a tip
can be seen by clicking on the button to the right of it. (Figure 14)

Figure 14

Contests/Achievements

This screen shows the wall of the user's achievements. Each achievement is represented by a badge, and the progress toward it is shown in a bar below the badge. Achievements are earned through various methods that show the user is improving financially. (Figure 15)

Figure 15

Evaluation and Next Steps

AM+A interviewed one financial planner to learn her reactions to the interview questions and to an earlier version of the white paper explaining the project. We plan to interview others. Using the user-centered design approach described above, we plan to continue to improve the Money Machine. Tasks include the following:

- Revising personas and use scenarios
- Conducting user evaluations
- Revising information architecture and look and feel
- Building initial working prototype (*e.g.*, for phone/tablet, or other platforms)
- Evaluating the Money Machine across different cultures
- Developing the Money Machine for business use as well as personal use
- Researching and developing improved information visualizations.

AM+A's long-term objective is to create a functional working prototype to test whether the application can actually persuade people with wealth-management challenges to exercise greater fiscal control, increase healthier wealth-management habits, and pursue a more financially sound lifestyle under real use conditions over the long term. If the theories are proven to be correct, this approach could have significant wealth-management benefits.

Acknowledgements

The author thanks his Associates, Hélène Savvidis, Catherine Isaacs, Chris Chambers, Carlene O'Keefe, and Tim Thianthai, for their significant assistance in planning, research, design, analysis, and documentation.

References

AARP Bulletin (2011), July-Aug. 2011, 52nd ed., sec. 6. Print.

AARP (2010). Approaching 65: A Survey of Baby Boomers Turning 65 Years Old. Washington: AARP.

Ameritrade. "Trade Architect." Web: <http://www.tdameritrade.com/tradingtools/tradearchitect.html>.

AVA Book (2005). *Designing fro Small Screens*. AVA Publishing SA.

Budvietas, Roberta. "Baby Boomers Use Social Media Differently than Generation X and Y." 12 Jan. 2011. Web: <http://www.sexysocialmedia.com/baby-boomers-use-social-media-differently-than-generation-x-and-y/>.

Carracher, Jamie (2011). "How Baby Boomers Are Embracing Digital Media." 6 April 2011. Web: <http://mashable.com/2011/04/06/baby-boomers-digital-media/>.

Coughlin, Joseph (2011). "Why US Baby Boomers Are Slow to Buy Smart Phones: Technophobes or Value Buyers?" 13 April 2011. Web: <http://bigthink.com/ideas/38209>.

Credit Loan. "Too Big to Fail: Inside America's Economic Downfall." Web: <http://www.creditloan.com/blog/2011/06/28/too-big-to-fail-inside-americas-economic-downfall/>.

Fidelity (2010). "Fidelity Enhances iPhone and iPod Touch Mobile App With Access To Workplace Retirement Plans." 22 June 2010. Web: <http://www.fidelity.com/inside-fidelity/employer-services/fidelity-enhance-iphone-and-ipod-touch-mobile-app>.

Fogg, B. J., and Eckles, D. (2007). *Mobile persuasion: 20 perspectives on the future of behavior change*. Palo Alto, CA: Persuasive Technology Lab, Stanford University.

Hartman, Blake (2011). "Retirement Plan – Alarming Statistics Of Middle-Income Baby Boomers Postponing Retirement Reported." 2 June 2011. Web: <http://starglobaltribune.com/2011/retirement-plan-alarming-statistics-of-middle-income-baby-boomers-postponing-retirement-reported-9202>.

Holiday Touch. "Video Games: No Longer Just for Kids." Web: <http://www.holidaytouch.com/Retirement-101/senior-living-articles/activities-and-lifestyle/video-games-not-just-for-kids.aspx>.

Junior Achievement. "Junior Achievement Programs." Web: <http://www.ja.org/Programs/programs.shtml>.

Lampa, Jason (2009). "10 Ways Financial Advisors Can Attract Baby Boomers in 2010." 25 Nov. 2009. Web: <http://www.producersweb.com/r/pwebmc/d/contentFocus/?pcID=99aeb af67fa527fec8cffb4286c7aa70>.

Jones, Matt and Marsden Gary. (2006). *Mobile Interaction Design*. John Wiley & Sons, Ltd.

Lehikoinen Juha, Aaltonon Antti, Huuskonen Pertti, Salminen Ilkka. (2007). *Personal Content Experience, managing digital life in the mobile age.* John Wiley & Sons, Ltd.

Lighthouse International. "Big Type Is Best for Aging Baby Boomers." Web: <http://www.lighthouse.org/accessibility/design/accessible-print-design/big-type/>.

Marcus, Aaron (2011a). The Money Machine. AM+A white paper. Available upon request.

Marcus, Aaron (2011b). The Health Machine. *Information Design Journal*, 19:1, 61-89.

Marcus, Aaron (2011c). Gaming the user experience. *User Experience Magazine*, 10(4), 32.

Marcus, Aaron and Jeremie Jean. (2009). Going green at home: the green machine. *Information Design Journal*, 17(3) 233-243.

Maslow, A. (1943). A theory of human motivation. *Psychological Review*, 50, 370-396.

Merrill Lynch. "What Matters Most To You?" Web: http://www.totalmerrill.com/TotalMerrill/pages/WhatMattersMostToYou.aspx

Newman, R. (2010). "Why Baby Boomers Are Bummed Out." 29 Dec. 2010. US News and World Report.

Norman, Joshua (2010). "Boomers Joining Social Media at Record Rate." 16 November 2010. Web: <http://www.cbsnews.com/stories/2010/11/15/national/main7055992.shtml>

Orlov, Laurie (2010). "AARP: Baby Boomers Are Not Comfortable with the Internet -- Really?" 10 June 2010. Web: <http://www.ageinplacetech.com/blog/aarp-baby-boomers-are-not-comfortable-internet-really>.

Perez, Sarah (2010). "Boomers Slowly Joining the Mobile Web." 4 March 2010. Web: <http://www.readwriteweb.com/archives/boomers_slowly_joining_the_mobile_web.php>.

Rao, Leena (2011). "Flurry: Time Spent On Mobile Apps Has Surpassed Web Browsing." 20 June 2011. Web: <http://techcrunch.com/2011/06/20/flurry-time-spent-on-mobile-apps-has-surpassed-web-browsing/>.

Samsung Electronics (2010). Persuasive Money Life. Toronto: SAIT. Computer Science Lab, Future Experience Part.

Silverman, Kevin (2011). "Medical Monday: Do Baby Boomers Use Social Media?" 7 February 2011. Web: <http://blog.ogilvypr.com/2011/02/medical-monday-do-baby-boomers-use-social-media-this-past-weekend-i-went-with-my-family-to-my-great-aunt%E2%80%99s-96th-birthday-the-whole-family-met-in-long-island-coming-in-from-other-parts-of/>.

Six, Janet (2010). "Designing for Senior Citizens / Organizing Your Work Schedule." 17 May 2010. Web:

      <http://www.uxmatters.com/mt/archives/2010/05/designing-for-senior-
      citizens-organizing-your-work-schedule.php>.
Social Security Administration (2011). Fast Facts & Figures About Social
      Security, 2011 (August 2011). Washington, DC: SSA Office of
      Retirement and Disability Policy, Office of Research, Evaluation, and
      Statistics. SSA Publication No. 13-11785.
      University of Maryland. "Visualization." Web:
      <http://www.cs.umd.edu/hcil/research/visualization.shtml>.
Usability Professionals' Association (2002). Web: <http://www.upassoc.org/>
Weiss, Scott. (2002). *Handheld Usability*. John Wiley & Sons, Ltd.
iPhone Mobile/Website Money Applications URLs
(Retrieval date: 07 July 2011)

http://www.advisorsoftware.com/products/ASIwealthManager.asp
http://www.goalgami.com/content/index.php
http://www.iggsoftware.com/ibank/
http://investoscope.com/
http://www.ipadappsdude.com/update-wealth-manager-finance/
http://itunes.apple.com/us/app/property-evaluator-real-estate/id335518202?mt=8
http://mastock.michelmontagne.com/
http://www.microsoft.com/money/default.mspx
https://www.mint.com/
http://mportfolio.umich.edu/
http://www.mvelopes.com/
http://quicken.intuit.com/
https://www.schwab.com/public/schwab/home/welcomep.html
http://www.smartmoney.com/
http://www.syniumsoftware.com/ifinance/
http://www.tdameritrade.com/welcome1.html
http://www.youneedabudget.com/

Case 2: The Story Machine

Introduction to the Story Machine

Finding a life-enhancing way to share family wisdom (history, lore, facts,
traditions, and beliefs) among generations is a 21st century global challenge,
especially in the USA, where geographically distributed, asynchronous, merged
families, with diverse cultural heritages constitute a significant portion of the
population. Many in the older generation are not as familiar with mobile- and
Web-based tools to manage their media and storytelling as their children and
grandchildren. Nevertheless, they want to and need to share important stories
about the past, perceptions about the present, and predictions of the future.

Story/memory management products, and services, are available to increase
people's awareness of family history, personalities, and issues, and to encourage
awareness and change, but they do not focus on innovative data visualization, and
they lack persuasive effectiveness to convert family members to preserve family

wisdom. Communicating family facts, concepts, and emotions, helps build awareness and identity, but does not result automatically in effective behavioral changes. The question then becomes: How can we better motivate, persuade, educate, and lead people to manage their stories, media, and time, thereby preserving their legacy for future generations?

The Story Machine project of 2011 researched, analyzed, designed, and evaluated powerful ways to improve inter-generational story-sharing behavior by persuading and motivating people to increase story generation, and to increase story sharing with other family members by means of a well-designed mobile application (for smart phone, tablet, and associated Web portal) concept prototype: the "Story Machine."

The author's firm, AM+A, previously designed and tested similar concept prototypes: the Green Machine (Marcus and Jean, 2009), oriented to persuading home consumers to make energy conservation behavior changes; the Health Machine (Marcus, 2011), oriented to avoiding obesity and diabetes through better behavior regarding nutrition and exercise; and the Money Machine (see previous case study), targeted to baby boomers and oriented to their managing their wealth better. The Story Machine uses similar principles of combining information design/visualization with persuasion design. AM+A's workshop paper explains the development of the Story Machine's user interface, information design, information visualization, and persuasion design.

User-centered Design Process Steps

As with all the AM+A Machine projects, the user-centered design (UCD) approach links the process of developing software, hardware, and user-interface (UI) to the people who will use a product/service. UCD processes focus on users throughout the development of a product or service.

In order to have a clearer vision of the target users for the Story Machine, AM+A conducted qualitative market research with potential customers.

AM+A conducted surveys in order to find out more about the motivations and behaviors of people when it comes to use of technology, family bonds, family physical interaction, and family legacies. AM+A submitted two questionnaires, one for the generation of baby boomers aged 47 and older, the second one for the younger generations. Each of the questionnaires had a total of 50 respondents. The objective of these questionnaires was to understand as much as possible about the needs and wants of people regarding their memory/story sharing. AM+A constructed draft and revised versions of questions after brainstorming internally about the questions. AM+A gained insights into definitions of families, family structure, need for story sharing, and preferred modes of communication. These insights led to construction of personas and user scenarios for the Story Machine.

AM+A developed four personas for men and women, that is, textual summaries of their lives and design summaries of the implications of the personas on the target concept design. The ages of the personas ranged from 20-65.

AM+A also constructed user scenarios that fit the personas and the results of the market studies. The following use scenario topics are drawn from the four preceding personas. However, some specific examples might be relevant only to a particular age group, education level, gender, or culture.

- Video Memories
- Personal Timeline
- Video Chat
- Social Media
- Photography Software
- Family Trades
- Media Specific to Time/Place
- Gamification
- General Behavior Change

AM+A also carried out competitive research with approximately 10 Apple iPhone applications and Android-based applications on other platforms. From our research, we determined that our concept designs needed to use persuasion theory, to provide games and competition, and to be appealing, not only easy to use.

In alignment with Fogg's persuasion theory (Fogg, 2007), Cialdini's work on persuasion (Cialdini, 2001), and Maslow's research on motivation [Maslow, 1943], we defined five key processes to create behavioral change via the Story Machine's functions and data:

- Increase frequency of using application
- Motivate changing story sharing habits
- Teach how to change story sharing habits
- Persuade users to plan short-term change
- Persuade users to plan long-term change.

We designed an information architecture that incorporate these concepts, designed initial sketches, reviewed them informally with potential users, and designed revised screens.

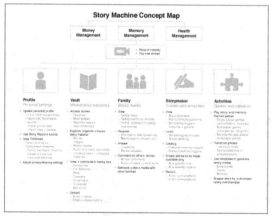

Figure 16: Information Architecture of the Story Machine

The primary modules, visualized by the icons in the diagram of the information architecture and the icons at the bottom of the screens, show dashboards depicting the current situation, a process model that encompasses the future, social networking among a dedicated user community, tips and advice, and challenges such as games and competition. A few example screens are shown.

Figure 17: Social Networking Screen. This screen shows family a member, favorites associate with that person, and news.

Figure 18: Memory Game Screen. This screen shows possible challenge to recognize specific family members and to gain points by completing recognition within certain time limits.

Figure 19: Recording Story Screen. This screen shows the video camera immediately available to record a story, together with time elapsed and the ongoing key-words that the phone has identified from the speaker's answers. These can be selected and used to auto-tag the interview, together with a GPS location and time-date stamp.

Figure 20: Activities Screen. This screen shows individuals that may be engaged in different family group activities, such as cookbook contributions; different family crests being created or reviewed; and other activities in which users may participate.

Sample Screens

These sample revised screen designs of the Story Machine for mobile phone platform show a family network, a memory game to identify family members, automatically generated tag words derived from family interviews, and an activities summary that shows family crests that can be designed in a family-crest-design tool.

These sample screens indicate how the Story Machine makes it easy and quick to create, tag, and store stories, and to access them. We also designed initial versions of activities that provide incentives for users to collect and share stories.

Next Steps

AM+A plans to interview potential users to gain specific feedback from the designs, then revise them further. Of special interest is how different cultures react to the particular concepts, functions, contents, and imagery. The Story Machine is an ongoing development project.

Acknowledgements

The author thanks his Associates, Mr. Chris Chambers, AM+A Designer/Analyst; Ms. Catherine Isaacs, AM+A Designer/Analyst; Ms. Carlene O'Keefe, AM+A Designer/Analyst; Ms. Helene Savvidis, AM+A Business-Development/Projects-Management Assistant; and Mr. Tim Thianthai, AM+A Designer/Analyst, for their significant assistance in the preparation of materials for this case study.

References

Cialdini. R. (2001). "The Science of Persuasion." *Scientific American.* February 2001, pp. 83-99.

Fogg, B. J., and Eckles, D. (2007). *Mobile persuasion: 20 perspectives on the future of behavior change.* Palo Alto, CA: Persuasive Technology Lab, Stanford University.

Marcus, A., & Jean, J. (2009). Going green at home: The green machine. *Information Design Journal, 17,* 233-243.

Marcus, A., (2011). The Health Machine. *Information Design Journal, 19,* 69-89.

Maslow, A. (1943). A theory of human motivation. *Psychological Review, 50,* 370-396

Conclusions

Each of the Machine projects is an ongoing work in progress. Development teams have taken each Machine as far as time permitted during an initial R+D period, which included initial competitive market research, development of personas and use scenarios, design of overall information architecture, design of sample screens, and, in some cases, initial review with potential users. Each of the projects deserves specific testing, design refinement for particular ages or cultures of users, and further investigation of information visualization. Nevertheless, the Machine projects thus far demonstrate a holistic approach to combining information design with persuasion design, leading to behavior change. The projects have been presented worldwide since the completion of each Machine. Based on feedback from reviewers, potential users, and subject-experts, AM+A plans to take each Machine further toward commercial implementation, as circumstances permit.

Biographical Note

Mr. Aaron Marcus is the founder/President of Aaron Marcus and Associates, Inc. (AM+A). A graduate in physics from Princeton University and in graphic design from Yale University, in 1967 he became the world's first graphic designer to be involved full-time in computer graphics. In the 1970s he programmed a prototype desktop publishing page layout application for the Picturephone (tm) at AT&T Bell Labs, was the first visual designer to program virtual reality spaces while a faculty member at Princeton University, and directed an international team of visual communicators as a Research Fellow at the East-West Center in Honolulu. In the early 1980s he was on the faculty of the University of California at Berkeley, became a Staff Scientist at Lawrence Berkeley Laboratory, founded AM+A, and began research as a Co-Principal Investigator of a project in computer-program visualization funded by the US Department of Defense's Advanced Research Projects Agency (DARPA). He has held leading roles at the ACM/SIGGRAPH 1980, the ACM/SIGCHI 1999, and the UPA 2005, the Usability Professional's Association's annual conference.

He is AIGA Fellow, and Member of the ACM's CHI Academy. He has received honors and awards from computing and design organizations. He is now the Editor-in-Chief *Emeritus* of *User Experience.* He is also an Editor of *Information Design Journal,* and was a regular columnist of *Interactions* for five years. He is on the Editorial Boards of *Visible Language, Universal Access Journal,* and the *International Journal of Human-Computer Interaction.* He is a Visiting Professor of the IIT Institute of Design, Chicago.

Mr. Marcus has written over 300 articles and chapters; written/co-written/edited eight books, including Human Factors and Typography for More Readable Programs (1990), Graphic Design for Electronic Documents and User Interfaces (1992), The Cross-GUI Handbook for Multiplatform User Interface Design (1994), and Mobile TV: Customizing Content and Experience (2010). Mr. Marcus focuses his attention on the Web, mobile devices, and social networks, helping the industry to learn about user-centered user-interface and information-visualization design, and providing guidelines for globalization/localization, cross-cultural communication design, and persuasion design.

Mr. Marcus has published, lectured, tutored, and consulted internationally for 45 years and has been an invited keynote/plenary speaker at conferences internationally.

Chapter 11: The Rhetoric of Redesign in Bureaucratic Settings

Karen Schriver

Abstract

Although information designers are typically skilled in imagining innovative solutions to problems of poor communications, they may underestimate the importance of making their rhetorical work visible and valued within organizations. This "before" and "after" case shows there is much more to information design than re-envisioning visual and verbal content. It demonstrates how redesign projects can be derailed and even rejected when information designers have not sufficiently understood the relative power held by various stakeholders within the organization—power that determines how decisions get made and what activities are deemed of value.

Background and Goals

This project got its start when the mayor of New York City signed an executive order requiring all city agencies to improve customer service by providing better access to their public documents. The mayor wanted better access not only for English speakers, but also for speakers of six other languages spoken frequently in New York: Spanish, Chinese, Russian, Korean, Italian, and French Creole (Bloomberg, 2008, July 22). According to city records, nearly one-half of all New Yorkers speak a language other than English at home, and 25% of City residents do not speak English as their primary language. City officials recognized that many government services require comprehending complex texts and graphics, filling-in forms, interpreting procedures, or understanding rules, regulations, and laws.

Officials found that many of the city's essential public documents were not well written in English, making them difficult and costly to translate. The motive for the executive order was to provide people who experienced difficulty with speaking, reading, or writing English with interpretation services so they would have better access to city government information. City government offices were charged with offering onsite help with translating or interpreting public documents and were directed to make their written documents more accessible. But before essential documents could be translated into the six target languages, the text and graphics needed to be clear in English first.

Many public documents from agencies across New York City were targeted for revision. The case presented here was initiated by the Department of Transportation, with the goal of clarifying documents that had been found to be confusing for native English speakers. The department requested a revision of a set of documents based on best practices in plain language and on research in information design. Due to space constraints, this case study focuses on one document that sheds light on some of the issues discussed earlier in this book.

Purposes for the Original Document

The original document (Figure 1) is an application for a permit to install "temporary festival lighting" on the streets of New York City. Suppose, for example, that a non-profit group wanted to raise awareness for their cause by hosting a "street party," requiring several New York City streets to be blocked off. To make the atmosphere more festive, the group might want to string colorful party lights all along the streets. And in fact, any New York City resident or group may get permission to install temporary festival lighting on the streets, but to do so, they must apply for a permit from the city government. The original document was a hardcopy text that had three purposes:

- To instruct applicants about how to get a permit for installing temporary lighting
- To provide a form to be filled in, which then had to be approved by the city government
- To detail the legal rules and regulations that must be followed when installing the lighting

Acquiring a permit is a staged process, which takes about three months and involves approvals from several city government offices. The city's primary concern was that applicants prove their ability to install the lighting safely and within the city's regulations for electrical wiring. Above all, the city was concerned with avoiding fires caused by overloaded electrical circuits due to careless or incompetent installation of high-wattage lighting.

Figure 1. A portion of the original document: Applying for a permit for installing temporary lighting.

How the Project Began: Stakeholder Analysis

The project began with a stakeholder analysis of the content. We considered two groups of stakeholders for the document:

- *Internal stakeholders*: Government employees (who worked at the Department of Transportation) who were decision makers and gatekeepers. These stakeholders were adamant about three issues: (1) that applicants follow city regulations in applying for the permit, (2) that the language of the forms preserve the legal intent of the law in order to protect the city from lawsuits, and (3) that the forms could be updated from hardcopy documents to online documents.
- *External stakeholders*: Individuals and groups who needed to comply with the New York City regulations for obtaining a permit for installing temporary lighting, including: (1) filling-in the application form, and (2) designing a plan (usually with the help of electrical contractors) for their activity that the city would approve.

We evaluated the original document by asking internal stakeholders to read and assess the document, scrutinizing its parts. We also conducted interviews with managers within the Department of Transportation regarding their impressions of what led an application to be rejected. Decision makers from the city government detailed incidents that led them to reject an application or ask for a resubmission.

Our team had also planned to assess the original documents with external stakeholders by employing a variety of reader-focused usability methods (Schriver, 1989). Our contention was that only by understanding the applicant's perspective (their cognitive and emotional responses) would we gain insight into why so many people found the instructions, forms, and regulations to be confusing. Unfortunately, our clients within the NYC Department of Transportation could not secure funding for usability testing. They advised that we postpone usability testing until our revised documents passed the scrutiny of their legal department. The city's lawyers believed that the most important aspect of the content was whether it accurately characterized the city's codes and regulations.

Our team heartily agreed that the documents should reflect the law, but we were more focused on designing usable documents organized from the perspective of the user. Our concern was not only with whether people could fill-in the forms correctly and understand the city's rules, but also on how people would feel about dealing with the New York City government as a result of their interaction. Put simply, we were interested in promoting a positive and painless user experience.

We hoped citizens' experience in using the redesigned communications might generate a long-term favorable "halo effect" about engaging with the city government. (The "halo effect" is the tendency to generalize a value judgment about a person, product, service, or experience to another. For example, when people have a positive experience with a service or product, they are likely to think well of the organization or brand that created it.) Ultimately, we strove to encourage city residents to perceive the city government as helpful. Our aim was to redesign the documents so it would be easy to engage with the city's policies and procedures. In this way fewer citizens would make mistakes or simply give up because engaging with the bureaucracy was too complicated and irritating.

With these goals in mind, we supplemented the internal stakeholder analysis with an *expert review* focused on issues of information design and plain language. Here, we drew on our substantial prior experience in usability in order to predict aspects of the content that would likely create difficulty for citizens. Together, the stakeholder analysis and the expert review allowed us to identify a number of deficiencies in the original and set some explicit goals for the revision.

Observations from Expert Review

Our expert review revealed problems of content, organization, writing, and design—each of which is explained briefly next.

Problems of Content and Organization

- The content was disorganized and not presented in the order the applicant needed it. In short, the forms and their instructions had problems of information flow (Jansen & Steehouder, 1992; Jarrett & Gaffney, 2009).

- The procedures and advice were often ambiguous, unclear, or missing. For instance, in interviews with the managers who approved the permits, they reported that applicants often failed to include in the plans they submitted information about how they would attach their electrical wiring to buildings or telephone poles. When applicants failed to include this information, the form would be returned to them for resubmission, delaying approval of their project. This and other types of planning advice about how to specify their project were missing in the original instructions, a major omission of content. As anyone who has used poor instructions would attest, trying to carry out procedures with missing steps challenges even the most patient of us. Put differently, problems of omission are often worse than those of commission (Schriver, 1992).

Problems of Writing

- The writing style was antiquated and legalistic, with heavy-handed use of the imperative voice. For example, the word "shall" was employed 32 times (e.g., all work shall conform…).
- There were archaic word choices. For example, the word "festoon" was chosen as a keyword in the form's title ("festoon lighting"), even though *festoon* is a rarely used word in American English. In fact, the Corpus of Historical American English indicates that between 1810 and 2009 the word *festoon* appeared only 99 times per 400 million American English words (Davies, 2010). Instead of using the low-frequency *festoon,* we chose the more common "festival," which is among the top 5,000 most frequent words in American English, appearing 12,198 times per 400 million words (Davies & Gardner, 2010, p. 152). Research shows that high-frequency words are easier to recognize than low-frequency words (Carpenter & Just, 1983; Hudson & Bergman, 1985; Zipf, 1949). We can conclude that it is important to choose short, familiar, high-frequency words rather than long, complex, or low-frequency words.
- Diverse content (e.g., steps, advice, rules, regulations) was presented in numbered lists, which grossly distorted the hierarchy of the content and implied that each item was an ordered step. The failure to group similar content and to signal the groups visually and verbally according to rhetorical function (e.g., procedures, tips, rules and regulations) made it hard for readers to discern what they "must do" from what they "needed to know before doing."
- The tone was distant and unfriendly, projecting a rigid bureaucratic persona.

Problems of Design

The application and the form had an uninviting appearance. The negative impression was created by characteristics such as the following:

- The form design was randomly organized and visually chaotic, employing a layout reminiscent of the typewriter era.
- The rules and regulations were presented on the same pages as parts of the form. Only the form needed to be submitted to the city government. The form should have been displayed separately. This would have avoided confusion for the user and irrelevant content for the government employee reviewing the form. The jumbled format failed to promote efficient reading and was unsuitable for displaying the content either on paper or online (Schriver, 2010).
- There was not enough space for applicants to write the answers to questions (Summers, Summers, & Pointer, 2014).
- The form had problems of alignment, grouping, and contrast.
- The visual organization did not reveal the structure of the content (Sless, 1999).
- The size of the typography violated principles of readable design (Schriver, 1997). For example, the list of conditions was displayed in type too small for comfortable reading. The text overused underlining. Enumerated items were randomly bolded.

The problems of the original document led us to develop goals for our revision, including goals for stakeholders as well as for the design of the content itself.

Goals for External Stakeholders (The Audience)

To help applicants
- Apply for a permit without making errors caused by confusing questions or by the wording of instructions, advice, rules, or regulations;
- Plan a project that would abide by the city's laws, rules, regulations;
- Fill in the form quickly and easily; and
- Understand the process of obtaining a permit and what happens in each stage of approval.

Goals for Internal Stakeholders (The Client)

To help the client
- Build good will between the New York City government and the citizens of New York;
- Make the text plain and clear in English in order to support an efficient translation into different languages; and
- Generate a template for use in designing a set of interactive online documents.

Goals for the Redesign

- To use design to reinforce the text's hierarchy and suggest an appropriate sequence for reading;

- To segment the content into meaningful groups and help applicants negotiate the application process;
- To rewrite the text using plain language in order to make the laws, rules, and regulations clear; and
- To use tables instead of prose to enable efficient decision making

Moreover, we embraced the idea that shorter is not better if making a shorter document means omitting crucial content. Figure 2 presents a two-page spread from the redesigned application.

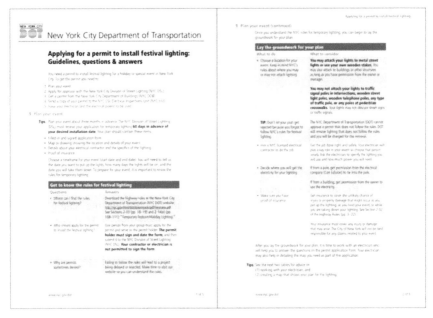

Figure 2. A portion of the redesigned application for a permit to install festival lighting.

As shown in the top left portion of Figure 2, we grouped the content according to five steps required for a successful application. Figure 2 shows the first step, "plan your event." Our approach was to segment the content into logical groups and organize it from the perspective of external stakeholders, using reader-friendly headings (e.g., "Questions" and "Answers"). We also reconceived the information display, shifting most of the content from prose to tables. This information design strategy of grouping, organizing, and signaling made the procedures stand out, enabling users to know what to do and what to focus on (Schriver, 2013). Each table has a clear structure (e.g., "What to do" and "What to consider") and is designed to walk the applicant through the process, making the steps more conspicuous and intelligible.

Figure 3 presents our revised form. In the redesign we created a strong vertical alignment for the headings, questions, and form fields for answering. Unlike the original, the revision provides applicants with sufficient space for writing or typing their answers.

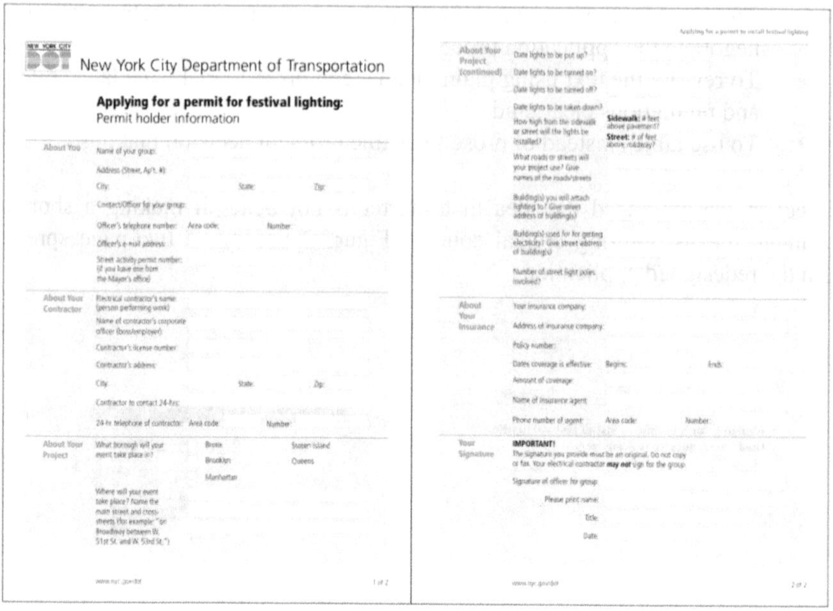

Figure 3. A revised form for applying for a permit.

As shown in Figure 3, we separated the content into logical groups, making it easy to scan. The redesign cues the applicant regarding the categories of questions that must be answered (e.g., "about your insurance"). It also orders the content in a way that applicants would likely expect and poses the questions more clearly (see those listed under "about your project"). Additionally, the form was made easier to use online by adding interactive fields.

Client Feedback on the Design

Once the revisions were complete, we solicited feedback from our client team. The response from internal stakeholders was extremely positive. As one team member (who worked on processing forms) said, "Could this actually be a form from NYC government? Wow, this is great!"

Although we were very gratified with the positive response, our enthusiasm waned when we did not get approval to test our revision. We were unable to move forward with a user-based assessment of the redesign because of internal problems within the organizational structure.

Our supervisors on the project—who were staunch advocates of plain language—ran into difficulties when they presented our redesign to the city's legal team. We had assumed that our project supervisors had apprised the city's legal team of the redesign concept as it progressed. The design had gone through four iterations prior to the semi-final version, with each iteration receiving extensive client feedback.

Like many information design teams, we worked remotely through electronic means and had never met face-to-face. We collaborated through email and conference calls, but because the legal team did not have (or make) time to participate, we had no access to their opinions.

Months after the redesign had been approved for publication by our project supervisors and collaborators, lawyers for the city voiced skepticism about three aspects of the redesign. First, lawyers argued that they could have done a better job of making a plain English version. They criticized the revision because it did not use the same legal language as the original. Second, they contended that if the redesign was actually better, it should have been shorter not longer than the original. And third, they also admonished us that the city did not need to provide advice about planning a festival lighting project and that such information was unnecessary.

In our opinion, underlying these three claims were serious empirical questions that could only be answered by engaging potential users of the content. From an information design perspective, clarifying the legal language was a virtue not a shortcoming. We also adhered to the principle that a document's length should be a function of the content audiences need or expect. In this case, as mentioned earlier, much of the content was unclear, ambiguous, or missing. With regard to the critique about our including advice about planning a festival lighting project, we contended that applicants needed guidance about planning their project because, as our interviews with staff indicated, a poor plan had often led to a rejected application. These controversies about the adequacy of the redesign could have been resolved through usability testing, but instead the legal team derailed the project.

Retrospective

In retrospect, our team had not anticipated the legal team's rejection of a citizen-oriented revision. We had interpreted the mayor's executive order to promote access to public information as a call for clarifying legal language. We also believed it meant giving citizens the content they needed for supporting an error-free application process, which could have saved the city the time and money associated with answering phone calls and re-reviewing rejected applications (Schriver, 1993).

This case study shows that although we were quite skilled in redesigning the documents and in negotiating with the team members we worked with, we were unable to gain support for our activities within a powerful segment of the larger organizational culture. Information designers can draw a lesson from this case.

It is important to understand the needs of all internal stakeholders for a redesign, not only the immediate team members and managers, but also those who may play a role in approving a project directly or indirectly. Information designers must acquire skills in "reading the context." We need to understand the relative power held by various stakeholders within the organization—power that determines how decisions get made and what activities are deemed of value. Information designers must acquire deep knowledge of the broader context in which design takes place in order to anticipate reactions of those who may wield control over their work; for a discussion, see Schriver (2012).

Although it may not be possible to engage all decision makers collaboratively, it may be possible to get their feedback and buy-in on a project before it is too far along toward completion. When people who can exert control over a project do not feel part of design decisions (even if they had opportunities to collaborate and did not), they are more likely to derail or even reject a design solution.

Additionally, the outcome of the project might have been different had we been able to meet our clients face-to-face rather than by collaborating at a distance through email and conference calls. Although we had built good relationships with those team members we had the chance to converse with, there were no opportunities to understand the hierarchy of the organization and the varied internal stakeholders for the project. We assumed the client team had given the legal department progress reports on the project. At the same time, we concluded the legal team would be only concerned with whether the revisions presented the city's codes, rules, and regulations in a clear and accurate manner. We knew they needed to review the final product but did not realize the legal team had authority over whether the redesign would be published. As collaboration expert from Harvard University Richard Hackman points out, distributed teams face unique challenges, making "it is hard to coordinate at a distance if it is unclear who is actually on the team" (Hackman, 2011, p. 33).

In hindsight we should have insisted on at least one face-to-face meeting with all internal stakeholders, including the legal team. If the project had been planned with all decision makers meeting face-to-face, we could have built up a sense of team cohesion, trust, and respect. Had we been able to help the team focus its goals, our final redesign could have been assessed on the basis of those shared goals and values. And if we had been able to garner support for usability testing our prototypes, we would have had empirical evidence for the efficacy of the redesign rather than having it evaluated on the basis of seemingly idiosyncratic criteria.

The larger lesson we can draw from this study of the rhetoric of redesign is that to be effective in bureaucratic settings, information designers must be skilled in three interdependent activities:

- Constructing content (generating ideas for visual and verbal artifacts);
- Connecting content (shaping artifacts rhetorically to meet external stakeholders' needs); and
- Contextualizing design activity (engaging in advocacy to orchestrate buy-in from all important internal stakeholders, with the goal of making design activity visible and valued within the organization).

As information designers develop sophistication in carrying out these activities, they stand a much better chance not only of creating good designs, but also of seeing the fruits of their labor make a difference.

References

Bloomberg, M. R. (2008, July 22). Executive Order No. 120: Citywide Policy on Language Access to Ensure the Effective Delivery of City Services. Retrieved from http://www.nyc.gov/html/om/pdf/2008/pr282-08_eo_120.pdf

Carpenter, P. A., & Just, M. A. (1983). What your eyes do while your mind is reading. In K. Rayner (Ed.), *Eye movements in reading: Perceptual and language processes* (pp. 275-307). NY: Academic Press.

Davies, M. (2010). Corpus of historical American English: 400 million words, 1810–2009 (Linguistic database). Retrieved August 11, 2014, from Brigham Young University, Department of Linguistics and English Language http://corpus.byu.edu/coha/

Davies, M., & Gardner, D. (2010). A frequency dictionary of contemporary American English. New York, NY: Routledge.

Hackman, J. R. (2011). Collaborative intelligence: Usi*ng teams to solve hard problems*. San Francisco, CA: Berrett-Koehler Publishers.

Hudson, P. T. W., & Bergman, M. W. (1985). Lexical knowledge and word recognition: Word length and word frequency in naming and decision tasks. *Journal of Memory and Language, 24*, 46-58.

Jansen, C. J. M., & Steehouder, M. (1992). Forms as a source of communication problems. *Journal of Technical Writing and Communication, 22*, 179–194.

Jarrett, C., & Gaffney, G. (2009). *Forms that work: Designing web forms for usability*. Burlington, MA: Morgan Kaufmann Publishers.

Schriver, K. A. (1989). Evaluating text quality: The continuum from text-focused to reader-focused methods. *IEEE Transactions in Professional Communication, 32*(4), 238–255.

Schriver, K. A. (1992). Teaching writers to anticipate readers' needs: What can document designers learn from usability testing? In H. Pander Maat & M. Steehouder (Eds.), *Studies of functional text quality* (pp. 141–157). Amsterdam: Rodopi Press.

Schriver, K. A. (1993). Quality in document design: Issues and controversies. *Technical Communication, 40*(2), 239–257.

Schriver, K. A. (1997). *Dynamics in document design: Creating texts for readers*. New York, NY: John Wiley & Sons.

Schriver, K. A. (2010). Reading on the Web: Implications for online information design. *Ljubljana Museum of Architecture and Design Lecture Series on Visual Communications Theory: On Information Design*. Retrieved from http://videolectures.net/aml2010_schriver_rotw/

Schriver, K. A. (2012). What we know about expertise in professional communication. In V. W. Berninger (Ed.), *Past, present, and future contributions of cognitive writing research to cognitive psychology* (pp. 275-312). New York, NY: Psychology Press.

Schriver, K. A. (2013). What do technical communicators need to know about information design? In J. Johnson-Eilola & S. Selber (Eds.), *Solving problems in technical communication* (pp. 386-427). Chicago, IL: University of Chicago Press.

Sless, D. (1999). Public forms: Designing and evaluating forms in large organizations. In H. Zwaga, T. Boersema & H. C. M. Hoonhout (Eds.), *Visual information for everyday use: Design and research perspectives* (pp. 135-153). London: Taylor & Francis.

Summers, K., Summers, M., & Pointer, A. (2014). When you need the medicine but can't understand the form: Making prescription medicine available to low-income patients. *Intercom, 61*(2), 11-15.

Zipf, G. K. (1949). *Human behavior and the principle of least effort.* Cambridge, MA: Addison-Wesley.

Biographical Note

Karen Schriver, PhD, is a designing woman on a mission. She helps organizations around the globe realize the social and economic benefits of excellence in information design. As an information designer with an empirical bent, Karen advocates for evidence-based decision-making in writing and visual design. Karen is a former professor of rhetoric and communication design at Carnegie Mellon University (Pittsburgh, Pennsylvania), where she co-directed the graduate programs in professional communication and document design. She created some of the first courses in the United States on integrating word and image, usability testing, and information design. For the past two decades Karen has led her own research and consulting firm, Karen Schriver Associates (KSA), which specializes in improving the quality of communications in technology, science, education, and health. Karen brings expertise in designing content that is clear, usable and memorable for expert or lay audiences—from websites to instructions to educational tools to forms to marketing materials. Karen challenges organizations to re-imagine their design strategies on the basis of research into their everyday practices of writing and design. Karen's clients include Microsoft, Sony, Apple, ATT, IRS, US Postal Service, Sprint, Fujitsu, Mitsubishi, Lutron Electronics, IBM, MIT Press, Hoffman-LaRoche, and the New York City Department of Transportation. Karen's book, *Dynamics in Document Design: Creating Texts for Readers* (New York: Wiley)—now in its 9th printing—is regarded as an essential work in the field. An internationally acclaimed leader in the field, Karen has been a guest speaker for writers and designers in Japan, South Africa, Brazil, France, Netherlands, Belgium, UK, Canada, Spain, Portugal, and Slovenia. Winner of 11 national awards for her research and communication design, Karen has appeared on TV, radio and websites. Karen has served on the Board of Directors for the Center for Plain Language (Washington, DC) and is a Fellow of the Communication Research Institute (Melbourne, Australia). Her ongoing research investigates (1) the nature of expertise in information design, and (2) how reading online is shaped by the design of text and graphics.

Chapter 12: The Development of Visual Information about Medicines in Europe

Karel van der Waarde & Carla Spinillo

Abstract

In Europe, the design of information about medicines as it appears on medicine boxes and package leaflets is strictly regulated. 'Design' is seen as important because it is mentioned in both legislation and guidelines. The European law, Directive 2004/27/EC, and the Readability Guideline of 2009 advises recognize information design and encourages companies "to ensure that the design facilitates navigation and access to information." The inclusion of design in these legal documents is fairly unique. The chapter will explore the design relevant existing regulations and the intricacies of their implementation.

European Laws Appreciate Design

In Europe, the design of information about medicines as it appears on medicine boxes and package leaflets is strictly regulated. 'Design' is seen as important because it is mentioned in both legislation and guidelines. The European law (Directive 2004/27/EC) states that *"The package leaflet must be written and designed to be clear and understandable, enabling the users to act appropriately, when necessary with the help of health professionals."* The Readability Guideline of 2009 advises that *"Companies are encouraged to seek advice from specialists in information design when devising their house style for the package leaflet to ensure that the design facilitates navigation and access to information."* The inclusion of design in these legal documents is fairly unique: very few laws acknowledge the role of design in the development of visual information.

Practical Implications: Medicines and Information

In order to register a medicine, it is necessary to provide all the information about a medicine to the Regulatory authorities. These authorities carefully check if the benefits of a medicine outweigh the risks, and if a medicine is really safe enough to be given to patients. Apart from the medico-pharmacological decisions, these authorities also have the responsibility to check wether the visual information is correct and if it is suitable for patients. In the last two decades, a range of guidelines, templates and advice was published that should help the pharmaceutical industry to write, design and test visual information. These documents should also help the authorities to check if visual information conforms to these guidelines.

After about fifteen years of substantial efforts, the package leaflets in Europe do not seem to have improved very much. They still follow the description that Walter Modell – editor of Clinical Pharmacology Therapeutics - provided in 1967: "The stuffers are generally printed in Lilliputian type of bible paper, hard to handle and very difficult to read."

Despite the attention for design in the legislation, it seems unclear why we do not develop information that really enables people to use medicines and why it takes so long to improve matters. Two examples provide a glimpse of the reasoning behind this.

Example 1: Design of a Pictogram

The first example describes the reaction of the authorities and pharmaceutical industry about a pictogram. This pictogram was drawn for a medicine that is only given in a hospital as an infusion ("a drip"). It would never be used on its own, but always with an accompanying text: "Farnilon is given to you through a drip in a vein (an infusion)."

Farnilon is given to you through a drip in a vein (an infusion).

Figure 1: A combination of a pictogram and text to indicate how a medicine is given to patients.

The combination of this text and pictogram indicates that the medicine would be given as an infusion. Furthermore, the visual prominence of the pictogram, as it was the only pictorial element on a package leaflet, would attract the attention of a patient immediately. This makes it easier for patients to interpret the information in the leaflet, because it implies that the medicine will be given by a nurse and that there is no need to consider the correct dosage, time of taking it or frequency. If the pictogram is not included, patients assume that they have to take this medicine themselves. This would lead to confusions like "why does this leaflet state in the instructions that I must calculate the dose, while it is given by a nurse?"

The reaction of 60 patients during a readability test indicated that the combination of the text and the pictogram was well understood. Most participants gestured with the index finger of their right hand to a vein in their left arm to indicate where the needle would be inserted.

When the pictogram was submitted, both the pharmaceutical company and the regulatory authorities objected. The first main objection was that the pictogram suggests that an infusion is always given in an arm. Although this is the most likely vein, it is sometimes necessary to use another vein. In those situations, the pictogram is incorrect. A second objection was that – if this pictogram was approved – it might be used by other infusion medicines too. Approving this pictogram creates a precedent and makes this pictogram the standard. It cannot be assumed that this is the best possible pictogram: there might be better alternatives. On the basis of both these objections, the pictogram was rejected.

Example 2: The Materials of a Readability Test

The second example describes the assumptions of the authorities about a readability test. The European legislation makes it obligatory to conduct usability tests on package leaflets. The official phrase is: *"The package leaflet shall reflect the results of consultations with target patient groups to ensure that it is legible, clear and easy to use."* Again, this is a laudable attempt to make sure that package leaflets are usable. The readability guideline advises: *"User testing means to test the readability of a specimen with a group of selected test subjects."*

Until recently (June 2010), it was acceptable to use mock-ups of leaflets in a readability test. These were high-quality double-sided laser prints on thin paper (60-70 grams). People who take part in a readability test have to handle these mock-ups: they have to find specific information in the leaflet and they have to be able to explain in their own words what this information means to them. The number of interviews is usually limited to 5 interviews in a pilot test and two series of ten people in the main test. After the pilot test, details of the text and the design of the leaflet are modified. In most user tests, two versions of leaflets are therefore used: the pilot test leaflet, and the modified leaflet for the main test of 20 interviews.

Since the end of July 2010, the European Medicines Agency (EMA) requires to use printed specimen for a readability test. A printed specimen is a leaflet that is printed on a production press. This is based on the assumption that people would be able to distinguish between a mock-ups and a specimen and that this difference has an effect on the results of the readability test. Unfortunately, there is no evidence that this is the case. The practical costs and time-delays to make 5 prints – and after some corrections another 20 prints – on a production press are substantial.

Current Situation: Fundamentally Different Assumptions?

These two examples are part of a pattern. Both examples highlight that there is a difference in perspective about the value of empirical arguments during the development of information about medicines. The process for the *approval of medicines* is used as the starting point. This approval requires substantial and reliable empirical evidence as it can be provided by scientific experiments. A scientific study on a limited number of people or products might not reveal major issues and is unlikely to produce reliable findings. Asking for production specimen does make sense in a scientific environment.

In contrast, the process for the *approval of information* requires reliable empirical evidence that shows that the majority of the problematic issues has been eliminated. A readability study that involves a limited number people will reveal the majority of the issues related to finding, understanding and application of information. The above mentioned pictogram – with the accompanying text - was understood by all test-participants when they looked at a high quality laser print. More test participants or a better print quality would not have altered the results.

At the moment, according to the regulatory authorities, 'information' needs to be supported by empirical evidence that is comparable to the evidence that is required for the registration of medicines. This is not only required for 'pictograms' and 'test materials' but also applies to visual elements like 'typeface,' 'typesize,' 'the use of bold and italic type,' and 'colour.'

Unfortunately, it would be very hard to conduct all the necessary experiments that could support all the decisions that are required to design a leaflet. A question like: "can you provide statistical evidence that bold type attracts the attention of elderly people" baffles designers, but is normal from a regulatory point of view.

For this reason, most designs of package leaflets and packaging follow existing examples and the readability guideline as closely as possible to avoid having to supply additional supportive evidence that is unlikely to be available. The result of this approach is that patients do not receive information in a format that is optimally useful in a specific situation.

Results: And a Way Forward

It is fairly easy to learn some lessons based on this European experience. If it is necessary to provide patients with appropriate information about their medicines, then it seems worthwhile to carefully consider at the following four points:

1. It is necessary to develop a "writing-designing-testing-process" in such a way that it incorporates all stakeholders. The assumptions of these stakeholders must be clarified.
2. The legislation and guidance must be performance based. The criteria for acceptable arguments need to be spelled out.
3. The legislation and guidance must allow for – and probably even stimulate – improvements and innovation.
4. The legislation and guidance must start from "best practice" and it should be tested before they are implemented.

These four points require a shift from "clear and understandable" to "enabling the users to act appropriately." Until that is accepted, it is likely that patients will receive poor, non-personalized, hard to update, text-oriented, context-free information about their medicines. In order to provide patients with information that suits their needs, it seems necessary to reconsider the prevailing assumptions and develop alternative prototypes that show that changes are required and possible.

Biographical notes

Karel van der Waarde studied graphic design in the Netherlands (The Design Academy, Eindhoven) and in the UK (De Montfort University, Leicester and the University of Reading). He received his doctorate in 1994 for a dissertation entitled: *An investigation into the suitability of the graphic presentation of patient package inserts.*

In 1995, he started a design - research consultancy in Belgium specializing in the testing of information design. His company develops patient information leaflets, instructions, forms, protocols, and the information architecture for websites. Most of the projects are related to information about medicines for patients, doctors and pharmacists.

Avans University of Applied Sciences (Breda, The Netherlands) appointed him as scholar in Visual Rhetoric between 2006 and 2014. It was a research post to investigate the development and use of visual communication with a longer term aim to support the relations between practice, research and education.

Karel van der Waarde frequently publishes and lectures about visual information. Publications have appeared in Dutch, Polish, Japanese, English, Spanish, Turkish and Portuguese.

Van der Waarde is a life-Fellow of the Communications Research Institute (Melbourne, Australia), a board member of International Institute for Information Design (IIID, Vienna, Austria) and editorial board member of *Information Design Journal*, *Journal of Visual Communication*, the *Poster* and *Visible Language*.

Carla Spinillo's biographical note appears in page 265.

Chapter 13: Regulating Information for People—How Information Design Has Made a Difference in the Ways in Which Governments and Industry Regulate Information

David Sless

Abstract

The Communication Research Institute (CRI) has been at the forefront of medicine information reform since 1985. Their research in the 1980s revealed that many of the problems related to poor usage of medications and non-compliance of medicines instructions were due to the content-based approach of regulations that underpinned the poor design of medicine information on labels and leaflets. Instead, CRI insisted that regulators should adopt a performance-based, not a content-based, approach. Achieving such a radical paradigm shift in regulators seemed almost impossible, but using information design principles and methods dating from the 1970s, CRI developed a systematic and rigorous process of testing and redesigning to ensure that information reached an acceptable level of performance and compliance, and showed that the only way to reach such a level was by ignoring the existing regulations.

The success of their designs led, in 2004, to a change in the Australian regulations for the labelling of non-prescriptive medicines. Now, ten years later, it is possible that the regulations will revert to a content-based approach. Sless calls for vigilance on the part of all information designers in the face of this retrograde step.

One of my main activities over the last 40 years has been to help organisations develop regulations that can lead to good information design: designs which respect and value the people who have to use the information, and which lead to measurable improvements in the ongoing dialogue between organisations and the people they serve.

Governments and industry regulate a great deal of information that people use in daily life: product labelling, instructions, contracts, policies, letters, bills, forms, statements, web sites, highway signs, public information symbols; the list goes on...

I am going to focus on one area where my colleagues and I have had some modest success, namely medicine information—in particular medicine labelling and medicine information for patients and consumers.

This is not easy work. It is at the site of conflicting interests between regulators, industry, consumers, and health professionals. Within pharmaceutical companies there are tensions between marketing and regulatory affairs departments. From a design point of view it is highly constrained work with little room for radical innovation. There are many barriers to achieving good outcomes and many failures along the way; but it is not impossible, and it is important.

Medicines are information-dependent products. Without information, they can be dangerous, harmful, even lethal. According the FDA (2013), citing an Institute of Medicine Report, medication errors are a significant public health concern that account for an estimated 7,000 deaths annually in the United States. The report cited labelling and packaging issues as the cause of 33% of all medication errors and 30% of fatalities from medication errors.

With easily usable information medicines can be safe, helpful, even life saving.

I am focusing on this area because information designers now have a substantial body of practice and research to give an overview that can be used in this and other areas where organisations seek to regulate information for public use.

Starting Point and Precedents

In 1985 I was invited by government and industry to set up the body that became the Communication Research Institute (CRI). Our remit was to help industry and government improve their communication with the public.

The CRI research was able to draw on a substantial body of prior research in design methods (e.g., Jones 1970), document designs (e.g., Felker et al 1980) and specifically in information design (e.g., Easterby & Zwaga 1984). Moreover, a growing number of significant case histories published in *Information Design Journal* provided an emerging view of professional practice in the field (e.g. Goodwin 1984, Tomaselli & Tomaselli 1984, Waller 1984). This early work suggested the possibility of a unified set of highly productive information design methods whose quality could be measured (Wright 1979).

We first demonstrated this publicly in a model case history (Fisher & Sless 1990); by 1992, it was possible to suggest that the resulting design methods had a wide general application to information design (Sless 1992).

One of the areas we looked at was the package labelling of such things as medicines, garden products and household chemicals. Our investigation of the problem domain in Australia (Shulman & Sless 1992) revealed that both the content and appearance of the information on these products were totally constrained by UK and USA government regulations, which had originated in the 19th century in the attempt to control access to dangerous chemicals in the UK, and to control the purity of chemicals available to the public in the USA. The dominant professions within these regulatory bodies were (and still are) pharmacists, doctors and chemists.

These regulations determined how such products could be made available to the public: by special license, through a doctor's prescription, by a pharmacist, or on open shelves in retail stores. The regulations prescribed the exact content, layout, typography and colours that could be used on the labelling. The result, as you would expect, were blind to information design (ID) considerations. You can see this in Figures 1 and 2.

In Figure 1, a page from the regulations of the 1990s, the heavy use of all caps and the specification of font sizes in millimetres is a clear indication of the absence of ID expertise.

SCHEDULE 2

ACETIC ACID (excluding its salts and derivatives) and preparations containing more than
    80 per cent of acetic acid, CH_3COOH for therapeutic use.

ALOXIPRIN.

ANTAZOLINE in eye drops.

ASPIRIN **except:**

    (a)   when included in Schedule 4 or 6;

    (b)   in individually wrapped powders or sachets of granules each containing
        650 milligrams or less of aspirin as the only therapeutically active constituent
        other than an effervescent agent when enclosed in a primary pack that:

        (i)   contains not more than 12 such powders or sachets of granules;

        (ii)   is labelled with the warning statement:

            WARNING - THIS MEDICATION MAY BE DANGEROUS
            WHEN USED IN LARGE AMOUNTS OR FOR A LONG
            PERIOD; or

            CAUTION - THIS PREPARATION IS FOR THE RELIEF OF
            MINOR AND TEMPORARY AILMENTS AND SHOULD
            BE USED STRICTLY AS DIRECTED. PROLONGED USE
            WITHOUT MEDICAL SUPERVISION COULD BE
            HARMFUL; and

        (iii)   includes in the directions for use, in capital letters not less than
            1.5 mm in height, the warning statements:

            CONSULT A DOCTOR BEFORE GIVING THIS
            MEDICATION TO CHILDREN OR TEENAGERS WITH
            CHICKEN POX, INFLUENZA OR FEVER; and

            CAUTION - DO NOT GIVE TO CHILDREN UNDER TWO
            YEARS OF AGE EXCEPT ON DOCTOR'S ADVICE; or

Figure 1: Australia regulations on aspirin labelling, 1990.

The crude design of the prescribed layout further indicates this absence (Figure 2).

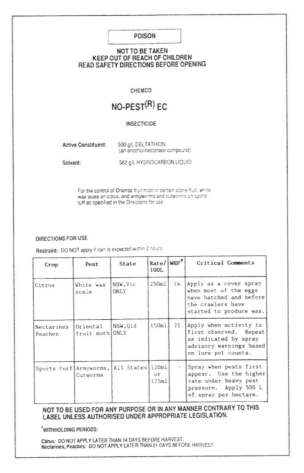

Figure 2: The Australian prescribed layout for an insecticide.

The issue ran deeper. In correspondence and discussions with regulators, we began to see other aspects of the issue. In response to a letter we wrote to a senior regulator about the usability of current labelling, we were firmly but politely told that:

> ...the purpose of the label is to conform with the regulations.

In 1988, at a joint seminar with regulators, after we pointed out that some of their typographic decisions made the labels potentially more difficult to use, one of the senior technical staff asked:

> Are you trying to suggest that we make the labels easier for consumers to use?

When we replied "Yes!" he said:

> *Gosh, that is radical!*

I often repeat that story in my meetings with regulators today and ask them whether they are ready to embrace such a radical change. Too frequently, they answer:

> *No!*

or

> *Not entirely.*

An increasing number, however, do want to reform the regulatory process and its outcomes.

This then is the environment into which we have continued to intervene on behalf of the public. To do so we have needed three things: a clear strategy for moving forward, committed supporters from within the community of stakeholders, and financial support to enable us to undertake the work.

Moving Forward

Art Shulman and I (Shulman & Sless 1992) suggested the following by way of redefining the problem:

> ...the central problem with the current regulation and design of labels is that it seeks to control and manage the wrong thing. It seeks to control content: that is, the information on the label. It does not seek to manage the dynamic relationship between label and consumer. Until both regulation and design concentrate on what actually happens when people use information, rather than just look at the information alone, we will only ever get partial control, leading perhaps to the appearance of good labelling (readability and presentation), but not the substance (comprehension and appropriate action). (Shulman & Sless 1992, p70)

We suggested a way forward:

> If industry, government and consumer groups can agree that a central purpose of labelling regulation is to ensure that consumers can use products appropriately, then the regulations should focus on the making it possible for consumers to behave appropriately.

> If this strategy were adopted, label designers would have to satisfy regulators on this central question: Can consumers use the product appropriately by reading the label? To answer the question, the designer

would be required by regulation to provide test results that show whether a particular label satisfies predefined criteria of appropriate product use.

Although this is a radically new way of regulating labelling, there is nothing inherently novel about this approach to regulation. Regulations require that the drugs and chemicals available to consumers have to go through testing processes before they are approved. Drugs and chemicals are tested for their performance, not just their content.

To make the contrast between the old and the new, we distinguished between the two approaches: the existing approach as *content-based regulation*, and the new approach as *performance-based regulation*.

Performance-based Regulation

The idea of performance-based regulation was not new. Many of us in information design had been working on it for some time.

For example, in the field of public information symbols, standards organisations at the national and international levels had been working on developing methods for designing and testing symbols for public use since the mid sixties, and the methods being used had by the 1970s achieved some degree of maturity (Zwaga & Easterby 1984).

The performance criterion in that case was whether people could comprehend a particular symbol at an adequate level, so that it could be used in public places. This work subsequently led to a large body of standards, both national and international (Adams 2011).

At CRI, we were able to build on this work in a number of high profile projects which we published as case histories, all of which used performance-based rather than content-based criteria to determine whether or not the designed information had reached an acceptable level of performance (Fisher & Sless 1980, MacKenzie 1992, Sless 1992).

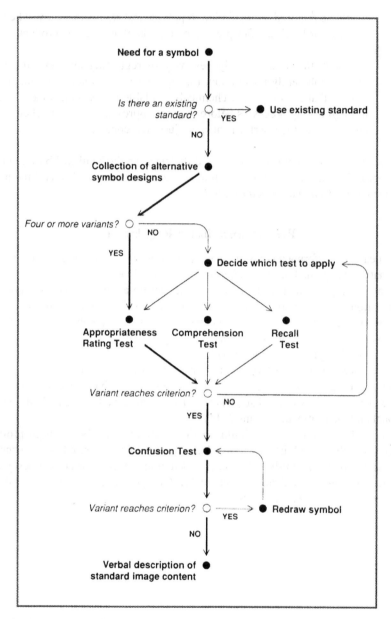

Figure 3: Procedure for the development of public information symbols (Zwaga and Easterby 1984).

Building on this work in later projects, we found that the best way of achieving these performance outcomes was by using a systematic and rigorous process, applied to and refined across a wide range of industries. We have articulated this process as a diagram (Figure 4).

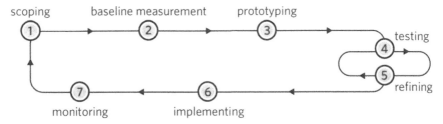

Figure 4: the CRI information design process.

For a detailed discussion of some of this work, its consequences and implications, see Sless (2008) and Tyers (2008).

The Paradigm Shift from Content to Performance

We have discovered that regulators find the shift from content to performance extremely difficult, particularly as all the available precedents are content-based within a scientific rather than design paradigm. Moreover, there is an implicit assumption in content-based regulation that if you control the content, you somehow control people's behaviour and they will use the information appropriately. In part, this derives from the legislative and legalistic framework within which the regulations are formulated—in which meaning and control are *in the words*—and there is an obvious tendency among regulators to focus on careful and precise specification of content.

The implicit belief in the control of content also derives from the human factors, social science, and applied science research literature from which regulators typically draw. These disciplines traditionally work with the assumptions of a mechanistic stimulus-response paradigm, using controlled experiments to determine the effects on behaviour of isolated variables—in the case of information, variables such as word size and colour. The regulations that result from this approach consist of a collection of content specifications on the assumption that if you get the individual parts right, the appropriate consumer behaviours will follow.

Figure 5 gives a typical example from a recent draft of Australian Medicine Regulations,

6.1 Prescription medicines

6.1.1 Font size of names

For registered medicines with less than four active ingredients, the name and quantity of the active ingredients is to be in a sans serif font at least the equivalent of 15 point Arial on the main label [subsection 9(7)(a)].

For prescription medicines with at least four active ingredients, the active ingredient names and quantities must be in a sans serif font that is the equivalent of at least 12 point Arial on the main, side or rear label [subsection 9(8)(a)].

Figure 5: Extract from *Guidelines for the Labelling of Medicines* Draft – Version 1.0, August 2014, TGA.

Two typographical features (sans serif font, and point size) are specified. I could spend the whole of this chapter explaining why, from an information design point of view, this is inadequate and will not guarantee the desired outcome, but instead I shall use an extract from a recent FDA (USA) draft regulation on the same subject, which sums up the problem, if not the solution, in relation to text in general (Figure 6).

> **Readability:** *Readability* refers to the ease with which a reader can scan over paragraphs of type. Readability is dependent on the manipulation or handling of the type. A highly legible typeface can be made unreadable by poor typographic design. Factors that affect readability include: line lengths, point size, leading, typeface selection, spacing, type alignment, and background.

Figure 6: Guidance for Industry. Safety Considerations for Container Labels and Carton Labeling Design to Minimize Medication Errors. DRAFT GUIDANCE. FDA April 2013.

These guidelines mention seven typographical features. Here is an acknowledgement that poor typographic design can lead to undesirable outcomes, and provides a reason why the Australian example is worse than useless. The FDA also summarises some of the factors involved. Unfortunately, it stops short of saying what is good typographic design. Indeed, this is the nub of the problem for regulators: with a professional background in pharmacy, medicine and chemistry they are unlikely to also have a professional background in typographic design, let alone information design, or even a sensitivity to what these might involve.

The difficulty lies, in part, in the immense effort required by regulators to cast aside their reliance on scientific methods offering piecemeal generalisations that cannot be demonstrated to work in particular contexts, and embrace instead those craft-based design processes and methods which offer the possibility of evidence-based outcomes.

Regulatory Requirements in a Performance-based and Evidence-based Approach

The performance-based approach starts with the question: What are the tasks we want consumers to perform with the labelling?

This work is undertaken at what we call the scoping stage (see Figure 4) and is discussed in detail in Sless (2004). The beauty of this approach, if regulators could be persuaded to embrace it, is that they can abandon their amateur attempts at typography that are doomed to fail, concentrate on specifying the outcomes they want to achieve, and learn how to read and evaluate evidence-based test results.

Figure 7 shows a generic set of performance requirements taken from the Australian Self Medication Industry (ASMI) Code of Practice:

PERFORMANCE TASKS. ASMI CODE OF PRACTICE 2004

IDENTIFY & SELECT	USE	STORE	DISPOSE OF
AT THE POINT OF SALE	*AT THE POINT OF USE*		
1. can locate and read product name	5. can locate, read and understand product description	10. can locate, read and understand storage instructions	11. can locate and read expiry date
2. can locate and read quantity	6. can locate and read product ingredients		
3. can identify what the product is used for	7. can locate, read and understand dosage and usage instructions		
4. can identify circumstances under which the product should not be used	8. can locate, read and understand any warnings		
	9. can locate and read information/enquiry number		

Figure 7

Figure 8 shows an elaboration and refinement of the above generic performance requirements developed specifically to account for the situation where consumers need to differentiate between a range of products within an umbrella brand. The differentiation tasks are shown in yellow.

1. IDENTIFY	**2. SELECT**	**3. USE**
1. Locate, read and recognise brand	3. Locate and read brand	14. Locate and explain new product description
2. Locate and read product names	4. Locate and read new product name	15. Locate and read new product ingredients
	5. Locate, read and explain new product strength	16. Locate, read and explain dosage and usage instructions
	6. Identify what symptoms the new product is used for	17. Locate, read and explain any warnings
	7. Differentiate between the products in the range	18. Locate and read information/ enquiry number
	8. Explain circumstances under which to choose the new product	**4. STORE**
	9. Identify under what circumstances the new product should not be used	19. Locate, read and explain storage instructions
	10. Locate and read active ingredients of new product	**5. DISPOSE**
	11. Locate, read and explain dosage and usage instructions of new product	20. Locate and read expiry date
	12. Locate and read quantity	
	13. Locate and read expiry date	

Figure 8: Consumer performance tasks for choosing and then using an OTC medicine that is part of an umbrella brand.

By way of contrast, Figure 9 shows a set of performance requirements for credit card statements.

IDENTIFICATION TASKS	BASIC USAGE TASKS	INTERACTIVE TASKS
Identify what the document is (a credit card statement)	Find and explain the date range covered by the statement	Find and explain how to make a payment*
Find and identify who is providing the statement (company name)	Find and explain the opening balance	Find and explain how to find more information
	Find and explain the closing balance	
Identify who the credit card statement is for (name, address, account number)	Identify the total of any cash advances for the statement period and the interest rate that applies*	
Find and explain the statement period (i.e. monthly statement, annual statement)	Identify the total of any purchases for the statement period and the interest rate that applies	
	Find and explain any interest that has been charged to the account	
	Identify any transaction dates	
	Find and explain any transaction descriptions	
	Find and explain the overall credit limit	
	Find and explain any available credit	
	Find and explain any payments that have been made*	
	Find and explain any payments due (when, how much, any overdue amounts)*	
	Find and explain any terms and conditions*	
	Find and explain how many pages are included in the statement	

Figure 9: Performance requirements from an international study of credit card statements (Sless 2009).

Lists like those above are developed in consultation with all the stakeholders from government, industry and consumers. They become the core of the regulations alongside a statement about the target performance level that these stakeholders want to achieve.

Figure 10 shows a typical target performance-level statement.

what should people be able to do with labels

Figure 10: Target performance level for OTC medicines in Australia.

Once all stakeholders have agreed the performance requirements, we apply rigorous information design methods to develop a solution. This is tested with consumers and refined until it reaches the point where it is possible to demonstrate with evidence that consumers can perform these tasks at the specified level.

The Model Projects

Outside the area of medicines information design, we had long before demonstrated the practical value of this performance-based and evidence-based approach. However, we needed to satisfy the many stakeholders that this approach was applicable to regulating medicines information

Patient Leaflets and Writing about Medicines for People

Our first project opportunity came when we were awarded the contract to develop usability guidelines for consumer medicines information (CMI). This resulted in the publication of *Writing about medicines for people* (Sless & Shrensky, 2006, 3rd edition). A detailed account of the methods used to develop the original guidelines (1994) was published by the Australian Language and Literacy Council as an example of best practice in accessible documents in the private sector (Penman, Sless, & Wiseman, 1996).

From our point of view, as information designers, three important findings came out of this work:

1. The main factor that affected people's ability to use CMI was the order of the headings under which information was presented. This is shown in the first column of Figure 11, and contrasts sharply with the conventional order still in use today by regulators.

Optimum structure for consumers (1994) tested for usability	Conventional order used by Regulators (2014) untested for usability
Before you begin to use this medicine	Ingredients,
What [this medicine] looks like	Uses OR What this medicine is used for
What [this medicine] does	Warnings,
When you must not take [this medicine]	Directions for use
Before you use [this medicine]	Other information.
How much of [this medicine] to take	
When to take [this medicine]	
After you use [this medicine]	
Other things you must do while taking [this medicine]	
Things you must be careful of doing/must not do while taking [this medicine]	
What to do if you forget to take [this medicine]	
What to do if [this medicine] does not work	
Side effects	
What to do if somebody accidentally swallows [this medicine]	
What to do if someone takes too much of [this medicine]	
Where to keep [this medicine]	
What to do with [this medicine] when you have finished with it	
Ingredients	
Further information	

Figure 11: The optimum order of headings in CMI contrasted with the regulators' preferred order.

Not surprisingly, the regulators (using no test data) put the ingredients at the top of the list, while consumers (based on our test data) find it easier if it is at the bottom of the list.

Notice how the consumers' optimum order is based on the temporal sequence of tasks they undertake in using the medicine, whereas the regulators' order follows their view of what they regard as most important. Moreover, consumers have a much more elaborated and rich sense of the tasks they have to perform with the medicine compared to the regulators' impoverished view. These differences give you a direct sense of the political background against which consumer medicine information is fought over, and the conflicting positions adopted by information designers representing medicine users and regulators representing their scientific interests in medicines.

2. In other work we had undertaken, most notably in forms design, we developed a technique of writing highly usable document grammars: a set of carefully developed and user-tested rules for combining the different functional elements within a document into consistent patterns that enabled readers to effectively navigate through documents, and to read the information that helped them perform tasks with the document.

In the case of CMI this came down to three main features in the following order:

*   Headings: used to navigate through the document
*   Instructions: telling you what to do
*   Explanations: explaining and elaborating the instruction

The most important rules governing these elements was the order: headings first, followed by instructions, and, where needed, explanations.

You can see this document grammar at work in Figure 12 in three different extracts for CMI.

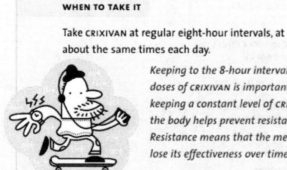

WHEN TO TAKE IT

Take CRIXIVAN at regular eight-hour intervals, at about the same times each day.

Keeping to the 8-hour interval between doses of CRIXIVAN is important because keeping a constant level of CRIXIVAN in the body helps prevent resistance. Resistance means that the medicine may lose its effectiveness over time.

How to take YAZ

→ **Take your first pink (active) tablet from the green area on the blister pack corresponding to the day of the week.**
Each blister pack is marked with the day of the week.

→ **Swallow the tablet whole with a glass of water.**
It does not matter if you take this medicine before or after food.

> ### STORAGE
> Keep Coumadin in the bottle until it is time to take it.
>
> Do not store Coumadin, or any other medicines, in the bathroom or near a sink.
> *Heat and dampness can ruin some medicines.*
>
> Keep Coumadin in a cool, dry place where the temperature stays below 30 degrees C.
>
> Do not leave the tablets in the car or on a window sill on hot days.
>
> Keep it where young children cannot reach it.
> *A locked cupboard at least one-and-a-half metres (5 feet) above the ground is a good place to store medicines.*

Figure 12: Three CMIs using different typography and layouts but the same document grammar.

While each of these examples show quite different fonts and weights, they still follow a consistent pattern of headings, instructions and, where necessary, explanations. Each functional element plays the same part in a CMI, even though their appearances differ. They each answer a different question for the reader.

- Heading: where am I?
- Instruction: what should I do?
- Explanation: why?

When we looked into the technical constraints on CMI production—most of which would be made available to consumers on demand at the point of dispensing rather than as package inserts—we discovered that the print engine to be used was limited to certain standard laser printer fonts—Times Roman and

Helvetica—and the typographic control of the output was limited something equivalent to WinWord 3.0, which came out in 1992. To this day, this remains the platform on which CMI are printed and made available to the public online as pdf files (TGA, 2014). Figure 13 shows the basic typographical styles and layouts available for CMI, and you can see the styles of headings, instructions and explanations available even in this crude typography.

Figure 13: Typographical styles available for CMI printed in Australian pharmacies.

Despite many attempts, we have failed to persuade the industry or the regulators to update this design, which was already out of date with available technology when we first introduced it in 1994. This gives you a further insight into the constraints surrounding this type of work.

Meanwhile, in the European Union (EU), large sections of *Writing About Medicines for People* were copied by EU regulators and used as the basis for EU regulations. Because the original 'copying' was informed neither by information design principles nor by a performance based approach to regulation, it led to many implementation problems; the document has gone through multiple revisions and is still best seen as a work in progress. You can see the latest iterations of the templates here: http://www.ema.europa.eu/ema /index.jsp?curl=pages/regulation/document_listing/document_listing_000134.jsp &murl=menus/regulations/regulations.jsp&mid=WC0b01ac0580022c59

Medicine Packaging: Proving that ID Leads to Improvement

There had been some attempts by industry to develop better packaging labels by applying what they described as 'Plain English.' We suggested that they could do better, and obtained an Australian government grant from the government to demonstrate this. Like the last project, this one was highly constrained—but because we were working with packaging, we could use professional graphics packages that had been unavailable to us in the CMI project (Rogers et al 1995).

Figure 14 shows the designs and results for one of the packages we tested, showing the percentage of consumers who gave correct responses to the 15 critical performance tasks associated with using these labels.

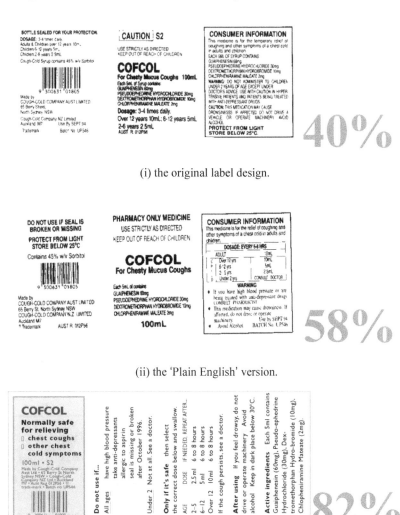

(i) the original label design.

(ii) the 'Plain English' version.

(iii) the CRI version.

Figure 14: Three labels tested by CRI and their performance (1995).

We also demonstrated in this project that in order to make the labels usable we had to violate the current labelling regulations. The point was not lost on industry, consumers, or government.

Our findings were taken up by two government inquiries (Industry Commission 1995, Federal Bureau of Consumer Affairs 1995). We were funded by these inquiries to hold a forum at which we invited all the key interests in labelling regulation—consumer groups, industry, and the regulators—to discuss the future of labelling regulation in Australia (Seymour 1996).

As a result of that process, the then Minister for Small Business and Consumer Affairs (Geoffrey Prosser) announced a major initiative to overhaul the regulations, talking about a new era of *Performance-Based Labelling*. Unfortunately (for us and consumers), he had to resign from his Ministerial position in July 1997 because of improper business dealings, and the bureaucrats in Consumer Affairs quickly changed the initiative to *Performance-Based Labelling Regulation*— not quite the same thing—and quietly forgot about the new era.

Therefore, it goes.

However, the medicine regulators, industry and consumers did not forget.

Medicine Packaging: Evidence from ID That Changed the Regulations

In 2002 we were invited by Glaxo Smith Kline (GSK) to undertake a project to redesign Panadol labelling. Panadol is a well-known brand of paracetamol, widely available in pharmacies and retail outlets in Australia, the UK and other jurisdictions. Our work went through four stages.

In the first, we developed a set of performance requirements for Panadol: tasks that consumers should be able to perform with the packaging and agreed to by GSK. We tested the existing Panadol packaging with consumers.

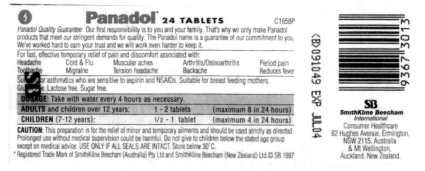

Figure 15: the existing Panadol packaging.

Using the results, we develop a new pack that was more likely to meet the performance requirements, unconstrained by the then current labelling regulations. To remove any strong association with the brand, we rebranded the pack to look more generic, and tested the new label with consumers.

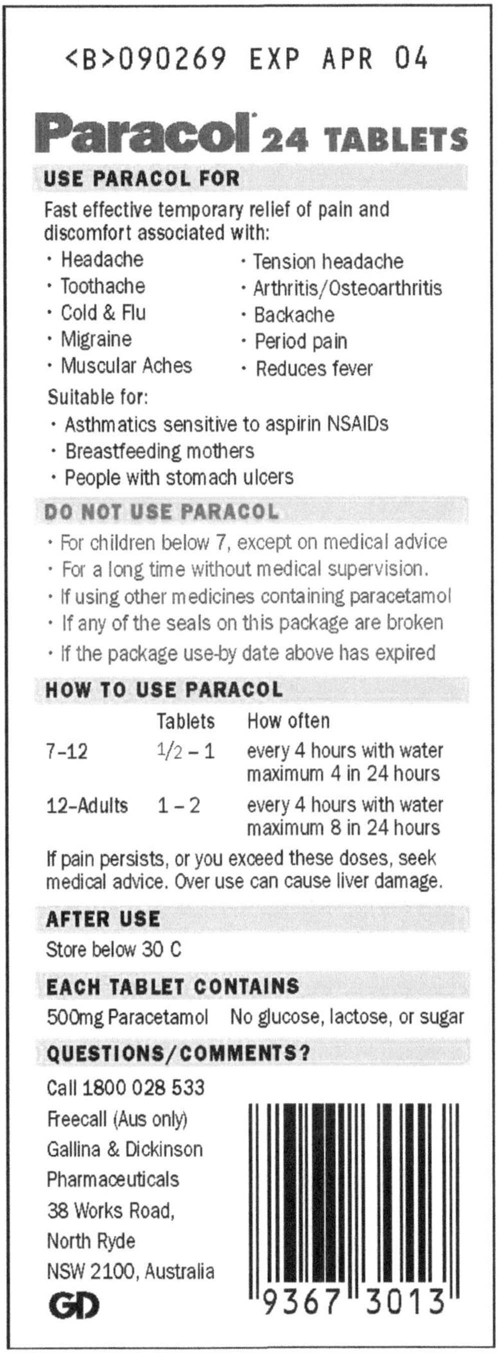

<B>090269 EXP APR 04

Paracol 24 TABLETS

USE PARACOL FOR

Fast effective temporary relief of pain and discomfort associated with:

- Headache
- Toothache
- Cold & Flu
- Migraine
- Muscular Aches
- Tension headache
- Arthritis/Osteoarthritis
- Backache
- Period pain
- Reduces fever

Suitable for:

- Asthmatics sensitive to aspirin NSAIDs
- Breastfeeding mothers
- People with stomach ulcers

DO NOT USE PARACOL

- For children below 7, except on medical advice
- For a long time without medical supervision.
- If using other medicines containing paracetamol
- If any of the seals on this package are broken
- If the package use-by date above has expired

HOW TO USE PARACOL

	Tablets	How often
7–12	1/2 – 1	every 4 hours with water maximum 4 in 24 hours
12–Adults	1 – 2	every 4 hours with water maximum 8 in 24 hours

If pain persists, or you exceed these doses, seek medical advice. Over use can cause liver damage.

AFTER USE

Store below 30 C

EACH TABLET CONTAINS

500mg Paracetamol   No glucose, lactose, or sugar

QUESTIONS/COMMENTS?

Call 1800 028 533
Freecall (Aus only)
Gallina & Dickinson
Pharmaceuticals
38 Works Road,
North Ryde
NSW 2100, Australia

GD

9367 3013

Figure 16: New (generic) packaging, non-compliant with the regulations.

Finally, we created Panadol packaging that incorporated our findings from both the existing and generic packaging, but this time complying with the then current regulations. As before, we tested the packaging with consumers.

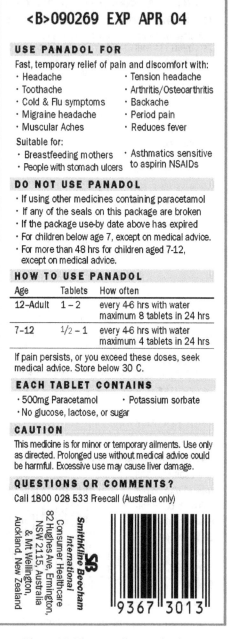

Figure 17: The compliant packaging.

The results showed that both the new generic and the compliant instructions performed above the existing instructions. But it also showed that the compliant instructions gave rise to some difficulties that were not present in the new instructions.

TASK	CURRENT DESIGN (%)	NEW DESIGN (%)	COMPLIANT DESIGN (%)
Finding information	87	97	92
Using information	72	96	89

Figure 18: Results from the testing of different Panadol packaging

These results were made available to the regulators, consumer groups, industry and other stakeholders, and a committee was established under the auspices of the Australian Self Medication Industry (ASMI) to develop an industry code of practice. This was published by CRI in 2004 (ASMI 2004). At the same time, the regulator published a new set of regulations, which for the first time were performance based.

Figure 19: the first-ever performance-based regulations for information, 2004.

Since then we have been helping industry develop new designs that comply with this code of practice.

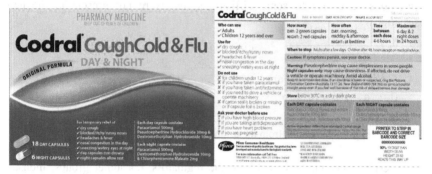

Figure 20: Example of CRI-designed package label developed after 2004 (enlarged).

Gloomy Prospects

Nothing stays the same, and change is not inevitable. We are today in danger of losing many of the advances we have made over the last thirty years. As I write, the Australian medicines regulator—the TGA (2014b)—has just put out a draft of a new set of labelling guidelines that, if implemented, would reverse almost all the gains of the last few years. The retrograde step back to a content-based set of regulations is evident in this document.

So our achievements may well be ephemeral. This in itself should be an object lesson to all information designers who undertake their work because they want to help people. If you wish this work to continue, you will have to fight for it.

Committed Supporters

We started this work at a time when the medicines policy settings in Australia went through a major reformation as a result of a report to government on medicines evaluation and use (Baume1991). The new policy went under the name of Quality Use of Medicines (QUM) and covered all aspects of medicine use, including the medicine information available to consumers. Baume made it clear that people had a right to information about their medicines. This assertion as part of QUM was the framework within which our work was legitimised.

The body that was set up to turn this policy into practice was called (somewhat inelegantly) Pharmaceutical Health and the Rational Use of Medicine (PHARM). Through that body we began the process of setting up our relations with all the stakeholders. We were privileged and fortunate to meet and work with people who shared our passion for making medicines information usable. Without dedicated and committed people sharing a common purpose, projects like this do not happen. I would like to thank them all for the opportunity we have had to work together on improving the quality of medicines information:

Alex Tyers, Darryl Reed, Elizabeth Gipps, Ian Adams, Jan Donovan, Juliet Seifert, Ken Lee, Lloyd Sanson, Marisa Walker, Mary Emanuel, Mary Murray, Maureen Mackenzie, Pam Quane, Paul Archer, Rob Wiseman, Robyn Penman, Ruth Shrensky, Steven Scarff, Susan Parker, Yong Kwok, Zephanie Jordan

References

Australian Self Medication Industry (2004). *ASMI labelling code of practice.* Canberra: Communication Research Institute. http://communication.org.au/product/labelling-code-of-practice/

Baume, P. (1991). *A question of balance.* Report on the future of drug evaluation in Australia. Commissioned by the Minister for Aged, Family and Services. Canberra: AGPS.

Easterby, R. & Zwaga, H. (1984). *Information Design.* London: Wiley.

Faulkner, L. (2003). Beyond the five-user assumption: Benefits of increased sample sizes in usability testing. *Behavior Research Methods, Instruments, & Computers* 2003, 35 (3) 379–383.

Felker, D. B., Pickering, F., Charrow, V. R., Holland, M., and Redish J. C. (1981). *Guidelines for document designers.* Washington, DC: American Institute for Research.

Fisher, P. & Sless, D. (1990). Information design methods and productivity in the insurance industry. *Information Design Journal* 6(2), 103–129. http://communication.org.au/product/information-design-and-productivity/

Food and Drug Administration (2013). Draft guidance for industry on safety considerations for container labels and carton labeling design to minimize medication errors. http://www.fda.gov/downloads/Drugs/GuidanceComplianceRegulatoryInformation/Guidances/UCM349009.pdf

Goodwin, P. (1984). Manuals for health workers. *Information Design Journal* 4/2 118–130.

Jones, C.J. (1970). *Design methods: Seeds of human futures.* London: John Wiley.

Penman R Sless D & Wiseman R 1996. Best practice in accessible documents in the private sector. In *Putting it plainly: Current developments and needs in Plain English and accessible reading materials.* Canberra: Australian Language and Literacy Council. http://communication.org.au/product/best-practice-information-design/

Rogers, D., Shulman, A., Sless, D., and Beach, R. (1995). *Designing better medicine labels: Report to PHARM.* Canberra: Communication Research Institute of Australia. http://communication.org.au/product/designing-better-medicine-labelling/

Seymour, E. (Ed) 1996 *Rethinking Labelling Regulation and Practice: Report of the forum.* Canberra: Communication Research Press http://communication.org.au/product/rethinking-labelling-regulation/

Sless D. (2004). Designing public documents *Information Design Journal + Document Design Journal* 12(1) 24-35

Sless, D. (1992). The Telecom bill: redesigning a computer generated report. In R. Penman & D. Sless (eds) *Designing information for people* Canberra: Communication Research Press 77-98.
    http://communication.org.au/product/designing-information-for-people/
Sless, D. & Shrensky, R. (2006). *Writing about medicines for people.* Sydney: Australian Self Medication Industry.
    http://www.communication.org.au/publications/bookshop/
Sless, D. Measuring information design. *Information Design Journal* 16(3), 250–258
TGA (2014a).
    http://www.tga.gov.au/consumers/information-medicines-cmi.htm#.U_675ESSyyN
TGA (2014b). *Guidelines for the labelling of medicines: Draft Version 1.0, August 2014.*
    http://www.tga.gov.au/pdf/consult/consult-labelling-medicines-140822-guideline.pdf
Tomaselli, K. G. and Tomaselli, R. (1984). Media graphics as an interventionist strategy. *Information Design Journal* 4 /2 99–117.
Tyers, A. Performance-based design. *Information Design Journal* 16(3), 202–215
Waller, R. (1984). Designing a government form: A case study. *Information Design Journal,* 4, 36–57.
Wickert, R. (1989). *No single measure : A survey of Australian adult literacy.* Canberra: Commonwealth Department of Employment, Education and Training.
Wright, P. (1979). The quality control of document design. *Information Design Journal* 1(1), 33–42.
Wright, P. (1979). The quality control of document design. *Information Design Journal,* 1, 33–42.
Zwaga, H. & Easterby, R. (1984). *Developing effective symbols for public information.* In H. Zwaga and R. Easterby (eds), *Information Design,* 277–298. Chichester: John Wiley.

Biographical Note

David Sless is director of the Communication Research Institute, visiting professor of information design in the Design Institute at Coventry University, vice president of the International Institute for Information Design, and an adjunct professor at the Australian National University.

David graduated from Leeds University in 1965. In 1975 he was awarded an MSc by Durham University for research in information design methods.

In 1985 he was invited to set up the organisation that became the Communication Research Institute, a not-for-profit body that undertakes research and provides information design services and advice to over 200 government and industry organizations around the world.

David is an advocate for evidence-based information design. David's main research has been in information design methods. In Australia, he is best known for his pioneering work on medicine information.

David is a frequently invited keynote speaker at international conferences, and is the author of over 200 publications.

Chapter 14: Transforming Government Letters: Design and Writing Working Together

Rob Waller and Jenny Waller

Abstract

Information designers apply user centred design processes to all aspects of communication – to the language as well as the visual appearance. This case study looks at how a set of complex letters were improved by graphic editing – this means adding visual structure to a verbal document in order to break up its content into manageable chunks, showing their different status. It means looking for opportunities to use lists, tables and other graphic forms to reveal systematic structures within the content, and using a layout that encourages strategic reading.

Introduction

Information designers apply user centred design processes to all aspects of communication – to the language as well as the visual appearance. In this chapter we present two case studies that show how complex official letters were improved by graphic editing – this means adding visual structure to a verbal document in order to break up its content into manageable chunks, showing their different status. It means looking for opportunities to use lists or tables to reveal systematic structures within the content, and using a layout that encourages strategic reading.

An important aspect of both of these projects was to the use of simple techniques and commonly used software, so that office staff in our client organizations could create clearer communications for citizens, without specialized design training.

Are Letters Still Important?

Although the digital age is now firmly established, official letters still survive, and they seem likely to survive for some time to come.

A letter can be sent to an address, even if you do not know who lives there. The receiver gets the same communication, in the same format, that was sent, with no need to have the right device or the right software. A letter is less likely to be mistaken for spam, or imitated by spammers. For the citizen, the letter has physical permanence, and can be stored, written on, and shared with other people to get advice. It does not change shape or lose content because they are reading it on a smartphone rather than a laptop.

And, importantly for government, it reaches people who are not yet digitally connected: a declining group, perhaps, but one that includes many people who are dependent on government support because of age, disability or poverty.

Case 1: Letters about Social Security Benefits and Pensions

Our client for this project was the Department for Work & Pensions (DWP), the UK government department that is responsible for social security benefits. They send out over 150 million letters a year to pensioners, and to people who receive benefits for disabilities, or unemployment. These letters are system-produced, which means they are assembled from a bank of standard messages according to conditional rules, and merged with personal data about citizens.

The Original Letters

Over the years the letters had become long and unwieldy, as more information was added through changes in regulations. DWP asked us to work with their internal project team tasked with designing a better format.

The letters have to incorporate a range of different kinds of information, including:

- personalized information about the amount of benefit the citizen would receive
- reasons for any changes in the amount
- how the calculation was done
- standard text about the process for asking questions or appealing
- standard text that communicates about other benefits people might be entitled to.

These different types of information were mostly undifferentiated in the old letters, so their length was off-putting and it was hard to distinguish between the most relevant and personalized information, and standardized text that has to be there in case you need it (for example, outlining the appeals process).

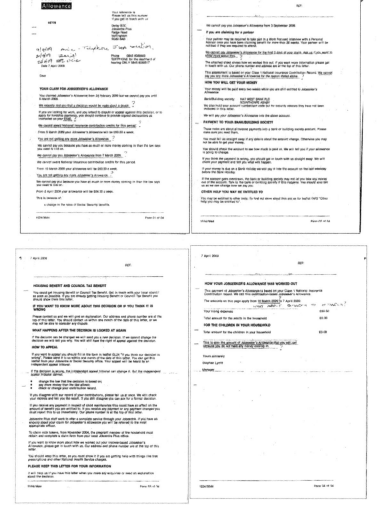

Figure 1. The original letters combined a series of personalized but unconnected messages with standard boilerplate text.

Although civil servants are often accused of using bureaucratic language, the original letters are written in plain English. But taken as a whole the letters are disjointed and poorly structured. Plain language is not enough if the document is visually disorganized, or if it does not work as a coherent message addressed to an individual reader.

The New Letters

The new letters are designed to encourage strategic reading. Strategic reading means reading with a purpose, varying your pace, ignoring information you do not need, and looking for answers to questions that form in your mind as you read.

Figure 2. The new letter template.

The new letters (Figure 2) start with a dominant heading that conveys the key message, together with a subheading that adds extra information. Between them, the heading and subheading always include two key pieces of information: firstly, the reason DWP is writing; and secondly, the name of the person the letter relates to (it is important this is prominently established, as these letters are also used as proofs of entitlement, and therefore as passports to other benefits).

Then each letter summarizes the situation using as few words as possible. Ideally we would like each letter to be no more than a page long, so people can get an overview of the whole situation before drilling down to deeper information to answer their questions.

If the department can predict more than one future change in the benefit that is payable, then this is shown in a clear table, with dates and amounts. The amounts are in bold so they can be quickly spotted – they are the key information people are looking for.

Headings are also used where appropriate – for example, to draw people's attention to action they need to take.

In order to keep the main letter short, more detailed information is provided on separate detail pages.

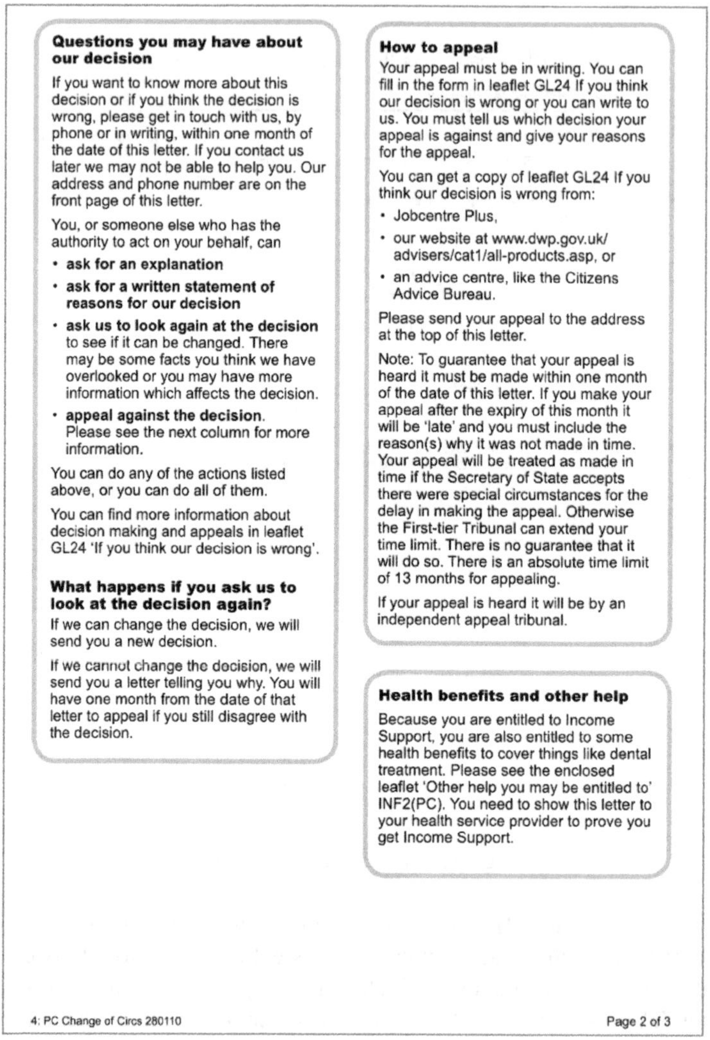

Questions you may have about our decision

If you want to know more about this decision or if you think the decision is wrong, please get in touch with us, by phone or in writing, within one month of the date of this letter. If you contact us later we may not be able to help you. Our address and phone number are on the front page of this letter.

You, or someone else who has the authority to act on your behalf, can

- **ask for an explanation**

- **ask for a written statement of reasons for our decision**

- **ask us to look again at the decision** to see if it can be changed. There may be some facts you think we have overlooked or you may have more information which affects the decision.

- **appeal against the decision.** Please see the next column for more information.

You can do any of the actions listed above, or you can do all of them.

You can find more information about decision making and appeals in leaflet GL24 'If you think our decision is wrong'.

What happens if you ask us to look at the decision again?

If we can change the decision, we will send you a new decision.

If we cannot change the decision, we will send you a letter telling you why. You will have one month from the date of that letter to appeal if you still disagree with the decision.

How to appeal

Your appeal must be in writing. You can fill in the form in leaflet GL24 If you think our decision is wrong or you can write to us. You must tell us which decision your appeal is against and give your reasons for the appeal.

You can get a copy of leaflet GL24 If you think our decision is wrong from:

- Jobcentre Plus,

- our website at www.dwp.gov.uk/advisers/cat1/all-products.asp, or

- an advice centre, like the Citizens Advice Bureau.

Please send your appeal to the address at the top of this letter.

Note: To guarantee that your appeal is heard it must be made within one month of the date of this letter. If you make your appeal after the expiry of this month it will be 'late' and you must include the reason(s) why it was not made in time. Your appeal will be treated as made in time if the Secretary of State accepts there were special circumstances for the delay in making the appeal. Otherwise the First-tier Tribunal can extend your time limit. There is no guarantee that it will do so. There is an absolute time limit of 13 months for appealing.

If your appeal is heard it will be by an independent appeal tribunal.

Health benefits and other help

Because you are entitled to Income Support, you are also entitled to some health benefits to cover things like dental treatment. Please see the enclosed leaflet 'Other help you may be entitled to' INF2(PC). You need to show this letter to your health service provider to prove you get Income Support.

4: PC Change of Circs 280110   Page 2 of 3

Figure 3. A panel page, with unconnected generic information.

Panel pages (Figure 3) include standardized text that is necessary, but which previously made the letters seem overlong and impersonal. By placing them in panels, the text is signalled as optional reading, with bold headings to help you decide. The most commonly used panels are about asking questions and appealing decisions.

The use of panels also helps get over the problem that each panel contains text from a different source, and that has been negotiated and agreed separately. Because they are in separate panels, readers should not expect a narrative that flows.

This is an example of layered text. This means writing and designing a document so it can be read strategically at different levels – you can read quickly at a summary level to get an overall understanding, followed by detailed inspections of extra information if you need it. It is a structure that has become very familiar in online information, where you click on a link to read more detailed information. But it is also effective in printed text, using page design to achieve a similar effect.

Figure 4. The calculation page.

Calculation pages (Figure 3) show the sum – how the total payment was decided, with a separate table for each time period. The calculation is expressed in a narrative format, with clear explanations of each amount, and link words such as 'less' and 'so'.

Case 2: Letters for Bereaved Families of Veterans

Our second case is a project for Veterans UK, a government agency that manages pensions and compensation for veterans and their families. They asked us to help them with a project to review and improve their correspondence with recently bereaved families. Their audience includes elderly widows of World War II veterans who have died in old age, but our special focus was on letters to families of military personnel who have recently died in service.

The key issue for this project was that extremely complex content had to be communicated to people whose cognition is impaired through stress and grief.

We found that widows might get 30 or 40 different letters in the first two months following bereavement, for example about arrangements for pensions, compensation, housing, children's education, personal possessions, memorials, medals and other things. So many well-intentioned organizations exist to help, that these letters might be accompanied by 10-12 leaflets about help that is available, or about coping with bereavement.

We consulted several organizations who help bereaved service families, many of them run by people who have been through the experience themselves. They told us that the families are overwhelmed by the amount of the information they get, and that information may not be processed in the order it is received – people typically sit down several weeks later and try to 'catch up.' or they may hand all the letters to someone who is advising them.

Interestingly, they were very clear that they did not want to receive continuing condolence messages from everyone who writes to them, but that they wanted letters to be businesslike and clear.

For their part, the civil servants who write these letters are very mindful of the state of mind of their audience, but have experiences of dealing not only with grief but also anger. Their past experience of appeals and disputes means that they have to be careful to communicate accurately about what the regulations say, and they are often focused on the complex rules of the schemes they administrate.

Figure 5 shows an excerpt from a particularly complex letter, to illustrate the problem:

AFPS 75 TOP UP AWARD CALCULATION

You.have been awarded a Temporary Allowance for Widow's benefit under the War Pensions Scheme (WPS) and this is Payable for the first 26 weeks of bereavement, payment of Armed Forces Pension Scheme (AFPS) benefits is deferred until the 27th week of bereavement, unless the WPS and AFPS benefits combined are more beneficial. In this instance a supplementary award equal to the shortfall will be made. This is called a TOP UP and will be awarded by the Service Personnel and Veterans Agency (SPVA) Glasgow. If your TAW is paid over a period when a pension increase is awarded (April of each year) then this shortfall is recalculated because TAW is not subject to increase but War Pensions and Armed Forces Pensions are.

The following calculation explains how this department has calculated your shortfall:

A Annual Rate of TAW = £12,259.00

B Period of Temporary Allowance for Widows (TAW) = 21 December 2011 to 19 June 2012.

C Period of Short Term Family Pension Entitlement (STP) 182 days =18 December 2011 to 17 June 2012

D Annual Rate of Short Term Family Pension (STP) = £12,043.29

E Annual rate of Short Term Family Pension (STP) from 9/4/12 = £12,669.54

F Annual Compensation Payment of £10,688.47 from 18/12/11.

G Annual Compensation Payment increasing to £11,244.27 on 9 April 2012.

H Annual Rate of War Widow's Pension (WWP) = £6,311.17

I Annual Rate of War Widow's Pension (WWP) after increase on 9 April 2012 = £6639.90

As your TAW did not start until 21/12/11 you were entitled to your STP of £12,043.29 per annum for the period 18/12/1 1 to 20/12/11.

For the period 21/12/11 to 08/04/12 D+H minus A = £6095.46 per annum this represents the amount of TOP UP due.

For the period 09/0412 to 17/06/12 E+1 minus A = £7050.44 per annum this represents the amount of TOP UP due.

For the period 18/06/12 to 19/06/12 G+I minus A = £5625.17 this represents the amount of TOP UP due.

Annual Compensation Payment payable from 20/06/12 = £11,244.27 per annum.

5

Figure 5. Excerpt from a letter addressed to a recently bereaved widow.

By any standards, this information is very complex – several different schemes are mentioned, and a range of time periods. Some of the payments change on 9 April, reflecting annual inflation-linked increases. A further difficulty is that all amounts are expressed as annual figures, even when they will only apply for a few days.

Our view, reinforced by feedback from users, was that the main focus of the reader is "how much money will I get, and when?" So we reorganized the information around time periods and actual amounts.

The pension you will receive

Period	Amount	What this represents	Comments
18 Dec 2011 to 21 Dec 2011	**£100.36** single payment	Short Term Family Pension	This payment covered the first few days before your Temporary Allowance for Widows started
21 Dec 2011 to 9 Apr 2012	**£1,529.54** per month	£1,021.58 of this is your Temporary Allowance for Widows

£507.96 of this is your Short Term Family Pension Top Up | |
| 10 Apr 2011 to 17 Jun 2012 | **£1,609.12** per month | £1,021.58 of this is your Temporary Allowance for Widows

£587.54 of this is your Short Term Family Pension Top Up | This change is because pensions rates increase in April |
| 18 Jun 2012 to 19 Jun 2012 | **£15.41** single payment | Short Term Family Pension Top Up | |
| 20 Jun 2012 until further notice | **£n,nnn.nn** per month | £553.32 of this is your War Widow's Pension

£nnnnn.nn of this is your Family Forces Pension

£932.02 of this is your Annual Compensation Payment | |

About the different schemes

Service pensions are very complicated, because several schemes run in parallel, and have different rules. It is particularly complicated in the early months following bereavement, while we calculate your entitlements.

Temporary Allowance for Widows (TAW)

This is part of the War Pensions Scheme, and runs for 26 weeks following bereavement. This is to give you an income while we are calculating your entitlement for the longer term.

Short Term Family Pension

This is part of the Armed Forces Pension Scheme, and runs for 91 days. Because you also qualify for the Armed Forces Attributable Benefit Scheme, it is extended by a further 91 days. If it is higher than the TAW, we pay you a Top Up amount.

Annual Compensation

This payment is made because your husband's death was attributable to military service. It is paid annually as a lump sum. [QUESTION: what scheme is this part of?]

2

Figure 6. Our draft of the same information, explained as a table using time as the organizing principle.

Designing for Strategic Reading

Strategic reading describes the set of skills used to read and use complex information. Effective readers are better able to look for the structure of a document, and to change their reading style according the kind of information they see. They may focus on different parts of the text on different occasions. When they get a letter about their benefits, they will naturally look for the amount first. If it is unexpected, they will look for the reasons. If they are in doubt, or just want to be sure, they will look for how it is calculated. Then later, if they have questions, they will look for answers or information about where to find out more. Because their reading is fluent, the most effective readers can do this with linear text that is graphically undifferentiated. They can remember the location of key content, and (so long as the text is logically structured) they can detect the structure of content well enough to search within it to find answers to their questions. We call this style of reading 'strategic' because it is done with a purpose in mind, which shapes the order and depth in which each element of text is attended to.

Less skilled readers, on the other hand, tend to read line by line, and may not read with a positive purpose in mind. Much of their cognitive effort is spent understanding unfamiliar words and working out the structure of complex sentences, and they may be less familiar with the fact that official texts have multiple authors and multiple purposes (and so are less coherent).

These readers may not have the confidence to park or ignore parts of the content that seem less relevant to them, so our new letters are designed to allow them – to encourage them, or at least to give them permission – to treat different parts of the text differently.

Strategic reading is an important aspect of functional literacy, which goes beyond the basics of prose literacy (deciphering the words and sentences) to describe the purposeful use of information sources to solve real world problems. While levels of prose literacy are very high (around 97%) in most western countries such as the UK, levels of functional literacy are worryingly low. A number of countries took part in the International Adult Literacy Survey (IALS) in the late 1990s, under the auspices of the OECD, which defines five levels of functional literacy. But although Level 3 is "a suitable minimum for coping with everyday life and work in a complex, advanced society," around 50% of the UK population was found to be below that level, and the proportion is higher among disadvantaged groups such as the long term unemployed. For more information about IALS see Murray, Kirsch & Jenkins (1998). The methodology is controversial, however, so for a balanced view see also Blum, Goldstein & Guérin-Pace (2001), or Hamilton & Barton (2000).

How We Worked

The Importance of Effective Teams

Traditionally, graphic designers take a brief from their client, and go away to develop a creative solution. Many information design projects involve a much greater level of co-designing alongside the client, and their users. They have a much greater level of detailed knowledge about content, and about the processes that documents are part of. The team for the DWP project included experts in social security legislation, administrative processes and IT systems. And the Veterans UK team included their internal design team, content experts, a serving soldier and customer-facing staff.

In our experience, the way that teams work together is critical to the success of projects like this. Although, in both projects, members of the team were based in different offices around the UK, they got together regularly for workshops. When people work in the same physical environment, the inevitable departmental positions become less important, as the team develops a shared understanding of different points of view and different business pressures.

In the case of Veterans UK, there was a conscious effort to create a 'community of practice' across the organization, so that letters sent by different departments speak with a single voice.

User Consultations

Ideally we would recommend quite detailed and extensive performance testing of document such as these. However, system-produced letters have hundreds of potential combinations of content, and it is not realistic to test them all. Instead, in both projects we consulted small groups of users, and expert staff, and it is important after launch to monitor any problems that emerge.

Dynamic Documents

The system letters in the DWP project are examples of 'dynamic documents' – these are automatically generated using business rules to select the data and text to merge. Each customer gets a personalized version of the document, with information only included that is potentially relevant to them.

A business rule is typically in the form: "if there is a Welsh postal code print a message about the Welsh language call centre," or "if the amount is zero, do not include information about payments." It might be driven by the data (such as date or amount) or it might use a data flag that is put there to instruct the system. For example, there is a code that represents the reason someone's benefit has changed – this is translated into a phrase such as "because you are no longer working" or "because your savings have gone down."

Patterns We Used in This Project

We use a pattern library approach to giving guidance about document design. It is a way to describe solutions to common problems, that can be used as a design tool by others faced with a similar problem. A typical example of a design pattern is the '1, 2, 3' numbered steps used in instruction manuals. Each time you see the pattern in use, signalled by the use of numbers, often with diagrams, with the steps graphically separated, you know how the writer intends you to use the information. And although each example might be different in execution, it has to follow certain guidelines if it is to work – for example, the numbers need to be prominent, and the beginning and end of the sequence have to be clear.

Guidelines about document design have often been communicated in a fragmented way in the past – separately addressing issues such as writing style, line length, typeface, or document structure. The pattern approach is more holistic, combining recommendations about a range of issues.

The pattern method originated with the architect Christopher Alexander (1977), but has since been more widely used in software engineering and interface design (Tidwell, 2005). So using this method for information design more generally will help the inevitable convergence of interaction design and information design as digital communications continue to evolve.

Some patterns we used here are:

News Headlines

As the name suggests, this kind of headline is designed to engage the reader with the text – it focuses on what is interesting and relevant, and may be in two parts: a heading and subheading (which expands on the heading, often emphasizing an action that is required, or a key aspect of the content). They solve the problem "people need to understand the main point quickly." The prompted reading strategy is: glance at the headline, and only read further if you need more information.

Panels

Panels are blocks of text that stand alone from the main narrative. They are used in many publications to contain specific messages that do not fit easily into the main text, or which need to be accessed easily. They solve the problem "there is optional text that is not part of the main narrative." The prompted reading strategy is: there is no particular order to read the panels – just note the content and read if and when it is relevant to you.

Summary Table

Tables are a fundamental graphic pattern and hardly need justification. They show systematic relations among the content – in this case, the dates and amounts. They solve the problem "there is a rhythm within the content – each element has the same structure." They prompt the reading strategy: scan each row or column, comparing information systematically; or if there are headings: use the headings to identify the row and column you need, then read the content where they intersect.

Narrative Sum

The calculation pages use a pattern that is probably more familiar in a school maths textbook – it talks you through the sum using ordinary language in much the same way as you might talk someone through it face-to-face. The prompted reading strategy is: do not panic – work your way systematically through each line, and we will explain as we go how the sum works.

Conclusion

Through two simple projects that improve communication from government to citizens, we have focused on some important themes for the practice of information design within organizations.

In both of these projects, the content is about regulations, about money and about time periods. For the writers, regulations come first – from them they derive messages about money and time. But the users it is the other way around. In a communication about benefits or pensions, the first thing they need to know is "how much?" The regulations then explain 'why that amount?', and the user only needs to understand them if they are considering a challenge.

Message to Designers: Information is Verbal as Well as Visual

Information design is not exclusively visual. Although in recent years the terms 'information design' and 'visualization' have become interchangeable, we prefer to see information design as the application of design thinking to information in what form it is best communicated. Graphic designers do themselves and their clients a disservice if they see words as a given that they cannot challenge or that necessarily exist in a purely linear form.

Information designers can influence even those communications where words must continue to carry the greatest part of meaning – designers do not always have to use alternatives to words, but can work with writers to make words more accessible. Digital communications have taught people to skim the surface of communications, so we can no longer rely on content being closely read (and perhaps we never could).

Message to Writers: Information is Visual as Well as Verbal

Both of the organizations we worked with have made considerable efforts to introduce plain English, through training and guidance. In the case of DWP, there were few problems with the language of the letters we reviewed – at the level of words and sentences, that is. But it was not enough to make sure the documents were easy to understand.

Plain language is important because, in most industrialized nations, levels of literacy are unevenly spread across society. Literacy researchers typically distinguish between three kinds of literacy: prose literacy (reading the words), document literacy (reading documents critically, and for practical purposes) and quantitative literacy (understanding numbers). Plain English alone only addresses the first of these. Information design addresses the other two, and it is our concern to find ways to make its techniques more accessible to information writers who have not had specialist information design training.

References

Alexander, C., Ishikawa, S., & Silverstein, M. (1977). *A pattern language. Towns. Buildings. Construction.* Oxford University Press.

Blum, A., Goldstein, H., & Guérin-Pace, F. (2001). International Adult Literacy Survey (IALS): An analysis of international comparisons of adult literacy. *Assessment in Education: Principles, Policy & Practice, 8*(2), 225 - 246.

Hamilton, M. and Barton, D. (2000). The International Adult literacy Survey (IALS): What does it really measure? *International Review of Education,* 46 (5): 377-389.

Murray, T. S., Kirsch, I. S. and Jenkins, L. B. (1998). *Adult literacy in OECD countries.* Washington, DC, National Center for Education Statistics.

Tidwell, J. (2005). *Designing interfaces: patterns for effective interaction design.* O'Reilly.

Biographical notes

Rob Waller was one of the pioneers of the new discipline of information design: the structuring and communicating of complex information. He is founder and Director of the Simplification Centre, a London-based organization campaigning for clearer public information.

Rob started his career as a researcher with the Open University, which developed distance education in the UK using innovative multi-channel teaching techniques. He was part of the multidisciplinary research effort in the UK in the 1970s and 80s, which brought designers, psychologists and others together in joint research programmes. His research still focuses on the relationship of graphic design to language and comprehension, the subject of his doctorate from the University of Reading.

In 1988 Rob started Information Design Unit, a consultancy that became the leading UK information design company, specializing in personalized customer communications, wayfinding, user research and management communications. IDU's client list included numerous well-known brands in the financial services, telecommunications, energy and retail sectors, as well as many government departments, hospitals and museums. In 2001 the business was sold to WPP, one of the world's largest marketing services groups, and Rob became Head of Information Design in the global branding agency Enterprise IG.

In 2007 Rob returned to an academic career at the University of Reading, as Professor of Information Design, teaching postgraduate students at PhD and MA level. While at Reading he started the Simplification Centre, which works with government departments and financial services companies to create clear communications. In 2011 Rob left the university to focus on developing the Centre as an advocacy group, exploring co-designing with user communities.

Rob has also been closely associated with the creation of an institutional framework for the development of information design. In 1979 he founded Information Design Journal, which was instrumental in defining the term itself; he co-founded the Information Design Association in the UK, which he currently chairs; and he has co-organized a series of international Information Design Conferences from 1982 to the present

Jenny Waller is an information writer, researcher and educator. She holds a degree in English Language and Literature from Trinity College, Dublin, and an MBA from Cranfield University. After teaching in secondary education for twelve years, she developed a career in management consultancy, specializing in change communications and information writing. She is the author of two textbooks on quality management.

Jenny has wide experience of every variety of information writing, and every variety of audience: forms and user guides for customers; technical manuals for software developers; strategy documents for senior managers; change communications for steel workers facing reorganization; information architecture for the UK government tax website. Her clients have included Unilever, the National Health Service, AAA, Guinness, DHL, British Steel, and several UK government departments.

Jenny has long experience in integrating language into the information design curriculum. In the mid 1990s she was Head of Information Design at Coventry University, and taught students on the BA Technical Communication programme, which combined technical writing with graphic design. In recent years she has been training director at the Simplification Centre, and developed an innovative training programme, accredited by the University of Reading, aimed at professionalizing document writers and designers working in large organizations. The curriculum combines writing, design and project management, and blends theoretical and practical approaches. She is now moving this to an e-learning platform.

Chapter 15: Information Design in the Development of Product Instruction Manuals in Brazil—Can a User-centered Design Approach Make a Difference?

Carla G. Spinillo and Kelli C.A.S. Smythe

Abstract

Drawbacks in the graphic presentation of information in product instructions to users may affect not only comprehension but also the use of a product, leading to failure and frustration in product+user interaction. This paper discusses the relevance of a user-centered-design approach to the development of product instruction through case studies of redesign of stove and a wash machine manuals produced by a major international manufacturer in Brazil. Initially, the design process of instructional material for product users is presented, highlighting the functional, aesthetics and cognitive aspects. Then, the case studies are described which were based upon empirical research with users, focusing on their reactions to the manuals' design, and their task performances during product interaction. The results showed that users' information needs were not fully provided in the material and the graphic representation of information was not in alignment with users' viewpoints. Based upon the results, a redesign of the stove and wash machine manuals was developed and guidelines for instructional materials are proposed. As a conclusion, users should be involved in the beginning of the design process of instructional material to promote effectiveness in comprehension and success in the user+product interaction: a lesson to be learned.

Introduction

From an information design perspective, a product instruction manual is a graphic artifact that mediates the user+product interaction – i.e., it is a graphic information mediator for task performance. When following instructions users engage in cognitive and motor activities which begin with (a) reading the manual (text, pictures), (b) integrating the information extracted from the manual to the product in hand and to their prior knowledge (of the product and/or task) to build a mental representation of the task which will lead (c) to constructing an action plan to carry out the steps, and (d) finally, performing those steps (Ganier, 2001, 2004). In this regard, most activities pertain to the cognitive domain, indicating the relevance of information design in instruction manuals to successful task performance. In the cognitive process, product users deal with instructional information in a subconscious manner towards its interpretation/comprehension. On the other hand, in the metacognitive process users are conscious of their understanding, that is, they monitor their behavior during the instructional information process (Spinillo, et. al, 2011; Spinillo, 2011). The graphic presentation of instructions plays an important role as a metacognitive resource to users as it facilitates the information processing (Spinillo, 2011). The typographic structure of the text and the design of pictorial instructions provide support to users during their metacognitive process when users interact with product manuals.

Moreover, reading instructions in order to perform steps can be seen as a problem-solving activity, which involves searching and using information to achieve the goal of utilizing a product correctly. According to Wilson (2000), how individuals interact with an information system or artifact determines their information searching behavior; and their physical and mental actions when they integrate information to current knowledge determine the individuals' information use behavior. This seems to be related to the cognitive and motor activities users engage in when following instructions, as well as to users' metacognitive process, as mentioned above.

By considering these aspects, it is possible to infer that when the graphic presentation of instructions in manuals presents drawbacks, not only users' comprehension of information may be affected but also task performance, resulting in failure and/or frustration during the interaction with a product. Thus, the design process of instructions should focus on the users so as to reach effectiveness in the product usage.

User-centered Design in Product Instruction Manuals

The participation of users in the design process is a matter of economic as well as social importance. Smythe (2014) claims that users' involvement may occur through iterative processes, methods, techniques and procedures which take into account the users' experiences in order to enhance the project requisites. Moreover, Maguire (2001) considers that a user-centered design approach may increase productivity and system/product acceptance, reduce errors and may also improve a company's reputation in the market. Nevertheless, the user-centered-design approach requires companies/manufactures to rethink the way they do business, develop products and think about their customers. According to Rubin and Chisnell (2008) a user-centered-design approach requires a significant change in the culture of companies/manufacturers. This may imply a shift from an immediate response from the market to solid initiatives/institutional programs built over time.

In relation to the development of product instruction manuals, the user-centered design approach is particularly relevant to the use of house appliances of daily use, due to its growth in the world economy. In Brazil the house appliances market has driven the industry's sales in both the internal and external markets. Between 1992 and 2014 the number of washing machines sold in Brazil increased from 24% to 51% and stoves are present in 98.8% of the Brazilian households (IBGE, 2014). House appliances represent 59% of the value of exports of the electronic industry in Brazil. However, the increase in the sales of house appliances in Brazil has not resulted in a more efficient user+product interaction. Several problems have been reported to the manufacturers' customer services and/or registered on websites for consumers' complaints.

Despite the relevance of product instruction manuals to the use of house appliances, research on users' information needs in task performance is yet incipient, at least from an information design perspective. Most studies on this topic consider users' interaction with the product/house appliance (e.g., Vasques *et al*. 2010), but they ignore the role that graphic presentation of information may play in task performance.

Designing helpful instructions to support user+product interaction is not only one of the aims of information designers, but also a matter of social responsibility. In this regard, Pettersson (2007) proposes design principles which consider the users' information needs and aims to support reasoning and reflections during the design process. These principles are grouped as following: functional, aesthetic, cognitive and management principles. Each type of principle takes into account aspects which need to be considered when designing information for users (Figure 1).

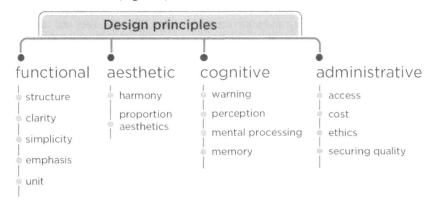

Figure 1: Diagram of Design Principles based on Pettersson (2007).

Considering the aspects presented above, this chapter discusses the relevance of a user-centered design approach to the development of product instructions. This will be done by means of discussing two case studies. Both case studies involve the redesigning of instructional manuals produced by a major international manufacturer in Brazil, the first one for a stove and the second one for a washing machine.

Case Studies: The Stove and Washing Machine Manuals for Users in Brazil

The case studies consist of empirical research with potential users of a washing machine and a steam stove. Both case studies focus on the users' reactions to the product instructions during task performance. These were the instructions presented in the redesigned versions of the original manuals.

In order to produce the redesigned versions, the original manuals were assessed taking into account recommendations found in the literature (e.g., Ganier, 2001; Spinillo & Dyson, 2000, 2011; Wright, 1999, 2007). This allowed the identification of drawbacks in the typographic articulation of the manuals and their pictorial instructions. The outcomes of the assessment showed deficiencies in the visual instructions (e.g., lack of figure-ground contrast, misuse of arrows, poor depiction), and lack of typographic articulation (e.g., emphatic cues, hierarchy, sequencing). Based upon these results, the stove and washing machine manuals were redesigned according to Pettersson's (2007) functional, aesthetic and cognitive principles. These principles were adapted to fit instruction manuals, as follows.

- Structure: organization/hierarchy of elements in space in order to facilitate identification of functional groups (levels and types of information) and the navigation system in the manuals.
- Clarity of presentation of elements: unambiguous representations to distinguish the different parts of the instructional message.
- Simplicity: conciseness, consistency and accuracy in order to improve the flow of reading and understanding of procedural images and texts.
- Emphasis: resources to highlight the most important elements to attract, to direct and to maintain the user's attention when interacting with the instructional material.
- Harmony: visual organization of elements in a pleasing and integrated manner.
- Unit: global coherence, elements should belong to the same level/type of information in the manual.
- Attention: resources to catch the user's eye when interacting with the manual.
- Perception: features to ease detection and identification of information.
- Processing: resources to promote the information flow so as to facilitate the understanding of pictorial and textual messages.

- Memory: resources to promote retention/storage of visual/verbal information.

In addition to the above, the redesigned versions should also be easy to handle and accessible in the context of use. Thus, illustrated pocket guides (Figures 2 and 3) to be displayed/available in the kitchen (stove) and/or utility area were produced (washing machine).

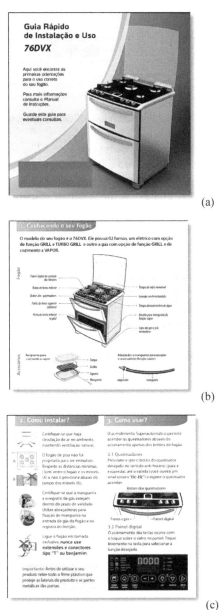

(a)

(b)

(c)

Figure 2 (a) (b) and (c): The cover and inside pages of the stove pocket guide.

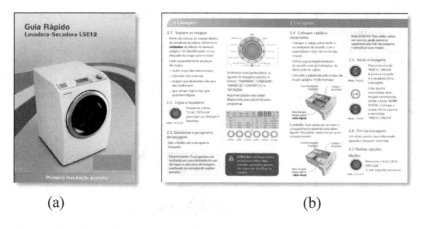

(a)   (b)

Figure 3 (a) and (b): The cover and inside pages of the washing machine pocket guide.

Validating the Redesigned Manuals/Pocket Guides: A User-centered Design Approach to the Stove and Washing Machine Instructions

The validation of the pocket guides for the washing machine and the stove aimed to verify their effectiveness in communicating the instructions and supporting the tasks, as well as participants' satisfaction with the proposed redesigns. Data was collected through task observation and verbalization during interaction tests, and follow-up interviews.

Participants and material: 12 adults (over 18 years old) took part in the stove interaction tests, and 13 adults took part in the washing machine tests. The material tested consisted of the pocket guides, the washing machine and the stove. An interview protocol was also used by the researchers.

It is worth mentioning that both appliances had digital displays containing features which were unknown to consumers (i.e., yet to be launched in the market). The stove had a steam function which required the use of a reservoir to boil water, and two ovens, one with grill function. The washing machine had a dryer and a timing function which allowed to dry different types of clothing and to program the washing. All of these were new features.

Procedures: for the stove's and the washing machine's interaction tests each participant was given the pocket guide and asked to perform all the instructions provided in it, verbalizing their actions during the tasks. When necessary, the researchers encouraged verbalization, asking questions to the participants. The tests were conducted individually, in laboratory conditions at the manufacturer's premises. After the completion of the tasks, a follow-up semi-structured interview was conducted.

Analysis of the results: The results were analyzed using a qualitative approach, but figures were considered only to indicate possible trends in the results. The following classification was used to identify errors in the tasks undertaken by the participants: errors of Information Processing (understanding of the information provided in the pocket guides) and Errors of Action (performing the steps). These categories were based on Barber and Stanton (1996), and Rasmussen (1986) taxonomies for human errors.

Main Results of the Pocket Guides' Validation with Participants

Case 1: The Stove

Most participants were female (N = 10) – only two males – and their ages ranged from 18 to 50 years old. All participants were literate and had stated that they read instruction manuals when buying new products.

Overall, the results showed that all participants made errors when performing the tasks presented in the pocket guide. Errors in information processing occurred mainly with regard to the use of the steam function, setting the clock on the digital display, and using the stove for the first time. These were due to (a) the omission of steps and sub-steps of the tasks, (b) wrong information sequencing (both in the text provided by the manufacturer) and (c) lack of clarity in some of the instructional images (steam oven). Similarly, the action errors concerned mainly the tasks related to using the steam function, and were made by all participants. Eleven out of twelve participants failed to empty the water reservoir of the steam function. This failure would have resulted in the users burning themselves in a real situation. All participants complained about the procedures for cleaning the reservoir (using the pipe and a container to drain the water from the reservoir). Some participants (N = 5) also reported having difficulty using the glass bow for steam cooking. Others also expressed their concern with the potential risk of burns in a real situation.

(a)

Figure 4 (a) and (b): Participants using the stove steam function mediated by the pocket guide during interaction tests.

The results of the interviews showed that the participants reacted satisfactorily to the instructions presented in the pocket guide, particularly for the stove installation and cleaning procedures. However, when using the steam function, participants made mistakes when carrying out the task despite understanding the instructions on how to use the steam function. The lack of familiarity with this function and the omission of detailed information to support task performance has certainly contributed to these results.

It is interesting to note that participants made negative comments on the graphic presentation of the pocked guide based on their experience with the stove in the interaction test. This indicates that the information drawbacks influenced the participants' value judgment of the graphic presentation of the pocket guide. Thus, it can be assumed that the aesthetic appreciation of an instructional document can be affected by its efficiency in supporting task performance. Further empirical investigation is required to sustain this assumption.

Case 2: The Washing Machine

Similarly to the stove interaction test, 10 out of 13 participants were women, their ages ranging from 31 to 40 years old. They also stated that they read instruction manuals when purchasing new products.

During the interaction tests, most errors were related to difficulties in using the digital touch display of the washing machine. Information processing errors were observed mainly with regard to finding information within the guide, and understanding labels and icons on the digital touch display depicted in the guide. This was mainly for the function 'Delay Start,' which allows users to program the washing machine time. It is worth mentioning that the label and the icon for this function, both shown on the digital touch display, were inaccurate in the instructions provided in the manufacturer's guide. When setting the time for laundering, the digital display shows the time the washing process *ends*, but its label suggests the time the process would *start* ('Delay Start' function). This discrepancy caused great confusion in task performance. Because the information on the label was inadequate, it led to lack of understanding by all participants.

Other aspect that caused action errors regards participants' integration of their previous experience with washing machines to the actual tasks. The sequence of the tasks presented in the guide instructing participants how to use the washing machine basic functions (simply laundering) did not correspond to the sequence of actions adopted by most of the participants (N = 10) when using a washing machine in their lives. This led to difficulties in finding/searching information within the pocket guide, affecting participants' reading strategy.

In relation to the follow-up interviews, participants' responses corroborated the errors identified during the interaction testing. The main difficulties regard the use of the digital display, particularly the 'Delay Start' function. Almost all participants (N = 12) felt that it assisted them when using the washing machine. However, more than half of the participants (N = 7) reported difficulties in locating information in the guide, particularly information presented in boxes labeled as 'Important,' which were used to highlight relevant parts of the guide text. These results indicate that the use of generic labels such as 'Important' to highlight contents was ineffective, therefore not contributing to participants' searching strategies. Finally, participants suggested improvements on the pictures and labels of the digital display, claiming that more clarity in the instructions for the 'Delay Start' function was needed.

General Discussion and Improvements on the Pocket Guides

The outcomes of the interaction tests and interviews indicated that the pocked guides presented flaws in their information content and graphic presentation, which seem to have affected participants' information searching and use behaviors (Wilson, 2000).

Moreover, since following the instructions provided in the guides was a problem-solving activity whose goal was to use the stove and the washing machine correctly, the drawbacks identified certainly affected participants' use behavior. This possibly affected the participants' construction of action plans to carry out the tasks (Ganier, 2001; Spinillo, 2011). The action plans may also have been influenced by the fact that participants' previous knowledge (of similar products and/or tasks) could not be integrated into the information extracted from the pocket guides.

Though, it is important to stress that some of the errors in task performance were due to deficiencies in the products' design. Inaccurate representation of information on the digital display of the washing machine and the stove precarious appliances for steam cooking are examples of product design shortcomings. In this regard, one may dare to say that not even good information design instructions for product use can solve the problems created by poor product design. They can only help users to deal with these problems.

As for the interviews' outcomes, participants' complaints and suggestions to improve the pocket guides indicate their awareness of their information needs to promote their understanding of the instructions. This regards participants' metacognitive process when interacting with the information systems for using the stove and the washing machine. Hence, the metacognitive process plays an important part in assessing communication effectiveness of product instructions, as in the case of the pocket guides.

Improving the Redesigned Pocked Guides: Benefits of a User-centered Design

Considering the results of the interaction tests and participants' responses in the follow-up interviews, adjustments were made in the pocket guides for the washing machine and the stove. Since these adjustments required reviewing and adding new information content to the guides, the manufacturer team was asked to rewrite and produce new contents to meet the users' information needs identified in the interaction tests. Thus, the content and the graphic presentation of the pocket guides were improved – i.e., their structure, clarity, and emphasis (functional principles) – so that they would be better perceived by users (cognitive principle). The following figures show the main improvements made to the pocket guides.

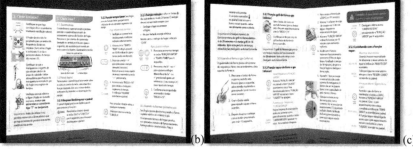

Figures 5 (a) (b) and (c): The amended versions of the cover and inside pages of the stove pocket guide.

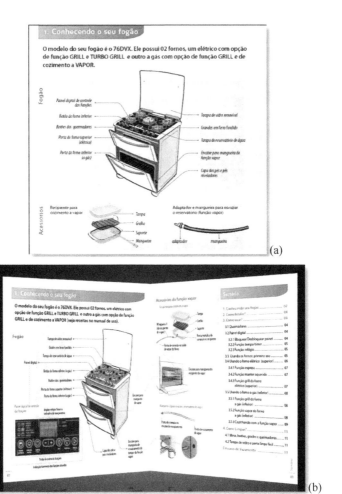

Figure 6: Detail of the pocket guide showing the inventorial image of the stove (a) before and (b) after validation with participants.

(a)

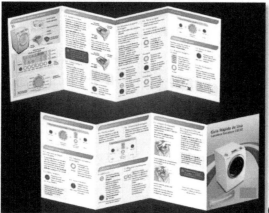

(b)

Figures 7 (a) and (b): The amended versions of the cover and inside pages of the washing machine pocket guide.

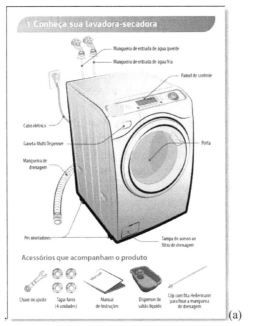

(a)

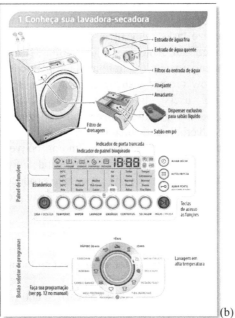

(b)

Figure 8: Detail of the pocket guide showing the inventorial image of the washing machine (a) before and (b) after validation with participants.

Conclusion and Final Considerations

The main conclusion that can be drawn from the outcomes of the validation of the pocket guides is that in order to meet users' information needs with regard to using the stove and the washing machine, users had to be consulted in the design process of the pocket guides. As a result, improved versions of the pocket guides were produced by the manufacturer and distributed with the products in the Brazilian market. Moreover, the manufacturer also made improvements to the appliances themselves (the stove and the washing machine). These improvements were based on the outcomes of the pocket guides' validation with participants.

However, it is important to stress that users' involvement in the design process of product instructions is not only a matter of respect to them, but a manufacturer's social and economic responsibility. If users are misinformed or have not received all the information they need to allow them to use a product correctly and safely, this will lead to injuries and/or damage the product. This will be considered neglect on the part of the manufacturers and they can be sued for that.

Some Recommendations for the Design of Product Instructions for Users

Based upon the outcomes of the cases reported here and the relevant literature, recommendations are proposed to the design of product instructions for users. They aim (a) to prioritize tasks relevant to the use of the products to promote understanding of instructional contents; (b) to facilitate users' search strategy to find information, avoiding anxiety/frustration when interacting with instructional material; and (c) to allow prompt visualization of the essential steps for using products to optimize users' information processing. Accordingly, the recommendations regard the graphic-information structure of the instructional artifact/document; the verbal and pictorial representations of contents; the schematic elements/cues used to emphasize and/or convey information; and navigation elements/cues to aid users to search/find information within the document. They can be used in the design process to produce prototype versions of instructional material to be validated with users, and are presented next.

1. Information-graphic structure
   - Choose a format/size ease to handle by users
   - Design a page grid consistent for setting text and images
   - Use visual separation cues for warnings
   - Provide a clear sequence of tasks to be carried out
   - Introduce the main/new functions of the product in the beginning of the document

2. Verbal representation
   - Choose a typeface of good legibility and typographic range to allow variation in typesetting
   - Establish typographic hierarchy to heading levels and sequence them with numbers (up to three levels preferably)

- Align text left to promote legibility
- Use numbers to order the steps
- Use simple bullets to list items
- Use signal words to indicate warnings (e.g., caution, warning, attention)

3. Pictorial representation
- Use inventorial image (visual overview of the product to users) as it may aid users' action plan
- Place texts near the images they refer to (caption and/or labels) as it may promote users' information processing
- Choose picture styles that promote clear visualization of the product/its parts (photographs may be not be suitable due to its visual complexity)

4. Schematic elements
- Use arrows to convey action/movement (not emphasis)
- Use only one type of semantic mark for negation (X or /) and color it in red to indicate prohibition
- Use emphatic devices consistently throughout the document (e.g. color, boxes) according to the content to be called attention to (e.g., box for warnings, bold for keywords within the text)
- Visually differ rows to ease table reading

5. Navigation elements
- Provide a table of contents to documents with many pages
- Provide vertical and horizontal space to separate blocks of text
- Provide information on the page margins (e.g., headings) to aid information searching in brochures
- Use keywords (in bold and/or color) to aid users to find information within the text

It is therefore important to highlight that poor content development by the manufacturer team may jeopardize efficiency in the design process of instructional material. Inaccurate instructional information and lack of communication between experts in the manufacturer team (e.g., product engineers and computing engineers) with regard to the product use are examples of drawbacks which may jeopardize efficiency in the management of the content of instructional material. Thus, to reach effectiveness in product instructions for users, manufacturers should not only adopt a user-centered approach to the design of information but also an integrated policy on content development management. This would advance manufacturers' view on product instructional material for users: from a mandatory technical document to an artifact that is part of the branding of the company. This would also improve the company's image with its customers.

Acknowledgement

Thanks are due to the participants who volunteered in the studies and to the manufacturer of the stove and washing machine for their support. Due to contractual requirements their name remains confidential.

References

Barber, C. & Stanton, N. A. (1996). Human error identification techniques applied to public technology: predictions compared with observed use. *Applied Ergonomics*, v.7. N.2, p. 119-131.

Ganier, F. (2001). Processing text and pictures in procedural instructions. *Information Design Journal* 10(2), 146-153, John Benjamins Publishing Company.

Ganier, F. (2004). Les apports de la psychologie cognitive a la conception d'instructions procedurales. *InfoDesign- Revista Brasileira de Design da Informação* 1, v.1.pp 16-28. www.infodesign.org.br

IBGE- Instituto Brasileiro de Geografia e Estatística. (2014). *Séries históricas e estatísticas.*   Available   at: <http://seriesestatisticas.ibge.gov.br/default.aspx> Accessed: June 2014

Maguire, M. (2001). Methods to support human-centred design. *International Journal of Human-Computer Studies*. v. 55, Issue 4, p. 587-634, October.

Pettersson, R. (2007). *It Depends: ID – Principles and guidelines* (2nd Edition). Tullinge: Institute for Infology.

Rasmussen, J. (1986). *Information Processing and Human-Machine Interaction: An Approach to Cognitive Engineering.* New York: Elsevier Science Inc.

Rubin, J. & Chisnell, D. (2008). Handbook of usability testing: how to plan, design, and conduct effective tests. (2nd Edition) New York : John Wiley & Sons, 1st ed. 1994.

Smythe, K. C. A. S. (2014). Inclusão do usuário na fase inicial do processo de design para sistemas de wayfinding em ambientes hospitalares já construídos. Unpublished Master Dissertation. Universidade Federal do Paraná, Curitiba, Paraná.

Spinillo, C. G. & Dyson, M. C. (2000). Facilitating participatory design through a framework for analysing procedural pictorial sequences. S. A. R. Scrivener, L. J. Ball, A. Woodcock (Eds). *Co-designing 2000 Adjunct Proceedings.* Coventry: Coventry University Press, v. 1, p. 13-16.

Spinillo, C. G. (2011). Animated visual instructions: can we do better? *Proceedings of The Society for Technical Communication's 58th Annual Conference. Sacramento?* STC, p. 128-134.

Spinillo, C. G.; Souza, J. M. B ; Storck, G. R. & Pottes, A. (2011). Aspectos sobre os modos de representação e o processamento da informação em instruções visuais animadas. Anais do 11° ERGODESIGN/USIHC. Manaus: UFM v.1, p. 15-26.

Vasques, R.; Loureiro, D.; & Padovani, S. (2010). Uso compartilhado de máquinas de lavar roupas: um estudo exploratório centrado na satisfação do usuário. In: Anais 9° P&D 2010. Congresso de Pesquisa e

Desenvolvimento em Design. Available at: http://blogs.anhembi.br/congressodesign/anais/artigos/69711.pdf Accessed: June 2014.

Wilson, T. D. (2000). Recent trends in user studies: action research and qualitative methods. *Information Research,* 5(3). Available at: http://informationr.net/ir/5-3/paper76.html. Accessed: March 2014

Wright, P. (1999). Printed instructions: can research make a difference? H. J. G. Zwaga, T. Boersema, & H. C. M. Hoonhout (eds.) *Visual Information for everyday use: design and research perspectives.* London, UK: Taylor & Francis, p. 45-67.

Wright, P. (2007). Cognitively congenial interfaces for public information. C. Spinillo, P. Farias and S. Padovani (Eds). *Selected Readings of the 2nd Information Design International Conference.* Curitiba: SBDI-The Brazilian Society of Information Design, p. 110-116.

Biographical Note

Carla G. Spinillo holds a PhD from The University of Reading (UK, 2000) and is a lecturer and researcher at The Federal University of Paraná, Brazil. She is the general editor of the Information Design Journal (2014-2016) and former co-editor of the Brazilian Journal of Information Design (2003-2013). She is also a member of the editorial policy board of the Journal of Visual Literacy and Associate Editor of the Books of Selected Readings of The International Visual Literacy Association (USA) conferences.

Kelli C. A. S. Smythe holds a Master's degree in Design from The Federal University of Paraná (Brazil) where she is currently undertaking her doctoral studies with a grant from the Ministry of Education. Since 1999 she has been an adviser to Aurus Design Studio and to a number of product manufacturers in Curitiba, Brazil, developing projects and conducting research on instructional information design, wayfinding and sustainability with user centered approach.

Chapter 16: Typography for People with Aphasia: An Exploratory Study

Guillermina Noel

Abstract

In this chapter, I present an exploratory study that was carried out to determine which typographic families could facilitate reading for people with aphasia (a communication disability caused by brain damage). During the writing of my doctoral thesis, I identified the need to develop evidence that will allow informed design decisions to be made for the presentation of printed text to people with aphasia. Given this need, I developed an exploratory study in an attempt to obtain evidence regarding typefaces and other factors that could facilitate reading for people with aphasia.

To do this, I selected two short paragraphs from the website of an Italian aphasia group (my thesis was completed in Italy). These paragraphs were presented to readers with aphasia, using four different typefaces and two different spaces between the lines. The task presented to the readers was to read until they found a target word in the paragraph.

This study provides valuable insight into the reading difficulties and limitations faced by people with aphasia. It suggests that texts for people with aphasia should be relevant to them, should avoid long and unfamiliar words, and should also have a high level of predictability. In addition, this study helps to identify strategies that readers with aphasia use when confronted with difficult words, such as substituting, rereading, and breaking words into parts.

Problem Statement

The legibility of a typeface affects reading (Slattery & Rayner, 2009). Legibility is understood here as the level of recognizability of the shape of a letter. The shape should clearly represent the letter that it intends to represent so that the character is easily read. All the letters should have the same style, but they must be easy to differentiate them from each other. Unfortunately, there is little information regarding legibility for people with aphasia. Generally, the information about typography for people with aphasia is imprecise, insufficient and inapplicable.

For example, articles related to "aphasia friendly" material suggest the use of "large and standard fonts" to facilitate text comprehension (Rose, Worrall, & McKenna, 2003; Brennan, Worrall, & McKenna, 2005). Unfortunately, the lack of precision of the information provided renders it impossible to implement. How large should large be? Hartley (1994), in relation to the design of text for older readers (most people with aphasia are elderly), concluded that "larger type-sizes lead to less words per given line-length, and this might cause problems with more complex typography. In addition, lengthy texts become bulkier and heavier, factors that might cause problems for the elderly" (p. 176).

To determine if some typefaces are easy to read for people with aphasia, it is necessary to use familiar text typefaces and to use them in sizes that are comfortable to read. Waller (2007) stated that "experience shows that it is quite hard to show significant and noticeable differences in legibility between normal (that is, not decorative or distorted) typefaces when displayed in good reading conditions" (p. 2). Finding which typefaces facilitate the reading of short paragraphs for people with aphasia will allow us to make informed design decisions and to present texts that are adequate to these readers.

Another difficulty is the length of the text, given that fatigue is a problem for people with aphasia. Thus, the presentation of long texts to people with aphasia is not advisable. As Waller (2007) suggests, it is possible to study typefaces for reading "by giving people a text to read that takes several minutes, and timing them" (p. 2). As we can see, the needs of people with aphasia seem to be incompatible with the need for long texts to study typefaces for reading. Thus, it seems to be necessary to find adequate ways to study typography for people with aphasia.

Because most people with aphasia have some kind of reading comprehension difficulty, the task to perform in this study is not reading to comprehend but reading to locate a word in the text. Guthrie (1988) suggests that searching a word within a document is a cognitive process that is closer to reasoning than to language processing. According to the author, locating a word in a document entails forming a goal, selecting a category, extracting information, integrating information, and recycling (checking that the information fits the goal).

Finding words within a text is also an everyday need. For example, stroke patients might need to search the information leaflet of ibuprofen, a drug used for moderate pain, to corroborate that this drug will not interact with other drugs that they are taking. A common feature in reading to find information is the need to reread the text. Going back to the example provided above, after confirming that they can take ibuprofen, stroke patients might read the leaflet again to find out how to take this medicine. Rereading the text implies a learning effect. It is expected, for example, that the reader will become familiarized with the text and structure of the document (Guthrie, 1988); thus, a learning or practice effect is expected to be found in this study.

In sum, there is a need for evidence that will allow informed design decisions to be made about typeface selection for people with aphasia. As Waller (2007) said, however, finding significant differences in typefaces for text is difficult. In addition, the approach used to obtain noticeable differences might not be adequate for people with aphasia because most have some kind of reading comprehension difficulty. All this makes the study of typefaces for people with aphasia hard; nevertheless, this study makes a first attempt to obtain evidence regarding typefaces for people with aphasia. The next section outlines the methodology that was followed.

Methodology

Participants

Six people with aphasia participated in this study. The participants were three women and three men, ranging in age from 39 to 82, and all having Italian as their first language. One participant could not complete the reading of all the texts; however, the information resulting from the first reading session was considered valuable and was therefore included. The data regarding the first reading session of another participant were lost. The remaining data were considered valuable and were included in the analysis of the findings.

Materials

Interest is an essential component in text processing. If the text is interesting, it can prompt a person to increase the cognitive effort required for reading (Hidi & Baird, 1986). Thus, two short paragraphs were selected from the website of an Italian aphasia organization called Aphasia Forum. This website is directed at people with aphasia, at their family members, and at health professionals working with people with aphasia. In this chapter, the paragraphs are referred to as text A and text B. Please read text A (a translation of the original Italian) for an idea of the topic and of the level of difficulty of the texts. Text A:

> The association was born from the experience of a small group of aphasic persons, family members and health professionals that since 1996 has worked in the national territory to disseminate information about aphasia and to organize sustaining initiatives.

The total number of words in text A was 29, and in text B it was 43. The words to identify were *familiari* (family members), *operatori* (health professionals), *disabilità* (disability), *barriera* (barrier), *esperienza* (experience), *piccolo* (small), *ostacolo* (obstacle) and *insieme* (together).

Four typefaces were selected to display the paragraphs: Times, Georgia, Arial and Verdana. There were two main typeface selection criteria: availability and legibility. In terms of availability, because most speech therapists use Microsoft Office in their job, it was assumed that they had access to Times, Georgia, Arial and Verdana. In terms of legibility, these four typefaces have

- a consistent style,
- a consistent character width,
- a good x-height,
- recognizable ascenders and descenders,
- they are well spaced and kerned (Kern: space between pairs of letters such as VA that needs to be increased or reduced to achieve a consistent balanced spacing), and
- distinguishable letters.

Avoiding letter confusion is indispensable when designing text for readers with aphasia. Tinker (1963) explains that poor readers "must distinguish between similar word forms by discriminating between certain letters. Examples are … 'these' and 'there'" (p. 37).

The x-height was adjusted to 2.55 mm in the four typefaces. This is within the range recommended by organizations such as the British Dyslexia Association and Lighthouse International. Figure 1 shows the four typefaces in their actual x-height and their legibility features.

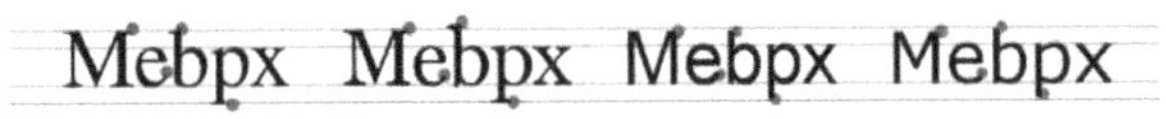

Mebpx Mebpx Mebpx Mebpx

Figure 1. From left to right: Times, Georgia, Arial, and Verdana.

The number of characters per line was about 32. The number of lines per paragraph was between six and nine. The paragraphs were set flush left.

Procedure

The meetings with the people with aphasia to evaluate the text material were held individually. People with aphasia were informed that the goal of the meetings was not to evaluate their reading comprehension abilities, but instead to assess the performance of the material.

The activity to evaluate the visual materials was conducted by Serena De Pellegrin, the speech therapist in the Department of Neurology of Padua University Hospital. I was observing, taking notes, and handling the materials.

To avoid memorization of the texts by the participants, activities such as evaluating prototypes and a brief interview about two different informed consent layouts were alternated with the reading of the brief texts.

The reading task was organized into two sessions. For example, participants read first text A (29 words) in Times and Georgia with a space between lines of 20 points, and then text B (43 words) in Times and Georgia with a space between lines of 24 points. After this, the participants did the word-picture matching activity used to evaluate a prototype and a brief interview about the word-picture matching prototypes. Next, the participants read text A (29 words) in Arial and Verdana with a space between lines of 20 points, and then text B (43 words) in Arial and Verdana with a space between lines of 24 points.

The speech therapist instructed the participants to read aloud until they found the target word. The reading of the six participants was audio-recorded. Reading accuracy was measured by the number of errors made, and reading ease was measured by the number of words that presented difficulties to the readers. The total time that each participant took to find the target word was recorded in seconds.

Findings

The results show a consistent pattern of difficult words across the participants regardless of the typeface and the line space used. It seems that the paragraphs did not meet the cognitive requirements of readers with aphasia. It might seem also that Georgia is better than Arial, but the time difference is too small to make this conclusion. Although the difference is small, which means that we should be cautious about the results, these preliminary findings still deserve attention.

The analysis of the audio-recording allowed the identification of errors and difficult words. Table 1 shows the errors made and the difficult words encountered by the participants according to typeface, line space, and type of text (Text A and Text B).

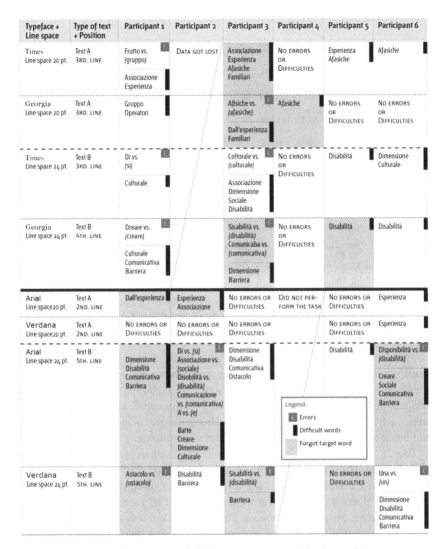

Typeface + Line space	Type of text + Position	Participant 1	Participant 2	Participant 3	Participant 4	Participant 5	Participant 6
Times Line space 20 pt.	Text A 3RD. LINE	Frutto vs. (gruppo) [E] Associazione Esperienza	DATA GOT LOST	Associazione Esperienza Afasiche Familiari	NO ERRORS OR DIFFICULTIES	Esperienza Afasiche	Afasiche
Georgia Line space 20 pt.	Text A 3RD. LINE	Gruppo Operatori		Afisiche vs. (afasiche) [E] Dall'esperienza Familiari	Afasiche	NO ERRORS OR DIFFICULTIES	NO ERRORS OR DIFFICULTIES
Times Line space 24 pt.	Text B 3RD. LINE	Di vs. (si) [E] Culturale		Coltorale vs. (culturale) [E] Associazione Dimensione Sociale Disabilità	NO ERRORS OR DIFFICULTIES	Disabilità	Dimensione Culturale
Georgia Line space 24 pt.	Text B 4TH. LINE	Dreare vs. (creare) [E] Culturale Comunicativa Barriera		Sisabilità vs. (disabilità) [E] Comunicaba vs. (comunicativa) Dimensione Barriera	NO ERRORS OR DIFFICULTIES	Disabilità	Disabilità
Arial Line space 20 pt.	Text A 2ND. LINE	Dall'esperienza	Esperienza Associazione	NO ERRORS OR DIFFICULTIES	DID NOT PERFORM THE TASK	NO ERRORS OR DIFFICULTIES	Esperienza
Verdana Line space 20 pt.	Text A 2ND. LINE	NO ERRORS OR DIFFICULTIES	NO ERRORS OR DIFFICULTIES	NO ERRORS OR DIFFICULTIES		NO ERRORS OR DIFFICULTIES	Esperienza
Arial Line space 24 pt.	Text B 5TH. LINE	Dimensione Disabilità Comunicativa Barriera	Di vs. (si) [E] Associazione vs. (sociale) Disobilità vs. (disabilità) Comunicazione vs. (comunicativa) A vs. (e) Batte Creare Dimensione Culturale	Dimensione Disabilità Comunicativa Ostacolo		Disabilità	Disponibilità vs. (disabilità) [E] Creare Sociale Comunicativa Barriera
Verdana Line space 24 pt.	Text B 5TH. LINE	Astacolo vs. (ostacolo) [E]	Disabilità Barriera	Sisabilità vs. (disabilità) [E] Barriera		NO ERRORS OR DIFFICULTIES	Una vs. (un) [E] Dimensione Disabilità Comunicativa Barriera

Legend.
[E] Errors
◼ Difficult words
▨ Forgot target word

Table 1. Reading errors and difficulties encountered by the participants.

As might be expected, long words caused errors and slowed down the reading pace (Rayner & Pollatsek, 1989; Slattery & Rayner, 2009). For example, the word "disabilità" (disability) presented most difficulties to the readers, followed by the word "comunicativa" (communicative). Figure 2 shows text B with the target words in italics and the difficult words readers encountered highlighted in yellow.

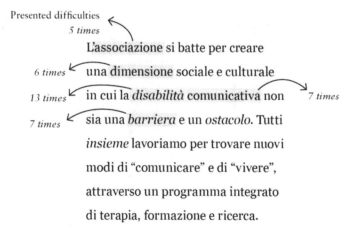

Figure 2. Example of how text B was presented to the readers.

Translation into English: The association struggles to create a social and cultural dimension in which the communication disability would not be a barrier or an obstacle. All of us together work to find new ways to "communicate" and to "live" through an integrative program of therapy, education and research.

The participants who had more difficulties reading long words, such as "comunicativa," read like this: "comu" / "comunica" / "comunicativa." Breaking a word into parts is a well-known strategy that readers use when they encounter difficult words (Brown, Pressley, Van Meter, & Schuder, 2004). In addition, when reading the word "afasiche" (aphasic), Participant 2 said: "Aphasic? How strange, I never saw that word before." This comment suggests that "aphasic" could be an unfamiliar word for some readers with aphasia.

The fact that the participants had similar difficulties despite their different reading impairments seems to indicate that the paragraphs were too demanding for readers with aphasia. Perhaps the difficulty was caused not only by the level of difficulty of the words but also by the low level of predictability of the text (Rayner, Reichle, Stroud, Williams, & Pollatsek, 2006). It is well-known that less skilled readers benefit from texts in which the context helps to predict what is coming next. As Stanovich and West (1981) stated, "since poorer readers have slower word recognition times, it is likely that this additional source of facilitation [contextual information] is implicated in their performance" (p. 668).

Given that the two paragraphs were selected from an aphasia website, their level of difficulty was not evaluated using readability formulas. In addition, readability formulas were not applied because they ignore meaning. The meaning of the text is an aspect that cannot be ignored when selecting readings for people with aphasia. As was previously mentioned, the text has to be relevant to them. Hartley, Trueman, and Burnhill (1980) suggested that, to evaluate the level of difficulty of a text, it is more valuable to ask the readers to examine the text and to provide their opinions than to apply readability formulas. The authors explained that consulting with the users is more valuable than applying readability formulas because it provides information about why and where to improve the text. Perhaps this is one of the values of the findings of my study: to inform where and why people with aphasia encountered difficulties.

Audio-recordings also allowed the identification of a behavior pattern. In many cases, after the therapist informed the participant which word was the target word, for example, "*operatori*," the participant asked: "operatori?" and the therapist responded: "yes, operatori." In other cases, the participant repeated the target word by breaking it into parts, for example: "di" / "sa" / "bi" / "li" / "tà," and the therapist confirmed: "yes, disabilità." This might indicate, as suggested by Guthrie (1988), that the person was encoding the information to be found, in other words, forming the goal.

In one case only was there an indication of the extraction of information. On this occasion, the participant asked the therapist: "Obstacle? With "O"?" After the therapist confirmed that the target word was obstacle with "o," the participant repeated: "o - o - o - o." This might suggest that the participant was storing in mind the details of the category.

As can be seen in Table 1, on thirteen occasions the participants could not complete the task successfully, that is, the readers forgot the word they had to find. This problem occurred even when the word to locate was in the second line. This might indicate a reduced working memory capacity. The attention limitations of people with aphasia compromise their language skills (Murray, 2002). In this case, attention and working memory limitations seem to compromise the capacity to locate a particular word in the text. According to Just and Carpenter (2004), "heavy processing requirements in a given task may decrease the amount of information that can be maintained, perhaps by generating too many competing structures or by actively inhibiting the maintenance of preceding information" (p. 1186). Thus, it might be that the difficult words block the maintenance of the target word in working memory. Alternatively, Guthrie (1988) proposes that, when searching information, the text one is reading must be integrated with the goal. The author called this process "integration," and explains that:

> A person who has failed to integrate at this point in reading is likely to be confused or disoriented. In this state of disintegration, it is reasonable to return to the original question. By making this move, the reader may enter (or reenter) the question in memory.... A high number of returns-to-question signifies a low level of integration skills (p. 188).

This might suggest that the working memory limitations of people with aphasia might affect their ability to locate information in a brief text. This, perhaps, has implications for speech therapists. Because searching a text is a frequent need, it might be necessary to assess searching abilities in people with aphasia.

The average time in seconds to locate the target word was used to explore

- whether the time is affected by the position of the word in the paragraph, and
- whether difficult words slowed down reading.

Table 2 presents the average time that it took for the participants to locate the target word, depending on the position of the word in the paragraphs.

Position of the word	2nd line	3rd line	4th line	5th line
Average time (in seconds)	5.1	14.8	16.6	30.6

Table 2. Time to locate the word depending on its position in the paragraphs.

The data in Table 2 show that the position of the word in the paragraph affects the average time taken to read. The average time increased from 5.1 seconds for words in the second line to 30.6 seconds for words in the fifth line. The difference is smaller between the third and fourth lines. Notice, however, that words were located in the third line in the two texts (A and B). Given this, Table 3 shows the average time, depending on the position of the word, and the number of readings for texts A and B.

	Reading 1	Reading 2	Reading 3	Reading 4
Position 2nd line			4.6	5.6
Position 3rd line	14	15.2		

Table 3. Time to locate the word in text A.

Table 3 shows that, when reading text A, both practice and the position of the target word affect the time taken to find the word in the text. The time to locate the word decreased from 14 seconds in the first reading, when the word is in the third line, to 5.6 seconds in the last reading, when the word is in the second line. Notice that the time increased from the first reading to the second reading, when the word is in the third line. This increment is probably due to Participant 4, who in the second reading had difficulties with the word *aphasic (afasiche)*, as shown in Table 1. The time from reading 3 to reading 4 increased, even though most participants did not encounter difficulties. Perhaps this could be caused by fatigue.

The total time to locate the word in text B is reported next in Table 4.

	Reading 1	Reading 2	Reading 3	Reading 4
Position 3rd line	15.2			
Position 4th line		16.6		
Position 5th line			30.22	29.2

Table 4. Time to locate the word in text B.

Table 4 shows that, when reading text B, the position of the target word affects the time taken to find it in the text. The practice effect cannot be observed given that every new line presents new text. In this case, though, the new text has only a few words. From reading 1 to reading 2, there are 5 new words to read, but from reading 2 to reading 3, there are only 3 new words to read (see Figure 2). This might suggest that it is the difficulty caused by words such as *disability* that affects the time taken to find the word, perhaps even more than the position. Given this, Tables 5 and 6 present the number of difficult words encountered and the time taken to locate the word to see whether difficult words slowed down reading.

Number of difficult words	0	1	2	3	4
Average time (in seconds)	6.1	8.4	11.3	23	20

Table 5. Time to locate the word depending on the difficult words in text A.

Table 5 shows that the number of difficult words slows down reading. The time taken to read increased from 6.1 seconds when no difficult words were encountered to 20 seconds when four difficult words were encountered. Next, Table 6 presents the data for text B.

Number of difficult words	0	1	2	4	5	9
Average time (in seconds)	5	12.7	25.2	33	24.3	39

Table 6. Time to locate the word depending on the difficult words in text B.

Table 6 shows that, when reading text B, the number of difficult words slows down reading. The time taken to read increased from 5 seconds when no difficult words were encountered to 39 seconds when nine difficult words were encountered.

These results suggest that the level of difficulty of the text did not match the needs of readers with aphasia. Difficult words (long and unfamiliar) require rereading and breaking into their parts, and this translates into longer reading times. Next, Table 7 presents the reading time per word, depending on the typeface.

	Times	Georgia	Arial	Verdana
Time x w. Text A	1	1	0.9	0.7
Time x w. Text B	1	0.8	1.3	1.2
Total	2	1.8	2.2	1.9

Table 7. Reading time per word depending on the typeface.

Table 7 shows the average reading time per word in seconds for each typeface. It seems that Georgia is the most legible and Arial is the least legible. Although the difference is small, which means that we should be cautious about the results, these findings still deserve attention. As Figure 3 shows, Georgia has better apertures (openings of letters such as "a," "c" and "e") than Arial. Open apertures favor legibility, facilitating the recognition of similar letters such as "c" and "e." Georgia also has better ascenders and descenders than Arial, and good ascenders and descenders facilitate the recognition of the word profile. As is known, the word profile is information that improves word recognition (Haber, Haber, & Furlin, 1983).

Figure 3. On the left, aperture, ascenders and descenders in Arial. On the right, aperture, ascenders and descenders in Georgia

The results might indicate that Georgia and Verdana (which also has better apertures, ascenders and descenders than Arial) at 2.55 mm are more legible, and hence more appropriate for the presentation of short paragraphs to readers with aphasia. Based on these results, however, it is not possible to make conclusions regarding line space, that is, whether it is more beneficial to use 20 or 24 points.

This is, indeed, a first step toward the study of typeface legibility and of readers with aphasia. The limitations of the study are discussed next.

Limitations

There are several weaknesses in this study. Despite having chosen the texts from an aphasia website, the texts (A and B) were too difficult for these readers with aphasia. More accurate findings might have been obtained if the texts had been more appropriate to the readers. Future studies should begin by evaluating the match between the texts and the readers.

Another limitation is the inadequacy of the texts selected to perform reading to locate information. These texts lacked clear categories of information, as well as headings and keywords that would have helped to identify them. A text with clear categories and structure would have provided more accurate results.

A further limitation is the use of reading aloud as applied in this study. More accurate results would have been found if the readers had been allowed to start reading and searching for the target word following their own strategies, instead of instructing them to start reading aloud the whole text from the beginning. It would also be advisable to control the position of the target word.

Another relevant aspect to consider is the nature of the activity to perform. Frascara (1984) demonstrated the importance of the situation of use or activity for the processing of information. Similarly, Jonassen, Lee, Yang, and Laffey (2005) argued that, after cognitive abilities, performance is most affected by the nature of the task. Mayer (2005) makes a distinction between being behaviorally active (that is, writing, pointing) and cognitively active. The activity in this study, I believe, did not promote the readers' engagement in problem solving, finding, for example, if clopidrogel (a drug taken by some stroke patients) interacts with ibuprofen. The activity did not support, moreover, the cognitive process of the readers. The task in this study was limited to reading until the readers found the target word. This promoted the reader to be behaviorally active, but not cognitively active. This interferes with measuring which typeface is more effective. A task that promoted active cognitive processing would have provided more realistic results.

A final limitation relates to the number of participants, because a larger number would have allowed more accurate findings.

Conclusions

The goal of this exploratory study was to take the first step in an attempt to obtain evidence that would allow informed design decisions to be made to facilitate reading for people with aphasia. As expected, it was not easy to provide evidence regarding typeface legibility for readers with aphasia. Hartley (1994) stated that "experiments on type-sizes and old age are difficult to carry out, and it is never fully clear whether one is investigating the effects of visual impairment or old age, or both, or indeed other factors" (p. 176).

The results of this study show that designers and other professionals who work with people with aphasia should be sensitive to the needs and cognitive limitations of these readers. Plain language experts and designers, in collaboration with therapists and in consultation with people with aphasia, should create the texts for websites, informed consents, patient information leaflets, and other documents directed at these readers. Of course, these texts should then be evaluated after with the users. This would improve the quality and adequacy of the texts.

This study provides insight into the reading difficulties and limitations faced by people with aphasia. It suggests that texts for people with aphasia should be relevant, should avoid long and unfamiliar words, and should also have a high level of predictability. The results also help to identify strategies that readers with aphasia use when confronted by difficult words, such as substituting, rereading, and breaking words into their parts.

The study suggests that words related to "living with aphasia" are the most difficult for people with aphasia. Many studies have demonstrated the need to provide information regarding this disorder to people with aphasia, but there still seems to be a need to find adequate ways to communicate this aphasia-related information.

Finding out ways to study typography for people with aphasia is a primary task to tackle in the future. The combination of eye-tracking technology, with verbal protocols, and qualitative methodologies such as observation and interviews might be a promising strategy to obtain useful evidence.

Implications and Recommendations

There are many factors that can allow or interfere with studying typeface legibility for readers with aphasia. Designers and other researchers who are studying this problem should, in addition to the issues outlined in the problem statement, consider the following:

- Select a text that is relevant to the readers, matches their needs, and is adequate to perform the reading task.
- Select a task that supports the location of information, that is real and meaningful, and that promotes active cognitive processing.
- Perform first a preliminary study to identify text difficulties, and then follow this with a second independent study to investigate typeface legibility when locating information.
- Use a text structure that shows clear categories of information.
- Provide instructions that support the task, and that guide and prompt searching.
- Use verbal protocols and audio-recording to reveal valuable insight about reading to locate information.
- Have two reader groups: one in which the texts are assigned in a randomized order, and another in which the texts are presented in the same order. This would allow a better study of typeface legibility.

This first step was indeed an exploration, and I hope that the information provided will contribute to future studies. Knowing what works and what does not work in typeface legibility for readers with aphasia is essential to facilitate their reading and to arrive at effective and clear communications.

References

Brennan, A., Worrall, L., & McKenna, K. (2005). The relationship between specific features of aphasia-friendly written material and comprehension of written material for people with aphasia: An exploratory study. *Aphasiology, 19*(8), 693-711.

Brown, R., Pressley, M., Van Meter, P., & Schuder, T. (2004). A quasi-experimental validation of transactional strategies instruction with low-achieving second-grade readers. In R.B. Ruddell & N.J. Unrau (Eds.). *Theoretical models and processes of reading* (5th ed.), (pp. 998-1039). Newark, DE: International Reading Association.

Frascara, J. (1984). Design principles for instructional materials. In R. Easterby & H. Zwaga (Eds.), *Information design* (pp. 469-478). New York: Wiley.

Guthrie, J. T. (1988). Locating information in documents: Examination of a cognitive model. *Reading Research Quarterly, 23*(2), 178-199.

Haber, L. R., Haber, R. N., & Furlin, K. (1983). Word length and word shape as sources of information in reading. *Reading Research Quarterly, 18*(2), 165-189.

Hartley, J. (1994). Designing instructional text for older readers: A literature review. *British Journal of Educational Technology, 25*(3), 172-188.

Hartley, J., Trueman, M., & Burnhill, P. (1980). Some observations on producing and measuring readable text. *Innovations in Education and Teaching International, 17*(3), 164-174.

Hidi, S. & Baird, W. (1986). Interestingness–A neglected variable in discourse processing. *Cognitive Science, 10,* 179-194.

Jonassen, D.H., Lee, C.B., Yang, C., & Laffey, J. (2005). The collaboration principle in multimedia learning. In R.E. Mayer (Ed.), *The Cambridge handbook of multimedia learning* (pp. 247-270). New York: Cambridge University Press.

Just, M.A., & Carpenter, P.A. (2004). A theory of reading: From eye fixations to comprehension. In R.B. Ruddell & N.J. Unrau (Eds.), *Theoretical models and processes of reading* (5th ed.), (pp. 1182-1218). Newark, DE: International Reading Association.

Mayer, R.E. (2005). *The Cambridge handbook of multimedia learning.* New York: Cambridge University Press.

Murray, L. L. (1999). Attention and aphasia: theory, research and clinical implications. *Aphasiology, 13*(2), 91-111.

Rayner, K., & Pollatsek, A. (1989). *The psychology of reading.* Englewood Cliffs, NJ: Prentice-Hall.

Rayner, K., Reichle, E.D., Stroud, M., Williams, C., & Pollatsek, A. (2006). The effect of word frequency, word predictability, and font difficulty on eye movements of young and older readers. *Psychology and Aging, 21,* 448-465.

Rose, T., Worrall, K., & McKenna, K. (2003). The effectiveness of aphasia-friendly principles for printed health education materials for people with aphasia following stroke. *Aphasiology, 17*(10), 947-963.

Slattery, T.J., & Rayner, K. (2009). The influence of text legibility on eye movements during reading. *Applied Cognitive Psychology, 24*(8), 1129-1148.

Stanovich, K.E., & West, R.F. (1981). The effect of sentence context on ongoing word recognition: Tests of two-process theory. *Journal of Experimental Psychology: Human Perception and Performance, 7*(3), 658-672.

Tinker, M. A. (1963). *Legibility of print.* Iowa: Iowa State University Press.

Waller, R. (2007). Comparing typefaces for airport signs. *Information Design Journal, 15*(1), 1-15.

Biographical note

Guillermina Noël holds a PhD in design sciences from the University IUAV of Venice, Italy, and a Master of Design from the University of Alberta, Canada. She has worked on the design of materials for people with severe speech and reading impairments, interacting with neurologists, educational psychologists, and speech therapists, emphasizing the importance of user-centered design and design for users with special needs.

Among her publications are: Frascara, J. & Noël, G. (2011). Evaluation and design of a blood components transfusion request form. *Information Design Journal*, 18.3, 241-249; Frascara, J., Della Puppa, A., Noël, G. & De Pellegrin, S. (2011). A critique of visual materials in 'Evidence for an occipito-temporal tract Underlying visual recognition in picture naming.' *Clinical Neurology and Neurosurgery*, 9.13, 80-81; Frascara, J. & Noël, G. (2009). "User-Centered communication" in S. Heller, & L. Talarico (Eds.), *Design school confidential* (pp. 118-121). Beverly, MA: Rockport Publishers; Noël, G. (2008). "Language impairment, family interaction and the design of a game" in *Visible Language*, 42.2, 143-157; and Noël, G. (2006). "Creating Possibilities" in J. Frascara (Ed.), *Designing Effective Communications* (pp. 57-62). NY: Allworth Press.

She has participated in conferences and delivered lectures and workshops in Argentina, Italy, Switzerland, Brazil, Canada, USA, Paraguay, Sweden, Spain, Cuba and Mexico. She has taught design at the University of La Plata, at the University of Alberta, at the University of La Matanza, and at the Universidad de las Americas Puebla, and works professionally in visual communication design since 1997. Since 2003 her practice focuses on health related design issues. She is now an Adjunct Researcher at the Health Design Lab at Emily Carr University, Vancouver, Canada.

Chapter 17: Design as a Catalyzer

"The tragedy is not to aim high and miss, the tragedy is to aim low and hit."

—Michelangelo Buonarroti

Ronald Shakespear

Abstract

Innovation–particularly in Argentina–has not been a simple process during the last fifty years: the relation between design and the reality of Latin America pushed us to invent new ways to cope with recurrent crises. Design acts, like in chemistry, as a catalyzer. The chapter exemplifies these and other fundamental concepts through the work of my studio, specialized in branding and way finding systems for large spaces.

I met Max Bruinsma at the Icograda São Paulo Conference, Fronteiras 2004. There, I heard him saying that design acts as a catalyzer. A catalyzer is a chemical substance that, simple or compounded, intensely modifies the speed of a reaction, intervening in it but without getting to necessarily be in its results. Catalyzers are defined by two variables: their active stage and their selectivity. Activity and selectivity, and even the life itself of the catalyzer, directly depend on the active stage used. The Merriam-Webster Dictionary says: "An agent that provokes or speeds significant change or action."

During a long time, signage was a term given to a residual sub-activity neighboring hardware. The culture of the information and persuasion instruments of large public spaces required many decades and not a few efforts to acquire professional standing. It is however still possible to find a pay phone public sign above a pay phone, or the sign for a mailbox above a mailbox. The phone and the mailbox *are* the signs.

Things have not changed that much through the centuries, and it would have been reasonable to infer that there was a growing discipline if one considers that the hieroglyphs, the smoke, the arrow, the foot print and the drum foretold the human will to communicate.

During a long time the language of the pyramids was ignored, and it was usual to assign to the hieroglyphs a cosmetic role, related to the fear of empty spaces more than to a visual grammar. The horror of empty spaces also produces the need for an overdose, understandable in some cultural contexts. Then the public signs epidemic rears its ugly face.

In the hard job of constructing Stevens, that wonderful character of the butler, for the film *The Remains of the Day*, Anthony Hopkins suffered the usual anxieties of the case. James Ivory, the director, advised him to have a chat with an old Windsor butler, now retired.

Hopkins and the man met for tea, of course, and engaged in a charming and long conversation. However, when the man was about to leave, Hopkins had the feeling of having gotten nothing worthwhile. Already at the door, the actor burst: "But tell me, finally, what is a butler?" The butler hesitated a bit and then said: "A butler is someone that, when he enters in a room, he makes the room seem emptier than before."

Throughout the years, in this hard job of making public spaces legible, of producing communication responses and constructing identities, I have come to the conclusion that this charming tale by Anthony Hopkins, somehow summarizes the nature and essence of our task. Obsessed by the need to establish the sequentiality of the signs, so as to attain the predictability of the messages, obsessed by the results of the endeavor, we have conceived many of the stimuli implemented in the urban space, forgetting that these should act in silence, without screaming. Like people's servants.

Visual Plan for Buenos Aires City (Design: Ronald Shakespear & Guillermo González Ruiz, 1971-72)

"The best way to predict the future is to design it." *Buckminster Fuller*

Every designer coins–not without difficulty–a theory of his practice, and this learning emerges necessarily from the empiricism of the practice itself. A complex dexterity is required to read a space, and its learning takes both time and effort. Trial and error. These large scale projects are extremely complex by their own nature, due to the number of accumulated requirements, due to their interdisciplinary character, and to the changing socioeconomic conditions within which they develop. From a historical point of view there are paradigmatic projects, and the international experience often confirms that they have played an epic role in the history of design.

This permanent call that takes design to the public space and makes it land on the urban space and activates the lives of cities and their people, gives sense to our work and naturally turns into a way of perceiving our trade.

"It has been said that humankind has the public signs it deserves, although it is almost a sure thing that the Roman Empire did not deserve something so beautiful as Trajan's typographic frontispieces. Facing such an assignment," adds

Jock Kinneir, "is a moment of truth for any designer, because it challenges his skills, integrity, and power of permanence. It is the moment in which every premise must be questioned and in which ignorance is a marvelous state of independence from traditional rules." Jock Kinneir had a profound significance for us, back then in the seventies. All the epic narrative of his program for the highways of the UK made him a referent for us. The subtle threads with which he managed his relations with traffic engineers, architects, urban planners and civil servants, are meaningful acts of design that the professional community acknowledges to him with praise: the magnificent typographic proposal–for the first time in the history of lowercases; the organization of the informational plane; his bright and efficient analysis of the factors letter/speed/distance; his fantastic translation of the vehicular flow onto the vector sign (surely, from a historic perspective, his greatest contribution to design); his chromatic proposal and, of course, the technology.

These words from the master sound so familiar, describe so well that moment–almost forty years ago–when starting with the Buenos Aires Visual Plan, that it seems pertinent to cite him here with the conviction that he not only was premonitory of our work, but also of that of many designers around the world that saw themselves, some time, compelled to transfer a constellation of graphic responses to large public spaces.

The designers of signage systems must decipher the codes of the public. Signs form part of the daily life of citizens, and not only stand there; they must be a-temporal and act as if they had always stood there. They must become visible when one has to find a destination; they must do their job and then merge back as part of the surroundings.

> "Man speaks in lowercase letters. He shouts in capitals," Jock Kinneir used to say.

Every transportation system is formed by two basic dimensions. In the first place, there is an infrastructure, and all its components involved; the integral service network. Secondly, there is communication, that through diverse functional elements, allows users to understand and use the service. We call this second dimension "the semiotic network." Pragmatic communications happen through an efficient signage system.

Since the creation of the railways, the airports, and the bus stations, as means for mass transportation, maps have been a preoccupation and a challenge for engineers, managers and design professionals.

Illustrious predecessors like the "Tube" map (Henry Beck), or New York's subway's (Massimo Vignelli) have transformed this particular element into a classic, a prototypical expression of the social function of design, and paradigm of both design for the masses and rationalist treatment of information.

This graphic configuration shows the navigational "menu," destinations and connections for public use, with significant perceptual benefits. It establishes a way of "reading" the place. Sensible and intuitive signage systems are the creation of designers that understand the complexity of the public space, the specific environment of the project in question, and the performance and the functions that are expected from the signs.

At the beginning of 1971, the then "Estudio Shakespear y Gonzalez Ruiz," received from the City of Buenos Aires the design commission of what later became "The Visual Plan for the City of Buenos Aires." The plan shaped a unique situation in our context. Not precisely because of its scale, surely without local or regional precedent. It was unique from the dynamic perspective it created with the client and from a series of fundamental decisions that made not only possible the execution of the project but also its survival. The decision to realize all the experimental prototypes for a field test and the subsequent pilot plans for the Avenues Libertador and Figueroa Alcorta, within the General Maintenance Direction, was a bright act: the signs went onto the streets, into the public domain. They existed.

After this foundational act, let us say, the administrative rails did the rest right up to our days. The images that accompany this chapter come from the *Standards Manual* (out of print for a long time) and are well known by now. It is to be noted that the problems of inserting our work in public spaces reiterates the same syndrome in every country of the world, be it first or third.

The typology of instruments that form the system is based of four basic signs: names of streets and avenues; transit system stops; squares and parks; and taxi stops.

Figure 1: Taxi stop sign

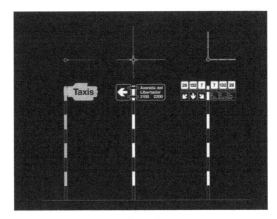

Figure 2

Figure 3: Streets and avenues names

Our devotion for Helvetica took us to choose it as the font for all communications of the City, including posters, signs and texts of all type and function. It was surely the first time that Max Miedinger's beautiful alphabet for Haas walked around Latin American streets.

The signs' names were originally blue, as it is required by the traffic code for information signs. Thereafter bureaucracy required them to be black, and be attached to existing traffic light columns (striped black and yellow). This decision, however, was later abandoned by the City, when seeing that attaching diverse stimuli to the same column made them attack one another and weakened their visibility. Overlapping two or more stimuli is a communicational failure.

Signs and People in Power

"When I use a word," Humpty Dumpty said… "it means just what I choose it to mean."

"The question is," said Alice, "whether you can make words mean so many different things."

"The question is," said Humpty Dumpty, "which is to be master–that's all."

—Lewis Carrol

We have always wondered, and want to emphasize this topic here, how was really the relation between Leonardo and Ludovico il Moro; or Michelangelo with Pope Julius II; or Raymond Loewy with NASA. Out of all our daily obsessions (intensified by the large scale-projects, naturally), i.e., vandalism, climatic factors' erosion, distances for perception in motion, installation subsystems, the letters, the color or the technology, just to name a few, the relation with the client is for us today the subject of utmost preoccupation.

Trying to justify his crimes, Harry Lime (Orson Welles) tells Holly Martins (Joseph Cotten), in *The Third Man*, "For thirty years in Italy, under the rule of the Borgias, there were wars, terror and killings, but Michelangelo, Leonardo and the Renaissance flourished. In Switzerland they have had five hundred years of brotherly love, democracy and peace, and what have they produced? The cuckoo clock."

The productive act–in final analysis, people and their circumstances–has always happened in contexts imposed by reality. The clients are the clients. They are those and no others, and Ludovico il Moro and Cesare Borgia made it finally possible for humanity to be privileged by the works of Leonardo. And the fundamental reason for so many virgins to be painted, is not based on the presumed devotion of the Masters, but–and very simply–on the client that commissioned virgins.

The striking of a flexible and creatively divergent relation with whom commissions the work and with all his management teams, is effectively a design act: it is part of the project and defines, without a doubt, the result. To make the city legible implies deciphering its codes.

The reality is that the decibels of visual contamination are colossal. The semiotic noise attacks daily life in the cities and, in that context, public information taking form in signs, struggles to be heard. To harmonize the integration of outdoors advertising with the signs calls for an urban master plan with precise regulations and the possibility to make them be observed. Cantilevered signs that reach across half the street and marquises out of any code can be found in many cities. We call that "urban rape."

Most design education programs are focused on preparing students for jobs in the industry forgetting that Rembrandt's light, Oscar Wilde's language, and Orson Welles' film editing are infinitely more important than mastering the computer. I have tried to narrate these contingencies in my book *Señal de Diseño*, with the hope that this "memoir of the practice" be of use for somebody. It would be for me a privilege. In the end, if design is not good at helping people live better, then it is not good at all.

The Fundamental Fact of this Type of Project is Order

An important requirement of this type of system is a very clear visual structure that could permit the user access the information immediately and with precision. Predictability and sequential logic are essential to facilitate a rapid learning of how the semiotic network works, where users establish a pragmatic relation with the signs and choose their options. This is crucial in what refers to placing, size, colors, and pictogram and text messages. With the passing of time, our information eager society has turned more complex and has generated a need for more and better information vehicles, to achieve a better understanding. This process has never been simple. On the contrary, the amount of unnecessary information always exceeds the amount of pertinent information. Our visual surrounding mirrors that complexity.

"The point of view changes the perspective" *Leonardo Da Vinci*

When NASA commissioned Raymond Loewy–surely one of the most important design pioneers–the interior design of the Skylab capsule, Loewy was about 70 years old. To live in his own flesh the behavior of an astronaut on board, Loewy wrapped himself in the pressurized spatial outfit to get in a zero gravity chamber. It was Loewy, whose tenacity and energy in pursuit of achieving his objectives were proverbial, who persuaded the engineers about the imperative need to install a porthole in the capsule.

Back home, the astronauts paid homage to Raymond Loewy. It was that vision of earth, through the porthole, what kept them–so they said–in the right emotional condition to face the outer space stress.

These infrequent dexterities that were manifested by pioneers like Alvar Aalto or Raymond Loewy in pursuit of producing multiple responses to design problems are the salt of life. But what is to be rescued from here is not NASA's space craft porthole, that permitted the astronauts, in an illusory fantasy, watch home while in orbit. The significant element is the designer's attitude, that allowed him to detect a need while, at the same time, solve the problem of the user and the client. If we establish the idea that design is not drawing but a mental plan, as defined by the Oxford dictionary, and agree that design is at the base of every human activity, all the concept of design gets definitely redefined for the whole of society.

Design is neither connected to the idea of art nor with that of beauty. It is connected to the idea of generating pragmatic things from which it is expected, it is demanded, a given result. When this condition is fulfilled, when the result produces better quality of life, the design is, surely, beautiful.

The Buenos Aires Subway (Design: Lorenzo, Juan & Ronald Shakespear. Diseño Shakespear, 1995-2008)

"If you don't know where you are going, any road will get you there."
Lewis Carroll

A transportation signage system demands a specific and deep study that takes into account the contexts in which the signs will be used. This means, the architectonic limitations, the lighting conditions, the circulation complexity, the right placement of the signs, and the quality of the messages directed at a multi-segment public of users.

Graphic, Typographic, Chromatic, Technological and Placement Sub-systems

These five subsystems, acting as a group or individually, determine the efficiency of a signage system. The graphic subsystem aims at establishing the visual power of the tools used; the typographic subsystem determines the legibility of the messages; the chromatic subsystem determines the capacity for encoding in a pragmatic form; the technologic subsystem determines the strength and the quality of the signs. Finally, the placement subsystem defines the most effective positioning of the signs in terms of perception and self-protection, to avoid destruction and deterioration.

Figure 4: Carlos Pellegrini station. Behind, the obelisk.

Figure 5: Access to Carlos Pellegini station before 2004

Figure 6: Facultad de Medicina station platform.

Figure 7: Bolívar station. Behind, the Cabildo (historic government house) and Buenos Aires Cathedral.

Today the signs are seen as a vital need in any transportation system in terms of organizing the flow of users, but they constitute as well an important element in a plan that could pretend to renew "the landscape." Historically, this landscape was contaminated by numerous non-planned elements. In an integrated project, where advertising and shops have a strong presence, signs are the voice of the place and form its identity. In recently implemented re-branding of the Buenos Aires subway system, Diseño Shakespear rescued from the first moment the popular word "Subte" (short for "subterráneo" that is, "underground"). "Subte" is anchored in the collective memory of the city, and is the denomination that emerges from the people. In this re-branding (that follows the one done by us in 1995) the color palette has been intensified to provide identity to the different lines. The focus groups organized by *Metrovías* (the private company running the system) clearly express the vocation of the users. Many people define their daily use as "I take the green one." "I take the red." "I take the blue."

The emotional capitalization of the Subte is enormous and its relation with the people is expressed in terms of ownership. The access points have then been characterized by a true urban rainbow where the brand is always the same but with the specific color of each line. The Visual Plan of Buenos Aires beloved Helvetica was replaced by the efficient and austere Frutiger. The team also worked on the protocols for the implementation and the technology of the signs, their sequentiality, and, above all, their predictability. In the Subte's platforms we replaced the "epidemy of little signs" with a continuous band that runs along the 220 meters of the station. Thus we made a sort of continuum belt that ties the network, like Hansel and Gretel's bread crumbs.

The map of the network was originally vertical. The so called Christian West reads horizontally, from left to right. Only some oriental people read and write vertically or from right to left. The horizontalization and schematization of the network implies, naturally, a modification in the habits of people. This certainly requires a learning process, that requires, like all change of habit, a decoding effort. Finally everybody takes their time.

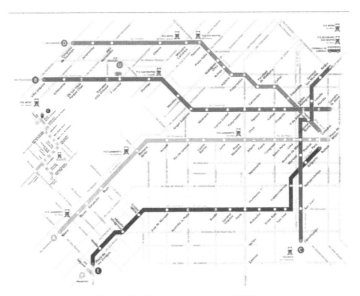

Figure 8: Current *Subte* map (2008).

Figure 9. Former *Subte* map (2004).

"Despite the horrors of the bureaucratic process involved in the development of a design program for a transportation network, the reward that offers the design of a better graphic system that affects millions of people, is enormous" says Massimo Vignelli.

In the new map for the *Subte*, the juxtaposition of the railways network to the urban network–a reference–allows the possibility to relate the city's landmarks with the *Subte's* service menu. This is also stimulating, because it promotes in the user the connectivity between the "the ground and the underground."

These large scale-projects in the cities' landscapes are usually called "signage systems." In the Anglo-Saxon countries they are called "wayfinding" or, more recently, according to Per Mollerup, "wayshowing," that possibly better expresses its nature and function. An excellent book that includes our work (*Follow me)* has been published in China. Also, the *Subte* project can be seen in Rob Carter's book *Typographic Design, Form and Commmunication*, recently published by Wiley & Sons.

I have always thought that good architecture requires only a few signs, and, personally, I have emphasized two fundamental aspects: the sequentiality and predictability of the signage systems. The first establishes the cyclic reiteration of the stimulation, and the second constructs a predictable cultural rhythm to read the city. In addition, although the fundamental role of the signs is to organize the flow of cars and people, its major contribution is the construction of an identity for the place.

The sign is a promise. And it must be fulfilled.

> "In theory, theory is exactly the same as practice. In practice it's not."
> *Rob Roach*

Biopark Temaikén (Design: Lorenzo, Juan & Ronald Shakespear. Diseño Shakespear 2002/2003)

The strong constraining elements of the urban landscape, and especially, the extended presence of advertising and the proliferation of shops, force designers to make certain decisions that give the communications the distinctiveness and the identity they need. In this context, this can only be achieved through the scale, the repetition and the right placement. One has to generate a communication channel that establishes the tone and the voice of the sender departing from a constant location–and hence, predictable–so as to give priority to the information and the connection with the public.

Design + Preservation + Amusement

"The main purpose of the Temaikén Foundation–says Lorenzo Shakespear–is to honor the privileged place we have in this world and generate a new consciousness of importance of preservation and the stewarding of nature. Tem (earth) and aikèn (life) are two *Tehuelche* terms that speak with clarity about the intentions of this thematic bio-park." (*Tehuelche*: aboriginal people from the Argentine pampas).

At Temaikén human progress has been put to the service of nature. The best technology, the highest scientific rigor and the possibilities of design in the service of communication have allowed the realization of a world-class park where every species finds itself in its natural surroundings. To align *Temaikén* with its essence and objectives, and at the same time build an efficient instrument for public recognition, Diseño Shakespear developed a total visual identity project.

Figure 10: Logo Temaikén.

The logotype, embryo of the Temaikén project, was conceived with a malleable and organic typeface, and expresses the phonetics of the name in a color range of sepias and earth tones, linked to land and nature. These colors invaded all communications systematically. A symbol was also designed, that evokes the logo, capturing its initial letter and inserting it in a circular container that alludes to the earth's sphere.

This triad of basic identity elements–logo, symbol and color–form a recognition and value unit of the *Temaikén* brand. Diseño Shakespear articulated them to reflect a friendly, warm and not screaming image that summons a more intimate dialogue between the park and its visitors.

Like in our design for the Buenos Aires Visual Plan (*Plan Visual de Buenos Aires*, Shakespear/González Ruiz) in 1971, the Municipal Hospitals (*Hospitales Municipales*, 1978/1982, Ronald and Raúl Shakespear), the Train of the Coast (*Tren de la Costa*, 1992/1995), the Sun Highways (*Autopistas del Sol*, 1996), or the Buenos Aires Subway system (*Subte de Buenos Aires*, 1995/ 2008, with Lorenzo and Juan Shakespear, like the previous two projects), the visual language used responded to the peculiarities of the surroundings, to the nature of the project, and to the profile of its public.

The House Style

Every signage system for mobility networks must meet two conditions, regardless of the particular nature of the space:

- It must be easy to locate the signs and their place must be predictable. To do this they must segregate from the surroundings, but without screaming so as to avoid reducing the protagonist role of the space. They also must appear, like a work of magic, at the decision moments, fulfill their mission and then merge in the environment again.

- The signs must be easily understood. Their capacity to resolve with precision the uncertainty that motivated the creation of a sign depends on the professional ability to anticipate the need and to offer the solution with economy of words (in a verbal system) or with high iconic value (in a pictographic system).

The *Temaikén* signage was conceived as an active manifestation of its identity. The various signs, far from being just signs, form a typology of instruments that goes way beyond resolving specific situations of traffic or communication flow: they express a house style, a tone of voice, and a dialogue with the public.

The consistency in the implementation (consistent and predictable placing of the signs, clear chromatic codes, pictographic, typographic and technological integration) is crucial to guarantee the efficiency of the system and of any signage system.

The semiotic structure of the *Temaikén* signage system is built on five classic sub-systems as it was already mentioned: graphic, typographic, chromatic, technologic and positioning. The building technology for all the system is extremely simple and complements well the rest of the architecture for the park. The Project Manual was prepared so that the Park administration could execute a perfect implementation and maintenance of the visual identity and signage system. The scientific interpretation signs contain information about each species and provide additional data such as maps of the original habitats along with the levels of danger of extinction of each species.

During the last decades, the value given to the phonetic names of business and products, expressed through clear and memorable typographic strategies, has produced a clear emphasis of the brands that have a strong verbal presence in the contaminated universe of corporate identities. We are culturally conditioned to the images. The election of a pictographic system responds to the clear premise to offer to the users a short-cut of nonverbal communication. A morphologically simple, almost gestural family of highly recognizable pictograms was designed to synthetically represent the different species of the fauna, keeping in mind the children, and their capacity for decoding.

Lance Wyman recounts that at the Washington Zoo, once the system was completed by his studio, a little boy asked his mother looking at the animals' footprints painted on the floor: "Tell me mom, are birds really so BIG in this place?"

The unease of the child is quite understandable. In order to gain a high presence for his project, Wyman, as surely other designers would have done, did not consider the scale for the footprints of birds, and gave them the same size as those of the pachyderms.

A charming sign in a highway that goes through the Arizona desert reads: "Boring, isn't it." Another in downtown Manhattan reads: "Don't even think about parking here." There is another similar sign in California: "Lost parents: your children are waiting for you at the nursery."

Figure 11: Bat identification sign: 3D pictogram.

The idea of two superimposed aluminum discs, separated by a 5 cm space and colored with two of the basic colors (to provide contrast) gives movement to the otherwise static pictograms. The mast that holds them, made of steel and tinted with a third color completes the group. The result has a high innovative value and a robust presence. Nevertheless the sign maintains its secondary role in the landscape and does not deteriorate the views. The pictograms have been cut with a laser plotter to achieve a pristine finish. The signs were painted with powder paint and covered by a UV lacquer to protect them from the sun and environmental agents.

While the images of the animals provide a visual link with their habitats, a glance at the map is enough to find the path toward whatever point in the park. The directional signs offer alternatives for the flow of the public and the planning of their placement provides agile responses in the knots and bifurcations where decisions have to be taken.

The parking area signs, as much as those for the main access, and those of the sectors biosphere, aquarium and Patagonia, link with the same design matrix. Communications in the so called "dark areas," like the aquarium, were solved with acrylic sheets printed in high contrast, four-color process. Mounted in internally lit boxes, the information seems to float on the "windows" of each area, keeping the ambient light unaltered.

The Master Map for *Temaikén* shows the park as a bird-view, with attached architectonic elements in 3D, presenting in a transparent and simple form the "menu" of the proposal, its contents, placement and circulation. It works as a "pocket-map," as an independent sign, or as a totem of the kind "You are here" (placed at strategic points of the pedestrian paths).

Indispensable during the 40 hectares network of paths, the map offers architectonic, geographic and pictogrammatic references immediately recognizable by the visitor.

The relation between the reality, uncovered step after step in the route, and its cartographic representation was one of the major preoccupations of the design team.

Figure 12: Ronald, Juan and Lorenzo Shakespear in an exhibition of their work.

Corollary of an Already Long Road

"If your house were burning down, what would you rescue?" "The fire."
Jean Cocteau.

Bernard Shaw says that the great drama of communication is to think that it has been successful. To communicate innovation presupposes before anything that to innovate is to replace existing situations with preferable ones. The Brand is not a Logo. Is a behavior. And a promise. When it delivers what it promises, commercial, institutional, cultural, is building Brand.

The Logo is–in any case–the emblem of that promise. Brands are not. They are becoming. And, effectively, some brands go to Heaven.

A virtuous brand is that that fulfills its promises. An efficient brand is that which emits the right identity. A good brand collects affection. The dilemma of the three "I": Identity, Identification, Image. The first is in the belly of the transmitter. The second is the strategy to transfer that identity. The third is the fantasy that the public elaborates from the first.

Brands and their visual expression are not eternal, they live ever shorter cycles and they not only need a strong identification behavior, but, in addition, the capacity to collect affection, seduction, and, above all, persuasion. This is, the capacity to modify human behaviors. There resides the innovative value of brands. Finally, as Jorge Frascara says, "The mission of design is not to communicate. It is to produce responses."

Design has changed more in the last 20 years than in the preceding five hundred. It has turned into a hyper-dynamic discipline oriented at producing desired responses from increasingly more dissatisfied audiences. The zest for profits is the reason for its demand and the existence of globalization supposes–of course–the presence of the globalizer. He is also dissatisfied. It has been said that there are no longer technological frontiers and while the contraptions of simulation make dinosaurs jump on the screens faced by fascinated multitudes, we annihilate forests and whales.

My friend Alan Fletcher, that died a few years ago, told me a beautiful story that he had heard from someone else. In 53 BCE, Marco Casio invaded Parthia (currently Iraq) with an army of 40,000 and the goal of expanding the Roman Empire. The result was a disaster, mainly due to the design of the Parthian bow. The Parthian bow was a weapon built with a laminated spring, with a range and power that made Roman legions defenseless; 20,000 Romans died; 10,000 were taken prisoner. According to Alan, it is important to note that the Parthians did not prevail because they had a better General. They prevailed because they had a better designer.

Finally, what are we doing here? Fifty years have passed with brands and signs. And today I would say that they look much alike. Finally everything has to do with people.

Biographical Note

Ronald Shakespear was professor at the Department of Design FADU / UBA and ADG president, Association of Graphic Designers of Buenos Aires. He founded his studio 50 years ago. Shakespear Design now runs with his son Juan.

He has been international jury member for the Art Directors Club of New York, the SEGD Design Awards (Washington DC), the poster for the Future (France) Citroen Prize, the Wolda Awards in Milan and is permanent Jury member for the Argentine Innovation Contest. He won the Lápiz de Plata as designer of the year, the Konex, Klaukol-CAYC Award for Lifetime Achievement, and the Golden Brain. He is a fellow of the Society of Environmental Graphic Design of the United States.

His latest book, *Señal de Diseño, Memoria de la Práctica*, has been re-published by Paidós. He has delivered lectures and workshops in thirty-three cities and his work has been published in many international books and magazines. His work has been exhibited in Washington, Richmond, Mexico, Buenos Aires, Paris and Milan.

His studio has designed many large signage systems as well as 1,600 brands over the last fifty years. His photographs were published by Jorge Alvarez Editor in 1966 in the book *Caras y Caritas* and are part of private collections and museums in Switzerland, Canada, USA and Italy. His portrait "Borges at the Library" (1966) is in the permanent exhibition of the Foundation Jorge Luis

Borges in Buenos Aires; and the poster for Hamlet, with Alfredo Alcon (1964), has been recognized in Mexico as one of the 100 best posters in history, and can be seen in the permanent collection of the Modern Art Museum of Buenos Aires. www.shakespearweb.com

Part V: Case Studies in Design Education

Design education is in dire need for adjusting to the contemporary demands emerging in the practice. The powerful Bauhaus model that enshrines visual innovation above anything else, where context, content and users are missing, is still surprisingly prevalent. This chapter discusses experiences in design education that foreground the role of design as a possible response to human needs, in projects that, without ignoring the importance of visual sophistication, put the emphasis on communication, on information management, on the dynamics of learning, on the use of research methods, and on an approach to design that is user centered, evidence based, and results oriented.

Values, objectives and educational approaches are realized in the classroom. There is where one can see systems in the act of becoming reality. A small collection is offered here as a hint of an area that can help understand how to implement a commitment to forming students in information design that works.

Chapter 18: Using Small Data for Big Change: Data Visualization for Frontline Healthcare Providers

Jonathan Aitken, Janet Joy, and Carmen Dyck

Abstract

Vancouver Coastal Health, a regional health authority in Vancouver, Canada, approached the Health Design Lab at Emily Carr University in 2013 with the goal of reimagining the presentation of specific datasets to front line medical workers, with the intention of improving the emergency treatment of heart, stroke, and sepsis patients in the earliest stages of their critical care. Current hospital practice collects high-level data that is designed to inform executives and senior leaders about the health system performance as a whole. The data show broad trends over a range of topics, but do not provide information that frontline clinicians can use to improve quality at the practice level. Clinicians need real-time data presented in a manner that can be understood quickly and applied to changes in protocols immediately. Two classes, a communication design and an interaction design class, considered the problem space and suggested solutions.

Introduction

Emily Carr University of Art + Design (ECUAD) has been engaged in designing for complex problems in healthcare for many years. Based on this history of success, the school recently formed a specific research area, the Health Design Lab (HDL), to collect such projects and initiatives into one centre. The HDL looks at large complex socio/health problems where design research and thinking can provide an "outside the box" perspective. Enthusiastic partners are key to this approach—from industry, government or the non-profit sector.

One of the Lab's most important partners is Vancouver Coastal Health (VCH). This publicly funded, regional health authority includes 13 hospitals ranging from rural community hospitals to large academic urban hospitals. VCH employs 22,000 full and part-time workers, plus 2,500 physicians and serves one million residents of British Columbia. Like healthcare systems everywhere, VCH struggles with a myriad of large, systemic problems, while striving to provide optimal patient care.

A typical hospital patient is complex, usually coping with multiple chronic conditions. In turn, a patient's care also becomes highly complex and is provided by many different professionals across many different settings. This complexity is further amplified by serial system changes, such as the introduction of disruptive innovations in the form of new medical technologies and treatments, frequent overhaul of organizational structures, and finally the evolution and expansion of information systems.

The Use of Big Data in Healthcare and the Need for Small Data Displays

The nature of healthcare information has changed dramatically in the last few decades. The increased ability to process large amounts of patient data has enabled the proliferation of administrative databases in which patient information is routinely collected and analyzed. Such databases have revolutionized healthcare. For example, without such databases the extent of medical errors documented in the 1999 report from the Institute of Medicine, "To Err is Human" (Kohn & Donaldson, eds., 1999) would never have been possible. That report, which described an average of 98,000 annual deaths due to medical errors in the U.S, led to a fundamentally new focus in healthcare which was the focus on Quality and Patient Safety—as well as much greater emphasis on using data as a tool for quality improvement. In 2004, Baker et al documented similar error rates in Canada.

This increase in available healthcare information has, in turn, changed our expectations about how healthcare is provided and measured. In the last 15 years, health systems have adopted the use of the Balanced Scorecards or something similar. Balanced score cards (Kaplan & Norton, 1992) measure overall system performance with a balanced set of metrics (both financial and strategic) to describe the range of system activities. For healthcare, this is big data—information aggregated across a system that provides "big dot," measures, such as mortality rates or hospital readmission rates.

Such report cards that summarize healthcare data are well-established tools to provide senior management with a high level view of system trends. In contrast, data reporting tools that are designed for frontline staff, i.e., those healthcare providers who directly contact patients or who directly affect their care—are not so well-established. Report cards don't allow frontline staff to pinpoint how their actions contribute to overall trends.

In focus groups conducted previously to this project, VCH staff asked, "How can we improve patient care if we don't know how we're doing?" Staff wanted to know if patients lived or died, if they missed certain steps in the protocols for care, or if they took too long to provide care. Staff wanted to know what happened to patients they sent for treatment at another hospital—did they get the procedure in time?

Project Rationale

This "gap" in the data forms the context for this project, where we chose to tackle how we could collect and display small data, i.e., data which healthcare professionals can immediately use to improve patient outcomes.

Healthcare performance data and measurement systems have historically been designed and developed by system planners, typically with backgrounds in accounting, management, or epidemiology—but rarely, if ever, information design. Moving the system towards providing data to frontline workers in a form they can immediately understand (Hildon et al., 2012) is uncharted territory for a healthcare system, and at this stage, VCH turned to Emily Carr for advice in how to structure both collection of, and dissemination back to, frontline staff.

VCH has been an enthusiastic partner with design students at ECUAD for several years, and values the relationship for its human-centered, and evidence-based approach to designing for innovative change. As VCH staff have been exposed to different ECUAD/VCH projects, their recognition of the potential for using design to improve healthcare has grown exponentially.

This paper presents a case study of one such project, completed during the 2013/2014 academic year, as a collaboration between VCH's Clinical Guidelines Initiative, a program that aims to facilitate the implementation and evaluation of evidence-based guidelines, and ECUAD design students.

Project Description

While the need for changes in data usage applies to many situations within the health authority, for this project the partner chose to focus on three specific scenarios where they wanted to effect a change in practice: stroke, sepsis and STEMI treatment (STEMI is a type of heart attack, known as an ST segment Elevation Myocardial Infarction). Currently, most of the data that VCH staff see are located in a scorecard that comes to staff about three months after care is provided, and only shows the data on a hospital level.

Dyck and Joy presented this challenge to two classes: the first, a communication design class, which was asked to consider ways to present information clearly and quickly in static, likely print-based outcomes; and the second, an interaction design class, which focused on both collection and display in an interactive digital platform. Students were given an example of a scorecard and asked to imagine the following scenario:

	Time Frame	Target	Year to Date	
Provide the best care				
SYSTEM LEVEL				
Emergency Patient Experience	Apr 2013 to Sep 2013	>= 90.0 %	89.7 %	△
Hospital Standardized Mortality Ratio	Apr 2013 to Sep 2013	<= 100.0	75.0	⬤
REDUCE UNNECESSARY VARIATION IN CARE BY USING EVIDENCE BASED PROTOCOLS				
Clostridium difficile Infection Rate	Apr 2013 to Dec 2013	<= 7.50	6.98	⬤
Hand Hygiene Compliance	Apr 2013 to Dec 2013	>= 85.0 %	74.8 %	◆
Percent of hip fracture fixations completed within 48 hours	Jan 2014 to Feb 2014	>= 90.0 %	90.4 %	⬤
Nursing Sensitive Adverse Events	Apr 2013 to Dec 2013	<= 10.0	29.3	△
IMPROVE CLINICAL INTEGRATION AND QUALITY BY BUILDING REGIONAL PROGRAMS, DEPARTMENTS AND PROCESSES				
Emergency Patients Admitted to Hospital Within 10 Hours	Apr 2013 to Feb 2014	>= 55.0 %	61.7 %	⬤
Surgery Wait Time	Apr 2013 to Feb 2014	>= 75.0 %	72.7 %	△
Surgery Wait Time Longer Than 52 Weeks	Apr 2013 to Feb 2014	<= 2.0 %	2.6 %	△
Unplanned Readmission Rate to Hospital	Apr 2013 to Sep 2013	<= 8.0 %	9.4 %	◆

Figure 1: Example of a Vancouver Coastal Health scorecard (March 2014).

Imagine a nurse who works in an emergency department. She has a 5 minute break, and is standing with her coffee in the staff room, which has this picture (Figure 1) displayed on the bulletin board. She looks at it—it is a document describing system level performance, but it does not tell her anything about how well or poorly her Emergency Department is providing care. She does not learn how many patients have come through with a certain condition, nor what happened to them. This visual—while helpful for senior leaders who monitor system performance—tells this nurse nothing about how exactly she and her colleagues can give better care to patients.

We asked the design students to imagine solutions that would improve this scenario of use — anything from posters to digital solutions. The students were introduced to the emergency department environment by presentations and tours, but they were not asked to constrain their ideas based on VCH's technological constraints. We wanted a "bottoms up" approach that might complement our top-down data reporting systems. It would be a short-loop data system with a shorter cycle time and tighter focus.

Design Research Process

The Health Design Lab bases most of its work on human-centered, participatory design research methodologies, such as those described by Sanders and Stappers (2013). With this project, co-authors Joy and Dyck had previously conducted research with frontline healthcare workers through focus groups, so it was not deemed a necessary step for the design students. Instead, the students reviewed this existing data and extrapolated from specific needs indicated by workers to more generalized principles that could be applied to designs. This type of affinity mapping is a key component of qualitative research, as it allows broad themes to emerge from experience-based knowledge.

These principles were then personalized through the use of invented personas—a shortcut that allows designers to make a sort of composite character that embodies some of the main themes from the research. In this case, students imagined a range of personas that represented nurses, administrators, and patients. This technique allowed students to consider their concepts from multiple perspectives. In doing so, they discovered the different "pain points" of their personas. Nurses, for example, have no time to decode data; administrative staff need training and support to enter and re-present data, and patients may ultimately want access to this information.

A review of the secondary research on information design and data visualization, supported with material from their faculty, gave the students a grounding in basic principles of data interpretation. A contextual review of other potential health systems solutions to the problem space revealed that little work exists within this area.

Some students also created a careful work and data flow analysis. This allowed for the integration of a proposed system of data collection and review to be placed within an existing context of work. This perspective was essential in the ultimate usability of the proposals—designs had to be easy to understand, as well as be accessible within their usual workday.

Results

Students from the communication design class explored traditional information design models. Grouping related information and organizing it spatially to create a timeline was a common response. This helped clinicians understand not only the sequences involved, but also key benchmarks at different stages of time sensitive treatment. Drawing from Tufte's principles of analytical design (Tufte, 2006), others understood the importance of showing comparative data. One example of this, (Figure 2) presents optimal time frames for treatment stages, and compares that to actual time frames reached by a specific team at one location. This "real-time" data could be automatically pulled into a pre-configured PDF from an Excel spreadsheet, and printed. Posted in a common staff room, this data can be comprehended quickly, and appropriate changes made by the team to improve best practices to improve compliance to targets.

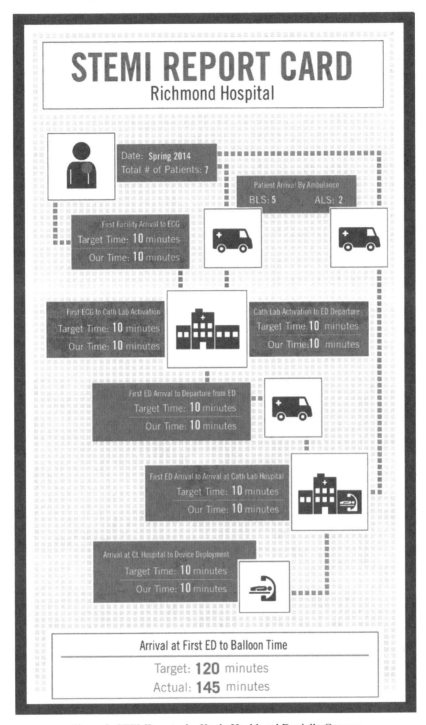

Figure 2: STEMI poster by Kayla Heald and Danielle Connor.

The interaction design students considered both the collection and visualization of data in a more seamless, digital workflow. In order to facilitate a wide exploration of outcomes, the partner intentionally put no technical constraints on the project. Students were free to consider and design for a wide variety of digital outcomes. Many landed on a tablet-based application. This hardware allows for easy disinfection—crucial for hospitals. Tablets are portable, light, and easy to navigate, sometimes with gloved fingers. They can communicate wirelessly with a larger database, pulling or pushing information.

In this example (Figure 3), data is collected simply through a combination of text fields and forced choices. The data is then pushed to a central server, where it is securely stored. When needed, the information is then "pulled" back to the tablet, after any personal identifiers have been stripped. The app then re-presents this data graphically—the patient journey is mapped, temporal comparators are indicated numerically, and other comparisons to targets can be made. Color coded graphics show at a glance whether targets are achieved, borderline, or the target time is not achieved. The huge advantage to this system is its flexibility and customizability. Users can define the time frame, switching between a specific day, week, or month. They can choose between mean and median numerical displays, a critical difference in a small dataset where one extreme number can skew results. Users can switch to pages showing progress over time in a traditional line chart, and select for more detail within that chart.

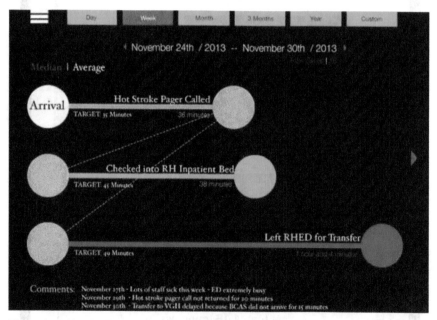

Figure 3: Tablet display of Stroke Care at a Community Hospital by Ben Westergreen and Scott Bell.

Another student group used a systems approach to repurpose existing data through an automated email system. Here their goal was to not add to the existing workload of the current data collectors. Instead, this proposal mined the existing "big data" for a specific subset, then automatically emailed it to the relevant team members. Deceptively simple, this direction had much promise. As it plugged into the existing workflow, no expensive changes needed to be made. Rather, using existing, and easily available digital tools such as MailChimp, it provided fast, inexpensive access to data, and could be rendered graphically.

Design Challenges

When the partners, Joy and Dyck, presented the students' work, the reaction of front-line staff were very positive. They were excited by the look and feel of the different options, yet concerned about the logistics of implementing them.

Frontline clinicians and managers appreciated that many of the data visualizations were:

- Visually appealing—the displays 'drew staff in' (with the use of bold colors and shapes)
- Easy to understand because the displays showed numbers in a 'count' format rather than a percentage or a rate (i.e., that 75 out of 100 patients got the right care vs saying that 75% of patients got the right care).
- Granular data: staff could drill down the data to see the performance of their unit to a specific date and time, and could compare it with past performance.
- Stage specific: staff could get performance data on discrete tasks within the process of care (i.e., length of time from triage to physician assessment)
- Contextually helpful: Some of the data tools even allowed the user to input other factors that helped to explain the data (i.e., delays could be because the Emergency Department was short-staffed or because the ambulance was delayed).

In short, staff said that these displays made data meaningful to them. Additionally, many staff were excited by the possibility of using technology such as apps and iPads so that data could be displayed in real-time, thus showing them *in the moment* where they needed to shift priorities to provide the best patient care possible.

Along with the initial positive responses, staff also expressed some concerns.

- Would the collection of this data fall to already overworked clinicians?
- Who would be responsible for aggregating the data and for coordinating the displays?
- To deal with hybrid environments, could data be 'pushed' to staff, through a variety of modalities (paper displays and electronic media)?
- What about data overload or display fatigue in a department with little wall space?

- What processes would be established to ensure that staff regularly review the data?
- What about patient privacy—if you only had one patient come in with a STEMI that week, then the data could identify a particular patient.
- How could the tools be created so that staff could easily move from one data recording event to another without relearning a new system?

Following the initial presentation of concepts, different groups asked for different changes and there was some confusion as to the workflow for eventual implementation. Several students were hired to facilitate these changes, but ultimately the faculty design lead, Aitken, asked to "pause" the process while some of these issues were sorted out.

As a first step, a meeting was organized with different groups within VCH: Information Technology (IT) administrative staff; Data Management leaders from Quality and Patient Safety; and Directors from Decision Support, which is the team that extracts data from databases and patient medical records (some of which are paper-based), and produces summary statistics and "scorecards" that are used by senior leaders. This meeting revealed several issues that would need to be addressed before we could effectively design for their specific local context.

First, the IT department does not currently support the development of apps for a tablet, nor would this be an easily implemented change. Like many health authorities in Canada, VCH struggles with older computers and an outdated Windows-based system. A mobile web app was suggested, as it could be designed and maintained by third party vendors, but this revealed further issues with the authority's system. Their current browser (as of January 2014) was Internet Explorer 6 (IE6), which was first released in 2001 and which precedes the advent of mobile web sites. Much of the HTML code used for mobile web sites will not run on IE6. Changes to this system would not have been possible during the time frame of this project, because numerous legacy systems, including critical clinical information systems were built to depend on IE6 and can only be replaced with enterprise-wide software. While this system and browser will be upgraded, it may still not be the ideal platform for web apps.

Second, privacy regulations require the storage of sensitive (i.e., patient) information on a secure central server, preferable within the hospital firewall. Nothing can be stored on the device itself. With the older, ethernet-wired desktop computers, this is not a simple connection.

The third issue is that tablets rely on a consistent wireless signal; wifi is not consistently available throughout all hospitals. This is by no means specific to healthcare, it is in fact a widespread issue in all buildings more than a few years old. Retrofitting buildings is expensive, and older concrete-dominant structures, like hospitals, are notoriously difficult spaces to set up a clear signal. As older buildings are retrofitted or replaced, this will improve, but it will be years before wifi is completely reliable within a hospital context.

Fourth, the advance of communications technologies inevitably progresses much faster than the policies needed to manage and support those technologies in healthcare settings. As a result, policies around the use of tablets or smartphones in the hospital workplace for work-related activities are unclear or inconsistent, and the adoption of communication technologies lags behind their potential. For example, unions and administration decided that staff should not use their own phones/tablets during work hours, but this rule was originally implemented to prevent their personal use. Restricting the potential application of these devices to improve patient care is an unintended consequence of this policy, and will likely be revised in the near future. Physicians are not regulated by these unions, and they routinely use tablets and smartphones.

These challenges are not unique to VCH. In fact they contribute to a generally poor understanding of the digital infrastructure needed within a healthcare system (Dexheimer & Borycki, 2014; Mosa et al., 2012; Wilcox et al., 2012, 2013). Peter Jones, in his book *Design for Care* (2013), indicated that while the implementation of electronic medical record systems is inevitable and will have wide economic and health benefits (p. 209), the proliferation of multiple systems and vendors render the possibility of a shared standard across the health system virtually impossible. This missed opportunity for a fully functional interconnected data system will take decades to correct. The noted physician and healthcare futurist Eric Topol (2012) expands on this theme, observing that most healthcare organizations operate as separate silos, with little sharing of patient information. Patients typically interact with more than one system, which increases the risk of adverse incidents, rendering useless the whole point of patient-centered health records.

Future Opportunities

While these challenges could have had a chilling effect on opportunities for changes to data collection and visualization, the enthusiastic response of staff to the students' initial concepts emphasized the need to proceed with the project. In order to meet some of the challenges, two strategies were chosen for further development of prototypes.

First, in order to fully understand the partner's specific context, we decided to implement a contextual review. Here, systems analysis will be employed to explicitly describe the constraints and possibilities within the system as a whole. Two systems analysis methods are appropriate to support the design of information visualization in this context: contextual inquiry and work domain analysis. Contextual Inquiry (CI) is a client-centered design process that is based upon a design team's in-depth understanding of how the client currently works and their ideas to improve that work in some way. Work Domain Analysis (WDA) is a method to identify the activity-independent capabilities and constraints that support and shape work. This will include a consideration of the IT structure that supports data collection and distribution, with a primary focus on which data collection and display methods could be implemented within the current VCH IT structure.

Second, the health authority's local context will allow for the implementation of a pilot in a limited fashion—no more than 8 devices. This provides an opportunity for the testing of new modes of data recording. Here, tablet computers could allow for on-site and in-the-moment data recording by the front line workers. This shift in data collection from administration personnel to clinicians may meet resistance. It will certainly affect their practice. But it may also have the benefit of effecting a shift in "ownership" of data from administration to clinicians. By engaging clinicians as co-creators in the rethinking of the data collection process within their established workflow, we can hope to engender a new sense of ownership and engagement *of* that process. In turn, this may also lead to better adoption of changes in practice from the clinicians, as they would see those changes as being self-directed, not imposed.

Conclusion

These issues typify the complexities involved in designing for healthcare. The public healthcare environment constrains information technology solutions in a variety of ways. Privacy regulations limit the publication and sharing of patient health information. Driven by vendor agreements set by Provincial regulations, hospital procurement policies necessarily provide strict limitations about purchasing computer equipment, tablets, and smartphones.

But interestingly, growing public access to their own "big data," generated by a myriad of newly available health and fitness apps and devices, is shifting the public discourse from one of wariness and caution around data sharing, to one of growing acceptance and understanding of its benefits. This new acceptance is leading to increased expectations around the implementation of technologies in many areas, and healthcare is no exception. We are now at a point where the public is asking for changes to how data is managed and shared by the healthcare system.

While this project is not yet "complete," it has been hugely successful in a few different ways. The initial assumption by the authors, that "small data" would be embraced by frontline workers as a tool to facilitate changes to best practice, has been shown to be true by their enthusiastic embracing of the project's prototypes. Rather than resistance from frontline workers, the project has more often been met with impatience—"why can't I have these tools right now!" was a more common response.

IT departments are now participating in discussions around how to implement change in smaller, manageable stages. While full scale changes to electronic records of all kinds is certainly occurring in most public health systems, their scale is so massive and expensive, that change here is ponderously slow. Instead, IT is suggesting that the constraints for prototypes and pilot projects are significantly less than those for solutions designed to be implemented on a broad scale.

Here is a window of opportunity—solutions that can be implemented on a small-scale, independently of larger policy constraints. Even when a potential solution would be most effective on a system-wide scale, the way forward is to first demonstrate its effectiveness in small-scale incremental steps. Here, user enthusiasm for novel approaches can be nurtured further, and contribute to the broader application of technologies aimed at the improvement of patient care.

References

Baker, G. R., Norton, P. G., Flintoff, V., Blais, R., Brown, A., Cox, J., et al. (2004). The Canadian Adverse Events Study: The incidence of adverse events among hospitalized patients in Canada. *Canadian Medical Association Journal,* 170, 1678-1686.

Dexheimer, J. W. and Borycki, E.M. Use of mobile devices in the emergency department: A scoping review. *Health Informatics Journal,* April 29, 2014. DOI: 10.1177/1460458214530137

Hildon, Z.; Allwood, D., and Black, N. Impact of format and content of visual display of data on comprehension, choice and preference: a systematic review. *International Journal for Quality in Health Care* 2012; 24 (1): pp. 55–64. 10.1093/intqhc/mzr072

Kaplan, R. S. and Norton, D.P.. The Balanced Scorecard: Measures that Drive Performance, *Harvard Business Review,* (January-February 1992): 71-79.

Kohn LT, Corrigan JM, Donaldson MS, editors. *To err is human: building a safer health system.* Washington, DC: National Academy Press, Institute of Medicine; 1999.

Jones, P. *Design for Care: Innovating healthcare experience.* (New York, Rosenfeld Media, 2013)

Mosa, A. S. M., Yoo, I. and Sheets, L. A. Systematic Review of Healthcare Applications for Smartphones. *BMC Medical Informatics and Decision Making,* 12:67 (2012). DOI: 10.1186/1472-6947-12-67

Sanders, L. and Stappers. P. *Convivial Toolbox: Generative Research for the Front End of Design* (Lausanne, Bis Publishers, 2013)

Topol, E. *The Creative Destruction of Medicine.* (New York, Basic Books, 2012)

Tufte, E. *Beautiful Evidence.* (Conn, USA. Graphics Press, 2006)

Wilcox, A. B.; Gallagher, K.D; Boden-Albala, B.; Bakken, S.R.. Research Data Collection Methods: From Paper to Tablet Computers, *Medical Care* Volume 50 (July 2012) Issue p S68–S73, DOI: 10.1097/MLR.0b013e318259c1e7

Wilcox, A. B.; Gallagher, K.; and Bakken, S.. Security Approaches in Using Tablet Computers for Primary Data Collection in Clinical Research, *eGEMs (Generating Evidence & Methods to improve patient outcomes)* Vol. 1: Iss. 1, Article 7(2013), DOI: http://dx.doi.org/10.13063/2327-9214.1008.

Biographical notes

Jonathan Aitken is the director of the Health Design Lab and Communication Design faculty at Emily Carr University of Art and Design. The Health Design Lab is a research centre that applies design thinking to healthcare, bringing human-centered design research methodologies to complex problems. Aitken's education in Communication and Industrial Design help him bring an interdisciplinary focus to his work. Currently teaching in the graduate and undergraduate programs, Aitken is particularly interested in how participatory design methodologies can facilitate design research into large, complex problems.

Dr. Janet Joy is director of Innovation and Evaluation at Vancouver Coastal Health (VCH). Her work focuses on supporting evidence-informed decision making. This has included knowledge translation, health technology review, program evaluation, and the implementation of system-wide clinical guidelines. Prior to working at VCH, she spent 10 years leading health policy studies at the Institute of Medicine in the U.S. She has a PhD in neuroscience and behavior, and is particularly interested in using visual tools to engage staff and support evidence-based quality improvement in healthcare.

Carmen Dyck, M.C., MPH, is a quality improvement advisor with Vancouver Coastal Health. First trained as a clinical counsellor with a focus on family systems therapy, she began her career as a program director with a provincial health focused non-governmental organization. Through work in Canadian and international contexts, she became a passionate advocate for health system improvement after seeing how patients and their families' lives changed when they were harmed by adverse events in health systems. She now works directly within the health system to help remove the barriers preventing health professionals from providing the best care possible.

Chapter 19: Maps as Stories—Designing Site Maps for the Huron River Watershed Council (HRWC)

Judith A. Moldenhauer

Acknowledgement: A version of this chapter appears as "Storytelling and Mapping: The Design of Site Maps for the Huron River Watershed Council (HRWC)" in *Applications of Information Design 2008: Selected papers from the international conference at Mälardalen University in Eskilstuna, Sweden 25-28 June 2008*, published by Mälardalen University in 2009.

Abstract

This chapter describes how a Wayne State University graphic design class used storytelling to re-design site maps for volunteers who monitor water quality for the Huron River Watershed Council. The original HRWC maps were difficult for the volunteers to use – difficult to know how get to a site, how to orient themselves to the physical reality of the sites, and how to select actual sample spots at the sites. Students worked in teams over the course of the semester to develop prototypes of map re-designs through the use of surveys, observation, and discussion with volunteers throughout the design process, and experimenting with various approaches to organizing and visualizing the information. The students accompanied the volunteers on a day of water sampling and observed how the maps were used (or not used) and the tasks the volunteers performed (or were not able to perform), and how their ability to use (or not use) the map affected the ease and completion of their task. The students then again accompanied volunteers on another day of sampling to test their designs and observe the use of the re-designed maps. Most student graphic design projects focus on the creation of the design, so students do not get to know if their designs would be successful outside of the classroom context. This project provided students with the important opportunity to test their concepts and know the level of their success in responding to the visual information needs of the volunteers; the volunteers' response was enthusiastic and they provided the students with suggestions for a few additional improvements.

Where Am I Going and How Do I Get There?

How often have you had trouble getting somewhere because of an inaccurate map and/or poor directions? You got lost (or at the very least were confused) because important information that you needed was omitted from the map or presented in a way that did not make sense to you. The problem that you encountered was that the information on the map – a combination of the words and visual cues about how to understand and use the map – did not meet your information needs. As Jef Raskin knows, "the way we represent information is of crucial importance in communicating the meaning of information." And as the linguist Leonard Bloomfield states, "Each person must necessarily refer language symbols to his or her own experience... but areas of general agreement permit the business of semantic transfer to go on and function." (Bloomfield 1984). But creating those "areas of general agreement" – especially how to create them – is the catch.

To ask for a map is to say, "Tell me a story." (Turchi, 2004, p. 11)

Maps are an example of information design. The best information design is rooted in the concept of user-centered design, that is, design based on the experiences of the people who actually have to make sense of and use information. The context of the design – what is to be communicated, how it is to be used, and by whom – is critical. The key to developing effective, user-centered information design is storytelling. By weaving together the "story" of the information with the "story" of the people using the information (their experiences, background, knowledge, emotions, etc.), information designers can create a new "story" that enables the information to be truly meaningful for the people who need to use it. (Moldenhauer, 2002/2003) Applied to map design, storytelling enables designers to relate an individual's experience of a space to the specific physical aspects of that space. The resulting map design enables a person to move confidently between places by successfully connecting real-time experience with navigational signals indicated on the map. User-centered design that responds to that individual's sense of orientation while moving through space is demonstrated in Thomas Porathe's 3-D ocean navigation system for Swedish shipping lines (Porathe, 2006; Figure 1), with Google maps that can pinpoint your location anywhere, and through maps that indicate "you are here." This understanding of user-centered design and the role of storytelling in information design was also the basis of the mapping project by Wayne State University graphic design students in Winter 2008 to re-design the Huron River Watershed

Council (HRWC) site maps for volunteers who use the maps to monitor water quality in the river and its tributaries.

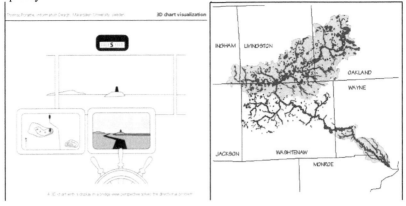

Figure 1. Thomas Porathe: 3-D ship navigation.

Figure 2. Map of the Huron River Watershed (upper, middle, and lower sections).

The Huron Watershed covers 900 square miles in southeast Michigan (Figure 2). HRWC sponsors a series of yearly events during which hundreds of volunteers monitor the water quality at 73 locations throughout watershed. WSU graphic design students accompanied groups of volunteers during the Stonefly count in January 2008 and the River RoundUp in April 2008. The Stonefly event documents the number of stonefly larvae in the streambed, and the River RoundUp event documents the variety and quantity of insect and larvae populations in the water. The presence of some species indicates good water quality (such as the Stonefly larvae: the more larvae the better the quality of the water) while the presence of other species indicates poor water quality. Each team of volunteers scoops up samples of river bottom, sifts through that material and then records the number and kinds of insects and larvae it finds. The Watershed Council provides the volunteers with maps of the sites to be monitored and of driving maps/directions to the sites.

The original site maps existed as 8-1/2x11 or 8-1/2x14 inch photocopies – high-contrast, black-and-white, on standard 20-lb weight photocopy paper – with a standardized, typeset top section in which the name of the location was written and a lower section in which the map itself had been placed (Figure 3). The maps were hand-drawn and all verbal commentary was hand-written. The drawing and words were done originally on grid paper, so the grid lines merged with the drawing and written comments in the photocopying process, making it hard to distinguish information. Occasionally, red pencil or highlighter pens were used to call out a path to the river or emphasize some information. The driving directions were 8-1/2x11 inch photocopies of sections of various commercially produced road maps (Figure 4). Most of these photocopied maps had a portion that was obscured by an overlaid block of typed, recommended directions leading from the Watershed Council's offices to the site (sometimes with additional hand-written annotations). Often the recommended driving route was visually called out with highlighter pen or added during an event by the volunteers assigned to the site.

Maps were re-used and new photocopies made as the old ones wore out or were lost. The result was maps that varied in quality and accuracy.

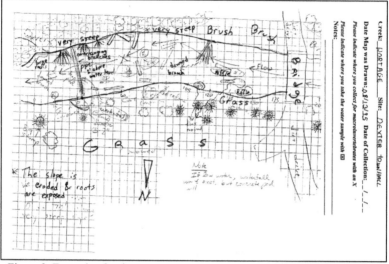

Figure 3: Example of a site map: Portage Creek at Dexter-Town Hall Road

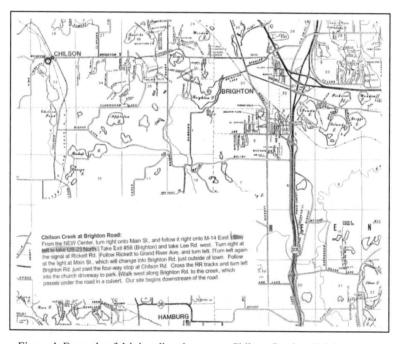

Figure 4: Example of driving directions map: Chilson Creek at Brighton Road

At the Stonefly event, each of the ten students in the class was assigned to a team of four to six volunteers to visit two sampling sites; thus twenty site maps and twenty sets of driving directions were used. The student observed the members of the team (those who were 18 years and older) using the maps who then filled out a questionnaire at the end of the event that asked about their experiences using the maps. A tally of the questionnaire responses from all teams about the maps for the twenty locations documented the following comments/issues.

- little or no information about where to park
- people wanted more specific instructions about where to take water samples
- little or no information about how to get to the spot to collect samples
- maps were hard to read because
    o they were hand-drawn and hand-written and
    o they were poor quality black-and-white photocopies
- people had difficulty in figuring out map orientation (e.g., no indication of north)
- maps lacked accuracy
- many maps were too detailed and too visually busy, yet some were not detailed enough for the task (related to lack of accuracy)
- poor driving directions to the sites
- the paper maps were dirty, damp or crumpled by the end of the event and lots of people suggested that the maps be laminated
- little or no sense of scale on the maps
- using color on the maps would help a lot
- people often had to guess at the meaning of the symbols
- maps were not up-to-date

With the data from their observations and from the questionnaire, each student worked on the re-design of the site maps (and their corresponding driving directions) for the two sites that she/he had visited during the Stonefly event. While each student developed his/her own map designs based on his/her data, she/he also worked in a three or four person group that collectively agreed on a few general visual approaches. For example, one group decided to use a barrel-fold brochure (two-fold, three-panel) format for their designs. Another group decided to use a common typeface on all their maps. Two of the three groups decided to laminate their maps. All of the groups decided to place the site map and driving directions on the same sheet of paper, to use color on the maps, and to design the maps using computer software that allows for easy updating of site information.

Over the course of the semester, two Watershed Council volunteers met three times with the students to provide feedback about the designs. It was through this interaction that the class learned that the HRWC site maps were actually done to record the habitat of each site – a different task than guiding volunteers to streambed collection spots (pools, riffles, etc.). Thus the comments and marks regarding collection activity were superimposed on and worked around the habitat information. The students also learned that two important and interrelated facts needed to be indicated on the map designs: 1) the collecting area and 2) the flow direction of the water. The collecting area at each site runs 300 feet along the stream (usually from the point of a bridge or highway overpass), and sampling activity is to begin downstream (somewhere within those 300 feet) because starting upstream would disturb the water downstream and thus skew the readings of those downstream samples. Everyone agreed that the new maps should indicate the collection area and the water flow direction. The original site maps created additional confusion with instructions to mark collection spots with an X (some maps already had Xs on them); in the field some teams marked spots on their maps but many did not. Since it was unclear whether to mark collecting spots, the students decided (and the volunteers agreed) to eliminate this reference on the maps. The volunteers also proofread the students' revised driving instructions, finding that Google-based directions referenced by the students were not always accurate or clear. These conversations shed light on some of the difficulties with the site maps and reinforced the importance of meeting the specific informational needs of the volunteers.

Of the twenty site maps re-designed by the students, thirteen were tested during the River RoundUp event at the end of April. Again, each student observed a team of four to six individuals (different from the Stonefly team) using the maps and whose members (again 18 years or older) filled out a questionnaire about their experience using the new maps. The testing of the students' designs was an important part of the design process to see if the students truly addressed the informational needs of the volunteers. A tally of the responses from all teams about the thirteen site maps documented the following comments/issues.

- maps were clear and easy to understand
- lamination of the maps was "great" (included comments about sturdiness)
- people appreciated the use of color
- good directions (both for site and driving maps) and people especially liked having site and driving directions together on one sheet
- words on the map were helpful (identification of objects, legends, comments on terrain)
- parking was clearly indicated
- people appreciated having a path to follow to get to the water (from the parking area)
- good map size
- map accuracy and details were good, especially the use of landmarks
- some improvements were needed on some maps
  - accuracy was not good when things left out or located incorrectly on map
  - some people wanted extra or more detail (landmarks) and a bigger detailed inset for driving directions
  - little or no sense of scale (measurement of distance – feet/mileage)

The following designs are examples of the thirteen new site maps and driving directions that were "road tested" in April. These examples explain how the students' maps sought to meet the informational needs of the volunteers through weaving the physical realities of each sampling site's story (e.g., distances, landmarks, terrain) with the stories of the volunteers' experience of the site (e.g., driving to the site, getting to the water, footing and obstructions in path, land contours). The original HRWC maps serve as a reference for the students' re-designs and highlight the communication issues faced by the students. The students' work, which incorporates Tufte's principles for envisioning information (Tufte, 1990) – macro/micro readings, layering and separation, small multiples, color and information, narratives of space and time – establish a clear sense of visual hierarchy with legible words and images that enable the volunteers to easily use the maps.

One of the important aspects of this project was that the students tested their designs. Most design student projects end with the production of concepts and include no opportunity to test the effectiveness of their designs. Nor are most student assignments framed by a research protocol approved by a university Internal Review Board (IRB) as was this one. There was no other way for the students to clearly understand the stories of the volunteers and the HRWC maps – and what happened when they came together – except through observation and surveys. Student course evaluations cited a new awareness of the importance of user-based design as something that the students would carry with them into their future work.

René Maldonado—South Ore Creek at Hamburg Road Site Map

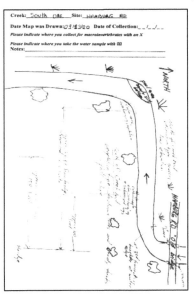

Figure 5. René Maldonado Original site map of South Ore Creek at Hamburg Road.

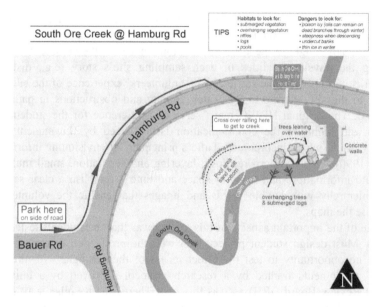

Figure 6. René Maldonado: Re-designed site map of South Ore Creek at Hamburg Road.

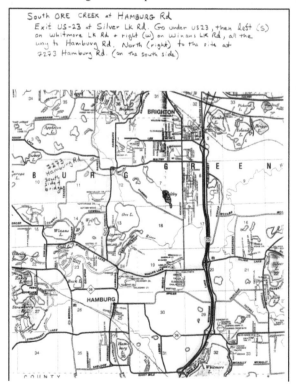

Figure 7. René Maldonado: Original driving directions map for South Ore Creek at Hamburg Road.

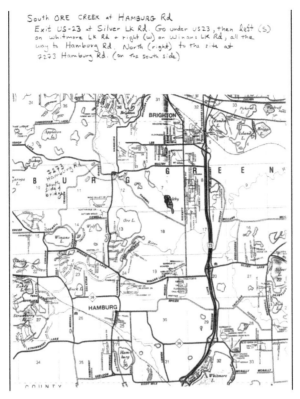

Figure 8. René Maldonado: Re-designed driving directions map for South Ore Creek at Hamburg Road.

René's laminated map design addresses the overall issues found in the initial questionnaire, but also specifically targets the comments made by his team and incorporates his observations of his team's experiences with the site. One questionnaire comment said, "the shapes of the stream beds are not always very accurate," and, indeed, the contour of South Ore Creek was incorrect on the original map but is now correct on René's new map. Another person commented that there was "not enough difference in lines to help determine their importance (i.e., thick lines for roads)" in the original map. René's new map uses color and shape to simplify, differentiate, and emphasize the important aspects of this site – the road, the water, where to collect, and what to expect of the landscape – and minimizes everything else. The road and creek stand out against the light green background, and the use of the word "Trees" replaces the visual clutter of the amoeba-like drawings and detailed hand-written commentary about different trees species and vegetation. The map does not employ a legend but instead identifies symbols as they appear on the map. At the Stonefly event, René's team had a hard time knowing where to park and where to cross the road to get to the creek; parking was not mentioned on either the site map or the driving directions. As a result, his map prominently calls out the parking and road crossing spots and uses a red line with arrows to show a path between these spots – no other element on the map uses red or emphasizes words in the same way.

Also derived from his site observations is the presence of concrete walls that probably supported the "old" Hamburg Road before the current road's configuration. The concrete walls are very evident at the site and probably are the square "transects" written next to "Hamburg Rd 'Old Bridge'" on the original map. The whole spatial orientation surrounding the label "Hamburg Rd 'Old Bridge'" is very confusing – the original map, which shows only one road, seems to conflate the contemporary Hamburg Road (which crosses the South Ore Creek) with a former configuration of the road that also crossed the creek. René's map simply concentrates on the features of the current site, which would correspond to the experience of the volunteers, and eliminates any reference to the "Old Bridge." René's map defines an "approximate sampling area" deduced from various distance marks on the original map. Within that sampling area, René points out potential collection spots – submerged logs, a pool with sand and silt, a calm spot in the flow of the creek, and overhanging trees that are prime locations for insects and larvae – with words and icons whose visual qualities stand out against their surroundings.

North is indicated by an "N" inside a large black triangle, responding to a questionnaire comment that the "compass point [was] not easily located" on the original map. Above the map is the name of the site in clear, large letterforms. Next to it are two categories of "Tips" – habitats and dangers. The dangers list is derived from the team's Stonefly experience, especially the "thin ice in winter" notation.

On the other side of the site map are the driving directions: a color Google map that highlights the route from the Watershed Council's offices to the site, flanked by step-by-step verbal instructions.

The response to René's new map was positive. His River RoundUp team said on the follow-up questionnaire that they very much liked the use of color on the map, that the map was very easy to read, that finding the site and the collecting area was very easy, and that overall the new map was much better than the original one. Additionally they appreciated the size of the map, the quality of the details and his use of "Tips." His group also noted some room for improvement: make the guardrail darker (more visible), actually show the steepness of the slope down to the creek on the map, visually emphasize the "Tips" area, and add the mileage to the driving directions.

Julieanne Franzen—Norton Creek at West Maple Road Site Map

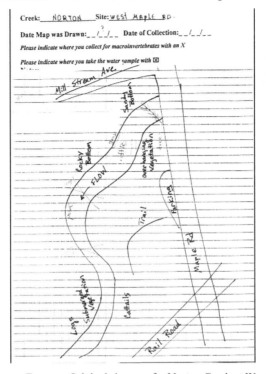

Figure 9. Julieanne Franzen: Original site map for Norton Creek at West Maple Road.

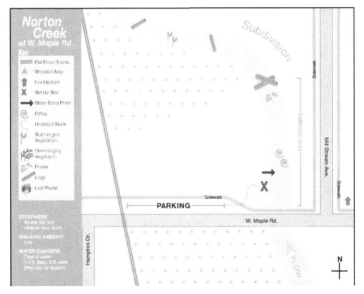

Figure 10. Julieanne Franzen: Re-designed site map for Norton Creek at West Maple Road.

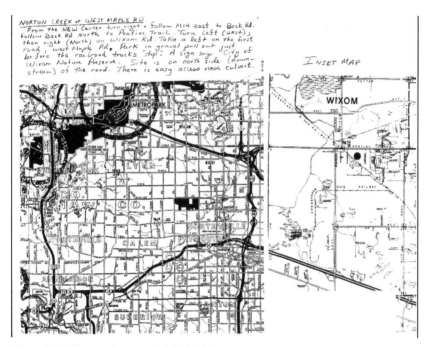

Figure 11. Julieanne Franzen: Original driving directions map for Norton Creek at West Maple Road.

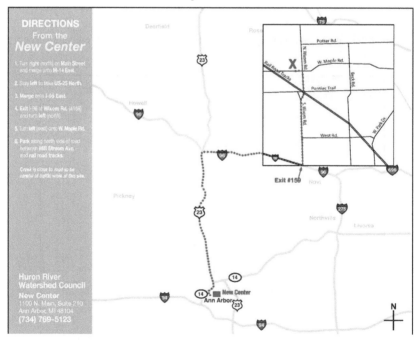

Figure 12. Julieanne Franzen: Re-design of driving directions map for Norton Creek at West Maple.

Julieanne's laminated map addresses many of the same issues as René's map but in some different visual ways. "The map doesn't tell us where to take samples" was a repeated comment on her team's Stonefly questionnaire. So while Julieanne shows the parking area and a path to the water, she additionally indicates the place for the volunteers to set up their monitoring station and the collection area; the monitoring spot is one of the most visually prominent points on her map. She uses a legend to identify the symbols on the map and even includes symbols in the legend that are not found on this map but could be found elsewhere, establishing a consistent legend for use on all HRWC site maps that would assist in comparing the characteristics of a variety of sites. On this map, Julieanne uses groupings of small green triangles across the map to represent wooded areas that communicate the experience of the physical differences between open and wooded spaces at the site. Another repeated comment on the questionnaire was that the original map was not accurate, especially the curves of the river. Julieanne corrects the visualization of the river and adds a north orientation (which was missing from the original map) and details such as the sidewalks and the presence of a subdivision.

The driving directions are on the reverse side of the site map. Julieanne simplifies a regional map to only show major highways for orientation to the area and then uses a red dotted line to call out the recommended route. At the highway exit, she inserts a box that continues to show the red dotted route to the site but at a detailed micro-scale. The yellow tint of the box interior contrasts to the white background of the area map behind it. Her treatment of the macro and micro views of the driving directions parallels the experience of shifts in distance, time, and attention that occur as a driver gets closer to the site.

The follow-up questionnaire responses to Julieanne's map were positive. Her design was often praised for the quality of the macro/micro driving directions, the size of the map, and having the site map and driving directions on the same sheet of paper. The lamination received good notice, too, as did her design of the legend. The need for a sense of scale on the site map was mentioned as a point of improvement.

The students' new map designs offer insightful suggestions for presenting information about the sites and how to get there in ways that more easily and accurately anticipate and address the experiences (i.e., the "stories") of future volunteers, and enable the volunteers to better locate the sampling sites, be prepared for the realities they will encounter at the sites, and more accurately locate the spots from which to collect streambed samples. While there is room for improvement on all the students' maps, the overwhelming response of the Watershed Council volunteers to the new maps demonstrates the effectiveness of user-centered design in meeting their informational needs.

With the student project completed, I will work with the Watershed Council staff and volunteers to incorporate the most effective aspects of the students' designs in establishing a common visual framework for all 73 HRWC maps. Only 53 more site maps to go!

References

Bloomfield, Leonard. (1984). *Language*. (Chicago: University of Chicago Press). Reprint: orginally published: New York: Holt, Reinhart, and Winston 1933.

Jacobson, Robert, ed. (2000). *Information Design*. (Cambridge, Massachusetts: The MIT Press).

Moldenhauer, Judith (2002/2003). Storytelling and the Personalization of Information: A Way to Teach User-based Information Design. *Information Design Journal*. Vol. 11, Issue 2/3, pp. 230-242

Tufte, Edward. (1990). *Envisioning Information* (Chester, Connecticut: Graphics Press, LLC).

Turchi, Peter. (2004). *Maps of the Imagination: The Writer as Cartographer*. San Antonio: Trinity University Press.

Porathe, Thomas. (2006). *3-D Nautical Charts and Safe Navigation*. (Doctoral dissertation, Mälardalen University). Mälardalen University Press.

Wilbur, Peter and Michael Burke. (1998). *Information Graphics*. (London: Thames and Hudson, Ltd.).

Biographical note

Judith A. Moldenhauer is associate professor for Graphic Design in the Department of Art and Art History and Interim Associate Dean for Student Affairs and Research in the College of Fine, Performing and Communication Arts at WSU. Her research and work focus on information design, especially for healthcare, and she has authored papers and journal articles on information design. Her professional work has included designs for several exhibitions at the Detroit Institute of Arts and educational materials for Healthy Start, a U.S. government program to reduce high infant mortality. She has collaborated with nursing colleagues to develop materials, including a smartphone app, that can help women recognize and seek help for postpartum depression. She has presented numerous papers for national and international conferences and authored journal articles on information design and design education. She was the WSU PI for the US FIPSE grant, "Seeing the Body Elsewise: Connecting the Life Sciences and the Humanities," and the US/EC FIPSE grant, "Development of Core Competencies and Student and Faculty Exchange in Information Design." Honors include several design awards, a Fulbright Fellowship to Sweden and selection as a Life Fellow in the Communication Research Institute, Australia. She serves as Education co-chair for the International Institute for Information Design and is a member of several other professional organizations such as the Design Research Society, AIGA, and the College Art Association.

Chapter 20: Context is King: A Graduate Course Exploring the Purpose, Effectiveness, and Contextual Issues of an Informational Graphic

Clinton Carlson and John Hicks

Abstract

This graduate student project is built on previous coursework in design research methods and anthropology to investigate the purpose, effectiveness, and contextual issues related to an existing informational graphic. The graphic was published by the Florida Keys Mosquito Control District (FKMCD) and intended to communicate the prevalence of mosquito larvae that could carry Dengue fever in the Key West community. The Field study included in-person surveys with the public, interviews with FKMCD staff, observation of FKMCD operations, and an audit of FKMCD communication materials. Results of the public survey suggested that the existing graphic was unclear. Through further research and collaboration with the FKMCD it was also determined that the graphic did little to initiate action from the community in the fight against Dengue fever. In response to these findings, a prototype informational graphic and communication plan were designed to deliver key information in a way that would associate actions that the public could take to fight Dengue (emptying standing water on their property) with a current habit (taking out the trash). This paper will present: (a) the research methods and tools utilized; (b) the results and conclusions from the field study; (c) the prototype graphic and plan; and (d) reflection on the value of real-world projects that allow for diverse research methods, broad contextual consideration, and flexible outcomes that focus on human-centered design.

Purpose

The performance of information graphics might be measured by the ability of the graphic to assist a user in achieving a task, increasing understanding, or making decisions. This performance however is often affected by many contextual elements that may not be represented in typical user-testing scenarios. It is possible that an information graphic perform at an acceptable level in lab-based user tests, but fail in actual application within a real-world context.

The project was part of a graduate applied design research course that integrated methods and approaches gained in previous courses. Its objective was to investigate the performance of an existing public health information graphic through broad qualitative methods that might reveal contextual factors and give the designer/student a baseline understanding of the graphic's effectiveness in informing the public of health risks. The purpose of this project was to give the student a guided experience with developing a research plan, determining methodology, designing research tools, collecting data, evaluating data, and reporting findings—all in a complex real-world setting.

Description

This course introduces graduate students to complex real-world design problems. Students are asked to apply research methods learned in previous coursework to a variety of topics in teams or independently. Typically, faculty form partnerships with public or private sector organizations to define the setting and scope of the student's work.

This particular student project was developed in cooperation with the Florida Keys Mosquito Control District (FKMCD). The FKMCD was confronting the first cases of dengue virus that had been seen in Florida in 70 years (Añez & Rios, 2013). FKMCD had initiated several efforts to communicate with the public about the risk and prevention of dengue virus, including placing a weekly informational graphic in the local newspaper. The Executive Director of the FKMCD was relatively new to the position and was interested in evaluating the efficacy of this graphic that had existed prior to his hiring.

MFA candidate John Hicks and Clinton Carlson, an assistant professor in communication design at the University of North Texas, collaborated to determine a research plan, develop necessary research tools, facilitate the on-location research, analyze the data, and report their findings back to the FKMCD.

Research Plan

The research plan included seven stages. The four middle stages (internal interviews, communication audit, observation of inspections, and the public survey) were done on site in Key West.

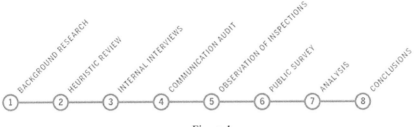

Figure 1

The plan was designed to obtain insight into the efficacy of the existing informational graphic through diverse qualitative methods. These methods were chosen to allow for greater exploration and understanding of broad contextual factors that might influence the effectiveness of the graphic. These factors included other competing public health communications, methods of generating the graphic, cost of publishing the graphic, internal support for the graphic, and existing public knowledge or beliefs on the topic.

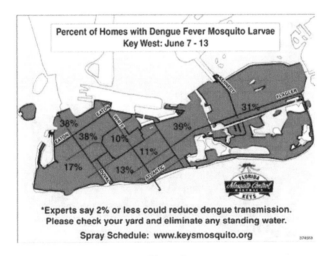

Figure 2

Background Research

Through online research and conversations with the Executive Director of the FKMCD, an understanding of the organization, dengue virus, mosquito vector, and the intent of the original graphic were established.

The FKMCD has over 70 full-time employees that facilitate mosquito control efforts throughout Monroe County. There are nearly 45 species of mosquitos in the Monroe County area, including the Ades aegypti vector that can carry the dengue virus (FKMCD, 2014). Dengue is a viral infection that is estimated to annually infect 50-100 million people worldwide (WHO, 2014). The infection exhibits severe flu-like symptoms for 2-7 days. Severe cases of dengue can be fatal.

Ades aegypti, the primary mosquito vector that carries dengue, is commonly found in water containers that are located near human residences. Natural or manmade containers that hold standing water can be ideal environments for Ades aegypti larva. Limiting habitat through reducing or treating standing water in common places such as planters, tires, buckets, and inactive wells is the primary method for reducing the threat of dengue.

A primary goal of the FKMCD is to inform the public on the need to eliminate standing water on their property on a weekly basis. The intent of the original informational graphic was to increase public awareness of the prevalence of Aedes aegypti and stimulate greater public participation in reducing the mosquito's habitat.

Heuristic Review

The combined experience we have with general design principles, information design, copywriting, and public health communications in various design settings allowed us to develop an initial analysis and a hypothesis as to the effectiveness of the information graphic.

FIGURE 3: HEURISTIC REVIEW OVERVIEW

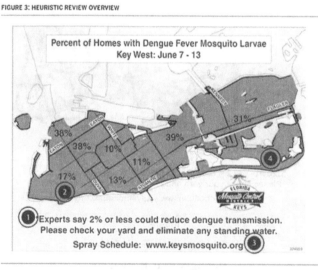

1. Lack of accessible language
2. Lack of meaningful measurements
3. Lack of clear call to action
4. Ineffective use of color coding

Figure 3

Our review of the map identified six primary problem areas that we felt could cause confusion with the public and reduce the graphic's efficacy. These included:

Lack of Accessible Language

The FKMCD informational graphic uses complex technical language that lacks context for reader comprehension or meaning. The graphic uses unnecessary technical terms such as transmission and larvae. The phrase "Experts say 2% or less could reduce dengue transmission," lacks clarity and context for many viewers to immediately understand who "experts" are and what the "2%" figure is referring to.

Lack of Meaningful Measurements

The graphic measures "percent of homes with Dengue Fever mosquito larvae". The graphic fails to give clear context for the level of risk these measurements pose to the public. The graphic also uses a unit of measurement that is more common to researchers than the general public.

Lack of Clear Call-to-Action

The call-to-action fails to clarify how often the public should "eliminate any standing water." This is critical information because the Aedes agypti larvae can reach adulthood in less than seven days. It also fails to give explicit information on why this directive should be followed and does not clearly convey the consequences of failing to take action.

General Clutter and Lack of Hierarchy

The graphic uses type that is the same size, weight, and color. This is particularly problematic in the bottom of the graphic where four different lines of text convey very different ideas. The lack of hierarchy hides the call-to-action in the midst of less critical information.

Ineffective Use (or Lack) of Color Coding

Although the map is designed to have color-coding to identify risk levels, the majority of maps reviewed showed only a single shade of red. The absence of a key to aid the viewer in understanding the meaning of the colors was also critical.

Placement Alongside Primarily Color Advertisements

Due to the fact that the graphic was reproduced in full-color, it was typically located on the back page alongside the only other full-color ads present in the newspaper. The graphic lacked the contrast to stand out from other elements on the page, reducing visibility.

Figure 4

Internal Interviews

Interviews with FKMCD employees helped us gain insight into the organizational beliefs and values regarding both the effectiveness of the newspaper information graphic as well as other communication efforts of the organization. We interviewed a variety of employees, including the Executive Director, Public Relations Director, Operations Director, Supervisors, and Inspectors. The questions and discussion gave us key insight into organizational factors that might impact the effectiveness of the informational graphic:

- If you could communicate one message to all Key West residents, what would that be?

The first question revealed that there was little consensus on what specific message should be the call-to-action for Key West residents. Answers ranged from the simple: "Dengue is dangerous" to the more complex: "Dengue is a serious health issue. Residents should be responsible for their yards." Several of the interviewees generally pointed to the need for residents to take action or reduce standing water, but they lacked a consensus to how this was stated and how much information was included in the message. Greater consensus and clarity of the message throughout the organization could help create greater repetition and memorability of a single public call-to-action.

- In your opinion, what are the most valuable communications or activities that you (FKMCD) do to encourage residents to take actions?

This question again revealed a wide variety of answers, however this time the answers largely correlated with the responsibilities of the interviewee. Inspectors felt that interaction with the public or inspection notifications were most effective. Directors felt that public campaigns or public engagement efforts were more successful in gaining public understanding and action. None mentioned the newspaper informational graphic.

- Do you think the online and print mosquito maps (informational graphic) are effective?

None indicated that the informational graphics were highly effective. They gave reasons such as a lack of explanation and complexity of information for the graphic's perceived shortcomings. One interviewee even suggested that the graphic did more harm than good.

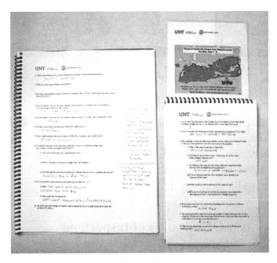

Figure 5

The interviews allowed us to understand organizational factors such as consistency of messaging, perceived value of existing communications, and time and financial cost of producing the informational graphic on a weekly basis. From the interviews we began to identify the consistency of messaging as a contextual issue that likely had an adverse impact on the effectiveness of the graphic. A consistent call-to-action that is simple, memorable, and effective in communicating what the public can do to reduce the risk of dengue transmission could increase the public's sense of self efficacy and further establish preventive patterns and habits within the general public.

Communication Audit

An audit of existing communication materials and efforts of the FKMCD allowed us to understand how consistent messaging was across many public touch points. The materials we reviewed included:

- A variety of door hangers that would inform homeowners

- Educational fliers for public events
- Educational materials for work with school-aged children
- Promotional items for public events
- The FKMCD website
- Inspection reports for homeowners
    - o   Vehicle graphics

Figure 6

Many of the materials exhibited a consistency of messaging, however a short, concise, accessible call-to-action was missing from many of the materials. One door hanger and leave-behind highlighted the text "Eliminate standing water in and around property immediately after it rains and/or once a week." We felt that this message could be slightly simplified and had the potential to be a valuable call-to-action across all public touch points.

Observation of Inspections

The FKMCD employs about 10 residential mosquito inspectors that are assigned to specific zones in which they inspect and treat property, and collect data. John and I individually rode with four different inspectors on their half-day routes through their zone. The properties inspected were a combination of proximity-based, historically problematic, and randomly assigned properties for research fidelity. Although approaches of the inspectors varied, it became clear that their vehicles, presence, and activities are a highly visible part of the FKMCD efforts. Some inspectors approached their inspections in a social manner that engaged residents in conversation, while others preferred to rely on detailed inspection reports to communicate with residents. Several inspectors voiced the belief that their efforts were the best opportunity to actually impact public self-efficacy and prevention efforts.

Figure 7

The observations gave us a deeper level of understanding and respect for the efforts of not only the inspectors but also the FKMCD as a whole. The effort required to capture the data, engage the public, and mitigate mosquito habitats is a time consuming and complex task that we felt reinforced the important role of inspectors in communicating to the public. We felt that there were opportunities to take further advantage of this interaction with the public through more consistent call-to-action messages on vehicles and inspection tags. It also helped us envision and consider additional opportunities to communicate with residents such as a campaign that would associate checking for water with taking the trash to the curb. We wondered if a sticker on city trash receptacles could reinforce the need for weekly property inspection and be an effective visual reminder. We felt that this approach had the potential to lead to habit formation that does not add a great deal of additional effort or cognitive load on residents.

Public Survey

During our observation of inspection routes, we were able to interview 18 residents. We gained insight into the efficacy of the informational graphic, as well as their general awareness of dengue prevention messages. Task-oriented survey questions allowed us to attain deeper understanding of how viewers might interpret the informational graphic. Open-ended questions allowed us to gauge their ability to recall previous prevention messages regarding dengue.

Respondents were asked to look over a reproduction of the informational graphic and its content. We then asked a series of questions to understand the levels of comprehension (Figure 8).

What is the map measuring or depicting?

One out of 18 respondents correctly verbalized that the map was measuring larvae. Two additional respondents said larvae with active dengue fever.

What does it mean when it says, "experts say 2% or less could reduce dengue transmission?

None of 18 respondents could correctly verbalize what the map was measuring.

According to the map and text, what is the most important thing that Key West residents should understand?

Eight of 18 respondents included some reference to reducing "standing water" in their answer.

Figure 8

Three alternative messages were presented to the viewer as different ways of communicating the need to eliminate standing water on a weekly basis. We asked respondents:

1. The main goal of this map is to encourage people to empty standing water on their property. Would any of the statements from the back of the card make that easier to understand or motivate you to do that more?

The respondents primarily chose versions (A and C), which highlighted a simple call-to-action through typographic hierarchy. Version C was the most chosen. It highlighted a simple but specific call-to-action, but also incorporated the most direct rationale or support for the call-to-action (Figure 9).

Version A	Version B	Version C
EMPTY STANDING WATER. We need your help to reduce these numbers to 2% or less to prevent dengue transmission.	By emptying standing water in your yard, you can help bring these numbers down. 2% or less can help prevent dengue transmission to humans.	Larvae can reach adulthood in less than 7 days. EMPTYING STANDING WATER EVERY 3-4 DAYS in your yard can reduce these numbers and reduce dengue transmission.

Figure 9

We also asked respondents to tell us what were typical reasons for not eliminating standing water on a regular basis. We asked them:

2. What do you think keeps people from taking actions such as checking for standing water?

Respondents identified a variety of reasons for not emptying standing water on a regular basis. The answers fell into four categories: A lack of information, lack of concern, lack of awareness, and forgetfulness.

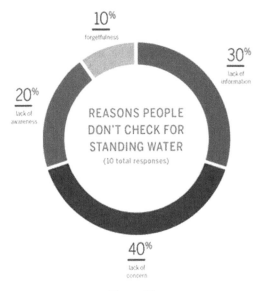

Figure 10

The survey largely corroborated our heuristic analysis of the information graphic, suggesting that graphic and written content were ineffective in communicating clear information and a call-to-action. It also reinforced the challenge of changing public behavior or habits. The last two questions suggest that a clear call-to-action, combined with relevant context for why that action is important may be helpful.

Analysis of Methods

Through an immersive research plan we were able to gain a great deal of contextual information to evaluate the performance of the existing informational graphic. We were also able to identify potential opportunities for alternative communication efforts. We could have rushed to more evidence-based methods of testing the informational graphic and failed to ask important contextual questions. However, each of the components of the research plan provided context and resulted in valuable information that informed our conclusions and recommendations for the FKMCD.

Conclusions

The heuristic evaluation and the public survey suggested that the existing FKMCD informational graphic was not effective in communicating informational content or a call-to-action. It appeared that the language was too complicated and not accessible. The graphic elements also seemed to be problematic in their lack of hierarchy and ineffective use of color. The proposed alternative call-to-actions, suggest that call-to-actions should be specific and accompanied by facts that give the reader more context as to why the actions are important.

The internal interviews, communication audit, and observation of inspections identified opportunities for greater consistency both in visual brand and in messaging. Seeing the inspectors make their rounds allowed us to conceptualize an alternative approach that focused on connecting mosquito control efforts with an existing habit—taking out the trash.

From the research we were able to give FKMCD the following recommendations:

- Discontinue current graphic use until a deeper analysis of public communication strategies could be done.
- Consider alternative methods of communicating call-to-action and supporting content.
- Develop greater consistency in call-to-action messages across all touch points.
- Establish a more consistent brand identity to increase connection between touch points.

Response

Executive Director of the FKMCD, Michael Doyle discontinued the use of the informational map in the newspaper and has considered unifying the FKMCD visual brand through a unique color and icon/logo that would be applied to vehicles, aircraft, and all materials. Additionally, our recommendation for the trashcan campaign was similar to a previous concept and was being considered by the FKMCD.

Reflection

The course gave MFA student John Hicks first hand experience with a variety of methods that would help gain critical contextual knowledge throughout the project. John's work with selecting research methods, developing research tools, conducting the research, and drawing conclusions from the data gave him experience with all stages of the design research process—within a limited amount of time. The portion of this project in Key West also allowed for sustained conversation about related research and design issues. Working with a real organization provided a great opportunity for growth in presentation skills, communication skills, and the ability to articulate the value of design research.

References

Germán Añez and Maria Rios, 2013. *Dengue in the United States of America: A Worsening Scenario?* BioMed Research International, vol. 2013, Article ID 678645, 13 pages, 2013. doi:10.1155/2013/678645

FKMCD, 2014. *Mosquitoes in the Florida Keys.* Florida Keys Mosquito Control District. Retrieved July, 2014 from: http://keysmosquito.org/about-us-2/about-the-keys-mosquito-control/

WHO, 2014. *Dengue and severe dengue.* World Health Organization. Retrieved July, 2014 from: http://www.who.int/mediacentre/factsheets/fs117/en/

Biographical note

Clinton Carlson is an assistant professor of communication design in the College of Visual Arts at the University of North Texas (UNT). He is also the Principal of the Tekzenit Innovation and Research Lab. Tekzenit is one of the fastest growing experience design firms in Texas. Clinton is working with current Tekzenit User Experience (UX) designers to start the xD Program which is a three-month apprenticeship program designed to transition recent graduates from related degree fields into a career in UX design. The program combines UX principles, practices, and human-centered research methods into its curriculum. Clinton's work is included in the AIGA National Design Archives and has been published and shown internationally. With an MDES in visual communication design from the University of Alberta and a BFA in visual communication design from the University of Nebraska-Kearney, Clinton has also taught at the University of Northern Colorado. His current research is focused on the use of co-creative and design-led research methods in the innovation of new solutions for cultural problems. He has been investigating how food recalls might be communicated better in the future for the last three years. Additionally, he is interested in the potential of participatory design methods to address public health issues in micro-communities. He lives in Denton, TX.

John Hicks is a visual designer, researcher and educator living in Fort Worth, Texas. By taking an empathic, participatory approach to design, he champions the needs of users and works to create meaningful experiences for them. His current research examines the professional deficiencies in hard and soft skill sets of entry-level communication designers. John earned his MFA in applied design research from the University of North Texas in 2014.

Chapter 21: Researching Learning and Memory[1]

Jorge Frascara

Abstract

In order to find out the best way of transmitting information in elementary schools, with the aim of developing guidelines for teaching aids, the effectiveness of three methods were compared: one based on observation, another on drawing, and the third on the use of a jigsaw puzzle.

Two kinds of questions, numerical and visual, were used in a response sheet. Results showed different performance of methods when comparing ages as well as when comparing short and long term retention. The jigsaw puzzle proved most effective when older boys answered numerical questions, and least effective among the youngest. Observation proved successful in short term, but drawing showed a much better long term retention level.

Project Description

The project was aimed at teaching design students to do field research, and, at the same time, to demonstrate the value of a user-centered, evidence-based approach to designing.

The project involved 372 school children aged 8, 10 and 12. The information to be learned was the names of 16 cuts of beef common in the city of Buenos

---

[1] A more extended version of this case study was first published as "The relative effectiveness of three methods for the transmission of information in relation to short and long term retention". *Design Papers 3,* Halifax, NS, Canada: Design Division, Nova Scotia College of Art and Design, 1981

Aires, where the study took place. Children were supposed to learn the name, the shape and a code number for each cut. The information was presented as a 70x100 cm poster, legible from across the room for the observation method, and in individual letter-size sheets for the other two methods (Figure 1). A learning period of 12 minutes was used for all conditions.

The content was chosen because of the following reasons:

a.   The amount of information was within the capabilities of all groups.
b.   Even though the information was familiar to all, it was unlikely that some would know the topic more than others.
c.   It was possible to learn the information through all three methods.
d.   No additional specific knowledge was required.

Method 1: Jigsaw puzzle

A 70x100 cm wall chart (Figure 1) was placed at the front of the room for twelve minutes. Every student received a letter-size printed sheet (Figure 2), plus an envelope containing sixteen pieces of cut out paper with the image of one cut of beef and its code number (Figure 3). The children worked for twelve minutes placing each piece on its place.

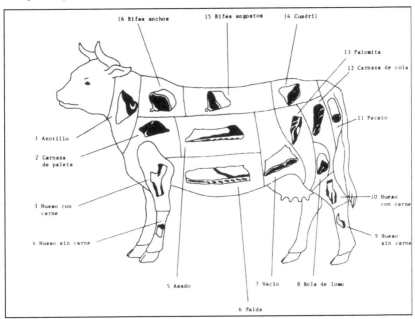

Figure 1

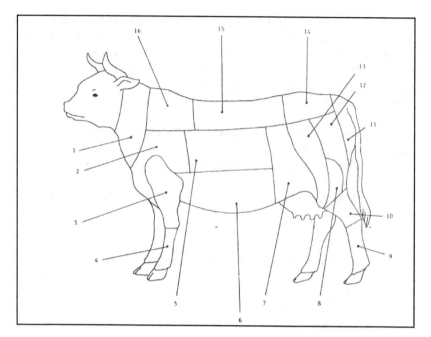

Figure 2

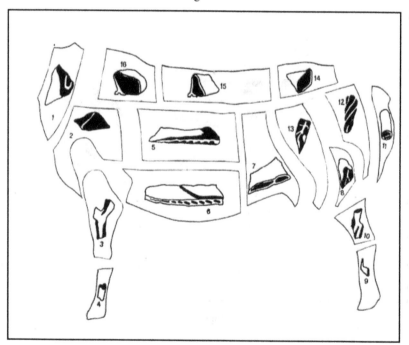

Figure 3

At the end of the 12 minutes the first wall chart was replaced by another to aid recall (Figure 4). The response sheet (Figure 5) was provided at the same time to the participants. Third grade children had 12 minutes to respond, while the others had 10.

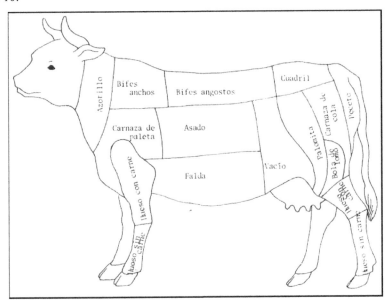

Figure 4

This response sheet was shown to the children during the study time so that they had an idea of what they were supposed to retain.

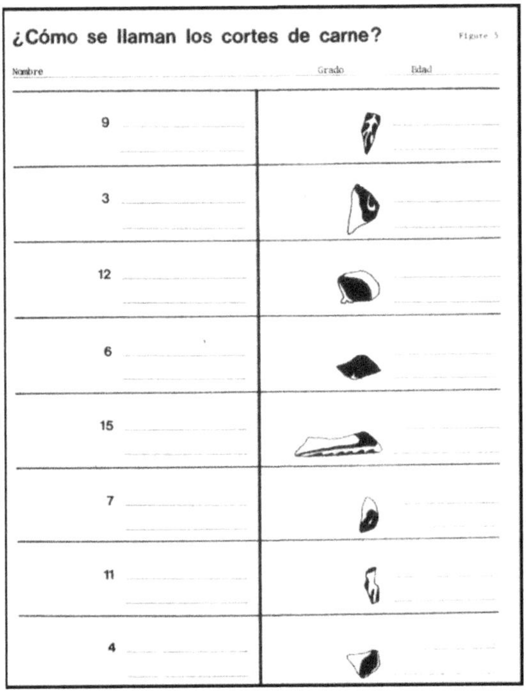

¿Cómo se llaman los cortes de carne?

Figure 5. Test sheet: Which are the names of the cuts of beef?

Method 2: Drawing

The same wall chart used at the beginning (Figure 1) was placed at the front of the room. Every student received a letter-size printed sheet of the same image (Figure 1), and a piece of tracing paper. They were asked to trace the shape, the number, and the name of each cut of beef. The response sheet was also shown during the learning period. At the end of the 12 minutes the letter-size sheet and the tracing materials were collected, and the first wall chart was replaced by another to aid recall (Figure 4). The response sheet (Figure 5) was provided at the same time to the participants.

Method 3: Observation

The initial wall chart was placed in front of the classroom (Figure 1). Students were asked to read aloud the name and the code number of each cut of beef along with the experimenter. When completing the first reading they were asked to remain silent and to observe each cut of beef. The response sheet was quickly shown to the students like in the other cases. The group then performed a second reading allowing time to attend to the shapes during the reading. At the end of the 12 minutes the wall chart was replaced by another to aid recall (Figure 4), and the response sheet (Figure 5) was provided.

Response Sheet (Figure 5)

The response sheet was designed to consider two kinds of questions: numerical and visual. Subjects were always supposed to write down the name of the cut of beef.

Long Term Retention

Without previous notice I returned to the schools one week later. Without refreshing the information the students were asked to complete a response sheet identical to the one completed the previous week. The second wall chart (Figure 4) was placed on the front of the room. A five-minute response time was allowed.

Population Studied

The subjects included 178 males and 194 females from grades 3, 5, and 7, attending three elementary schools in the city of Buenos Aires and its surrounding areas.

Variables Studied

Age, sex, and type of question (numerical or visual), to evaluate short term and medium term retention (immediate test or one week later without warning), related to three ways of presenting the information.

Methodological Considerations

    a. The experimenter was always the same, so that the problem was presented consistently to the different groups.

    b. Working with groups rather than with isolated individuals allowed some uncontrollable communication between subjects. However, the situation did not vary between methods, hence it is unlikely that it could have biased the results.

    c. It is possible that having placed the numbers column on the left side of the response form, response to numbers could have been favored.

    d. The retention aid wall chart might as well have enabled retention on the basis of numbers, and not on the basis of shapes.

    e. Several children thought that the number and the drawing found on the same line in the response sheet belonged to the same name. This caused some doubts and might have caused some mistakes, as well as loss of time (which was limited to five minutes).

    f. The complexity of the assignment seemed to be appropriate, since the three groups answered some questions correctly, and none responded well to all.

Results

Results showed that children were able to remember the verbal-visual information efficiently when tests were taken immediately after the learning process and the method used required observing a poster and repeating words aloud. Otherwise, tests carried out one week later demonstrated a major retention of the information initially memorized among the children that learned the information tracing it from the model sheet (Frascara 1981). This demonstrates the way in which the learning method affects retention.

    Regarding general average performance in immediate memory "Observation" was the best method, followed by drawing. Nevertheless, "Jigsaw puzzle" proved superior in grade 7, reaching 95% of correct answers for numerical questions among boys. This is an interesting result, because it goes against the common idea that younger children learn better with games while older ones can handle well more abstract information. The lowest was 10% (girls, 3rd grade, visual questions, jigsaw puzzle; and boys, 3rd grade, visual questions, observation).

Results I: Short Term Memory (Figure 6)

        Type of question: In every case it was easier to remember the name of the cuts based on the numbers than based on the shape, except for the 5th grade children using Drawing for input.

        Memorization: If one were to give a value of 100 to 3rd graders' memorization, this rose to 186 for 5th grade and to 280 for 7th.

        Sex: No significant differences were found for this variable.

Summary of results of the first test for each learning method, type of question, sex, and school grade of the children

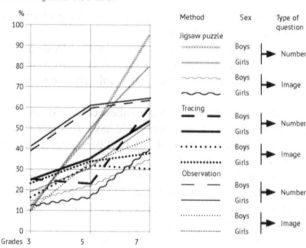

Figure 6

Results II: Medium Term Memory

Figure 7 shows comparisons between tests 1 and 2 regarding the input method used and the kind of question (unfortunately no second test was possible for children using the jigsaw puzzle input). It is to be noted how image recollection was better retained than number recollection.

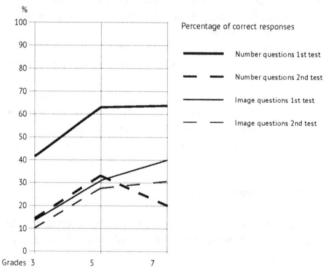

Figure 7

Concluding Comments

The decline of retention between the first and the second test was greater for numerical questions (30%) than for image questions (7%). This indicates the importance of long term retention testing when evaluating a teaching method: testing immediately after providing information might be misleading. The smallest loss of retention after one week (1%) involved the image questions among those using tracing as an input method (Figure 8).

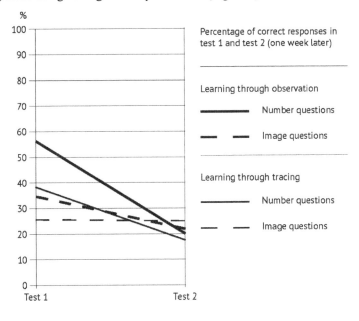

Figure 8

It is evident that the method used for the acquisition of information conditions retention in connection with the kind of question asked. It would be interesting to study which could be the input method that allows best retention performance for short and long term memory. As well, it would be interesting to look into the input method that allows the greatest flexibility to perform well when confronting different kinds of questions.

Chapter 22: Simple Visual Narrations

Krzysztof Lenk

Abstract

Learning about the possibilities and limitations of different methods of visually recording information is one of the pedagogical goals in the information design class. Only personal, tangible experience and success or failure in finding appropriate solutions will develop a student's mental framework for proper resolution of future design tasks.

I

It all started at my School of Design in Lódz, Poland. At the first meeting of a Fall semester, I asked students in class to speak in detail about their Summer vacation. Other students in the group had the right to ask the speaker for more details or better explanations. Students presented a variety of information about events, travels, adventures and moods. Some of them had experienced nice sunny weather, while others had the misfortune of rain. The form of a verbal narration reflected the personality of the narrator. Some orally talented students were unstoppable in telling their story, while other, more shy students had difficulty in putting words together and got a lot of questions from the audience.

After hearing from all the students, I asked them to write down their stories, no longer than 120 words. Transitioning from oral narration to written notation happened to be an interesting experience – one of filtering content from free, intuitive and informal story-telling to the much more rigid rules of grammar and syntax of written language. My request to contain the whole story into a limited space created pressure to focus on describing events most essential for the narration.

When all the typed stories were collected, I asked my students to take pencils and analyze the written text to find the smallest, primary bits of information. It then became apparent that some circled words were nouns, others were verbs, and some others were adjectives.

These circled bits of information became a good starting point for visual rendering. On my request, students had to draw each bit of information separately on a 25 x 25 cm piece of paper, using black and white plaka paint and a 2 cm wide brush. Now the real difficulties began. First, visual grammar has no verbs and they have to be substituted by other methods of indicating action. Next came the discovery that the library of visual adjectives is very limited. Very early into the process, students learned that a literal translation from verbal to visual narration is not possible, and that the visual narration has to be created practically from scratch. In order to do it, the designer has to find visual substitutions for verbal actions, and to simplify the use of adjectives.

II

When time came to organize the individual pictures into a sequential narration it became clear that the non-visible content implied in the breaks between the pictures is very important for a proper grasp of the story by the reader. These breaks shouldn't be too wide because the narration loses continuity, nor too narrow because the content of two neighboring pictures overlaps. When the pictorial narration had been arranged, it occurred to the students that the look of all the pictures in a sequence had to be unified. All pictures should be rendered in the same visual style. The final evaluation of each sequence happened after the pictures were reduced photographically to a size of 5 x 5 cm and the sequence was arranged on an A4 page.

Figure 1

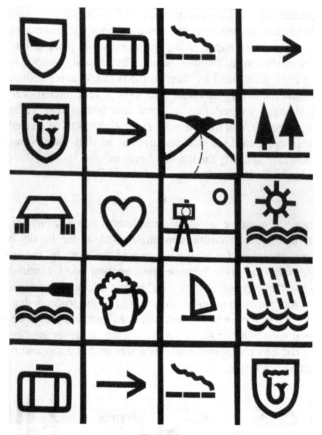

Figure 2

By participating in this project, students familiarized themselves with basic principles of the information capacity of oral, written and illustrative narrations. They had a chance to deal with the concepts of sign and significance. A dose of semiotic theory presented during the process helped them to see their practical experience in a broader intellectual and methodological context.

III

The exercise described above was a good introduction to methods of registering visual information. I started to use it in my information classes in Poland, as well as at Ohio State University, where I was invited to teach in 1979. The results were similarly interesting. What surprised me enormously was the fact that all my American students described their vacation experience as a time of hard work, while for Polish students vacations were a time of leisure and pleasure. I then had a reflection that maybe this is the reason why the United States is a rich country and Poland is a poor, though pleasant one.

Figure 3

Figure 4

Later, at Rhode Island School of Design, I conducted similar assignments in different configurations, like one where students had to build a kite, tested for its ability to fly. In the next step, students had to present a verbal description of the building process, and finish by drawing instructions as an obligatory sequence of sixteen pictures. In a similar tasks students had to present the content of a typical airplane safety instruction card in its most simplified form, or a process of tightening a knot.

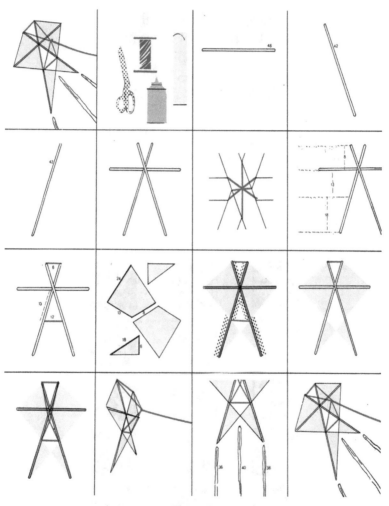

Figure 5

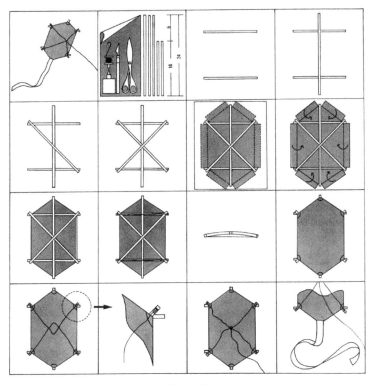

Figure 6

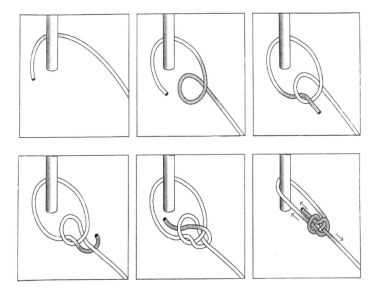

Figure 7

Students who passed these exercises had gotten a good understanding of the informational capacity and limitation of different channels of communication. They also learned how to develop coherent narrative sequences. It ought to be a valuable foundation for more demanding projects in the future.

Biographical note

Krzysztof Lenk is professor emeritus, Rhode Island School of Design. He studied graphic design in Poland, at the Academies of Fine Art in Warsaw and Cracow, and graduated in 1961 with an MFA degree in Graphic Design.

In 1968-69, he worked in Paris, first at the SNIP Agency, and later at the political weekly *Jeune Afrique*. After returning to Poland he became a creative director of the illustrated weekly *Perspectywy*, and a consultant to many newspapers and magazines.

In 1973, the School of Visual Arts in Łódz, Poland, invited Lenk to organize a teaching program of publication design, with a focus on modern periodical design. Lenk was twice awarded by the Polish Minister of Culture and Arts.

He has taught graphic design at RISD since 1982. This one-year invitation happened to turn into a permanent appointment.

In cooperation with Paul Kahn, from Brown University, in 1990 he founded the studio Dynamic Diagrams, specializing in information design. Their more than eighty clients include IBM, Netscape, Microsoft, Harvard and Yale Universities, The Holocaust Museum in Washington DC, Musee des Arts et Métiers in Paris, and the publications *Nature* in London and *Science* in Washington. In 2001 Krzysztof Lenk retired from the studio.

A book, *Mapping the Web*, by Kahn and Lenk, published in London in 2001, has been translated into five languages.

In 2010, Krzysztof Lenk retired from Rhode Island School of Design, after twenty-eight years of teaching.

Conclusion: Closing the Book, Opening the Agenda

Jorge Frascara

The reason for this book, as for all useful design projects, is the discovery of a need. In this case it is the need to understand the functioning of the hundreds of things we use in our contemporary life, from mortgage agreements or other legal documents, to things that should be very simple, such as the gas bill, the controls of a cell phone, or the dose of a pharmaceutical drug.

Fifty per cent of the people in the more developed countries have difficulties with reading comprehension; they cannot do what is called strategic reading, the quick reading that identifies the essentials of a text, extracts relevant content, and makes sense of it all. They read every word with the same attention, overloading working memory and, consequently, finding it difficult to get to the heart of a document. One-half of these people, in turn, are functionally illiterate, they can read words and phrases, but since their everyday life does not include reading or writing, they cannot understand the logical relations between paragraphs, and have problems with long sentences and unusual words.

At the other extreme, the population with high education continuously meets the barriers created by professional jargons: lawyers have their own language, and so do physicians, software developers, and politicians.

There is an urgent need to develop a culture of clear communication. Our profession has a mission to promote this culture in both its visual and its verbal form. To do this, not only it is necessary to be convinced of the value of clear communication: one has to acquire the tools to implement it. These tools, discussed in this book, allow us to practice the design that is needed: user-centered, evidence-based, and results-oriented.

Information design is an accountable practice, and evaluation of performance is an integral part of its processes. It does not have to do with styles, fashions, artistic intuitions or arresting personalities: its material is daily life and the possibility to improve it through a better way of managing information.

Thanks to the joint efforts of the authors, who collectively accumulate a vast experience in research, teaching, and practice of information design, this book can serve to delineate the territory, identify the strategies, and define the objectives for the task ahead.

Our collective goal is to improve the quality of information design – essential requisite for the effective functioning of all the communication systems that support contemporary life – and in this way contribute to the development of a healthy and fair society.

CPSIA information can be obtained at www.ICGtesting.com
Printed in the USA
LVOW02s0532040215

425607LV00012B/519/P